Being Alive

'For three decades, Tim Ingold's has been one of the most consistently exploratory and provocative voices in contemporary scholarship. This book leads us, in prose that is exactingly lucid and charged with poetic eloquence, on a journey through, amongst other things, Chinese calligraphy, line drawing, carpentry, kite flying, Australian Aboriginal painting, native Alaskan storytelling, web-spinning arachnids, the art of walking and, not least, the history of anthropology, none of which will ever look quite the same again! The work is at once a meditation on questions central to anthropology, art practice, human ecology and philosophy, a passionate rebuttal of reductionisms of all kinds, a celebration of creativity understood in the broadest possible sense and a humane and generous manual for living in a world of becoming.'

Stuart McLean, *University of Minnesota, USA*

'Simultaneously intimate and all-encompassing, Tim Ingold's second landmark collection of essays explains how it feels to craft an existence between earth and sky, among plants and animals, across childhood and old age. A master of the form, Ingold shows how aliveness is the essential resource for an affirmative philosophy of life.'

Hayden Lorimer, *University of Glasgow, UK*

'In these iconoclastic essays, Ingold breaks the dichotomies of likeness and difference to show that anthropology's subject, and with it that of the human sciences more generally, is not constituted by polarities like that of space contra place, but by a movement along paths that compose a being that is as alive to the sentient world as this world is to its human inhabitants.'

Kenneth Olwig, *Swedish University of Agricultural Sciences, Sweden*

Building on his classic work *The Perception of the Environment*, Tim Ingold sets out to restore life to where it should belong, at the heart of anthropological concern. Starting from the idea of life as a process of wayfaring, *Being Alive* presents a radically new understanding of movement, knowledge and description as dimensions not just of being in the world, but of being alive to what is going on there.

Tim Ingold is Professor of Social Anthropology at the University of Aberdeen, UK. He is the author of *The Perception of the Environment* and *Lines*.

Being Alive

Essays on movement,
knowledge and description

Tim Ingold

LONDON AND NEW YORK

First published 2011
by Routledge
2 Park Square, Milton Park, Abingdon, Oxon OX14 4RN

Simultaneously published in the USA & Canada
by Routledge
711 Third Avenue, New York, NY 10017

Routledge is an imprint of the Taylor & Francis Group, an informa business

British Library Cataloguing in Publication Data
A catalogue record for this book is available from the British Library

Library of Congress Cataloging in Publication Data
Ingold, Tim, 1948–
    Being alive : essays on movement, knowledge and description /
    Tim Ingold.
        p. cm.
    Includes bibliographical references and index.
    1. Anthropology–Philosophy. 2. Human ecology–Philosophy.
    3. Human beings–Effect of environment on. 4. Geographical
    perception. I. Title.
    GN33.I45 2011
    301.01–dc22   2010043941

ISBN: 978-0-415-57683-3 (hbk)
ISBN: 978-0-415-57684-0 (pbk)
ISBN: 978-0-203-81833-6 (ebk)

Typeset in Bembo by
HWA Text and Data Management, London

Printed and bound by CPI Group (UK) Ltd, Croydon, CR0 4YY

'It's my life'
Zack Ingold (aged 3)
to whom, with affection,
this book is dedicated.

CONTENTS

List of figures   *ix*
Preface and acknowledgements   *xi*

Prologue

1 Anthropology comes to life   3

PART I
Clearing the ground   **15**

2 Materials against materiality   19

3 Culture on the ground: the world perceived through the feet   33

4 Walking the plank: meditations on a process of skill   51

PART II
The meshwork   **63**

5 Rethinking the animate, reanimating thought   67

6 Point, line, counterpoint: from environment to fluid space   76

7 When *ANT* meets *SPIDER*: social theory for arthropods   89

PART III
Earth and sky   **95**

  8 The shape of the earth   99

  9 Earth, sky, wind and weather   115

10 Landscape or weather-world?   126

11 Four objections to the concept of soundscape   136

PART IV
A storied world   **141**

12 Against space: place, movement, knowledge   145

13 Stories against classification: transport, wayfaring and the
integration of knowledge   156

14 Naming as storytelling: speaking of animals among the
Koyukon of Alaska   165

PART V
Drawing making writing   **177**

15 Seven variations on the letter A   181

16 Ways of mind-walking: reading, writing, painting   196

17 The textility of making   210

18 Drawing together: doing, observing, describing   220

Epilogue

19 Anthropology is *not* ethnography   229

Notes   *244*
References   *254*
Index   *265*

FIGURES

2.1 Wet stone   19
2.2 Ladder   27
2.3 Dry stone   32
3.1 Skeletons of the gibbon, orang-utan, chimpanzee, gorilla and man   34
3.2 Hand (a) and foot (b) of chimpanzee; hand (c) and foot (d) of man   36
4.1 The correct way to hold a saw and how to use the thumb and left
     hand as a guide when beginning the cut   52
5.1 Radiating life: an acacia tree in Tsavo National Park, Kenya   71
6.1 A line of becoming, in relation to the localizable connection of
     A and B (distance), or in relation to their contiguity   84
6.2 'Loose' ligament tissue of the rat   87
7.1 ANT, the mound builder   89
7.2 SPIDER, the web weaver   90
7.3 The meshwork (spider/web/twig) and the network of relations between
     spider, web and twig   92
8.1 Mental models of the earth   100
8.2 (a) Ethan's drawing of the spherical earth surrounded by the 'sky';
     (b) Darcy's drawing of the sky, the ground (with houses) and the   103
     spherical earth
8.3 Examples of the picture cards used in the experiment by Nobes, Martin
     and Panagiotaki   106
8.4 Adults' drawings of the earth   107
9.1 The world brought indoors: René Magritte's *Poison* (1939)   118
9.2 The exhabitant of the earth (a) and the inhabitant of the weather-world (b) 120
9.3 A pencil sketch by Vincent van Gogh dating from summer 1889, of a
     wheat field with cypress trees   122
9.4 Withered grasses in frozen snow, Goodnews Bay, Lower Kuskokwim
     District, Alaska   123
9.5 Fungi breaking through asphalt   124

13.1	The dual inheritance model of genetic and cultural transmission	158
13.2	Story and life	161
13.3	Wayfaring (top) and transport (bottom)	163
15.1	'This is not an **A**': card, paper, ink and red cosmetic dye	182
15.2	**A**s in plastic, from an alphabet set for pre-school children	184
15.3	Ox-head A and a scene painted on the wall of the chapel of Djar in the city of Thebes	186
15.4	Gothic **A** and quill, showing approved penhold	187
15.5	A line of writing: typed and handwritten on ruled paper	189
15.6	The sound of **A**: musical score, phonetic articulation and tuning fork	192
15.7	An embroidered **A** with needle and thread in fabric	194
16.1	Words in pictures and pictures in words: a page from the Aberdeen Bestiary	201
16.2	Figurative and geometric motifs in Yolngu art	203
17.1	Sight lines as threads: two engravings by Abraham Bosse	219

PREFACE AND ACKNOWLEDGEMENTS

I am an anthropologist: not a social or cultural anthropologist; not a biological or archaeological anthropologist; just an anthropologist. And in this book I present a very personal view of what, for me, anthropology is. I do not pretend that it is in any way representative: to the contrary, anthropologists reading this book may feel that it strays rather far from their usual preoccupations, and that its centre of gravity lies closer to other fields such as art or architecture. It has indeed been part of my purpose to shift anthropology in this direction, a purpose founded on the conviction that the convention according to which anthropology is committed to observing and describing life as we find it, but not to changing it, whereas art and architecture are at liberty to propose forms never before encountered, without having first to observe and describe what is already there, is unsustainable. The truth is that the propositions of art and architecture, to the extent that they carry force, must be grounded in a profound understanding of the lived world, and conversely that anthropological accounts of the manifold ways in which life is lived would be of no avail if they were not brought to bear on speculative inquiries into what the possibilities for human life might be. Thus art, architecture and anthropology have in common that they observe, describe and propose. There is, perhaps, a discipline waiting to be defined and named where these three fields meet, and if some readers would prefer to regard this book as a kind of manifesto for that discipline, then I shall not object.

Nor would I object were anyone to consider my endeavour to be closer to philosophy than anthropology, save to say that I am no philosopher. I remain in awe of philosophers whose words I cannot even begin to understand, yet tantalised by the obscurity with which, so often, they seem to shroud their arguments. On reflection, however, I have been surprised by how much of the work that has influenced my thinking has come from philosophers rather than anthropologists. Indeed a quick count through the bibliography for this book reveals that of the works that can be definitively attributed to one particular discipline, almost as many are in philosophy as in anthropology. But if my kind of anthropology is actually philosophy, then it is a philosophy that has been pitched out of its traditional academic turrets and forced to do its thinking both in and with the very world of which it writes. In such a philosophy, the bibliography of a book offers a poor guide to the real sources of intellectual inspiration. Why do we acknowledge only our textual sources but not the ground we walk, the ever-changing skies, mountains and rivers, rocks and trees, the houses we inhabit and the tools we use, not to mention the innumerable companions, both non-human animals and fellow humans, with which and with whom we share our lives? They are constantly inspiring us, challenging us, telling us things. If our aim is to read the world, as I believe it ought to be, then the purpose of written texts should be to enrich our reading so that we might be better advised by, and responsive to, what the world is telling us. I would like to think that this book serves such a purpose.

In many ways the book is a sequel to my earlier collection of essays, *The Perception of the Environment*, published in 2000. Whereas that book brought together a selection of my writings from the last decade of the twentieth century, the present volume does the same for the first decade of the twenty-first. In *Perception*, I put forward a conception of the human being as a singular nexus of creative growth within a continually unfolding field of relationships. This process of growth, I suggested, is tantamount to a movement along a way of life. My work since then has been largely dedicated to following through the implications of this suggestion. In doing so, I have found myself returning again and again to the same themes: the idea of life as lived along lines, or wayfaring; the primacy of movement; the nature and constitution of the ground; the divergent perspectives of the earth as ground of habitation and as distant planet; the intercourse of earth and sky, wind and weather; the fluidity and friction of materials; the experiences of light, sound and feeling; what it means to make things; drawing and writing; and storytelling. One of the key concepts that I introduce in this book is that of the meshwork, understood as a texture of interwoven threads. But the book itself exemplifies the concept, in that it, too, is woven from the thematic threads that run through it. Each of the chapters is a particular knot. By following the threads they can, in principle, be read in any order. For the sake of convenience, however, and in order to highlight what I think to be the principal regions of convergence, I have grouped the chapters into five parts.

These parts are: 'clearing the ground', 'the meshwork', 'earth and sky', 'a storied world' and 'drawing making writing'. They are flanked by an introductory prologue and a final epilogue: the former places the volume within the context of the development of my own thinking; the latter places it in the context of the history of the discipline of anthropology and its future prospects. When I first planned the book, I thought it would be divided into three parts, corresponding to the three keywords of the subtitle: movement, knowledge and description. I soon discovered, however, that this would not work, since almost every chapter dealt with all three. The explanation for this lies in what, I suppose, can be taken as the major contention of the book, namely, that to move, to know, and to describe are not separate operations that follow one another in series, but rather parallel facets of the same process – that of life itself. It is by moving that we know, and it is by moving, too, that we describe. It is absurd to ask, for example, whether ordinary walking is a way of moving, knowing or describing. It is all three at once. This is so for one fundamental reason that is headlined in the title of this book. Philosophers have meditated at length on the condition of being in the world. Moving, knowing and describing, however, call for more than being *in*, or immersion. They call for observation. A being that moves, knows and describes must be observant. Being observant means being alive *to* the world. This book is a collection of studies in *being alive*.

British anthropologists like myself currently find themselves working in an academic environment that is profoundly hostile to the task of being alive. Crushed by an avalanche of mission statements, strategic plans, audit reports and review exercises, ideas born of the sweat and toil of an engagement that is nothing if not observant wilt and wither like plants starved of light, air and moisture. The prostitution of scholarship before the twin idols of innovation and competitiveness has reduced once fine traditions of learning to market brands, the pursuit of excellence to a grubby scramble for funding and prestige, and books such as this to outputs whose value is measured by rating and impact rather that by what they might have to contribute to human understanding. I am fortunate however to work in an institution – the University of Aberdeen – that has so far held out against the worst excesses of the business model of higher education. It is a place where ideas still count, and where intellectual life continues to flourish in a spirit of collegiality. In few other places, if any, would it have been possible to build up a programme of teaching and research in anthropology, as we have done in the past decade, starting from scratch, into the busy and thriving operation it is today. This is the decade, from 1999 to 2009, during which the essays comprising this volume were written.

The first three years were spent developing the programme, leading to the foundation of the Department of Anthropology in 2002. For the next three years I headed it, and for the next (2005-2008) I was largely on leave, thanks to the award of a Professorial Fellowship by the Economic and Social Research Council, for which I am profoundly grateful. Most of the work for this book was in fact completed during my tenure of this Fellowship. No sooner had it ended, however, than I was plunged into the maelstrom of my present position, as Head of the University's School of Social Science (which includes Anthropology, Sociology and Politics & International Relations). Once again, my reading, thinking and writing were muscled aside by the insistent and relentless demands of heavy-duty administration. This has been immensely frustrating. Every time I thought the skies might open to allow me just a few days to write, the clouds closed in again and blocked out the light. At length, and in some desperation, I hurriedly bundled up a sheaf of papers, packed them in a suitcase, and took off with my family for three weeks in a cottage by the shores of Lake Pielinen in eastern Finland. That was in July 2010. The place is well known and very dear to us: we have been going there, off and on, for the past twenty-five years. It is somewhere I can write, undisturbed save for the rustling of the wind in the trees, the singing of birds, and of course the itchiness of mosquito bites, which at least have the advantage of keeping one alert.

Thanks to the place, the cottage, and the forbearance of my family – who made no secret of their disapproval of the fact that I was continually 'working' when I should have been on holiday – I was able in those three magical weeks to convert my disorganised bundle of papers into a virtually finished book. Of place, cottage, and family, the last has of course been a source of continual support, and not just on holiday. My wife Anna, who has had to tolerate a husband often so cocooned in his own thoughts as to be unreachable by any known means of human communication, has worked tirelessly to keep me at least marginally in touch with reality, while my daughter Susanna, who has grown from a little girl to a young adult over the years during which these essays were written, has enlivened us all thanks to her indomitable spirit and a regular regime of family hugs. But during this period the Department of Anthropology, too, has grown, not only through new appointments but also through the arrival of many children, all of whom – parents and children alike – have brought a special vitality to an exceptionally happy and vigorous anthropological community. I thank them all, especially the children, for keeping me young, as I do the many students with whom I have been privileged to work. Their questioning, criticism and insight have been a never-failing source of inspiration. Finally, I thank my cello, which has been a constant if temperamental companion over more years than I can remember. It has, in that time, become so much a part of me and of the way I am that when I think and write, it thinks and writes in me. To that extent, it is truly a co-author of this book.

The majority of the essays making up the book have been previously published. All, however, have been more or less extensively revised for the present volume, principally in order to remove overlap or duplication of material.

Chapter 1 started life as a Distinguished Lecture presented to the General Anthropology Division (GAD) of the American Anthropological Association during the AAA Meetings in Philadelphia, on 4 December, 2009. A highly abbreviated version of the lecture is published in the GAD Bulletin, *General Anthropology* (Volume 17(1), 2010, pp. 1-4). I am grateful to the committee of the GAD, and especially to Emily Schultz and Pat Rice, for inviting me to present the lecture.

Chapter 2 has evolved from a lecture originally presented as part of an advanced undergraduate course at the University of Aberdeen, on *The 4 As: Anthropology, Archaeology, Art and Architecture*, and I thank the students taking the course for their inspiring feedback. I also want to thank Stephanie Bunn, whose ideas have greatly influenced my own, and who has been generous in sharing her knowledge and experience as a craftsperson through the workshops she has delivered over the years as part of the *4 As* course. Having converted the lecture into an academic paper, I initially presented it at the 2004 conference of the Theoretical Archaeology Group at the University of Glasgow, and subsequently at the seminar on *Materiality in Society and Culture* held at the University of Oslo in November 2005. I thank the participants on both occasions, as well as the staff and students at Stanford University's Department of Archaeology with whom I discussed the paper in February 2006, for their helpful comments. I went on to present it, in what felt at the time like an intellectual suicide mission, to the material culture seminar at University College London. Though my arguments were blown up, I survived, and the paper was eventually published as a discussion article 'Materials against materiality', in the journal *Archaeological Dialogues* (Volume 14(1), 2007, pp. 1-16), together with critical comments from Christopher Tilley, Carl Knappett, Daniel Miller and Björn Nilsson, and my response. I am grateful to all four commentators for their insightful criticisms, to the journal's associate editor Peter van Dommelen and two anonymous reviewers for their excellent advice, and to Cambridge University Press for permission to reproduce the article in its present form. I also thank David Nash for supplying and allowing me to use the photo that appears as Figure 2.2. The photos for Figures 2.1 and 2.3 were taken by Susanna Ingold.

Chapter 3 was originally written and presented as the Beatrice Blackwood Lecture at the Pitt-Rivers Museum, Oxford, on 16 May, 2001. I am most grateful to the Friends of the Pitt-Rivers Museum, and especially to Rosemary Lee, for inviting me to present the lecture. It was subsequently revised and published in the journal *Material Culture* (Volume 9(3), 2004, pp. 315-340). I am grateful to SAGE for permission to reproduce the article in its present form. In revising it for publication I benefited from the advice of many people, including David Anderson, Hastings Donnan, Brian Durrans, Junzo Kawada, John Linstroth, Hayden Lorimer, Katrin Lund, Edward Tenner and Jo Vergunst, along with two anonymous readers. My thanks to all.

Chapter 4, like Chapter 2, evolved from a lecture for the *4As* course, and was subsequently presented at a research seminar on *Technology and its Social Forms* held at the University of Bergen, Norway, in March 2006. It was written up for publication as a chapter in the volume edited by John R. Dakers, *Defining Technological Literacy: Towards an Epistemological Framework*, published in 2006. For ideas and advice, I am grateful to Brenda Farnell, Charles Keller and François Sigaut, and for permission to reproduce the chapter I thank the volume's publishers, Palgrave Macmillan (New York).

The essay which now forms **Chapter 5** was first presented at a special symposium in Stockholm to mark Vega Day, 24 April 2004, organised by the Swedish Society for Anthropology and Geography, on the occasion of which I was awarded the Society's Retzius Medal in Gold. I have benefited greatly from conversations with my fellow contributors to the symposium – Alf Hornborg, Nurit Bird-David and Colin Scott – and thank them for their support. The essay was first published, alongside the other three symposium papers, in the journal *Ethnos* (Volume 71(1), 2006, pp. 9-20). I am grateful to the publishers, Routledge, for permission to reproduce it in its present form, and to Agence Altitude for permission to reproduce the image in Figure 5.1, from the work of the aerial photographer Yann Arthus-Bertrand.

Chapter 6 was written for the conference *Neurobiology of 'Umwelt': How Living Beings Perceive the World*, sponsored by the IPSEN Foundation, and held in Paris on 18 February, 2008. The conference was a rather frustrating event. Ostensibly, its purpose was to review the concept of *Umwelt*, originally introduced into biology in the early decades of the twentieth century through the writings of Jakob von Uexküll, in the light of recent developments in neuroscience. However with one exception – the philosopher Anne Fagot-Largeault – none of the other contributors appeared to be have read or understood von Uexküll's work. Mistaking the *Umwelt* for an inner mental representation, they failed to appreciate the challenge that von Uexküll's approach to perception poses to mainstream neuro-cognitivism. As the only anthropologist among the speakers, my own contribution was quite out of kilter with the others. I am nevertheless grateful for the opportunity that the conference gave me to straighten out my ideas on perception as a life process. My contribution was subsequently published in 2009, as the final chapter (pp. 141-155) in a volume with the same title as the conference, edited by its organisers, Alain Berthoz and Yves Christen. I am grateful to the volume's publishers, Springer Verlag (Berlin and Heidelberg), for permission to reproduce the chapter in its present form.

Chapter 7 was originally written as a joke. I had been invited to write an epilogue for a collection of papers on the topic of 'material agency', put together by Carl Knappett and Lambros Malafouris. Reading through the papers, it struck me that their authors – many of whom were in thrall to actor-network theory and enamoured of its jargon – were taking themselves just a little too seriously. It would do no harm, I thought, to poke some gentle fun at the earnestness of their pretensions. The collection, entitled *Material Agency: Towards a Non-Anthropocentric Approach*, was published by Springer Science + Business Media (New York) in 2008, and my contribution appears on pages 209-15. I am grateful to the publishers for permission to reproduce it here, in a revised form.

Chapters 8 and **9** both began life at a conference on the anthropology of wind, held at the University of Oxford in June 2005. My contribution to the symposium, entitled 'Blowing life: sensing the wind in the animic cosmos', was in fact closely modelled on the essay included here as Chapter 5. It was at this conference, however, that I first produced the sketch that now appears as Figure 9.2, and the comments I received encouraged me to develop the idea further. Following the conference, and thanks to the stimulus it provided, I wrote the paper entirely anew, and presented it for the first time at the seminar on *Landscapes and Liminality*, held at the University of Turku's research station at Kevo, in Finnish Lapland, in January 2006. The paper, by then entitled 'Earth, sky, wind and weather', was first published, alongside other contributions to the original wind conference, in the 2007 special issue of the *Journal of the Royal Anthropological Institute* (pp. S19-S38), and in the subsequent volume *Wind, Life, Health: Anthropological and Historical Perspectives*, edited by Elisabeth Hsu and Chris Low (Oxford: Blackwell, 2008, pp. 17-35). I am most grateful to the volume's editors for their encouragement and support.

Even after it had been published, however, I was not entirely satisfied with the paper. It seemed to fall into two parts that addressed different issues and did not fit together properly. I therefore resolved to develop the first part as a separate essay. This has grown into Chapter 8. The inspiration for this essay goes back to one of a series of seminars on *The Interactive Mind*, sponsored by the Arts and Humanities Research Council, and held on that occasion at the University of Sheffield (April 2005). During the seminar I heard a presentation on 'Conceptual change in children' by Michael Siegal, and was intrigued by the psychological research he described on children's perceptions of the earth and the sky. I determined there and then to look further into this, and am grateful to Dr Siegal for pointing me towards the relevant literature, which has grown significantly in the intervening years. In developing the essay I have taken account of these further contributions. I presented the result for the first time at a seminar in the Department of Geography at the University of Glasgow on 9 March, 2010, and then as a lecture at the University of Minnesota on 2 April 2010. I am grateful to Hayden Lorimer and Stuart McLean for their respective invitations. In addition, I thank Elsevier for permission to reprint the illustrations that appear as Figures 8.1 and 8.2, from *Cognitive Psychology* 24 (S. Vosniadou & W. F. Brewer, 'Mental models of the earth: a study of conceptual change in childhood', pp. 535-585, 1992). I also thank Gavin Nobes for certain points of clarification and, with the British Psychological Society, for granting me permission to reproduce the image in Figure 8.3 from the *British Journal of Developmental Psychology* 23 (G. Nobes, A. E. Martin and G. Panagiotaki, 'The development of scientific knowledge of the Earth', pp. 47-64, 2005). Finally, I thank Benjamin Lazier for allowing me to see and refer to his inspiring but still unpublished paper, 'Earthrise, or the globalization of the world picture'.

In Chapter 9, I have taken the remaining sections of my original article, 'Earth, sky, wind and weather', and have revised and added to them by introducing material from another, subsequently published paper entitled 'Bindings against boundaries: entanglements of life in an open world' (*Environment and Planning A*, Volume 40(8), 2008, pp. 1796-1810), which was originally presented as one of a series of lectures at Linacre College, Oxford, in February 2007. I have retained the original title for the Chapter, and am grateful to John Wiley & Sons for allowing me to republish it in its present form. I also thank the Design and Artists Copyright Society (DACS) for permission to reproduce the painting by René Magritte in Figure 9.1, the van Gogh Museum, Amsterdam, for permission to reproduce the drawing by Vincent van Gogh in Figure 9.3, the Lower Kuskokwim School District, Alaska, for permission to use the image reproduced in Figure 9.4, and Klaus Weber for supplying and allowing me to use the photo in Figure 9.5.

Chapter 10 has not been previously published. It builds, however, on an earlier paper entitled 'The eye of the storm: visual perception and the weather', published in the journal *Visual Studies* (Volume 20(2), 2005, pp. 97-104). A first draft of the present essay was written for a multidisciplinary symposium on *Landscape in Theory*, held at the University of Nottingham on 26 June, 2008. I have however virtually rewritten it, yet again, for this volume. I am grateful to Stephen Daniels for inviting me to the symposium, to Kenneth Olwig for many inspiring conversations, and to John Thornes for an enlightening correspondence on the painterly rendering of sky and weather.

Chapter 11 began as an off-the-cuff commentary that concluded a landmark conference on *Sound and Anthropology* held at the University of St Andrews in June 2006. I wrote up my notes some months after the conference, and they were published in the following year under the title 'Against soundscape' in a volume edited by Angus Carlyle: *Autumn Leaves: Sound and the Environment in Artistic Practice* (Paris: Double Entendre, pp. 10-13). I have revised and retitled this brief essay for the present volume.

Chapter 12 has a long history. It was the first in this volume to be drafted, and one of the last to be published. It was initially prepared for a conference on *Space, Culture, Power*, held at the University of Aberdeen in April 2001. I subsequently revised it for a conference on *Space, Spatiality, Technology* held at Napier University, Edinburgh, in December 2004. Since then, it has undergone a number of further revisions, and was eventually published, in 2009, in a long delayed volume of contributions from the original 2001 conference, entitled *Boundless Worlds: An Anthropological Approach to Movement*, edited by Peter Wynn Kirby (Oxford: Berghahn, 2009). I am indebted to Berghahn Books for permission to reproduce the chapter here. It has once again been very much revised.

Chapter 13 was originally written for a session on *The Genealogical Model Reconsidered*, held at the 101st Annual Meetings of the American Anthropological Association in New Orleans, November 2002. It, too, has undergone numerous revisions, and was finally published in a volume of papers from the session, entitled *Kinship and Beyond*, edited by its original organisers, Sandra Bamford and James Leach (Oxford: Berghahn, 2009). Once again, I am grateful to Berghahn Books for permission to reproduce the chapter in this volume.

Chapter 14 was written for an international conference on *Animal Names*, held at the Istituto Veneto di Scienze, Lettere ed Arti, Venice, in October 2003. It was published by the institute in 2005, in an eponymous volume of papers from the conference, edited by Alessandro Minelli, Gherardo Ortalli and Glauco Sanga (pp. 159-172). In revising the paper for this volume, I was inspired by the poetry of Alastair Reid. I am grateful to Griet Scheldeman for bringing Reid's remarkable work to my attention.

Chapter 15 has its origins in an exhibition curated by Wendy Gunn, and held at Aberdeen Art Gallery from April through June, 2005. The exhibition, entitled *Fieldnotes and Sketchbooks: Challenging the Boundaries Between Descriptions and Processes of Describing*, was designed to coincide with the 2005 conference of the Association of Social Anthropologists, on *Creativity and Cultural Improvisation*, held that year at the University of Aberdeen. I subsequently wrote an essay based on my contribution to the exhibition, which appeared alongside papers from the other contributors in a volume with the same title, under Wendy Gunn's editorship. The volume was published in 2009 by Peter Lang. The title of my contribution (pp. 109-134), like that of my piece in the exhibition, was *12 As*. In revising the essay for the present volume, however, I have reduced the number of As from twelve to seven.

I am indebted to Wendy Gunn for her work in putting together both the exhibition and the subsequent book, and to Mike Anusas for introducing me to the work of the eccentric theorist of design, Vilém Flusser.

Chapter 16 was originally written for a special issue of the journal *Visual Studies* (Volume 25(1), 2010, pp. 15-23) on 'Walking, ethnography and arts practice', edited by Sarah Pink, Phil Hubbard, Maggie O'Neill and Alan Radley, and based on contributions to the Roam walking weekend organised by Radar, the Arts Programme of the University of Loughborough, in March 2008. Unable to attend the weekend myself, I first developed the ideas presented in this Chapter for the CUSO (Conférence Universitaire de la Suisse Occidentale) Doctoral Programme workshop on *Literature and the Environment* at the University of Geneva, 16-18 October 2009. I am grateful to the participants in the workshop for an inspiring discussion. Figure 16.1 is reproduced by permission of Historic Collections, King's College, University of Aberdeen, and Figure 16.2 by permission of the Buku-Larrnggay Mulka Centre, Yirrkala, Australia (on behalf of the Marrakulu clan) and of the University of Chicago Press. I thank the publishers of *Visual Studies*, Routledge, for permission to reproduce the article in its present form.

Chapter 17 was written for a special issue of the *Cambridge Journal of Economics* (Volume 34(1), 2010, pp. 91-102) on the ontology of technology, edited by Philip Faulkner, Clive Lawson and Jochen Runde. I wrote the first version in 2007, and revised it two years later in the light of the extremely helpful comments of three anonymous referees. I am grateful to Oxford University Press for permission to reproduce a revised version of the essay in this volume.

Chapter 18 is based on a paper originally written for the conference *Beyond the Whole? Anthropology and Holism in a Contemporary World*, held at Sandbjerg, Denmark, in July 2008. I am most grateful to the organisers of the conference for the invitation to attend, in extraordinarily distinguished company. The paper was subsequently revised in the light of helpful comments from Ton Otto, Nils Bubandt and Anna Tsing, and published (2010) in a volume of contributions from the conference, edited by Ton Otto and Nils Bubandt, entitled *Experiments in Holism: Theory and Practice in Contemporary Anthropology*. The paper has been very extensively revised for the present volume, and while I have kept the original title of 'Drawing together', I have changed the subtitle from 'materials, gestures, lines' to 'doing, observing, describing', so as to better reflect its current foci. I thank the editors of the original volume, and its publishers Wiley-Blackwell (Chichester), for permission to reuse this material.

Chapter 19 began life as the Radcliffe-Brown Lecture for 2007, presented at the University of Edinburgh on 12 March of that year, and at the British Academy in London two days later. It was subsequently revised for publication in the *Proceedings of the British Academy* (Volume 154, 2008, pp. 69-92). Many people assisted me both in the preparation of the lecture and in subsequently revising it for publication. They include Maurice Bloch, Philippe Descola, Keith Hart, Heonik Kwon, Paul Sillitoe, James Urry and David Zeitlyn. I thank them all. To Oxford University Press I am grateful for permission to reproduce the text in an only slightly revised form.

Tim Ingold
Aberdeen
September 2010

Prologue

1

ANTHROPOLOGY COMES TO LIFE

As individuals express their life, so they are. What they are, therefore, coincides with their production.

Karl Marx and Friedrich Engels (1977 [1845-6]: 42)

The only thing that is given to us and that *is* when there is human life is *the having to make it ... Life is a task.*

José Ortega y Gasset (1941 [1935]: 200)

The manner in which we humans *are* on the earth is *Buan*, dwelling. To be a human being means ... to dwell.

Martin Heidegger (1971 [1954]: 147)

For we are made of lines. We are not only referring to lines of writing. Lines of writing conjugate with other lines, life lines, lines of luck or misfortune, lines productive of the variation of the line of writing itself, lines that are *between the lines* of writing.

Gilles Deleuze and Félix Guattari (2004 [1980]: 215)

Anthropology, in my view, is a sustained and disciplined inquiry into the conditions and potentials of human life. Yet generations of theorists, throughout the history of the discipline, have been at pains to expunge life from their accounts, or to treat it as merely consequential, the derivative and fragmentary output of patterns, codes, structures or systems variously defined as genetic or cultural, natural or social. Born of nature, moulded by society, impelled by the promptings of genetic predisposition and guided by the precepts of transmitted culture, human beings are portrayed as creatures whose lives are expended in the fulfilment of capacities bestowed at the outset. Beginning, as Clifford Geertz famously put it, 'with the natural equipment to live a thousand kinds of life', each of us is supposed to 'end in the end having lived only one' (Geertz 1973: 45). Life, in this view, is a movement towards terminal closure: a gradual filling up of capacities and shutting down of possibilities. My own work, over the last quarter of a century, has been driven by an ambition to reverse this emphasis: to replace the end-directed or teleonomic conception of the life-process with a recognition of life's capacity continually to overtake the destinations that are thrown up in its course. It is of the essence of life that it does not begin here or end there, or connect a point of origin with a final destination, but rather that it keeps on going, finding a way through the myriad of things that form, persist and break up in its currents. Life, in short, is a movement of opening, not of closure. As such, it should lie at the very heart of anthropological concern.

Looking back on my efforts to restore anthropology to life, they seem to fall roughly into four phases, each of which revolves around a single key term. The first phase was about the meaning of *production*; the second was about the meaning of *history*. In the third phase I was preoccupied with the notion of *dwelling*. The latest phase – the one I am in now – is an exploration of the idea that life is lived along *lines*. Though they followed one another in time, these phases were by no means discrete. Rather, each carried over into the next. It all began with the question of what it means to say of human beings that they are the producers of their lives. But I did not cease thinking about this question as it gave birth to another: how is it that, in producing their lives, humans create history? How, if at all, is this history to be distinguished from the process of evolution in which all living creatures are supposed to be caught up? Nor did I cease thinking about history as I began to see, in what I called the perspective of dwelling, a way to overcome the entrenched division between the 'two worlds' of nature and society, and to re-embed human being and becoming within the continuum of the lifeworld. And I have not ceased thinking about dwelling in my current explorations in the comparative anthropology of the line, which grew from the realisation that every being is instantiated in the world as a path of movement along a way of life. Or to trace the progression of my thinking in reverse: to lay a path through the world is to dwell; to dwell is to live historically; every historical form of life is a mode of production. In what follows, I shall recapitulate the first three phases of this progression, in their original order, as an introduction to the fourth, which is represented by the essays that comprise the present volume.

Production

I came initially to the question of production through a reflection on how the ways of working of human beings differ from those of non-human animals (Ingold 1983). Over a century previously, Friedrich Engels had been pondering the same thing. In a draft introduction to his unfinished magnum opus, *Dialectics of Nature*, probably written in 1875-6, Engels argued that the works of humans differ fundamentally from those of other animals, in so far as the former are driven by an 'aim laid down in advance' (Engels 1934: 34). True, human activities are not alone in having significant environmental consequences; moreover the great majority of these consequences, as Engels was the first to admit, are unintended or unforeseen. Nevertheless, returning to the theme in an essay on 'The part played by labour in the transition from ape to man', written around the same time, Engels was convinced that the measure of man's humanity lay in the extent to which things could be contrived to go according to plan. 'The further removed men are from animals', he declared, 'the more their effect on nature assumes the character of premeditated, planned action directed towards definite, preconceived ends' (ibid.: 178). Finally, in another contemporary fragment, Engels conceded that it is the end-directedness of human action that qualifies it as production. 'The most that the animal can achieve is to *collect*; man *produces*, he prepares the means of life … which without him nature would not have produced' (ibid.: 308). To put it another way, irrespective of the actual impact of their activities, animals do not labour in their environment in order to change it. They have no conception of their task. But human beings always work with some notion of what they are doing, and why, even though the results never quite conform to expectations.

This, too, was the conclusion to which Karl Marx had moved in the first volume of *Capital*, published a few years earlier, in 1867. Unlike the spider weaving its web or the bee constructing its cell, the human labour process, said Marx, 'ends in the creation of something which, when the process began, already existed … in an ideal form' (Marx 1930: 170). Yet for Marx, this model of creation presented something of a dilemma. For if the form of a thing must already exist in the imagination before the work of production can even begin, where does this initial image come from? In notes published posthumously as the *Grundrisse*, Marx came up with his answer. It is consumption, he argued, that sets the aims of production. It does so by creating expectations about the forms things should take and the functions they should fulfil, and these expectations, in turn, motivate the productive process. 'If it is clear that production offers consumption its external object', Marx reasoned, 'it is therefore equally clear that consumption ideally posits the object of production as an internal image, as a need, as drive and as purpose' (Marx 1973: 91-2). Or in a nutshell, whereas producing things gives us objects to consume, consuming things gives us ideas of what to produce. The result is a closed circuit, of production and consumption, the one converting pre-existing images into final objects, the other converting objects into images. To ask which comes first, production or consumption, is to pose a chicken and egg question.

Herein lay Marx's dilemma. How could he prove, as his philosophy of materialism required, that production takes precedence over consumption? Allowing that production and consumption are but phases of one process, he continued to insist, in the *Grundrisse*, that 'production is the real point of departure and hence also the predominant moment' (1973: 94). If that were really so, however, then somewhere along the line products would have miraculously to appear that present to the consumer the need that subsequently motivates their production. In a well-known anthropological critique, Marshall Sahlins scorned Marx's tortuous and ultimately circular attempts to transform, as he put it, 'the pre-existing image of production into its objective consequence' (Sahlins 1976: 153). The source of Marx's discomfiture was a gift to Sahlins, who was out to show, quite to the contrary, that the finalities of production are pre-specified in the symbolic forms of culture. Marx's admission that every act of production has to begin with an image in mind, of what is to be produced, seemed only to prove Sahlins's point. Yet a moment's reflection reveals that Sahlins is trapped in exactly the same circularity as Marx, the only difference being that he has resolved to enter the circle at a diametrically opposed pole. Whereas Marx, the materialist, had to pull objects from a hat in order to set the ball rolling, the culturalist Sahlins has to conjure symbolic representations from thin air. Indeed so long as we assume that there is no more to production than converting images into objects, and no more to consumption that turning objects back into images, there appears to be no escape from the circle. Neither object nor image can take precedence, neither production nor consumption, when each is a precondition for the other.

Yet Marx himself, spelling out the elements of the labour process in *Capital*, hints that there is more. Images do not turn themselves into objects just like that. The process takes time, and as Marx observes, the producer's 'purposive will, manifesting itself as attention, must be operative throughout the whole duration of the labour' (Marx 1930: 170). Moreover as he labours, it is not only the materials with which he works that are transformed.[1] The worker, too, is changed through the experience. Latent potentialities of action and perception are developed. He becomes, even if ever so slightly, a different person. Perhaps, then, the essence of production lies as much or more in the attentional quality of the action – that is, in its attunement and responsiveness to the task as it unfolds – and in its developmental effects on the producer, as in any images or representations of ends to be achieved that may be held up before it. There is indeed a precedent for this view in the earlier collaborative writings of Marx and Engels. In a passage from *The German Ideology*, penned in 1846, they go so far as to equate production with life itself, and every mode of production with a mode of life. 'As individuals express their life', wrote Marx and Engels, 'so they are. What they are, therefore, coincides with their production, both with *what* they produce and *how* they produce' (Marx and Engels 1977: 42). Conceived as the attentive movement of a conscious being, bent upon the tasks of life, the productive process is not confined within the finalities of any particular project. It does not start with an image and finish with an object but carries on through, without beginning or end, punctuated – rather than initiated or terminated – by the forms, whether mental or ideal, that it sequentially brings into being.

Taken in this sense, as I argued in a lecture delivered almost thirty years ago,[2] production 'must be understood *intransitively*, not as a transitive relation of image to object' (Ingold 1983: 15). This is to set the verb 'to produce' alongside other intransitive verbs such as to hope, to grow and to dwell, as against such transitive verbs as to plan, to make and to build. And it is, once and for all, to restore to production the existential primacy that Marx had always sought for it (Ingold 1986: 321-4). Its primacy is that of life itself: of the processes of hoping, growing and dwelling over the forms that are conceived and realised within them. Yet this assertion of the priority of ongoing process over final form, as we shall see, poses a fundamental challenge to the very model of creation to which both Marx and Engels had appealed in order to characterise the distinctively human character of productive labour. Indeed, once we dispense with the prior representation of an end to be achieved as a necessary condition for production, and focus instead on the purposive will or intentionality that inheres in the action itself – in its capacity literally to *pro-duce*, to draw out or bring forth potentials in the person of the producer and in the surrounding world – then there are no longer any grounds to restrict the ranks of producers to human beings alone. Producers, both human and non-human, do not so much transform the world, impressing their preconceived designs upon the material substrate of nature, as play their part from within in the world's transformation of itself. Growing into the world, the world grows in them. And with this, the question concerning production gives way to another, this time about the meaning of history.

History

As he drafted the introduction to his *Dialectics of Nature*, Engels was well aware of the intimate connection between these two questions. There is a limited sense, he admits, in which animals produce, yet without ends in mind, their activity – more or less instinctive – does not really count as production. Likewise, animals may be said to have a history, but such history, Engels wrote, 'is made for them, and in so far as they themselves take part in it, this occurs without their knowledge and desire' (Engels 1934: 34). Only when human beings appear on the stage do we enter history proper: that is, a history they have made themselves in the conscious pursuit of predetermined aims.

Writing over a century later, Maurice Godelier returned to the same theme, in virtually identical terms. Introducing a collection of his essays on *The Mental and the Material* (1986), dedicated to the revival of a Marxian approach to anthropology, Godelier, too, grants that non-human species have histories of a kind. These natural histories, however, have come about not through any intentional activity on the part of non-humans themselves, but are rather compounded from the reproductive consequences of accidental variations and recombinations of hereditary material along lines of descent. Such histories, of what Charles Darwin had called 'descent with modification', and which his latter-day followers would call 'evolutionary', have taken place *in*, but are in no sense produced *by*, populations of organisms. The human species, of course, has an evolutionary history of this sort, which palaeo-anthropologists have been at pains to unravel. But alone among animals, Godelier insists, humans also have History, which he spells with an upper-case 'H' in order to distinguish it from the lower-case histories of variation under natural selection common to all living kinds (Godelier 1989: 63).

It is a fact about human beings, Godelier asserts (1986: 1), that 'they produce society in order to live'. By this he means that the designs and purposes of human action upon the environment – action that yields a return in the form of the wherewithal for subsistence – have their source in the domain of social relations. But although Godelier takes his inspiration from Marx, in fact Marx does not say that humans produce society. He says they produce themselves and one another. They do so by reciprocally laying down, through their life activities, the conditions for their own growth and development. What they produce, in short, is not society but the ongoing process of social life. As Marx and Engels had put it, in *The German Ideology* (1977: 42), human beings are the what and how of their production: each is the instantiation of a certain way of being alive and active in the world. Or in the words of the philosopher José Ortega y Gasset, we should say 'not that man *is*, but that he *lives*' (Ortega y Gasset 1941: 213).

Ortega's writings were much cited by mid-twentieth-century cultural anthropologists in the belief that they lent support to the idea that culture, and not nature, shapes human experience. 'Man', Ortega had famously declared, 'has no nature, what he has is … history' (1941: 217). In an influential work from the same period, entitled *Theoretical Anthropology*, David Bidney objected that this presents us with a false choice. Human nature and cultural history, Bidney argued, are not mutually exclusive but rather complementary. Each depends on the other, and adequate self-knowledge required the comprehension of both (Bidney 1953: 154–5). In reality, however, Ortega's declaration was not about the primacy of culture; it was about the primacy of *life*. Humanity, he is telling us, does not come pre-packaged with species membership, nor does it come from having been born into a particular culture or society. It is rather something we have continually to work at. 'The only thing that is given to us and that is when there is human life', Ortega went on to say, 'is *the having to make it* … *Life is a task*' (Ortega y Gasset 1941: 200). For both Marx and Ortega, then, what we are, or what we can be, does not come ready made. We have, perpetually and never-endingly, to be making ourselves. That is what life is, what history is, and what it means to produce. And that, too, for these authors, is what it means to be human. To inquire into human life is thus to explore the conditions of possibility in a world peopled by beings whose identities are established, in the first place, not by received species- or culture-specific attributes but by productive accomplishment.

It was with these thoughts in mind that I returned to the work of Godelier. The thesis he sets out to prove, in *The Mental and the Material*, is that History is wrought in the human transformation of nature. Through their creative action upon the natural environment, Godelier claims, human beings bring about changes not only in their relations with that environment but also in the relations among themselves constitutive of society (Godelier 1986: 1). Entailed in this claim, however, lies a contradiction – perhaps the founding contradiction of the entire edifice of western thought – namely that it has no way of comprehending human beings' creative involvement in the material world, save by taking them out of it. In so far as humans are encompassed *within* this world they are objectively bound to the determinations of an evolved human nature which they had no hand in shaping; conversely they are able to shape their own destinies only in so far as they issue from a historical consciousness that is constituted *without* the material world, in an intersubjective or social domain of mental realities that stands over and above the sheer materiality of nature. Indeed the very concept of the 'human' seems to embody the abiding paradox of a form of life that can realise its own essence only by transcending it. My reflections on the concept of production, however, seemed to offer a potential resolution. If production is not, as Godelier would have it, about transforming the material world, but rather about participating in the world's transformation of itself, then could we not conclude that human beings produce themselves and one another by establishing, through their actions, the conditions for their ongoing growth and development? And might it not be in precisely this mutual establishment of developmental conditions that we find the meaning of history?

Human actions, of course, establish such conditions not only for other humans. They also do so for assorted non-humans. The farmer's work on the fields, for example, creates favourable conditions for the growth of crop plants, and the herdsman's does the same for domestic animals. Moreover, granted that not all producers are human, it is easy to turn the argument around and show how various non-humans contribute, in specific environments, not just to their own growth and development but also to that of human beings. It follows that human social life is not cut out on a separate plane from the rest of nature but is part and parcel of what is going on throughout the organic world. It is the process wherein living beings of all kinds, in what they do, constitute each other's conditions of existence, both for their own and for subsequent generations. In so far as the forms of beings arise within this process, it may be described as evolutionary. This argument, however, has a radical corollary, and it took some time before it fully dawned on me. It is that variation under natural selection, although it undoubtedly occurs *within* evolution, is *not*, in itself, an evolutionary process (Ingold 2001a: 125). The differential reproduction of organisms, competing for resources within a finite environment, leads to population-level changes in gene frequencies; evolution, however, is about the emergence of form within matrices of development. Genes are of course critical components of these matrices. They make a difference. But the forms of organisms are not compendia of difference but the ever-emergent outcomes of processes of growth.

The penny dropped thanks to my encounter with the work of the philosopher of biology, Susan Oyama. In her path-breaking book *The ontogeny of information* (1985), Oyama shows that mainstream evolutionary theory, modelled on Darwinian principles, is disabled by an elementary fallacy. The fallacy is to suppose that organic form pre-exists the processes that give rise to it (Oyama 1985: 13). Positing the objective consequence of ontogenetic development as a pre-existent design specification, technically known as the *genotype*, orthodox theory proceeds to account for organic form as the external, *phenotypic* materialisation of this inner design. The logical circularity entailed here is precisely the same as the one that I had already identified in Marx's discussion of production and consumption, whereby the product – the outcome of the productive process – is posited as an ideal form, an image, which precedes and underwrites its subsequent realisation. And the solution, in both cases, is the same: that is, to insist on the primacy of process over product; of life over the forms it takes, whether covert (as mental image or genotype) or overt (as material object or phenotype). Following Oyama, I argued that the forms of organisms are not genetically preconfigured but continually emerge as developmental outcomes within matrices comprised of mutually conditioning relations. Far from being confined to the transitive intervals between genotype and phenotype, life carries on in the unfolding of the relational matrices wherein organic forms are generated and held in place. Evolution is the name we give to this unfolding. It is, in Oyama's words (1989: 5), 'the derivational history of developmental systems'.

What has come to be known as 'developmental systems theory' (DST) remains something of a heresy in mainstream evolutionary biology. I was keen, however, to introduce DST to anthropology, since I saw in it a way to move beyond the traditional dualism which insisted, as in Godelier's formulation, on one kind of History for humans and another kind of history for the rest of the living world, and which set up an imaginary point of emergence at their intersection. With DST, it is possible to resituate the historical experience of human beings within the evolving matrices of development in which all living beings are immersed (Ingold 2001b). Homing in on any one such matrix, what we discover there is not so much an interplay between two kinds of history – the upper case History of humanity on the plane of society and the lower case history of nature – as a history comprised by the interplay of diverse humans and non-humans in their mutual involvement. In a prophetic paper written over three decades ago, in 1976, the geographer Torsten Hägerstrand already foresaw the collapse of the great divide between nature and society. We can bring these divisions under one perspective, he argued, by regarding every constituent of the environment as a path of becoming (Hägerstrand 1976: 332). There are human becomings, animal becomings, plant becomings, and so on. As they move together through time and encounter one another, these paths interweave to form an immense and continually evolving tapestry. Anthropology, then, is the study of human becomings as they unfold within the weave of the world. And it was this idea of history, evolution and social life as woven, rather than as either made by humans or made for them, that led me to dwelling.

Dwelling

I had been pondering the distinction between building and dwelling long before a chance conversation with a student of architecture, circa 1990, directed me towards the philosophical writings of Martin Heidegger on the subject. The distinction seemed to me to offer an exemplary instance of the contrast, to which I have already drawn attention, between transitive and intransitive senses of production. Thus it was Marx, not Heidegger, who set me thinking about it. Building, in Marx's celebrated fable of the human architect and the bee, figures as a transitive relation: the architect, you may recall, has already built the cell in his head before he constructs it in wax (Marx 1930: 169-70). Indeed the presumption that built form is the manifest outcome of prior design is implicit in the designation of the building as a work of architecture. Dwelling, by contrast, is intransitive: it is about the way inhabitants, singly and together, produce their own lives, and like life, it carries on. Critically, then, dwelling is not merely the occupation of structures already built: it does not stand to building as consumption to production. It rather signifies that immersion of beings in the currents of the lifeworld without which such activities as designing, building and occupation could not take place at all. As individuals produce their lives, Marx and Engels had declared (1977: 42), so they *are*.

In his seminal essay, *Building Dwelling Thinking*, Heidegger argued precisely the same point. His concern was to recover, behind the narrow, modernist identification of dwelling with occupation or consumption, its original and primary meaning as being, encompassing the entire way in which one lives one's life on the earth. Thus 'I dwell, you dwell' is identical to 'I am, you are' (Heidegger 1971: 147). Building, then, is not a means to dwelling, nor does dwelling fix the ends, or the designs, which building goes on to implement. For to build, as Heidegger put it, 'is in itself already to dwell ... Only if we are capable of dwelling, only then can we build' (ibid.: 160). In an earlier collection of essays on *The Perception of the Environment* (Ingold 2000a), I took this as the founding statement of what I called the 'dwelling perspective'. By this I meant a perspective founded on the premise that the forms humans build, whether in the imagination or on the ground, arise within the currents of their involved activity, in the specific relational contexts of their practical engagement with their surroundings. I opposed this to the 'building perspective' enshrined in the familiar model of making, according to which productive work serves merely to transcribe pre-existent, ideal forms onto an initially formless material substrate (Ingold 2000a: 178-87). To adopt a dwelling perspective is not, of course, to deny that humans build things. But it is to call for an alternative account of building, as a process of *working with* materials and not just *doing to* them, and of bringing form into being rather than merely translating from the virtual to the actual.

Another way of visualising this is to think of building, or of making more generally, as a modality of weaving. As building is to dwelling, so making is to weaving: to highlight the first term of each pair is to see the processes of production consumed by their final products, whose origination is attributed not to the improvisatory creativity of labour that works things out as it goes along, but to the novelty of determinate ends conceived in advance. To highlight the second term, on the other hand, is to prioritise process over product, and to define the activity by the attentiveness of environmental engagement rather than the transitivity of means and ends. Whereas the building perspective sets the maker, as a bearer of prior intentions, over and against the material world, the dwelling perspective situates the weaver in amongst a world of materials, which he literally draws out in bringing forth the work. He is, in that regard, a producer in the original sense of the term. Through this latter perspective I hoped to shift anthropology in general, and the study of material culture in particular, away from the fixation with objects and images, and towards a better appreciation of the material flows and currents of sensory awareness within which both ideas and things reciprocally take shape.

Though I have drawn on Heidegger for my discussion of dwelling, I am by no means a Heideggerian, and it has not been part of my project to elucidate what Heidegger really meant or to explain its significance for anthropology. I am more than content to leave that task to others. For me, two aspects of Heidegger's philosophy have proved especially troublesome. One concerns what it means to live and dwell in the open; the other, the particular mode of being attributed to humans as opposed to non-human animals. These aspects are connected, since it is Heidegger's contention that the world opens up to humans in a way that it does not, and cannot, to non-humans. He imagined this opening as a kind of clearing, freed up for such activities as building and cultivation, making things and growing things. Yet confined to its clearing, the taking place of human dwelling seems oddly circumscribed. The existence of non-human animals, by contrast, appears not to be so bounded, but rather spills out into its surroundings along whatever paths afford growth and movement. Heidegger's apparently paradoxical conclusion was that, whereas animal life – which knows no bounds – is closed to the world, human life – which opens to a world – is reined in and contained. The solution to the paradox lies in Heidegger's insistence that although the animal mingles freely in its environment, it lacks the capacity to apprehend the things it encounters there for what they are, *as things*. It has an environment, but remains deprived of a world (Heidegger 1995: 239). For humans however, precisely because of their capacity to break the bonds that hold the animal captive to its environment, a world of things opens up of which the animal knows nothing. The allegorical clearing in which dwelling takes place is a world thus revealed, and its boundaries are the limits of disclosure, at which things commence their presencing. Whereas the animal merely *exists* in its environment, within these limits it is possible for the human to *be*.

I would not myself go along with such a sharp division between human and animal, world and environment, being and existence. To the contrary, one of my aims in developing the dwelling perspective was to show that organism-and-environment and being-in-the-world offer points of departure for our understanding that are ontologically equivalent, and in that way to unite the approaches of ecology and phenomenology within a single paradigm. Heidegger's human, it seems to me, remains trapped in the dilemma of a creature that can know itself and the world of which it is viscerally a part – in which it lives and breathes – only by renouncing its very existence in that world. This may be a dilemma for philosophers but it is not, I think, a dilemma for inhabitants who fundamentally get to know the world by going about in it. Both humans and non-humans, I would contend, conduct themselves skilfully in and through their surroundings, deploying capacities of attention and response that have been developmentally embodied through practice and experience. The inspiration behind this contention came not from philosophy but from psychology, and specifically from the ecological approach to perception pioneered by James Gibson (1979).

As a hard-nosed, matter-of-fact realist, Gibson's position could hardly have been further removed from Heidegger's. His humans could just as well have been animals, and for humans and non-humans alike, Gibson took the world, revealed through the process of habitation, to be an environment. To place Heidegger and Gibson side by side is like comparing chalk and cheese. More by accident than by design, however, this is what I found myself doing. If it was from Heidegger that I borrowed the concept of dwelling, then it was from Gibson, at least initially, that I drew my theory of perception. And the key insight that I took from it was that perception is fundamentally about *movement*. Reacting against the cognitivism of mainstream psychology and the Cartesian premises on which it rests, Gibson insisted that perception is the achievement not of a mind in a body, but of the whole organism as it moves about in its environment, and that what it perceives are not things as such but what they afford for the pursuance of its current activity. It is in the very process of attending and responding to these 'affordances' (ibid.: 127-43), in the course of their engagements with them, that skilled practitioners – human or non-human – get to know them. Meaning, for Gibson, is drawn from these productive engagements.

A point of observation, set in motion, describes a path. The essence of Gibson's argument was that the shapes and forms of environmental objects are revealed by changes along this path in the pattern of light reflected off their outward surfaces, as it reaches the eyes of the moving observer, rather than by piecing together 'snapshots' taken from any number of fixed points en route. 'Observation implies movement', writes Gibson, 'that is, locomotion with reference to the rigid environment, because all observers are animals and all animals are mobile' (1979: 72). Yet something, I felt, was amiss here. It seemed that Gibson had succeeded in restoring perceivers to life at the expense of a sclerotisation of the environment. The moving observer of his account is like the lone survivor on a planet once bustling with life, which has been petrified by some great cataclysm. The *rigid* environment, cluttered with objects of all sorts, can be occupied, but it surely cannot afford dwelling. We need a different understanding of movement: not a casting about the hard surfaces of a world in which everything is already laid out, but an issuing along with things in the very processes of their generation; not the *trans-port* (carrying across) of completed being, but the *pro-duction* (bringing forth) of perpetual becoming.

To grasp this sense of movement I took a leaf out of the book of another philosopher: Maurice Merleau-Ponty's *Phenomenology of Perception* (1962). There was much on which Merleau-Ponty and Gibson were agreed, especially in their rejection of the Cartesian paradigm. But they differed in one fundamental respect. Gibson asked how it is possible to perceive things in the environment. But Merleau-Ponty took a step back, and asked what kind of involvement of the perceiver in the lifeworld is necessary for there to be things in the environment to perceive, and beings to perceive them (Ingold 2000a: 263). To cut a very long story short, his conclusion was that since the living body is primordially and irrevocably stitched into the fabric of the world, our perception of the world is no more, and no less, than the world's perception of itself – in and through us. This is just another way of saying that the inhabited world is *sentient*. It is not possible, Merleau-Ponty implied, to be sentient in an *in*sentient world – in a world, that is, which has turned its back on its inhabitants, exposing only its rigid, external surfaces to perceptual scrutiny. Such, as we have seen, was the environment envisaged by Gibson. To be sentient, to the contrary, is to open up to a world, to yield to its embrace, and to resonate in one's inner being to its illuminations and reverberations. Bathed in light, submerged in sound and rapt in feeling, the sentient body, at once both perceiver and producer, traces the paths of the world's becoming in the very course of contributing to its ongoing renewal.

Here, surely, lies the essence of what it means to dwell. It is, literally to be embarked upon a movement along a way of life. The perceiver-producer is thus a wayfarer, and the mode of production is itself a trail blazed or a path followed. Along such paths, lives are lived, skills developed, observations made and understandings grown. But if this is so, then we can no longer suppose that dwelling is emplaced in quite the way Heidegger imagined, in an opening akin to a clearing in the forest. To be, I would now say, is not to be *in* place but to be *along* paths. The path, and not the place, is the primary condition of being, or rather of becoming. For this reason, I have begun to wonder whether the concept of dwelling is, after all, apt to describe how humans and non-humans make their ways in the world. The concept carries an aura of snug, well-wrapped localism that seems out of tune with an emphasis on the primacy of movement. Looking back, I rather regret having placed so much weight on it, and now prefer the less loaded concept of habitation. Thus rephrased, my contention is that wayfaring is the fundamental mode by which living beings inhabit the earth. Every such being has, accordingly, to be imagined as the line of its own movement or – more realistically – as a bundle of lines.

Lines

In reaching this conclusion I had – without realising it at the time – stumbled upon a key insight of one of the late twentieth century's most influential, if idiosyncratic philosophers, Gilles Deleuze. This should have come as no surprise, in view of Deleuze's debt to the philosophy of Henri Bergson. For my part, I had first come across the writings of Bergson, along with those of his philosophical contemporary, Alfred North Whitehead, two decades previously, while I was working on my book *Evolution and Social Life* (Ingold 1986). Though deeply unfashionable at the time,[3] I was greatly inspired by what they had to say, and in my book I set out to link the sense of evolution (and concomitantly, of production) as a life process to the ideas of creativity and duration that I drew from their work. From Whitehead, I took the idea that the world we inhabit is never complete but continually surpassing itself. Creativity inheres in the movement of the world's self-surpassing, or in what Whitehead called 'concrescence' (Whitehead 1929: 410). Crucial to Bergson was the claim that in this movement of creation, of life and growth, lies the essence of time: 'Wherever anything lives', he wrote, 'there is, open somewhere, a register in which time is being inscribed' (Bergson 1911: 17). If there were no more to production than a transitive relation between image and object, then in theory, the time it takes could be compressed into an instant, and history itself would merely be a succession of such instants. But in reality, life goes on, forever overtaking the ends that may be held up within it. One may set out to build a house or to cultivate a field, and eventually lay down one's tools in the satisfaction of a job well done, yet in the doing, life and consciousness have advanced, and other goals already lie on the horizon. For the same reason that horizons cannot be crossed, it is impossible to reach the ends of life.

In his *Creative Evolution* of 1911, Bergson argued that every living being is cast like an eddy in the current of life. It is as though, in its development, it describes 'a kind of circle' (1911: 134). Returning full circle to Bergson in my own thinking, I found that I, too, had done the same. Were I, however, to draw this circle, using pencil and paper, I would no longer see – in the completed figure – the trace of the twirling movement that went into its formation. What stands out on the page is rather the outline of a geometrical form. With this figure, it seems that a division is set up between what is on the 'inside' and what is on the 'outside'. Likewise, says Bergson, we are inclined to treat the living being that has spiralled in upon itself as an externally bounded object, or as a container for life. Yet life, Bergson insisted, is not contained in things. It is movement itself, wherein every organism emerges as a peculiar disturbance that interrupts the linear flow, binding it into the forms we see. So well does it feign immobility, however, that we are readily deceived into treating each 'as a *thing* rather than as a *progress*, forgetting that the very permanence of its form is only the outline of a movement' (1911: 135). It would be wrong, then, to compare the living organism to an object, for 'the organism that lives is a thing that *endures*' (ibid.: 16). Like a growing root or fibre, it creates itself endlessly, trailing its history behind it as the past presses against the present (ibid.: 29).

It was in just this fashion that my roundabout way of thinking led me simultaneously back to Bergson and forth to Deleuze. Admittedly, my initial attempts to read Deleuze, prompted by the recommendations of many friends and colleagues, led nowhere. Finding the work all but incomprehensible, I abandoned these attempts in sheer frustration. As so often with philosophers, I had to wait until my own thinking had caught up with his before I could make any sense at all of what he was saying. But starting afresh, prepared with what I had vainly supposed to be my new vision of life as a phenomenon of lines, I was astonished to discover that it had already been forcefully enunciated by Deleuze, along with his collaborator, the psychoanalyst Félix Guattari, as long ago as 1980, in their book *A Thousand Plateaus*. 'Individual or group', they write, 'we are composed of lines … or rather, bundles of lines' (2004: 223). There are lines of life, lines of writing, lines productive of variation in lines of life or writing, lines of luck and misfortune, and so on (ibid.: 215). Deleuze and Guattari call them, interchangeably, 'lines of flight' and 'lines of becoming'. Imagine a river, flowing along between banks on either side. Suppose that the banks of the river are connected by means of a road-bridge. We could then cross by road from a location on one side to a location on the other. Thus the bridge establishes a transitive connection between the two locations. But the river, running under the bridge in a direction orthogonal to the road, does not connect anything to anything else. Rather, it just flows, without beginning or end, scouring the banks on each side and picking up speed in the middle (Deleuze and Guattari 2004: 28).

In this distinction between the linear connector that goes across from point to point, and the line of flight that runs along, pulling away at points on either side as it sweeps by, I found a precise parallel to my original distinction between transitive and intransitive senses of production. The point-to-point connector is transitive: it takes us from a starting point, such as an image of what is to be made, to an end point in the form of the completed object, or vice versa, from the ready-made object to a final image in the mind of a spectator or consumer. The line of flight, to the contrary, is intransitive: it carries on. Here, finally, lies the key to my project of restoring life to anthropology. We have, in effect, been concentrating on the banks while losing sight of the river. Yet were it not for the flow of the river there would be no banks, and no relation between them. To regain the river, we need to shift our perspective from the transverse relation between objects and images to the longitudinal trajectories of materials and awareness. Recall Hägerstrand's idea that everything there is, launched in the current of time, has a trajectory of becoming. The entwining of these ever-extending trajectories comprises the texture of the world. Whether our concern is to inhabit this world or to study it – and at root these are the same, since all inhabitants are students and all students inhabitants – our task is not to take stock of its contents but to *follow what is going on*, tracing the multiple trails of becoming, wherever they lead. To trace these paths is to bring anthropology back to life.

PART I

Clearing the ground

Anthropology is not usually regarded as an experimental science. Scholars in many other disciplines deliberately set up situations in order to study their outcomes, going on to compare the results with what had been predicted on the basis of speculative conjectures already arrived at through abstract, theoretical reasoning. Anthropologists, however, are enjoined to observe and describe the forms of life they encounter more or less as they find them, and to do their theorising after the fact. Of course they recognise, as many experimental scientists do not, that by the very fact of their presence, they cannot help but participate in the situations they observe. But it has been more common to interpret this involvement as a potentially problematic source of observer bias than as a procedure of discovery. Fearing that their observations might be contaminated by their own designs or preconceptions, and to avoid the charge of ethnocentricity, most anthropologists are keen to play down the experimental dimensions of their work in what they call 'the field'. Yet for the people who live there, quotidian life is experimental through and through. Inhabitants the world over grow into the knowledge of how to carry on their lives by trying things out for themselves, often guided by more experienced companions, in the anticipation of what the outcomes might be. And as self-confessed students of the everyday, anthropologists – in practice – do much the same. Is not experimentation, then, as fundamental to anthropological inquiry as it is to the ways of life it seeks to understand?

Anthropology's dilemma is that it remains yoked to an academic model of knowledge production, according to which observation is not so much a way of knowing what is going on in the world as a source of raw material for subsequent processing into authoritative accounts that claim to reveal the truth behind the illusion of appearances. This truth, it is claimed, is to be found on the library shelf, groaning under the weight of scholarly books and periodicals, rather than 'out there' in the world of lived experience. It is this model that underwrites the idea of the scientific experiment, the purpose of which is to yield the observational data needed to prove (or disprove) a hypothesis. Experimentation in everyday life, by contrast, is a matter not of testing conjectures in arenas of practice, but of enrolling practical activity in the very process of following a train of thought. It is to do our thinking in the open, out-of-doors. This, too, is what anthropology does. Anthropological experiments require no elaborate instruments that would deputise for the investigator, allowing the latter to hide behind the scenes and thereby to maintain the illusion of absence that underwrites the claim to objectivity. Nor do they require any laboratory within which to craft a simulacrum of the world designed to highlight only those variables that are subject to investigation. Rather, they place the investigator, in person, right in the midst of things. In terms of scientific protocols, these experiments break all the rules. That, perhaps, is why anthropologists are so shy about owning up to the experimentality of their discipline, and why they shelter behind the pretence that far from joining with the people among whom they work in a search for answers to the fundamental questions of life, all they are doing in the field is collecting ethnographic data – on what these people say and do – for subsequent analysis.

I believe that the experimental nature of anthropology is something to be celebrated rather than covered up, and in this part I suggest three very simple experiments that anyone can do. The first is to wet a stone, leave it to dry and observe what happens. The second is to remove one's shoes and go barefoot. And the third is to saw through a plank of wood. These experiments do not so much offer definitive results for further analysis as open up an entire terrain of inquiry, clearing the ground for an anthropological approach to life. The first experiment forces us to switch our attention from the stone as a material object to what happens to stone – a material – in the course of exchanges of substance across its surface with the surrounding medium of air. In place of the material world, populated by solid objects, our eyes are opened to a world of materials, including earth, air and water, in which all is in flux and transformation. The second experiment reveals the extent to which our understanding of that most fundamental surface of all, the ground, is moulded by the experience of walking in boots or shoes over paved surfaces. Barefoot walking reveals the ground to be composite and heterogeneous, not so much an isotropic platform for life as a coarse cloth or patchwork woven from the comings and goings of its manifold inhabitants. And it reveals, too, the extent to which our primary tactile contact with the environment is through the feet rather than the hands. The third experiment shows us how practical skill, in bringing together the resistances of materials, bodily gestures and the flows of sensory experience, rhythmically couples action and perception along paths of movement. Together, these experiments suggest that the entangled currents of thought that we might describe as 'mind' are no more confined within the skull than are the flows of materials comprising corporeal life confined within what we call the body. Both spill out into the world.

I begin with materials. They are what things are made of. As I show in Chapter 2, however, the focus – in anthropology, archaeology and material culture studies – has tended to be on the materiality of objects rather than on materials and their properties. The abstract concept of materiality, I argue, has actually hindered the proper understanding of materials. We would learn more by engaging directly with the materials themselves, following what happens to them as they circulate, mix with one another, solidify and dissolve in the formation of more or less enduring things. We discover, then, that materials are active. Only by putting them inside closed-up objects are they reduced to dead or inert matter. It is this attempted enclosure that has given rise to the so-called 'problem of agency'. It is a problem of our own making. How is it, we wonder, that humans can act? If we were mere lumps of matter, we could do nothing. So we think that some extra ingredient needs to be added to liven up our lumpen bodies. And if, as sometimes seems to us, objects can 'act back', then this ingredient must be attributed to them as well. We give the name 'agency' to this ingredient.

It is the supposed cause that sets otherwise inert matter in motion. But if we follow active materials, rather than reducing them to dead matter, then we do not have to invoke an extraneous 'agency' to liven them up again. The wind, for example, is not an object, nor does it tear at the trees because it is endowed with agency. It is an air current, materials-in-motion. We say 'the wind blows', because the subject–verb structure of the English language makes it difficult to express it otherwise. But in truth, we know that the wind *is* its blowing. Similarly, the stream *is* the running of water. And so, too, I *am* what I am doing. I am not an agent but a hive of activity. If you were to lift the lid off, you would find something more like a compost heap than the kind of architectural structure that anatomists and psychologists like to imagine.

In Chapter 3 I turn from the flows of materials to the movements of people. Studies of human cognition tend to assume that thinking and knowing are the achievements of a stationary mind, encased within a body in motion. This assumption, I suggest, has its foundation in three related areas of technological development that, in the history of western societies, accompanied the onset of the modern era. The first was in footwear, particularly in the constriction of movement and sensation imposed by the stiff leather boot. The second was in paving and road-building, leading to the creation of hard thoroughfares that remain unmarked by the passage of human life. The third was in transport, by which travellers could be 'carried across' from a point of departure to a destination, rather than making their own way as they go along. Together, they contribute to our ideas that movement is a mechanical displacement of the human body across the surface of the earth, from one point to another, and that knowledge is assembled from observations taken from these points. Of course there are forms of pedestrian movement, notoriously the so-called striding gait, that approximate to the ideal of pure transport. As a rigidly mechanical, straight-legged oscillation from the hips, with eyes gazing ahead rather than downcast, the stride only works with booted feet on a paved surface. It enacts a bodily image of colonial occupation, straddling the distance between points of departure and arrival as though one could have a foot in each simultaneously, encompassing both – and all points in between – in a single, appropriative movement. For the most part, however, humans have not so much stridden across the surfaces of the earth as picked their way with bare, sandaled or moccasined feet. It is in these dextrous movements along paths of life and travel, I contend, and not in the processing of data collected from multiple sites of observation, that inhabitants' knowledge is forged. Thus locomotion and cognition are inseparable, and an account of the mind must be as much concerned with the work of the feet as with that of the head and hands.

What goes for walking also goes for other skilled activities that have a similarly itinerant character. In Chapter 4 I draw on a detailed account of the task of sawing through a plank of wood to explore three themes of fundamental importance for the proper understanding of technical skill. These concern the processional quality of tool use, the synergy of practitioner, tool and material, and the coupling of perception and action. First, I show that sawing is processional in the same way as is walking: every step is a development of the one before and a preparation for the one following. Like going for a walk, the task has recognisable phases of getting ready, setting out, carrying on and finishing off. Secondly, I ask what it means to speak of the saw as a tool that functions to cut wood. I argue that the function of the saw lies not in its objective attributes but in stories of past use. Of these stories, however, the saw has no memory. The relation between hand and saw is therefore fundamentally asymmetrical. For the saw relies on the gestural movements of the hand, embodied through previous practice, for its stories to be told. Thirdly, as an instance of the 'workmanship of risk', sawing calls for manual dexterity. I contend that the essence of dexterity lies in the carpenter's capacity to bring into phase an ensemble of concurrent movements, both within and beyond the body. It is this attunement that makes the activity rhythmic rather than metronomic. Far from being merely habitual or 'done without thinking', such rhythmic activity calls for intense concentration. This concentration, however, is that of a consciousness that is not confined within the head of the practitioner but reaches out into the environment along multiple pathways of sensory participation. What, then, has been the fate of skill in an age of technology? Have skills given way to machines? I conclude that they have not, for two reasons. First, real machines, in operation, are open rather than closed systems; and secondly, as fast as machines take over operations once performed by skilled practitioners, further skills develop around the new machines.

2
MATERIALS AGAINST MATERIALITY

Before you begin to read this chapter, please go outside and find a largish stone, though not so big that it cannot be easily lifted and carried indoors. Bring it in, and immerse it in a pail of water or under a running tap. Then place it before you on your desk – perhaps on a tray or plate so as not to spoil your desktop. Take a good look at it. If you like, you can look at it again from time to time as you read the chapter. At the end, I shall refer to what you may have observed.

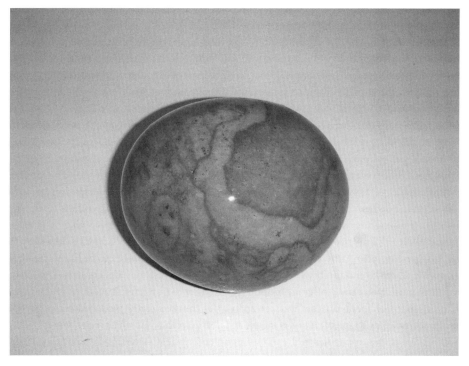

FIGURE 2.1 Wet stone (photo: Susanna Ingold)

Missing materials

I begin with a puzzle. It is that the ever-growing literature in anthropology and archaeology that deals explicitly with the subjects of *materiality* and *material culture* seems to have hardly anything to say about *materials*.[1] I mean by materials the stuff that things are made of, and a rough inventory might begin with something like the following, taken from the list of contents from Henry Hodges' excellent little book, *Artefacts*: pottery; glazes; glass and enamels; copper and copper alloys; iron and steel; gold, silver, lead and mercury; stone; wood; fibres and threads; textiles and baskets; hides and leather; antler, bone, horn and ivory; dyes, pigments and paints; adhesives; some other materials (Hodges 1964: 9).

This down-to-earth volume is packed with information about all sorts of materials that prehistoric people have used to make things. Yet I have never seen it referenced in the literature on materiality. Looking along my shelves I find titles like: *The Mental and the Material*, by Maurice Godelier (1986); *Mind, Materiality and History*, by Christina Toren (1999); *Matter, Materiality and Modern Culture*, edited by Paul Graves-Brown (2000); *Thinking Through Material Culture*, by Karl Knappett (2005); *Materiality*, edited by Daniel Miller (2005); *Material Cultures, Material Minds*, by Nicole Boivin (2008), and *Material Agency*, edited by Lambros Malafouris and Karl Knappett (2008). In style and approach, these books are a million miles from Hodges' work. Their engagements, for the most part, are not with the tangible stuff of craftsmen and manufacturers but with the abstract ruminations of philosophers and theorists. They expound, often in a language of grotesque impenetrability, on the relations between materiality and a host of other, similarly unfathomable qualities including agency, intentionality, functionality, spatiality, semiosis, spirituality and embodiment. One looks in vain, however, for any comprehensible explanation of what 'materiality' actually means, or for any account of materials and their properties. To understand materiality, it seems, we need to get as far away from materials as possible.

Why should this be so? Anthropology has long, and rightly, insisted that the road to understanding lies in practical participation. You would think, then, that as anthropologists, we would want to learn about the material composition of the inhabited world by engaging directly with the stuff we want to understand: by sawing logs, building a wall, knapping a stone or rowing a boat. A woodworker is someone who works with wood, yet as Stephanie Bunn has observed, most anthropologists would be content to look at the work in terms of the social identity of the worker, the tools he or she uses, the layout of the workshop, the techniques employed, the objects produced and their meanings – everything but the wood itself. The materials, it seems, have gone missing. Coming to anthropology from her background as an artist and craftsperson, Bunn was directed to the literature on material culture. But nowhere in this literature could she find anything corresponding to the 'bit she did': the working with materials that lay at the heart of her own practice as a maker (Bunn 1999: 15). This making is for her, as it is for many artists, a procedure of discovery: in the words of sculptor Andy Goldsworthy, 'an opening into the processes of life within and around' (Friedman and Goldsworthy 1990: 160). Could not such engagement – working practically *with* materials – offer anthropology, too, a more powerful procedure of discovery than an approach bent on the abstract analysis *of* things already made? What academic perversion leads us to speak not of *materials and their properties* but of *the materiality of objects*?

One clue to the answer lies in the title of a conference held at the McDonald Institute for Archaeological Research, Cambridge, in March 2003: *Rethinking materiality: the engagement of mind with the material world*.[2] The pretext for this conference came, in large part, from a reaction against the excessive polarisation of mind and matter that has led generations of theorists to suppose that the material substance of the world presents itself to humanity as a blank slate, a *tabula rasa*, for the inscription of ideational forms. An example is Godelier's argument in *The Mental and the Material*, to which I referred in the last chapter, that there can be no deliberate action of human beings upon the material world that does not set to work 'mental realities, representations, judgements, principles of thought' (1986: 11). Where, then, do these mental realities come from? Do they have their source, as Godelier intimates, in a world of society that is ontologically distinct from 'the material realities of external nature' (ibid.: 3)? At the Cambridge conference Colin Renfrew argued, to the contrary, that the kinds of representations and judgements to which Godelier refers are not so much imported into arenas of practical activity as emergent within them, arising from the very ways in which human beings are interactively involved with material substance (Renfrew 2004: 23; see also Renfrew 2001: 127). Yet in his formulation of what he now calls 'material engagement theory', the polarity of mind and matter remains. For the engagement of which he speaks does not bring the flesh and blood of human bodies into corporeal contact with materials of other kinds, whether organic or inorganic. Rather, it brings incorporeal minds into contact with a *material world*.

What, then, is this material world? Of what does it consist? For heuristic purposes, Christopher Gosden suggests, we could divide it into two broad components: *landscape* and *artefacts* (1999: 152). Thus it seems that we have human minds on the one hand, and a material world of landscape and artefacts on the other. That, you might think, should cover just about everything. But does it? Consider, for a moment, what is left out. Starting with landscape, does this include the sky? Where do we put the sun, the moon and the stars? We can reach for the stars, but cannot touch them: are they, then, material realities with which humans can make contact, or do they exist for us only in the mind? Is the moon part of the material world for terrestrial travellers, or only for cosmonauts who touch down on the lunar landscape? How about sunlight? Life depends on it. But if sunlight were a constituent of the material world, then we would have to admit not only that the diurnal landscape differs materially from the nocturnal one, but also that the shadow of a landscape feature, such as a rock or tree, is as much a part of the material world as the feature itself. For creatures that live in the shade, it does indeed make a difference! What, then, of the air? When you breathe, or feel the wind on your face, are you engaging with the material world? When the fog descends, and everything around you looks dim and mysterious, has the material world changed, or are you just seeing the same world differently?[3] Does rain belong to the material world, or only the puddles that it leaves in ditches and pot-holes? Does falling snow join the material world only once it settles on the ground? As engineers and builders know all too well, rain and frost can break up roads and buildings. How then can we claim that roads and buildings are part of the material world, if rain and frost are not? And where would we place fire and smoke, molten lava and volcanic ash, not to mention liquids of all kinds from ink to running water?

None of these things fall within the scope of Gosden's second component of materiality, namely, artefacts. Moreover the category of the artificial raises its own anomalies. In an experiment, I asked a group of undergraduate students to sort a motley collection of objects that they had found lying around outside into two piles, one of natural objects, the other of artefacts. It turned out that not a single thing could be unequivocally attributed to one pile or the other. If they seemed to vary on a scale of artificiality, it was only because for some more than others, and at different times in their histories, human beings had played a part in the processes that led to their being where they were, and taking the forms they did, at the moment when they were picked up. In this sense the bifacial stone hand-axe recently made for me by a professional flint-knapper is perhaps more artificial than the stone recovered from your garden that you have before you on your desk. But that does not make the former any more a part of the material world than the latter. More generally, why should the material world include only *either* things encountered *in situ*, within the landscape, *or* things already transformed by human activity, into artefacts? Why exclude things like the stone, which have been recovered and removed but not otherwise transformed? And where, in this division between landscape and artefacts, would we place all the diverse forms of animal, plant, fungal and bacterial life? Like artefacts, these things might be attributed with formal properties of design, yet they have not been made but have grown. If, moreover, they are part of the material world, then the same must be true of my own body. So where does this fit in? If I and my body are one and the same, and if my body indeed partakes of the material world, then how can the body-that-I-am engage with that world?

Medium, substance, surface

An alternative way forward is offered by James Gibson, in his pioneering work on *The Ecological Approach to Visual Perception*. Here he distinguishes three components of the inhabited environment: *medium*, *substances* and *surfaces* (Gibson 1979: 16). For human beings the medium is normally air. Of course we need air to breathe. But also, offering little resistance, it allows us to move about – to do things, make things and touch things. It also transmits radiant energy and mechanical vibration, so that we can see and hear. And it allows us to smell, since the molecules that excite our olfactory receptors are diffused in it. Thus the medium, according to Gibson, affords movement and perception. Substances, on the other hand, are relatively resistant to both. They include all kinds of more or less solid stuff like rock, gravel, sand, soil, mud, wood, concrete and so on. Such materials furnish necessary physical foundations for life – we need them to stand on – but it is not generally possible to see or move *through* them. At the interface between the medium and substances are surfaces. All surfaces, according to Gibson, have certain properties. These include a particular, relatively persistent layout, a degree of resistance to deformation and disintegration, a distinctive shape and a characteristically non-homogeneous texture. Surfaces are where radiant energy is reflected or absorbed, where vibrations are passed to the medium, where vaporisation or diffusion into the medium occur, and what our bodies come up against in touch. So far as perception is concerned, surfaces are therefore 'where most of the action is' (Gibson 1979: 23).

It is all too easy, however, to slip from the *physical* separation of gaseous medium from solid substance to the *metaphysical* separation of mind from matter. Thus the artefact is characteristically defined – as it is by Godelier – as an object formed through the imposition of *mental* realities upon *material* ones (1986: 4). The artisan, it is argued, begins work with an image or design already in mind of the object he plans to make, and ends when the image is realised in the material. For example, in the making of the stone biface mentioned above, the knapper must have begun – as Jacques Pelegrin says of his prehistoric counterpart – with a 'pre-existing mental image … deserving of being termed a "concept"' (1993: 310). Here the surface of the artefact is not just of the particular material from which it is made, but of materiality itself as it confronts the creative human imagination (Ingold 2000b: 53). Indeed the very notion of material culture, which has gained a new momentum following its long hibernation in the basements of museology, rests on the premise that as the embodiments of mental representations, or as stable elements in systems of signification, objects have already solidified or precipitated out from the generative fluxes of the medium that gave birth to them. Convinced that *all that is material resides in things*, or in what Bjørnar Olsen (2003) calls 'the hard physicality of the world', students of material culture have contrived to dematerialise, or to sublimate into thought, the very medium in which the things in question once took shape and are now immersed. Ironically, Olsen does just this when he accuses social scientists who take leave of the material world for the realms of cognitive experience of being guided by a hermeneutics in which 'all that is solid melts into air' (Olsen 2003: 88).[4]

Another example of this kind of slippage, from materials to materiality, can be found in an article by sociologist Kevin Hetherington, on the role of touch in everyday practices of placemaking. In the course of his argument,[5] Hetherington suggests that Gibson's theory of perception offers only 'a weak acknowledgement of the materiality of the world'. For whatever its virtues, the theory has so far failed to address 'what an encounter between the fingertip and the materiality of the world might have to tell us of a scopic we call place' (Hetherington 2003: 1938-9). Perhaps you might like to try touching the stone on your desk. To be sure, your finger has come up against a hard material – stone. It is cold to the touch, and perhaps still damp. But has touching this particular stone put you in touch with *the materiality of the world*? Is there nothing material that is not locked up in solid, tangible objects like stones? Are we really to believe that whatever lies on the hither side of such objects is immaterial, including the very air that affords the freedom of movement enabling you to reach out and touch them, not to mention the finger itself – and, by extension, the rest of the body, since fingers are not operated from the mind by remote control? Is the air you breathe an ether of the mind, and your finger but a phantom of the imagination? Gibson's whole point, of course, was that the surface separates one kind of material (such as stone) from another (such as air), rather than materiality from immateriality. It is precisely because of this emphasis on materials that Gibson downplays any notion of the materiality of the world.

Imagine you were a burrowing animal like a mole. Your world would consist of corridors and chambers rather than artefacts and monuments. It would be a world of *enclosures* whose surfaces surround the medium instead of *detached objects* whose surfaces are surrounded by it (Gibson 1979: 34). I wonder whether, if moles were endowed with imaginations as creative as those of humans, they could have a material culture. Anthropologically trained moles, of a philosophical bent, would doubtless insist that the materiality of the world is not culturally constructed but culturally *excavated* – not, of course, in the archaeological sense of recovering erstwhile detached, solid objects that have since become buried in the substance of the earth, but in the sense that the forms of things are hollowed out from within rather than impressed from without. In their eyes (if they could see) all that is material would reside *beyond* the objects of culture, on the far side of their inward-facing surfaces. Thus these objects could be phenomenally present in mole-culture only as material absence – not as concrete entities but as externally bounded volumes of empty space. The very idea of material culture would then be a contradiction in terms.

This example is not entirely fanciful, for in many parts of the world – including Mediterranean Europe, North and Central America, the Near and Middle East, China and Australia – humans have set up house in caves or other underground dwellings, often carving elaborate systems of interconnected rooms and passageways from the bare rock. Even today, an estimated five million cave dwellings are still in use, the vast majority of them in China (Mulligan 1997: 238–40). The mundane activity of their inhabitants, however, plays havoc with our established categories of thought. We say houses are built, but can you 'build' a cave? Whether constructing or excavating, much hard physical work may be involved. But whereas the house-builder erects an edifice, a monument to his labour, by the time the cave is finished all that seems to have been created is an unfurnished volume. In fact a great many cave dwellings incorporate constructed elements, such as a roofed frontage that may be built out from the rock face where the latter rises from level ground. The result is a well-integrated structure, not a peculiar hybrid. There must be something wrong with a way of thinking that forces us to treat only one half of the house positively as a material object, and the other half negatively as a hole in the ground. We need an alternative approach.

The source of the problem lies, once again, in the slippage from materials to materiality. It is this that leads us to suppose that human beings, as they go in and out of doors, live alternately on the inside and on the outside of a material world. It is as though this world were a Swiss cheese, full of holes yet nevertheless contained within the envelope of its outward surfaces. In the real world of materials, however, there are neither interior holes nor exterior surfaces. Of course there are surfaces of all sorts, of varying degrees of stability and permeability. But these surfaces, as Gibson showed, are interfaces between one kind of material and another – for example between rock and air – not between what is material and what is not. I can touch the rock, whether of a cave wall or of the ground underfoot, and can thereby gain a feel for what rock is like as a *material*. But I cannot touch the *materiality* of the rock. The surface of materiality, in short, is an illusion. We cannot touch it because it is not there. Like all other creatures, human beings do not exist on the 'other side' of materiality, but swim in an ocean of materials. Once we acknowledge our immersion, what this ocean reveals to us is not the bland homogeneity of different shades of matter but a flux in which materials of the most diverse kinds, through processes of admixture and distillation, of coagulation and dispersal, and of evaporation and precipitation, undergo continual generation and transformation. The forms of things, far from having been imposed from without upon an inert substrate, arise and are borne along – as indeed we are too – within this current of materials. As with the Earth itself, the surface of every solid is but a crust, the more or less ephemeral congelate of a generative movement.

The stuff of animals and plants

As they swim in this ocean of materials, human beings do of course play a part in their transformations. So, too, do creatures of every other kind. Very often, humans take over from where non-humans have left off, as when they extract the wax secreted by bees to make the cell walls of the honey-comb for further use in the manufacture of candles, as an ingredient of paint (alongside linseed oil, egg-yolk and a host of other concoctions), as a means of waterproofing and as a hardener in leatherwork. Another example is the production of silk, which begins with the consumption of mulberry leaves by the grubs of the moth *Bombyx mori*. Liquid secretions exuded from the grub's glands harden on contact with air to form filaments from which it winds its cocoon. To make silk, the filaments from several cocoons are unwound and reeled together, resulting in fibres of extraordinary strength. Then there is shellac, an essential ingredient of French polish. This material comes from the secretions of the lac insect (*Coccus lacca*), native to India. These secretions form a protective coating that covers entire twigs of the trees on which the insect larvae have settled. The twigs are collected, and the lac removed and purified by boiling in water. The lac itself, which is insoluble, is then concentrated by evaporation, and stretched into sheets which set hard when they cool (Hodges 1964: 125, 162-4).

Although insects are among the most prolific producers in the animal kingdom of materials subsequently taken up for human use, a full inventory of such materials would be virtually inexhaustible. As a small sample, just consider this list of materials traditionally used by nomadic pastoral people in making tents:

> *Skins:* these usually have to be softened by being scraped and beaten – a long and arduous task. Then they have to be cured by soaking in substances such as sour milk, camel dung or bark fermented in urine.
>
> *Wool:* in Central Asia wool is made into felt by pulling a long, waterlogged roll of five or more fleeces backwards and forwards for many hours.
>
> *Hair:* North African pastoralists make 'black tents' from goat hair which is spun on a drop spindle and woven on a ground-loom. Hair is also used to fill mattresses and to make rope, and is suitable for warp threads in weaving rugs and blankets. In addition, it is used for making paint brushes.
>
> *Bone:* used for tent frames, pegs and toggles, as well as for the needles used in sewing skins.
>
> *Horns, hooves and claws:* split into thin layers these can be used to make window panes.
>
> *Sinews:* used for sewing skins (with bone needles), or as warp-threads.
>
> *Feathers:* used for strengthening warp threads and for bedding (along with lambswool and camel hair).
>
> *Dung:* mixed with clay to form plaster (also acts as an effective insect-repellent).
>
> *Fish:* the bones, skin and offal may be boiled to produce glue. Adhesives can also be made from dried blood, animal skins, bones and horns, muzzles and sinews, and cheese and quicklime.
>
> *Eggs and dairy produce:* in painting, milk is used as an emulsifier while egg-yolk is mixed with pigments to form a medium for distemper.
>
> (paraphrased from Bunn 1997: 195-7)

Plants, too, provide an endless source of materials for further processing and transformation. One has only to enumerate, for example, all the different materials that can be derived from trees, including wood, bark, sap, gum, ash, paper, charcoal, tar, resin and turpentine. Other flowering plants and grasses give us cotton, flax, jute and papyrus. Nettles still grow widely in Britain because the fibres of their stalks were used in the Middle Ages for bowstrings.

Many materials in common use are derived from the unlikely combination of ingredients from an astonishing variety of different sources. Here are two examples from medieval and early modern Europe. The first is of the material used for stucco work in sixteenth century England. The basic ingredient of lime was mixed with the following materials of mostly animal origin: 'hog's lard, bullock's blood, cow dung, wort and eggs, wort and beer, milk, gluten, buttermilk, cheese, curdled milk [and] saponified beeswax' (Davey, cited in Bunn 1997: 196).

The second example is of ink, an essential material for the medieval scribe. Two kinds of ink were used. One was made of lamp-black mixed with gum. For the other, which came into general use from the twelfth century, the principal ingredient was the oak-apple. This is the round, marble-sized tumour that often grows on the leaves and twigs of oak trees. It is formed around the larva of the gall wasp that has laid its egg in the tree-bud. The oak galls are collected, crushed and either boiled or infused in rainwater (or white wine vinegar). The other main ingredient is copperas, manufactured by the evaporation of water from ferrous earth, or by pouring sulphuric acid over old nails, filtering the liquid and mixing it with alcohol. The copperas is added to the oak-gall potion and thoroughly stirred with a stick from a fig tree. This has the effect of turning the solution from pale brown to black. Finally, gum arabic – made from the dried-up sap of the acacia tree – is added in order to thicken the concoction (Hamel 1992: 32-3). The scribe now has his ink, but of course to write he still needs a pen, made from the feather of a goose, crow or raven, and parchment prepared by a lengthy procedure from the skins of calves or goats (ibid: 8-16, 27-9).

Bringing things to life

Now so long as our focus is on the *materiality of objects*, it is quite impossible to follow the multiple trails of growth and transformation that converge, for instance, in the stuccoed façade of a building or the page of a manuscript. These trails are merely swept under the carpet of a generalised substrate upon which the forms of all things are said to be imposed or inscribed. In urging that we take a step back, from the materiality of objects to the properties of materials, I propose that we lift the carpet, to reveal beneath its surface a tangled web of meandrine complexity, in which – among a myriad of other things – the secretions of gall wasps get caught up with old iron, acacia sap, goose feathers and calf-skins, and the residue from heated limestone mixes with emissions from pigs, cattle, hens and bees. For materials such as these do not present themselves as tokens of some common essence – materiality – that endows every worldly entity with its inherent 'objectness'; rather, they partake in the very processes of the world's ongoing generation and regeneration, of which things such as manuscripts or house-fronts are impermanent by-products. Thus, to cull one further example at random, boiling fish-bones yields an adhesive material, a glue, not a fishy kind of materiality in the things glued together.

   In this regard, it is significant that studies of so-called material culture have focused overwhelmingly on processes of consumption rather than production (Miller 1995, 1998: 11; though see Olsen 2003: 91-4 for a critical comment). For such studies take as their starting point a world of objects that has, as it were, *already crystallised out* from the fluxes of materials and their transformations. At this point materials appear to vanish, swallowed up by the very objects to which they have given birth. That is why we commonly describe materials as 'raw' but never 'cooked' – for by the time they have congealed into objects they have already disappeared. Thenceforth it is the objects themselves that capture our attention, no longer the materials of which they are made. It is as though our material involvement begins only when the stucco has already hardened on the house-front or the ink already dried on the page. We see the building and not the plaster of its walls; the words and not the ink with which they were written. In reality, of course, the materials are still there and continue to mingle and react as they had always done, forever threatening the things they comprise with dissolution or even 'dematerialisation'. Plaster can crumble and ink can fade.

FIGURE 2.2   Ladder (wood, four metres high, Lake Biwa, Japan) by David Nash (photo courtesy of the artist)

Experienced as degradation, corrosion or wear and tear, however, these changes – that objects undergo after they are 'finished' – are typically attributed to the phase of use rather than manufacture. As the underbelly of things, materials may lie low but are never entirely subdued. Despite the best efforts of curators and conservationists, no object lasts forever. Materials always and inevitably win out over materiality in the long term.[6]

This is a theme that has been taken up in the work of the sculptor David Nash. He makes things like boxes, ladders and chairs, but out of unseasoned timber, allowing the wood to live on beyond the life of the tree of which it was once a growing trunk or limb, without ever losing touch with its arboreal roots. Observing one of Nash's ladders, for example, the wood appears to body forth from the thing made from it, rather than retreating back-stage as is the case with its factory-made equivalent in the showroom. We see wood that has been made into a ladder rather than a ladder that has been made out of wood (Figure 2.2). Moreover, with the passage of time the wood – as it seasons – splits, warps and cracks, eventually settling into a shape quite different from that given to it by the sculptor's initial intervention. 'I keep my mind on the process', says Nash, 'and let the piece take care of itself' (cited in Warner 1996: 15). For beneath the skin of the form the substance remains alive, reconfiguring the surface as it matures. But in treating the wood as life-giving material rather than dead matter, Nash is only drawing our attention to what our predecessors already knew when they first coined the term 'material' by extension from the Latin *mater* ('mother'). As Nicholas Allen reminds us, the term 'has a complex history involving feminine-gender Latin and Greek words for wood … which is or has been alive' (Allen 1998: 177). Far from being the inanimate stuff typically envisioned by modern thought, materials in this original sense are the active constituents of a world-in-formation. Wherever life is going on, they are relentlessly on the move – flowing, scraping, mixing and mutating.[7] The existence of all living organisms is caught up in this ceaseless respiratory and metabolic interchange between their bodily substances and the fluxes of the medium. Without it they could not survive. This of course applies to us human beings as much as to organisms of other kinds. Along with all terrestrial vertebrates, we need to be able to breathe.

In the world of solid objects envisaged by material culture theorists, however, the flux of materials is stifled and stilled. In such a world, wherein all that is material is locked up in things, it would be impossible to breathe. Indeed neither life itself, nor any form of consciousness that depends on it, could persist. 'One cannot dream profoundly with *objects*', writes philosopher Gaston Bachelard. 'To dream profoundly, one must dream with *substances*' (1983: 22). Suffocated by the dead hand of materiality, 'strewn with unrelated things, immobile and inert solids, objects foreign to our nature' (ibid.: 12), the material world can only be brought back to life in the dreams of theorists by conjuring a magical mind-dust that, sprinkled among its constituents, is supposed to set them physically in motion. It has come to be known in the literature as *agency*, and great expectations have been pinned upon it. Action, we are told, follows agency as effect follows cause (Gell 1998: 16). Thus people are supposed to be capable of acting, and are not just acted upon, because they have acquired some of this agency.[8] Without it, they would be but things. By the same token, however, if agency is imaginatively bestowed on things, then they can start acting like people. They can 'act back'; inducing persons in their vicinity to do what they otherwise might not. In one of the most original and provocative discussions of materiality to have appeared in recent years, Peter Pels characterises the logic of this argument as *animist*: 'a way of saying that things are alive because they are animated by something foreign to them, a "soul" or … spirit made to reside *in* matter' (Pels 1998: 94). Whatever its source might be, this animating principle is understood here as *additional* to the material object on which it has been bestowed.

There is however, according to Pels, another way of understanding how things can act back. This is to say that the spirit that enlivens them is not *in* but *of* matter. We do not then look beyond the material constitution of objects in order to discover what makes them tick; rather the power of agency lies with their materiality itself. Pels characterises this alternative logic as *fetishist*. Thus the fetish is an object that, by virtue of its sheer material presence, affects the course of affairs (1998: 94–5). This argument is an important step in the right direction, but it takes us only halfway. On the one hand it acknowledges the active power of materials, their capacity to stand forth from the things made of them. Yet it remains trapped in a discourse that opposes the mental and the material, and that cannot therefore countenance the properties of materials, save as aspects of the inherent materiality of objects. Thus the hybrid quality that Pels attributes to the fetish – its capacity at once to set up and disrupt 'the sensuous border zone between ourselves and the things around us, between mind and matter' (ibid.: 102) – is in fact a product of the misrecognition of the active properties of materials as a power of the materiality of objects. There is nothing hybrid about one of Nash's ladders, however. Like the living tree in the ground from which it was made, it inhabits the border zone not between matter and mind but between substance and medium. The wood is alive, or 'breathes', precisely because of the flux of materials across its surface.

Bringing things to life, then, is a matter not of adding to them a sprinkling of agency but of restoring them to the generative fluxes of the world of materials in which they came into being and continue to subsist. This view, that things are in life rather than life in things, is diametrically opposed to the conventional anthropological understanding of animism, invoked by Pels (1998: 94) and harking back to the classic work of Edward Tylor, according to which it entails the attribution of life, spirit or agency to objects that are really inert. It is, however, entirely consistent with the actual ontological commitments of peoples often credited in the literature with an animistic cosmology (see Chapter 5). In their world there are no objects as such. Things are alive and active not because they are possessed of spirit – whether *in* or *of* matter – but because the substances of which they are comprised continue to be swept up in circulations of the surrounding media that alternately portend their dissolution or – characteristically with animate beings – ensure their regeneration. Spirit is the regenerative power of these circulatory flows which, in living organisms, are bound into tightly woven bundles or tissues of extraordinary complexity. All organisms are bundles of this kind. Stripped of the veneer of materiality they are revealed not as quiescent objects but as hives of activity, pulsing with the flows of materials that keep them alive. And in this respect human beings are no exception. They are, in the first place, organisms, not blobs of solid matter with an added whiff of mentality or agency to liven them up. As such, they are born and grow within the current of materials, and participate from within in their further transformation.

Properties and qualities

If, as I have suggested, we are to redirect our attention from the materiality of objects to the properties of materials, then we are left with the question: what are these properties? How should we talk about them? One approach to answering this question has been proposed by the theorist of design, David Pye (1968: 45-7). His concern is to examine the idea that every material has inherent properties that can be either expressed or suppressed in use. This idea is frequently enunciated by sculptors and craftspeople who assert that good workmanship should be 'true to the material', respecting its properties rather than riding roughshod over them. Suppose, then, that we take a metallic material like lead. Among a list of its properties we might include the following: ductility, heaviness, low melting point, resistance to electrical current, impenetrability to X-rays, and toxicity. Of these the first two might possibly be expressed artistically, but the others cannot. But if our aim is to be true to the material, then why, Pye asks, should we be content to select only certain aspects of the lead, according to choices that have been dictated by considerations that have nothing to do with it? Then again, some materials exhibit properties while being worked that they lose once the job is done. Red-hot iron at the forge has the consistency of beeswax, but if the smith seeks to bring out its softness and elasticity, then the result, once the iron has cooled, will express precisely those properties that the material, now hard and rigid, no longer possesses. Similarly, the rounded form of a clay pot, formed while the material was damp and pliable, can hardly be said to bring out the brittleness of clay that has been baked in a kiln. Nor can we deny the excellence of workmanship that allows a master sculptor to fashion the hardest of stone into surfaces that appear as soft and smooth as silken cloth, or an infant's skin.

On these grounds, Pye argues that it is not really the *properties* of materials that an artist or craftsperson seeks to express, but rather their *qualities*.

> The properties of materials are objective and measurable. They are *out there*. The qualities on the other hand are subjective: they are *in here*: in our heads. They are ideas of ours. They are part of that private view of the world which artists each have within them. We each have our own view of what stoniness is.
>
> (Pye 1968: 47)

The assertion, then, that a sculpture is good because it brings out the stoniness of stone cannot be justified on the basis of any properties of the stone itself that can be objectively known. It merely reveals our own personal preferences concerning the qualities we like to see in it. It is of course true that we may hold such preferences concerning the materials we use to make things. It is also true that these materials may be subjected to a battery of tests in order to measure such properties as density, elasticity, tensile strength, thermal conductivity, and so on. For an engineer setting out to design a structure and deciding what materials to use, such measurements – which can be as accurate and objective as current science and instrumentation allow – may be of critical importance. Yet the knowledge they yield is a far cry from that of, say, the stonemason, smith, potter or carpenter, which comes from a lifetime's experience of working *with* the material. This is a knowledge born of sensory perception and practical engagement, not of the mind with the material world – to recall Renfrew's (2001) 'material engagement theory' – but of the skilled practitioner participating in a world of materials.

It may seem pedantic to distinguish between the material world and the world of materials, but the distinction is critical to my argument. The trouble with Pye's dichotomy between properties and qualities is that it takes us straight back to the polarisation of mind and matter from which our inquiry began. Materials, for Pye, are varieties of matter, that is, of the physical constitution of the world as it is given quite independently of the presence or activity of its inhabitants. Thus their properties are properties of matter, and are in that sense opposed to the qualities that the mind imaginatively projects onto them. Following Gibson, I have chosen to concentrate not on matter as such, but instead on substances and media, and the surfaces between them.[9] These are the basic components, for Gibson, not of the physical or material world but of the *environment*. Whereas the physical world *exists* in and for itself, the environment is a world that continually *unfolds* in relation to the beings that make a living there. Its reality is not *of* material objects but *for* its inhabitants (Gibson 1979: 8, see Ingold 1992). It is, in short, a world of materials. And as the environment unfolds, so the materials of which it is comprised do not *exist* – like the objects of the material world – but *occur*.[10] Thus the properties of materials, regarded as constituents of an environment, cannot be identified as fixed, essential attributes of things, but are rather processual and relational. They are neither objectively determined nor subjectively imagined but practically experienced. In that sense, every property is a condensed story. To describe the properties of materials is to tell the stories of what happens to them as they flow, mix and mutate.

Living the stone

This is exactly what Christopher Tilley does in his book, *The Materiality of Stone* (2004). Focusing on ancient monuments of massive stone or rock – the Mesolithic menhirs of Brittany, the temple architecture of Neolithic Malta and the Bronze Age rock carvings in southern Sweden – Tilley devotes a great deal of attention to the properties of stone *as material*. He shows how its 'stoniness', if you will, is not constant but endlessly variable in relation to light or shade, wetness or dryness, and the position, posture or movement of the observer. To describe the properties of stone he has to follow these variations as he walks around or over each monument, or crawls through it, at different times of day, in different seasons, and under different weather conditions. Yet in the very title of his book, these properties of stone, as material, are recast as the materiality of stone. And in that move the stone is instantly swallowed up by the landscape whose surface marks an interface not between earth and air but between nature and culture, the physical world and the world of ideas – 'two sides of a coin which cannot be separated', but two sides nonetheless (Tilley 2004: 220, see Ingold 2005b). On the one side, as Tilley (2007: 17) explains in a response to an earlier version of this chapter, there is a world of stones that is 'oblivious to the actions, thoughts and social and political relations of humans'. Here, he says, we are dealing with 'brute materials'. These are what geologists study. For the geologist, a stone is a formless lump of matter. He might find forms *in* the matter, for example in its molecular or crystalline structure, but it is these, and not the outward form of the stone itself, that concern him. On the other side is a world in which stones are caught up in the lives of human beings, and given form and significance through their incorporation into the social and historical contexts of these lives. This is the world that calls for the interpretative work of the archaeologist or student of material culture.[11]

It is precisely in order to delineate this latter world, according to Tilley, that we require a concept of materiality – 'one that needfully addresses the "social lives" of stones in relation to the social lives of persons' (Tilley 2007: 17). Likewise, archaeologist Joshua Pollard states that 'by materiality I mean how the material character of the world is comprehended, appropriated and involved in human projects' (Pollard 2004: 48). The paradox inherent in both definitions is that materiality lies in the measure to which the socially and historically constituted, form-bestowing agency of human beings *transcends* what Pollard calls the world's 'material character', or what Tilley calls its 'brute materiality'. This paradox reminds me of much older debates for and against the '*human* nature of human nature', which likewise oscillated between a notion of brute animality common to all creatures and one of an essential humanity by which the social life of persons was thought to be raised onto a plane of being over and above the purely biophysical (Eisenberg 1972; Ingold 1994: 19–25). In speaking of the world of materials, rather than the material world, my purpose has been to escape from this oscillation, both by returning persons to where they belong, within the continuum of organic life, and by recognising that this life itself undergoes continual generation in currents of materials.

Considered as a constituent of the material world, a stone is indeed both a lump of matter that can be analysed for its physical properties and an object whose significance is drawn from its incorporation into the context of human affairs. The concept of materiality, as we have seen, reproduces this duality, rather than challenging it. But in the world of materials, humans figure as much within the context for stones as do stones within the context for humans. And these contexts, far from lying on disparate levels of being, respectively social and natural, are established as overlapping regions of the *same* world. It is not as though this world were one of brute physicality, of mere matter, until people appeared on the scene to give it form and meaning. Stones, too, have histories, forged in ongoing relations with surroundings that may or may not include human beings and much else besides. It is all very well to place stones within the context of human social life and history, but within what context do we place this social life and history if not the ever-unfolding world of materials in which the very being of humans, along with that of the non-humans they encounter, is bound up? My plea, in arguing for a return to this world, is simply that we should once more *take materials seriously*, since it is from them that everything is made.

FIGURE 2.3   Dry stone (photo: Susanna Ingold)

Now return to the stone that has been quietly sitting on your desk as you have been reading. Without any intervention on your part, it has changed. The water that had once covered it has evaporated, and the surface is now almost completely dry. There might still be a few damp patches, but these are immediately recognisable from the darker colouration of the surface. Though the shape of the stone remains the same, it otherwise looks quite different. Indeed it might look disappointingly dull. The same is true of pebbles washed by the tide on a shingle beach, which never look so interesting once they have dried out. Though we might be inclined to say that a stone bathed in moisture is more 'stony' than one bathed in dry air, we should probably acknowledge that the appearances are just different. It is the same if we pick up the stone and feel it, or knock it against something else to make a noise. The dry stone feels and sounds differently from the wet one. What we can conclude, however, is that since the substance of the stone must be bathed in a medium of some kind, there is no way in which its stoniness can be understood apart from the ways it is caught up in the interchanges across its surface, between medium and substance. Like Nash's sculptures of unseasoned wood, though much more quickly, the stone has actually changed as it dried out. Stoniness, then, is not in the stone's 'nature', in its materiality. Nor is it merely in the mind of the observer or practitioner. Rather, it emerges through the stone's involvement in its total surroundings — including you, the observer — and from the manifold ways in which it is engaged in the currents of the lifeworld. The properties of materials, in short, are not attributes but histories.

3

CULTURE ON THE GROUND

THE WORLD PERCEIVED THROUGH THE FEET

Is it not truly extraordinary to realise that ever since men have walked, no-one has ever asked why they walk, how they walk, whether they walk, whether they might walk better, what they achieve by walking, whether they might not have the means to regulate, change or analyse their walk: questions that bear on all the systems of philosophy, psychology and politics with which the world is preoccupied?

Honoré de Balzac (1938 [1833]: 614)[1]

On the rise of head over heels

In the course of human evolution, three developments took place that have made us creatures of a kind recognisably distinct from even our closest cousins among non-human primates, the great apes. The first was the enormous enlargement of the brain, especially the frontal regions. Compared with other mammals, the human brain is pretty large; compared with what would be expected for mammals of our size, it is massive. The second was the remodelling of the hand, and above all the development of that special ability we have of being able to bring the tip of the thumb into contact with the tips of any of our other fingers – an ability that allows us to carry out manual operations with a versatility and dexterity unequalled in the animal kingdom. The third consisted of a suite of anatomical changes – the rebalancing of the head upon the neck, the characteristic S-shaped curvature of the back, the broadening of the pelvis and the straightening of the legs – that underlie our ability to stand upright and to walk on two feet. In the second of his three essays on *Man's Place in Nature*, published in 1863, T. H. Huxley illustrated these changes through a comparison of the skeletons of the gibbon, the orang-utan, the chimpanzee, the gorilla and the human being (Figure 3.1). There is an engaging liveliness about this depiction: the human skeleton seems to be lightly stepping towards you, and preparing to shake you by the hand. Nevertheless the picture has been deliberately constructed to tell a story, one that has entered the textbooks and been retold on countless occasions ever since. It is the story of how man's eventual achievement of upright posture laid the foundations for his pre-eminence in the animal kingdom, and for the growth of culture and civilisation. In the

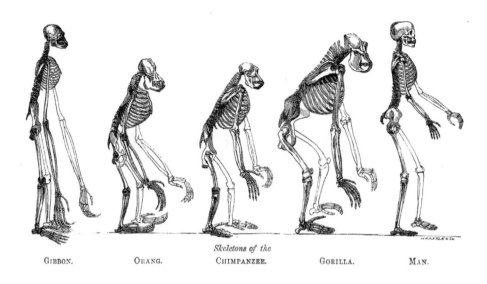

Skeletons of the
GIBBON.   ORANG.   CHIMPANZEE.   GORILLA.   MAN.

FIGURE 3.1 Skeletons of the gibbon, orang-utan, chimpanzee, gorilla and man, drawn from specimens in the Museum of the Royal College of Surgeons. Reproduced from Huxley (1894: 76).

picture, man marches confidently into the future, head high, body erect, while the stooping apes trundle along obediently behind (Huxley 1894: 76).

But if it was by standing up straight that our ancestors embarked upon the road to civilisation, it was not – according to this story – their feet that brought them there. It was their hands. In *The Descent of Man*, Charles Darwin drew particular attention to what he called the 'physiological division of labour' by which feet and hands came to be perfected for the different but complementary functions, respectively, of support and locomotion, and of grasping and manipulation. In apes this division was but imperfectly established, for while the feet, blessed with toes far more dextrous than ours, retained considerable powers of prehension, the hands continued to play a significant supportive role. By contrast the human foot, with its relatively immobile big toe, has all but lost its original prehensile function, becoming little more than a pedestal for the rest of the body, while all the important work of holding, feeling and gesturing is delegated to the hands. It must have been of great advantage to man, Darwin reasoned, 'to stand firmly on his feet', since this would have left the hands and arms free for the essential arts of subsistence and survival (Darwin 1874: 77). Above all, bipedal posture liberated the hands for the use and manufacture of tools. And it was the selective advantages conferred by tools, according to Darwin, that ultimately set up the conditions for the enlargement of the brain. The argument ran that the 'most sagacious' of individuals, having bigger and better brains, could design the most ingenious tools and use them to greatest effect. This, in turn, would confer a reproductive benefit, ensuring that intelligence-enhancing variations, more abundantly preserved in future generations, would be ratcheted up in the course of natural selection. Every incremental increase would lead to yet further advance in the technical sphere, and so on through mutual reinforcement (ibid.: 196–197).

Darwin's account, it must be said, did little more than embellish an old story with a newly conceived mechanism – that of natural selection – to drive it along. The idea that bipedal locomotion liberates the hands, and furthermore that the free hand endows human beings with an intellectual superiority over all other creatures, can be traced back to classical Antiquity. It is to be found in the writings of Xenophon, Aristotle, Vitruvius and Gregory of Nyssa, and was already commonplace among naturalists of the eighteenth and early-nineteenth centuries (Stoczkowski 2002: 87–88). Somewhat controversially, however, Darwin insisted that human superiority was not of kind but only of degree. The rudiments of intelligence, he claimed, can be found in the lowliest of animals, such as the humble earthworm (Reed 1982), while even the most civilised of men have not altogether escaped the determinations of instinct. As creatures advance along the scale of nature, the proportion of rational intelligence to natural instinct very gradually increases, but only with the emergence of humanity does the balance tip decisively towards the former (Darwin 1874: 98ff.). For Darwin, then, the descent of man *in* nature was also an ascent *out* of it, in so far as it progressively released the powers of intellect from their bodily bearings in the material world. Human evolution was portrayed as the rise, and eventual triumph, of head over heels.

This immediately enables us to make sense of Darwin's remarks concerning the relative significance of the hands and the feet. Unlike the quadruped, with four feet planted solidly in the ground of nature, the biped is held down only by two, while the arms and hands, released from their previous functions of support and locomotion, become answerable to the call of reason. Marching head over heels – half in nature, half out – the human biped figures as a constitutionally divided creature. The dividing line, roughly level with the waist, separates the upper and lower parts of the body. Whereas the feet, impelled by biomechanical necessity, undergird and propel the body *within* the natural world, the hands are free to deliver the intelligent designs or conceptions of the mind *upon* it: for the former, nature is the medium through which the body moves; to the latter it presents itself as a surface to be transformed. And in this potential for transformation, inherent in the coupling of hands and brain, lie the conditions for man's mastery and control over his material environment. 'Man could not have attained his present dominant position in the world without the use of his hands', says Darwin, 'which are so admirably adapted to act in obedience to his will'. He goes on to cite with approval the words of Sir Charles Bell, professor of surgery at the University of Edinburgh, from his Bridgewater Treatise of 1833. 'The hand supplies all instruments, and by its correspondence with the intellect gives [man] universal dominion' (ibid.: 76–77).

Boots and shoes

I shall return to Sir Charles in another connection, but at this point I want to pick up another strand in Darwin's discussion of the division of labour between hands and feet. Presented in an offhand manner, almost as an afterthought, it is of major significance for my argument. Having remarked upon the specialisation of the foot for support and locomotion, and the corresponding loss of its original grasping function, Darwin notes that 'with some savages … the foot has not altogether lost its prehensile power, as shown by their manner of climbing trees, and of using them in other ways' (ibid.: 77). He does not take the point further; indeed it must have seemed to him more or less self-evident. As the savage was regarded as anatomically intermediate between the ape and the civilised human, it would stand to reason that his feet would retain some vestiges of the ape-like form. T. H. Huxley, however, has rather more to say on the matter. He, too, observes that primitive people seem able to do things with their feet – his examples are rowing a boat, weaving cloth, and even stealing fishhooks – that might strike us civilised folk as extraordinary. But rather than being a function of their innate anatomical endowment, might this not have more to do with their habit of going barefoot? 'It must not be forgotten', Huxley warns us, 'that the civilised great toe, confined and cramped from childhood upwards, is seen to a great disadvantage, and that in uncivilised and barefooted people it retains a great amount of mobility, and even some sort of opposability' (Huxley 1894: 119). Paradoxically, it seems that with the onward march of civilisation, the foot has been progressively *withdrawn* from the sphere of operation of the intellect, that it has regressed to the status of a merely mechanical apparatus, and moreover that this development is a consequence – not a cause – of technical advance in footwear. Boots and shoes, products of the ever more versatile human hand, imprison the foot, constricting its freedom of movement and blunting its sense of touch.

Edward Tylor, in his *Anthropology* of 1881, takes these observations one step further. In order to make the now familiar point that the differentiation between the hand and foot is so much greater for the human than it is for the ape, he presents us with a picture in which the hand and foot of the chimpanzee, and of man, are placed side by side (Figure 3.2). But he hastens to add that the drawing of the human foot 'is purposely taken, not from the free foot of the savage, but from the European foot cramped by the stiff leather boot, because this shows in the utmost way the contrast between ape and man' (Tylor 1881: 43). The qualification is remarkable, since it amounts to an admission that the ideal-type human being, the gold standard against which similarities and differences between humans and apes are to be gauged, is one that has to a significant degree been forced into shape through the artificial application of a restrictive technology. Like Huxley, Tylor is able to come up with examples, albeit anecdotal, of the dexterity of the barefoot savage. 'With the naked foot, the savage Australian picks up his spear, and the Hindu tailor holds his cloth as he squats sewing.'[2] The boot-wearing European, Tylor admits, is helpless by comparison. His foot, the one illustrated in the picture, is nothing more than a 'stepping-machine'. Like Darwin before

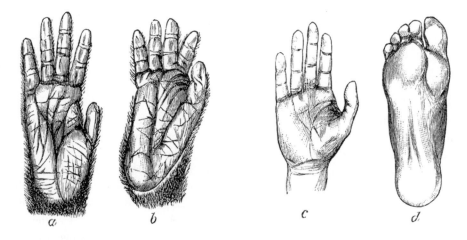

FIGURE 3.2 Hand (a) and foot (b) of chimpanzee; hand (c) and foot (d) of man. Reproduced from Tylor (1881: 42).

him, and of course Sir Charles Bell, Tylor was convinced that man's intellectual development was gained by the use not of his feet, but of his hands. 'From handling objects, putting them in different positions, and setting them side by side, he was led to those simplest kinds of comparing and measuring which are the first elements of exact knowledge, or science' (ibid.: 43–44). Thanks to his hands and his heavy boots the civilised man, it seems, is every inch a scientist on top, but a machine down below.

The effects of the boot on the anatomy and function of the foot were already well recognised by the time that Darwin, Huxley and Tylor were writing. In 1839 a paper was read before the Society of Arts for Scotland entitled 'Observations on Boots and Shoes, with reference to the Structure and Action of the Human Foot'. The author, a certain James Dowie, presented himself to the Society as the inventor, patentee and manufacturer of boots and shoes with elastic soles.[3] Explaining the advantages of his invention, Dowie drew attention to some remarks of Sir Charles Bell, the Edinburgh surgeon to whom I have already referred, in which he compares the Irish agricultural labourer, travelling to harvest barefoot, and the English peasant whose foot and ankle are tightly laced in a shoe with a wooden sole. Look at the way the Englishman lifts his legs, observed Bell, and you will perceive 'that the play of the ankle, foot, and toes, is lost, as much as if he went on stilts, and therefore are his legs small and shapeless' (cited in Dowie 1839: 406). Indeed, Bell was much in favour of James Dowie's patent elastic boots and shoes, going so far as to provide a public testimonial in which he not only affirmed the correctness of Dowie's understanding of the anatomical details, but also declared himself a highly satisfied user. 'I have worn your shoes with pliant soles', he wrote, 'and … find them pleasant and easy to the foot.' Yet for all that, the well-heeled of the western world have continued to strut about, in Bell's graphic phrase, 'as if on stilts', often to their considerable discomfort. To the affluent, the constriction of the feet remains as sure a mark of civilisation as the freedom of the hands. Is the conventional division of labour between hands and feet, then, as 'natural' as Darwin and his contemporaries made it out to be? Could it not be, at least in some measure, a result of the mapping, onto the human body, of a peculiarly modern discourse about the triumph of intelligence over instinct, and about the human domination of nature? And could not the technology of footwear be understood, again in some measure, as an effort to convert the imagined superiority of hands over feet, corresponding respectively to intelligence and instinct, or to reason and nature, into an experienced reality?

Leaving the ground

In what follows I shall argue that the mechanisation of footwork was part and parcel of a wider suite of changes that accompanied the onset of modernity – in modalities of travel and transport, in the education of posture and gesture, in the evaluation of the senses, and in the architecture of the built environment – all of which conspired to lend practical and experiential weight to an imagined separation between the activities of a mind at rest and a body in transit, between cognition and locomotion, and between the space of social and cultural life and the ground upon which that life is materially enacted. I begin with travel. What is of interest here is the way in which, in Britain and Europe from around the eighteenth century onwards, the business of travel came to be distinguished from the activity of walking. For most people in the British Isles, before the days of paved roads and public transport, the only way to get about was on foot. Walking was a mundane, everyday activity, taking them to work, market and church, but rarely over any great distance. Walkers did not travel. But by the same token, as Anne Wallace (1993) has shown in her fine study of the place of walking in English literature, travellers did not walk. Or rather, they walked as little as possible, preferring the horse or carriage, even though neither was much faster in those days, or any more comfortable (Jarvis 1997: 20–22). Travel was an activity of the well-to-do, who could afford such things. They considered walking to be tedious and commonplace, a view that lingers in the residual connotations of the word 'pedestrian'.[4] If they *had* to walk, they would do their best to blot the experience from their memories, and to erase it from their accounts.

The affluent did not undertake to travel for its own sake, however, or for the experience it might afford. Indeed the actual process of travel, especially on foot, was considered a drudge – literally a *travail* – that had to be endured for the sole purpose of reaching a destination (Wallace 1993: 39). What mattered was the knowledge to be gained on arriving there. Thus Samuel Johnson, relating his journey with James Boswell to the Western Isles of Scotland, recommended travel as the only way to test the conceptions we may have of places and landscapes against objective realities, and promptly went on to describe the view from a resting place in a beautiful mountain valley where he first had the idea of writing his narrative (Johnson and Boswell 1924: 35). His interest lay in the scene around him at that spot, not in how he came to it, about which he had virtually nothing to say. For men like Johnson, a trip or tour would consist of a series of such destinations. Were the experience of place-to-place movement to intrude overmuch into conscious awareness, they warned, observations could be biased, memories distorted and, above all, we might be distracted from noticing salient features of the landscape around us. Thus on a visit to the island of Ulinish, Johnson complains that his appreciation of a natural arch in the rock would have been greater 'had not the stones, which incumbered our feet, given us leisure to consider it' (ibid.: 67). Only when the mind is set at rest, no longer jolted and jarred by the physical displacements of its bodily housing, can it operate properly. As long as it is in between one point of observation and another, it is effectively disabled.

So it was that the elites of Europe – at least from the eighteenth century – came to conduct and write about their travels as if they had no legs. Skimming across the surface of the country, they would alight, here and there, to admire the view. The embodied experience of pedestrian movement was, as it were, pushed into the wings (Certeau 1984: 121), in order to make way for a more detached and speculative contemplation. Walking was for the poor, the criminal, the young, and above all, the ignorant (Jarvis 1997: 23). Only in the nineteenth century, following the example set by Wordsworth and Coleridge, did people of leisure take to walking as an end in itself, beyond the confines of the landscaped garden or gallery. For them pedestrian travel became, in the words of Rebecca Solnit, 'an expansion of the garden stroll' (Solnit 2001: 93). Yet the rise of the practice and theory of walking as an inherently virtuous and rewarding activity, despite presenting an apparent challenge to earlier ideas of destination-oriented travel, actually depended on material improvements in transport that greatly increased the volume of such travel, and extended its range and possibility (Wallace 1993: 65–66). For one thing, as public transport came to be affordable to ordinary working people, walking figured as a matter of choice rather than necessity, and the stigma of poverty formerly attached to its practitioners faded away (Urry 2000: 51). And for another thing, transport could take people to the places – the scenery – within and around which they wanted to walk. Thus the entire landscape became the destination at which one had arrived from the very moment of setting out on foot (Solnit 2001: 93).

If you could choose to walk, however, as well as select for yourself the places where your stroll or hike would begin or end, then the alternative must always have been available of sitting down, whether your seat be immobile or attached to a moving vehicle. Thus the most enthusiastic of peripatetics, even while extolling the physical and intellectual benefits of walking, did so from the comfortable vantage point of a society thoroughly accustomed to the chair. In the history of the western world, chairs made their first appearance as seats of high authority and did not come into widespread use, even in the most wealthy of houses, until around the sixteenth century. The 'sitting society' to which we are so accustomed today is largely a phenomenon of the last two hundred years (Tenner 2003: 105). It is probably no accident, nevertheless, that the civilisation that gave us the leather boot has also come up with the upholstered chair. Of course, human beings do not *need* to sit on chairs, any more than they need to clad their feet in boots and shoes. As the designer Ralph Caplan wryly remarks, 'a chair is the first thing you need when you don't really need anything, and is therefore a peculiarly compelling symbol of civilisation' (Caplan 1978: 18). Nothing, however, better illustrates the value placed upon a sedentary perception of the world, mediated by the allegedly superior senses of vision and hearing, and unimpeded by any haptic or kinaesthetic sensation through the feet. Where the boot, in reducing the activity of walking to the activity of a stepping machine, deprives wearers of the possibility of thinking with their feet, the chair enables sitters to think without involving the feet at all. Between them, the boot and the chair establish a technological foundation for the separation of thought from action and of mind from body – that is for the fundamental *groundlessness* so characteristic of modern metropolitan dwelling (Lewis 2001: 68). It is as though, for inhabitants of the metropolis, the world of their thoughts, their dreams and their relations with others floats like a mirage above the road they tread in their actual material life. A famous anthropological statement to this effect comes from Clifford Geertz. 'Man', he has declared, 'is an animal suspended in webs of significance he himself has spun.' I think we should perhaps amend this statement, to say that only booted and seated man, artificially insulated – whether in movement or at rest – from direct contact with the ground, would consider himself so suspended (Geertz 1973: 5, see Ingold 1997: 238).

In most non-western societies the usual position of rest to adopt, while awake, is the squat. 'You can distinguish squatting mankind and sitting mankind', wrote the ethnologist Marcel Mauss in his essay on body techniques (Mauss 1979: 113–114). My guess is that squatters still considerably outnumber sitters, despite the export of chairs around the globe. However, for those of us brought up to sit on chairs, to have to squat for any length of time is acutely uncomfortable. It seems that the chair has blocked the development of the normal capacity of the human being to squat, just as the boot has blocked the development of the prehensile functions of the foot. Only with much practice and training can these blockages be overcome. Yet in western societies, where uprightness or 'standing' is a measure of rank and moral rectitude, the squatting position is reserved for those on the very lowest rung of the social ladder – for outcastes, beggars and supplicants. Armed with a battery of devices from high chairs to baby walkers, western parents devote much effort to getting their infants to sit and stand as soon as is physically possible, and worry about any delay in their development.[5] Older children are urged to stand up straight, and to 'walk from the hips' with minimal bending at the knees. To succeed in this, they must be fitted with appropriate footwear. Indeed one of the most essential bodily skills that every child has to master before being able to make his or her way in a boot-clad society such as our own, is the art of tying shoelaces. With loose shoelaces, the walker can only prevent his shoes from falling off by adopting a shuffling gait that is widely regarded as a mark of impotence, infirmity or decrepitude. He is, moreover, at constant risk of tripping up. I was struck by a radio interview with one of ex-president Slobodan Milosevic's erstwhile friends and supporters, who was describing his circumstances in a Belgrade gaol. Of all the indignities he had to suffer, the interviewee said, the worst was that he had to go around in boots *without laces*.

The historian Jan Bremmer has traced the western ideals of upright posture, and a gait with long measured strides and straight legs, to the culture of ancient Greece, passed on to early modern Europe by way of the works of Cicero, Saint Ambrose and Erasmus. The origin of the Greek gait, Bremmer suggests, lies in an earlier age when every man had to carry arms, and be ready to fight to protect both reputation and possessions (Bremmer 1992: 16–23, 27). In this respect the positioning of the hands is particularly significant. Not only should they be ready for use, held slightly in advance of the trunk (an injunction that translates into contemporary disapproval of standing with one's hands in one's pockets), they should also be downturned. For a man with upturned hands would be one without weapons – one who had, by that token, symbolically abdicated his manhood, presenting himself in an effeminate pose. In addition the free man should keep his head erect, as Bremmer puts it, with 'the eyes openly, steadfastly, and firmly fixed on the world' (ibid.: 23). Now if we return to T. H. Huxley's comparative depiction of man and the great apes, with which I began (Figure 3.1), we find that the man is precisely in the recommended posture of ancient Greece. He is upright, proceeding forward with a measured gait. He is looking directly ahead, not downwards and, sure enough, the palms of his hands are downturned. Indeed, a man he most certainly is. For had the figure been of a woman, following the same conventions, the head and eyes would be downcast, the palms turned upwards, and the step smaller and more nimble.

Anthropologist Junzo Kawada (n.d.) has drawn a fascinating comparison between expected European (or, more particularly, French) ways of walking and carrying things, and those customary in Japan – roughly from the twelfth to the mid-twentieth century. Whereas the European, as I have already observed, walks from the hips while keeping the legs as straight as possible, Japanese people traditionally walked from the knees while minimising movement at the hips. The result is a kind of shuffle, not unlike that of a man who has lost his shoelaces, which to European eyes looks most ungainly. Walking from the knees, however, is very effective on rough or hilly terrain, since with the lowered centre of gravity the risk of tripping and falling is much reduced. It is also ergonomically consistent with the technique, once widely used in Japan, of carrying heavy loads suspended from a long, supple pole resting athwart the shoulder. Kawada is able to relate the postural difference in walking, respectively from the hips and from the knees, not only to alternative methods and devices for load carrying, but also to traditional dance styles, artisanal techniques and practices of child rearing. European dancers aspire to verticality, using their feet like stilts, a posture taken to its most stylised extreme in classical ballet where the female dancer balances on the tips of her toes, arms stretched heavenwards, while her male partner, with his leaps and bounds, temporarily loses contact with the ground altogether. Japanese dancers, by contrast, through flexible movement of the knees, drag their feet across the smooth floor in a shuffling motion, without ever lifting their heels (Suzuki 1986: 6). Again, whereas European artisans (with the singular exception of the tailor) work either standing or seated on a firm, raised support, their Japanese counterparts typically work from a squatting position, which confers no loss of status.

Finally, Japanese parents are glad to see their children crawling everywhere on all fours, displaying none of the anxiety of Europeans who regard crawling as a stage to be superseded as quickly as possible, through rigorous discipline and the use of artificial aids. Tadashi Suzuki, one of the foremost figures in contemporary Japanese theatre, writes with approval of 'the perception that our hands are also our feet', which comes, for example, from cleaning the floor with a polishing rag. A child who experiences this kind of 'floor-cleaning' movement, he observes, 'will understand, even after growing up, that parts of the body other than the feet can have a dialogue with the ground' (ibid.: 21). However, as traditional, wood-floored houses are giving way in Japanese cities to internally carpeted, western-style apartment blocks, in which one resident's floor can be another's ceiling, and in which floors are no longer polished on hands and knees but vacuumed from a standing position, the once strong and positive orientation towards the ground is being eroded. For Suzuki, this is a matter of regret. 'Because wooden hallways and passageways have disappeared', he laments, 'the feet and hands of modern man have been separated from each other; we have forgotten that mankind is one of the animals' (loc. cit.). But what Japanese people may be forgetting only in modern times, has a history of denial in the western world stretching back for over two millennia. Wiktor Stoczkowski has traced the symbolic valorisation of uprightness, still so prominent in palaeoanthropology, in a wealth of classical and early Christian sources: Plato, Xenophon, Aristotle, Pliny the Elder, Vitruvius, Ovid, Cicero, Prudentius and Gregory of Nyssa. The idea expressed throughout is that the human, by standing upright, can gaze heavenwards, know the gods (or God), and exercise dominion over all other creatures (Stoczkowski 2002: 73–74). For these western thinkers, quite unlike their historic Japanese counterparts, the achievement of bipedalism was critical to raising human beings above the threshold of nature and to establishing the superiority of the human condition over that of the animals. The quadruped, in their eyes, was necessarily a being inferior to man.

Walking the streets

The western proclivity to walk as if on stilts has of course been taken to its most absurd extreme in the military drill. This evoked some wry observations from Marcel Mauss, under the heading of 'walking':

> We laugh at the 'goose-step'. It is the way the German army can obtain maximum extension of the leg, given in particular that all Northerners, high on their legs, like to take as long steps as possible. In the absence of these exercises, we Frenchmen remain more or less knock-kneed…
>
> (Mauss 1979: 114–115)

Why do we laugh at the goose-stepping German soldier? Surely it is because his movements are so oddly mechanical. No one naturally walks like that; indeed if they did, they would forever be tripping over things. The goose step is only possible on the artificially monotonous surface of the parade ground.[6] Nevertheless, by public works, most metropolitan societies have transformed their urban spaces into something approximating the parade ground, by paving the streets. In so doing, they have literally paved the way for the boot-clad pedestrian to exercise his feet as a stepping machine. No longer did he have to pick his way, with care and dexterity, along potholed, cobbled or rutted thoroughfares, littered with the accumulated filth and excrement of the countless households and trades whose business lay along them. Dirt is the stuff of tactile (and of course, olfactory) sensation. It could trip you up, or soil your boots. But as the geographer Miles Ogborn has shown in his study of the paving of the streets of Westminster in the City of London, during the mid-eighteenth century, the construction of pavements offered pedestrians a street surface that was smooth and uniform, regularly cleaned, free from clutter and properly lit. Above all, the streets were made open and straight, creating a fitting environment for what was considered the proper exercise of the higher faculty of vision – to see and be seen (Ogborn 1998: 91–104).

John Gay's satirical poem *Trivia: or, the Art of Walking the Streets of London*, dating from 1716, presents a marvellous account of the pedestrian experience of those days, when the pavers were hard at work. Sensibly, Gay begins with some advice on footwear: 'Let firm, well-hammer'd Soles protect thy Feet' (Gay 1974: 136). And he recognises, too, that if we are to walk without tripping, soiling our clothes, or becoming drenched in water from overhead gutters, we need to mobilise all our senses – of smell and touch as well as vision – especially when out after dark.

> Has not wise Nature strung the Legs and Feet
> With firmest Nerves, design'd to walk the Street?
> Has she not given us Hands, to groap aright,
> Amidst the frequent Dangers of the Night?
> And thinks't thou not the double Nostril meant,
> To warn from oily Woes by previous Scent?
> (ibid.: 167)

Nevertheless, vision remains paramount. A way of walking is recommended, which, while preserving the independence and autonomy of the individual, maintains a constant visual vigilance – not of the ground surface but of *other people*.

> Still fix thy Eyes intent upon the Throng
> And as the Passes open, wind along.
> (ibid.: 160)

This vigilance extends, moreover, to the observance of a certain etiquette. One should make way for ladies, the old and infirm, the blind and lame, and the heavily loaded porter. It is also wise to give a wide berth to those who are liable to cover you with dust, from the toff with his fancy wig to the miller with his bags of flour.

> You'll sometimes meet a Fop, of nicest Tread,
> Whose mantling Peruke veils his empty Head…
> Him, like the *Miller*, pass with Caution by,
> Lest from his Shoulder Clouds of Powder fly.
> (ibid.: 145)

In nearly three hundred years, not much has changed, except that the 'throng' is more intense, you are more likely to find gangs of workmen digging up the streets than laying pavements, and the greatest threat to those who do not, as Gay puts it, 'maintain the Wall', comes from being driven over by an automobile rather than a horse and carriage.

Some of the most acute observations on walking the streets in a contemporary city come from the sociological writings of Erving Goffman. Indeed he begins his classic study, *Relations in Public*, with a detailed account of how the individual pedestrian, conceived as a pilot encased in the soft shell of his clothes and skin, succeeds in getting around without falling over or bumping into other people (Goffman 1971: 6–7). What is so striking about Goffman's account is that he describes walking, almost exclusively, as a *visual* activity. The pilot is supposed to use his eyes to guide his body about. He does this through a process that Goffman calls 'scanning'. Every individual continually scans or checks out an area that takes the form of an elongated oval, narrow at either side and longest in front. As other people approach, he checks their direction while they are still three or four pavement squares away, making any necessary adjustment in his own path at this stage. They can then be allowed to come nearer without further cause for concern, since any interference at such close range would require them to make a very abrupt turn. In order to maintain his scanning area, the individual may have to angle his head so that his visual field is not blocked by the pedestrian in front. But he also keeps an eye on the faces of those coming towards him, which, rather like a rear-view mirror, reveal in their expressions possible sources of interest and danger that have already passed behind his sight line (ibid.: 11–12). Finally, if the street is so crowded that normal scanning becomes virtually impossible, the individual has resort to a special manoeuvre that Goffman (following an earlier study by Michael Wolff) calls the step-and-slide – 'a slight angling of the body, a turning of the shoulder and an almost imperceptible sidestep' (ibid.: 14). It is, as Goffman notes, thanks to their ability to 'twist, duck, bend and turn sharply' that pedestrians are generally able to extricate themselves at the very last moment from impending impact (ibid.: 8). This advantage is not shared by the motorist nor, in the past, by the horse rider.[7]

What Goffman shows us, through his study, is that walking down a city street is an intrinsically social activity. Its sociality does not hover above the practice itself, in some ethereal realm of ideas and discourse, but is rather immanent in the way a person's movements – his or her step, gait, direction and pace – are continually responsive to the movements of others in the immediate environment.[8] Yet Goffman's walkers, each a 'vehicular unit' comprising the visually guided pilot within a soft bodily shell, still seem somehow detached from the solid ground beneath their feet. They could almost be floating in thin air. Admittedly Goffman does recognise – albeit in passing – that besides scanning for other people, the individual also scans the flooring immediately before him, in order to avoid small obstructions or dirt. Thus 'within the oval scanned for oncomers … is a smaller region that is also kept under eye' (ibid.: 16). There is some evidence that the intensity of the downward scan varies by age and gender, in a way that fully accords with established cultural conventions. Michael Hill, in a review of studies of pedestrian behaviour, reports on a psychological experiment that purported to show that women look down when they walk, more than men. But whether this was because they were walking more slowly and had more time to look, or because they were conforming to rules of female modesty, or because they were wearing dangerously impractical high-heeled shoes, the experimenters could not say (Hill 1984: 9–10). When it comes to children, Michael Wolff notes that city parents are inclined to treat under-sevens as 'baggage', dragged along by the hand rather like a suitcase on wheels. Often the children neither look nor even know where they are going, nor are they looked at by those coming in the opposite direction. Oncoming pedestrians, it appeared, 'would "sight" the adult and negotiate the right-of-way with him', while ignoring and being ignored by the child whose eyes, besides being at a lower level, would be resolutely downcast (Wolff 1973: 45). The child's-eye view of this has been immortalised in the lines of A. A. Milne:

> Whenever I walk in a London street,
> I'm ever so careful to watch my feet.[9]

The message of these lines is that before a child can begin to negotiate a right of way for himself, in horizontal eye-to-eye contact with others, he has to acquire a complex set of social skills: 'It's ever so portant how you walk' (Milne 1936: 12).

Nowadays, of course, the steadfastly forward-looking urban male is more likely to go by car, the female rather less so. The great majority of journeys by foot are made by children under the age of fifteen (Hillman and Whalley 1979: 34). They are the real walkers of our society. But my point has been that the reduction of pedestrian experience, that has perhaps reached its peak in the present era of the car, is the culmination of a trend that was already established with the boot's mechanisation of the foot, the proliferation of the chair and the advent of destination-oriented travel. I have but one further observation to make in this regard, which brings me back to the subject of paving. It is simply that boots impress no tracks on a paved surface. People, as they walk the streets, leave no trace of their movements, no record of their having passed by. It is as if they had never been. There is, here, the same detachment of persons from the ground that runs, as I have shown, like a leitmotif through the recent history of western societies. It appears that people, in their daily lives, merely skim the surface of a world that has been previously mapped out and constructed for them to occupy, rather than contributing through their movements to its ongoing formation. To inhabit the modern city is to dwell in an environment that is already built. But whereas the builder is a manual labourer, the dweller is a footslogger. And the environment, built by human hands, should ideally remain unscathed by the footwork of dwelling. To the extent that the feet *do* leave a mark – as when pedestrians take short cuts across the grass verges of roads, in cities designed for motorists – they are said to deface the environment, not to enhance it, much as a modern topographic map is said to be defaced by the itineraries of travel drawn upon it (Ingold 2007a: 85).[10] This kind of thing is typically regarded by urban planners and municipal authorities as a threat to established order and a subversion of authority. Green spaces are for looking at, not for walking on; reserved for visual contemplation rather than for exploration on foot. The surfaces you can walk on are those that remain untouched and unmarked by your presence.

Environment, technology, landscape

The groundlessness of modern society, characterised by the reduction of pedestrian experience to the operation of a stepping machine, and by the corresponding elevation of head over heels as the locus of creative intelligence, is not only deeply embedded in the structures of public life in western societies. It has also spilled over into mainstream thinking in the disciplines of anthropology, psychology and biology. I now turn to a brief review of three thematic areas in which this overspill has manifestly occurred. The first concerns the perception of the environment, the second the history of technology, and the third the formation of the landscape. For each of these areas I ask what the effect would be of overturning prevailing assumptions and of adopting, with the Japanese as described by Kawada, a fundamental orientation towards the ground. What new terrains would be opened up? Here I have more questions than answers, and my purpose in this section is less to state my conclusions than to set an agenda for future research. I shall return in the final section to the theme with which I began, of the evolution of human anatomy.

The perception of the environment

It is almost a truism to say that we perceive not with the eyes, the ears or the surface of the skin, but with the whole body. Nevertheless, ever since Plato and Aristotle, the western tradition has consistently ranked the senses of vision and hearing over the contact sense of touch. I shall not go into the relative standing of vision and hearing, since this is a lengthy and complex story in itself (Ingold 2000a: 243–287). But my first and most obvious point is that a more literally *grounded* approach to perception should help to restore touch to its proper place in the balance of the senses. For it is surely through our feet, in contact with the ground (albeit mediated by footwear), that we are most fundamentally and continually 'in touch' with our surroundings.[11] Of course matters are not quite that simple, for we touch with our hands as well as with our feet. By and large, however, studies of haptic perception have focused almost exclusively on manual touch. The challenge is to discover special properties of pedestrian touch that might distinguish it from the manual modality. Is it really the case for example, as intuition suggests, that what we feel with our hands, and through the soles of our feet, are necessarily related as figure and ground? In other words, is the ground we walk on also, and inevitably, a ground against which things 'stand out' as foci of attention, or can it be a focus in itself?[12] What difference does it make that pedestrian touch carries the weight of the body rather than the weight of the object? And how does the feel of a surface differ, depending on whether the organ of touch is brought down at successive spots, as in plantigrade walking, or allowed to wrap around or slide over it, as can be done with the fingers and palm of the hand? Further questions arise when we consider the involvement of the other senses in pedestrian experience. From Goffman's studies, we can recognise the importance of vision to the walker. But let us not forget the experience of the blind. I wonder whether manual and pedestrian touch are differentiated by blind persons to the same extent or along the same lines as they are by the sighted. Finally, apropos hearing, we should recall the involvement of the ear in maintaining balance, essential for standing and walking, and that persons who are deaf report being able to hear through the feet, provided that they are standing on surfaces, such as floorboards, that conduct vibration.

The bias of head over heels influences the psychology of environmental perception in one other way. We have already seen how the practices of destination-oriented travel encouraged the belief that knowledge is integrated not along paths of pedestrian movement but through the accumulation of observations taken from successive points of rest.[13] Thus we tend to imagine that things are perceived from a stationary platform, as if we were sitting on a chair with our legs and feet out of action. To perceive a thing from different angles, it is supposed that we might turn it around in our hands, or perform an equivalent computational operation in our minds. But in real life, for the most part, we do not perceive things from a single vantage point, but rather by walking around them. As the founder of ecological psychology, James Gibson, argued in his classic work on visual perception, the forms of the objects we see are specified by transformations in the pattern of reflected light reaching our eyes as we move about in their vicinity. We perceive, in short, not from a fixed point but along what Gibson calls a 'path of observation', a continuous itinerary of movement (Gibson 1979: 195–197). But if perception is thus a function of movement, then what we perceive must, at least in part, depend on how we move. Locomotion, not cognition, must be the starting point for the study of perceptual activity (Ingold 2000a: 166). Or more strictly, cognition should not be *set off* from locomotion, along the lines of a division between head and heels, since walking is itself a form of circumambulatory knowing. Once this is recognised, a whole new field of inquiry is opened up, concerning the ways in which our knowledge of the environment is altered by techniques of footwork and by the many and varied devices that we attach to the feet in order to enhance their effectiveness in specific tasks and conditions. Examples are almost too numerous to mention: think of skis, skates and snowshoes; running shoes and football boots;[14] stirrups and pedals; and of course the flippers of the underwater diver. Nor should we ignore hand-held or underarm devices that aid locomotion such as walking sticks, crutches and the oars of the rowing boat.

The history of technology

This brings me to my second theme. Nothing better exemplifies the assumed superiority of head and hands over feet, in human endeavour, than this wonderfully pithy statement from the *Grundrisse* of Karl Marx. Tools, he says, are 'organs of the human brain, created by the human hand; the power of knowledge, objectified' (Marx 1973: 706). For Marx, history is the process in which human beings, through their labour, have progressively transformed the world of nature and, in so far as they also partake of this world, have also transformed themselves. Recall that in the classic, dualistic view to which Marx fully subscribed, humans are in nature from the waist down, while the hands and arms impress the mind's intelligent designs upon the surface of nature from above. The foot, from this point of view, is not so much empowered by human agency as a force of nature in itself, which – as in numerous treadle-operated machines – may be harnessed to power the apparatus of manufacture. The hand makes the tool; the foot drives the machine. Men have made history with their hands; they have mastered nature and brought it under control. And the nature thus controlled includes the foot, increasingly regulated and disciplined in the course of history by the hand-made technology of boots and shoes.

To overturn the bias of head over heels is also to dispense with the dualism that underpins this argument. Rather than supposing that the hand operates *on* nature while the feet move *in* it, I would prefer to say that both hands and feet, augmented by tools, gloves and footwear, mediate a historical engagement of the human organism, in its entirety, with the world around it. For surely we walk, just as we talk, write and use tools, with the whole body. Moreover in walking, the foot – even the boot-clad foot of western civilisation – does not really describe a mechanical oscillation like the tip of a pendulum. Thus its movements, continually and fluently responsive to an ongoing perceptual monitoring of the ground ahead, are never quite the same from one step to the next. Rhythmic rather than metronomic, what they beat out is not a metric of constant intervals but a pattern of lived time and space. As I shall show in the next chapter, it is in the very 'tuning' of movement in response to the ever-changing conditions of an unfolding task that the skill of any bodily technique ultimately resides (see also Ingold 2000a: 353). I refer there to the example of sawing through a plank of wood, but the point applies just as well to walking through the terrain. Indeed it could be said that walking is a highly intelligent activity. This intelligence, however, is not located exclusively in the head but is distributed throughout the entire field of relations comprised by the presence of the human being in the inhabited world.

The formation of the landscape

What I have to say regarding my third theme follows from this. In conventional accounts of the historical transformation of nature, the landscape tends to be regarded as a material surface that has been sequentially shaped and reshaped, over time, through the imprint of one scheme of mental representations after another, each reshaping covering over or obliterating the one before. The landscape surface is thus supposed to present itself as a palimpsest for the inscription of cultural form. My argument suggests, to the contrary, that the forms of the landscape – like the identities and capacities of its human inhabitants – are not imposed upon a material substrate but rather emerge as condensations or crystallisations of activity within a relational field. As people, in the course of their everyday lives, make their way by foot around a familiar terrain, so its paths, textures and contours, variable through the seasons, are incorporated into their own embodied capacities of movement, awareness and response – or into what Gaston Bachelard (1964: 11) calls their 'muscular consciousness'. But conversely, these pedestrian movements thread a tangled mesh of personalised trails through the landscape itself. Through walking, in short, landscapes are woven into life, and lives are woven into the landscape, in a process that is continuous and never-ending (Tilley 1994: 29–30).

This idea may sound rather abstract, but can be readily grasped by reflecting on the phenomenon of footprints. 'You know my methods, Watson', says Sherlock Holmes in the case of *The Crooked Man*. 'There had been a man in the room, and he had crossed the lawn coming from the road. I was able to obtain five very clear impressions of his footmarks ... He had apparently rushed across the lawn, for his toe marks were much deeper than his heels.'[15] But if Holmes could recognise the man's gait from the patterns of his footprints, and even read off from them something of his intentions, this was not because the gait served to translate from a conception in his mind to an impression on the ground, but because both the gait and the prints arose within the intentional movement of the man's running. He was evidently in a hurry. Of course, as this example shows, pedestrian activities can mark the landscape. When the same paths are repeatedly trodden, especially by heavy boots, the consequences may be dramatic, amounting in places to severe erosion. Surfaces are indeed transformed. But these are surfaces *in* the world, not the surface *of* the world. Human beings live in, not on, the world, and the historical transformations they bring about are – as we saw in Chapter 1 (p. 6) – part and parcel of the world's transformation of itself.

On the evolution of human anatomy

To conclude, let me return to the observations of Darwin, Huxley and Tylor with which I began. Recall that Darwin regarded the relatively prehensile foot of the unshod savage as intermediate between that of the ape on the one hand, and the civilised man on the other. This view is no longer admissible today. We know that the boot-clad European is, genealogically speaking, no further removed from the ape than the barefoot Aborigine. Yet human feet do indeed vary a great deal, not just morphologically but in the operations they can perform. Describing a group of elderly Marquesan Islanders in his semi-fictional narrative of travel in the South Seas, *Typee* (1846), Herman Melville observed that

> ... the most remarkable peculiarity about them was the appearance of their feet; the toes, like the radiating lines of the mariner's compass, pointing to every quarter of the horizon. This was doubtless attributable to the fact, that during nearly a hundred years of existence the said toes had never been subjected to any artificial confinement, and in their old age, being averse to close neighbourhood, bid one another keep open order.
>
> (Melville 1972: 142)

Melville surely allowed himself some licence to exaggerate. Nevertheless there is ample corroborating evidence of a more scientific nature to suggest that the feet of unshod peoples are very differently formed from those of people who are accustomed to wearing shoes of various kinds. Research has shown that 'even the simplest footwear starts to rearrange the bones of those who habitually use it' (Tenner 2003: 58). The fourth and fifth toes of the normally bare foot, according to orthopaedist Steele Stewart (1972), have an unmistakable prehensile curl, and in walking they pick over the ground with almost manipulative precision (Carlsöö 1972: 12). In regular users of footwear – even rudimentary sandals – this trait is less developed. Wearing sandals tends to enlarge the gap between the big and second toe, but in other ways the form of the sandaled foot is closer to that of people who wear shoes, since both sandal and shoe wearers lose the characteristic rolling motion of the bare foot that starts from the heel and runs along its outer edge, ending with the ball of the foot and the toes (Ashizawa et al. 1997).

It is not only the morphology of the booted European foot that is peculiar – in the straightness and parallelism and of the toes, and the lack of space between them. Equally peculiar is the so-called 'striding gait' with which the walkers of western civilisation (especially men) have been enjoined since Antiquity to sally forth into the world, asserting as they go their superiority over subject peoples and animals. In a now classic study, palaeoanthropologist John Napier asserted that the stride 'is the essence of human bipedalism and the criterion by which the evolutionary status of a hominid walker must be judged' (Napier 1967: 117). This reification and universalisation of the striding gait as the quintessential human locomotor achievement betrays an ethnocentrism that, as John Devine shows, has long plagued the literature of human evolutionary biology. In fact, with their oddly formed feet and eccentric gait, 'Westernised men and women ... may present us with the exception rather than the rule in the area of locomotor skills' (Devine 1985: 554). It is not just that people around the world walk in all sorts of ways, depending on the surface and contours of the ground, the shoes they are wearing (if any), the weather, and a host of other factors including culturally specific expectations concerning the postures considered proper for people of different age, gender and rank. They also use their feet for sundry other purposes such as climbing, running, leaping, holding things down, picking them up, and even going on all fours. In emphasising these variations, my purpose is not to claim that the feet and gait of the barefoot hunter–gatherer who 'runs, creeps and climbs' (Watanabe 1971) are somehow more 'natural' than those of the striding, boot-wearing European. As Mauss recognised in his essay on body techniques, there is simply no such thing as a 'natural' way of walking, which may be prescribed independently of the diverse circumstances in which human beings grow up and live their lives (Mauss 1979: 102). But he could just as well have said that every existing technique is as natural as every other, in that it falls within the range of possibility and comes as second nature to its practitioners.

What would certainly be unnatural, however, and beyond the realm of possibility, would be for any human being to spend his or her life, when not sitting or lying down, either standing bolt upright on one spot, like a statue, or striding about without carrying any significant load on a hard level surface. The western body image, which underwrites so much of the discourse on human anatomical evolution, rests on an ideal that is practically unattainable outside the highly artificial setting of the laboratory. Yet it is in such laboratory settings that most systematic studies of bipedal locomotion have been carried out (Johanson 1994). These studies are often illustrated with pictures of more or less naked figures pacing a bare floor.[16] It is as though, by stripping the body of all appurtenances and the ground of all features, the universal essence of human walking will be revealed in a form untrammelled by the particularities of environment and culture. In truth, however, there is no such essence. For the experimental subjects of gait analysis already bring with them, incorporated into their very bodies, the experience of architecture, dress, footwear and baggage drawn from life outside the laboratory. Many of the earliest subjects to be roped into locomotion research were in fact soldiers, already trained in the routines of the drill. It is hardly surprising that when commanded to walk they stepped out as if on parade! As Mary Flesher (1997) has shown, the scientific study of human locomotion has its roots in military discipline.

We cannot, then, attribute bipedality to human nature, or to culture, or to some combination of the two. Rather, human capacities to walk, and to use their feet in countless other ways, emerge through processes of development, as properties of the systems of relations set up through the placement of the growing human organism within a richly textured environmental context. As psychologist Esther Thelen and her colleagues have shown in their studies of infant motor development, it is not possible to characterise 'bipedal locomotion' in isolation from the real-time performance of the manifold pedestrian tasks with which we have grown up (Thelen 1995: 83). In what sense, then, can we speak of the evolution of the human foot, or of bipedalism as a distinctively human achievement? If by evolution we mean differentiation and change over time in the forms and capacities of organisms, then we must surely admit that as fully embodied properties of the human organism, these traits have indeed evolved. We cannot, however, understand this evolution in terms of the genesis of some essential body plan, given for all humans in advance of the conditions of their life in the world, to which particular inflections are added by dint of environmental and cultural experience. For no such plan exists. There is no standard form of the human foot, or of bipedal locomotion, apart from the forms that actually take shape in the course of routine pedestrian operations. Two points of capital importance follow. First, an explanation of the evolution of bipedality has to be an account of the ways in which the developmental systems through which it emerges are reproduced and transformed over time. And secondly, by way of their activities, their disciplines and their histories, people throughout history have played – and continue to play – an active role in this evolutionary process, by shaping the conditions under which their successors learn the arts of footwork. Thus the evolution of bipedality continues, even as we go about our business on two feet. We have been drawn, in sum, to an entirely new view of evolution, a view that *grounds* human beings within the continuum of life, and that situates the history of their embodied skills within the unfolding of that continuum.

… and finally

The philosopher Jacques Derrida wondered how there could be a history or a science of writing, when the practice of writing is already implicated in the ideas of history, and of science (Derrida 1974: 27). For my part I wonder how there could be a cultural history of bodily techniques when the technology of footwear is already implicated in our very ideas of the body, its evolution and its development. Boots and shoes support our established notions of the body and of evolution, just as writing supports our notions of science and of history. To extricate ourselves from these circularities, we should perhaps take the advice of Giambattista Vico, offered in his *New Science* of 1725. To understand the origins of writing, Vico wrote, 'we must reckon as if there were no books in the world' (1948 §330). To understand the evolution of walking, likewise, we must imagine a world without footwear. For our earliest ancestors did not stride out upon the land with heavy boots, but made their way within it lightly, dextrously, and mostly barefoot.

4

WALKING THE PLANK

MEDITATIONS ON A PROCESS OF SKILL

> Was there ever a bookcase that gave a fraction of the satisfaction as the one fashioned by your own hands?
>
> The Editor, *The Handyman and Home Mechanic*

On sawing a plank

I am making a bookcase from wooden planks. Each shelf has to be cut to the right length. Marking the distance along the plank with a tape measure, I use a pencil and set square to draw a straight line across it. After these preliminaries I set the plank on a trestle, lift my left leg and kneel with as much of my weight as I can upon it, while keeping my balance on the ground with my right foot. The line to be cut slightly overhangs the right end of the trestle. Then, stooping, I place the palm of my left hand on the plank just to the left of the line, grasping it around the edge by the fingers. Taking up a saw with my right hand, I wrap my fingers around the handle – all, that is, except the index finger, which is extended along the flat of the handle, enabling me to fine-tune the direction of the blade (Figure 4.1, top).

Now, as I press down with a rigid arm on the left hand, I engage the teeth of the saw with the edge, at the point where it meets my drawn line, and gently nick the edge with two or three short upstrokes. To guide the saw at this critical juncture, I bend the thumb of my left hand, so that the hard surface of the joint juts out to touch the blade of the saw just above the teeth (Figure 4.1, bottom). Once the slot in the edge is long enough that there is no further risk of the saw jumping out and lacerating my thumb, I can begin to work it with downward strokes. At this point I have to attend more to the alignment of the blade than to the precise positioning of the teeth, in order to ensure that the evolving cut proceeds in exactly the right direction. To do this, I have to position my head so that it is directly above the tool, looking down. From this angle the blade appears as a straight line and I can see the wood on either side of the cut.

The first strokes are crucial, since the further the cut goes, the less room there is for manoeuvre. After a while, however, I can relax my gaze and settle down to a rhythmic up-and-down movement with long, smooth and even strokes. Though delivered to the saw

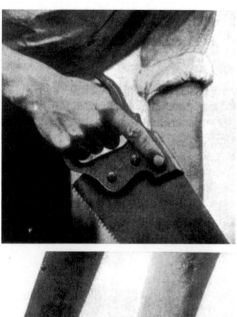
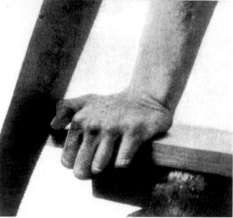

FIGURE 4.1 The correct way to hold a saw (top) and how to use the thumb and left hand as a guide when beginning the cut (bottom). Reproduced from *The Handyman and Home Mechanic* (London: Odhams Press).

through the right hand and forearm, the movement is actually felt throughout my entire body in the oscillating balance of forces in my knees, legs, hands, arms and back. The groove I have already cut now serves as a jig that prevents the saw from veering off the straight line. Because of the way the saw's teeth are cut, they slice the wood on the downward stroke, whereas the upward stroke is restorative, returning the body-saw-plank system to a position from which the next cycle can be launched. However, a good saw requires little or no pressure on the downstroke, and works under its own weight.

Although a confident, regular movement ensures an even cut, no two strokes are ever precisely the same. With each stroke I have to adjust my posture ever so slightly to allow for the advancing groove, and for possible irregularities in the grain of the wood. Moreover I still have to watch to make sure I keep to the line, since even though the saw is constrained to slide within the existing groove, the groove itself is slightly wider than the blade, allowing for some slight axial torque. This is where the index finger of my right hand, stretched along the handle of the saw, comes into play (Figure 4.1, top). In effect I use it to steer within the tight margins afforded by the groove. The actual width of the groove is determined by the setting of the saw's teeth, which are bent outwards, alternately to one side and the other of the blade. The point of this is that it allows clearance for the blade to slide within the groove. It would otherwise become jammed.

As I approach the end of the line, a marked drop in the pitch of the sound created by my sawing, caused by a loss of tensile strength in the plank, serves as an audible warning to slow down. Once again I have to concentrate on the cutting edge. For a clean finish, the last few strokes are as critical as the first. To prevent the free end from breaking off under its own weight, leaving a cracked or splintered edge, I must shift my left hand to the right of the groove, no longer pressing down on the plank but supporting it. At the same time I saw ever more slowly and lightly until, eventually, the cut end comes free in my left hand and I allow it to drop to the ground.

This description of a quite elementary episode of tool use might seem unnecessarily elaborate. It serves, however, to illustrate three themes of fundamental significance for the proper understanding of technical skill. These themes concern: (i) the processional quality of tool use, (ii) the synergy of practitioner, tool and material, and (iii) the coupling of perception and action. In the following sections I elaborate on each theme in turn, using the example of sawing a plank for purposes of illustration. I conclude with some remarks on the fate of skill in a world increasingly engineered to the specifications of technology.

The processional quality of tool use

The use of a tool is commonly understood as a discrete step in an operational sequence, a *chaîne opératoire*, one of a number of such steps that together comprise a schedule for the assembly of a complete object like a bookcase. It does not take just one step, however, to saw a plank. It takes many steps; moreover these steps are no more discrete or discontinuous than those of the walker. That is to say, they do not follow one another in succession, like beads on a string. Their order is processional, rather than successional. In walking, every step is a development of the one before and a preparation for the one following. The same is true of every stroke of the saw. Like going for a walk, sawing a plank has the character of a journey that proceeds from place to place, through a movement that – though rhythmic and repetitive – is never strictly monotonous.

The journey does have recognisable phases – of getting ready, setting out, carrying on and finishing off – and these lend a certain temporal shape to the overall movement. These phases are not, however, sharply demarcated. When, leaving the front door of my house, I turn the corner into the street, I alter my pace and gait, and lift my sights from the immediate vicinity of the doorstep to the longer vista of the pavement. The movement, nevertheless, is continuous. It is the same with sawing. Like turning a corner, the initial nicking of the edge of the plank leads into the smooth downward strokes of the cut through an unbroken transition. Only when I look back on the ground covered can I say that one phase of the process is finished, and another has begun. The same is true of the process as a whole. When do I begin to saw? Is it when I mark the line, when I rest my knee and hand on the plank, when I nick the edge, or when I commence the downward strokes? And when do I cease? Perhaps, having cut through the plank, I lay down the saw, but this may only be to pick up the next piece to be cut. In sawing as in walking, movement always overshoots its destinations.

Let us take a closer look at the four phases of the process, beginning with 'getting ready'. Even before setting out I need to have arrived at some overall conception of the task to be performed – of what is to be done, how to do it, and the tools and materials required. This conception covers an assortment of factors that are only loosely connected, and serves to guide the work rather than strictly to determine its course. Charles Keller, a pioneer in the anthropological study of cognition in practice, aptly calls it an 'umbrella plan', an idiosyncratic constellation – peculiar to each practitioner – of stylistic, functional, procedural and economic considerations assembled specifically for the task at hand (Keller 2001: 35). Though the composition of the umbrella plan calls for forethought, such thinking is itself a mundane practical activity, set in the context of the workplace, rather than a purely intellectual, 'inside-the-head' exercise (Leudar and Costall 1996: 164). It includes, for example, 'sizing up' the planks, deciding which to select for the shelf I want to cut and which to reserve for other purposes, so as to minimise the waste from offcuts. It also includes the retrieval of the saw and trestle from where I last put them, so that I have them to hand for when the cutting is to begin. Even drawing the line across the plank, with pencil and set square, can be understood as part of the planning process, a 'measuring out' that is done not in advance of engagement with the material but directly, at full scale, on the material itself. Crucially, the pencil line can be erased. While inscribed *on* the material, it is not, like the subsequent cut, indelibly incised *into* it. Evidently, then, the umbrella plan is in no sense confined within the mind of the practitioner. On the contrary, it is laid out over the workplace itself: in the marking up of the materials and in their disposition in relation to the body of the practitioner and the tools that he will bring to bear on them.

There is a critical moment, in implementing any task, when getting ready gives way to setting out. This is the moment at which rehearsal ends and performance begins. From that point on there is no turning back. Pencil marks can be rubbed out, but an incision made with the blade of a saw cannot be contrived to disappear. The skilled practitioner chooses his moment with care, knowing that to set out before one is ready, or alternately to allow it to pass unnoticed, could jeopardise the entire project. The Ancient Greeks had a word for this moment, namely *kairos*. As the classical scholar Jean-Pierre Vernant explains:

> In intervening with his tools, the artisan must recognise and wait for the moment when the time is ripe and be able to adapt himself entirely to the circumstances. He must never desert his post … for if he does the *kairos* might pass and the work be spoiled.
>
> (1983: 291–292)

This moment of setting out, however, is also marked by a switch of perspective, from the encompassing view of the umbrella plan to a narrow focus on the initial point of contact between tool and material. Thus my attention, in setting out to saw a plank, is fixed on that constricted space between where the teeth of the saw meet the edge of the plank, where the edge of the plank is gripped by the fingers of my left hand, and where the joint of my left thumb guides the blade of the saw (Figure 4.1, bottom). For that brief interval while I nick the edge with a series of short, upward strokes, my overall conception of the work fades into the background as I concentrate on the precise details of the emergent cut. There is a certain tension in these initial movements – each is like a gasp, a sudden intake of breath, that runs counter to the direction in which the saw is disposed to run, and in which the wood is disposed to receive it. The wood resists, and seems to want to expel the saw by causing it to jump out.

It is when I reverse the rhythm, cutting with downstrokes rather than upstrokes, that setting out gives way to carrying on. The reversal is somewhat analogous to what happens when I set out with a rowing boat from the shore, turning from the initial and rather awkward pushing of the oars in back stroke to the more comfortable and efficient movement of pulling once a sufficient depth of water has been reached. In sawing, as in rowing, from that moment on it seems that I am working *with* the instruments and materials at my disposal rather than *against* them. Although I am of course cutting the plank against the grain, the wood nevertheless 'takes in' or accommodates the saw along the line that I have already cut, and yields to its movement rather than repelling it. In duration the phase of carrying on is generally the longest, and it can call for considerable strength and endurance. But it is also the most relaxed, flowing in a smooth legato rhythm that contrasts markedly with the abrupt staccato passage of setting out. At the same time my focus also shifts, from the point where the drawn line meets the edge to its entire length, and from the detail of the saw's teeth to the alignment of the blade as a whole. So it continues, until I reach the phase of finishing off. There is no precise moment when carrying on ends and finishing off begins, but rather a point of inflection from which the movement is gradually retarded and its amplitude diminished. Simultaneously, my attention begins to shift from the line of the cut to its destination, where it intersects the trailing edge of the plank.

It is commonly supposed that each stage in the process of making an artefact is completed at the point when the material outcome precisely matches the maker's initial intention. Holding an image of the intended outcome at the forefront of his mind, the maker is said to measure his progress against the extent to which it has been realised and to cease once he has achieved a result congruent with the image. In practice, however, it is not the image of the end product that governs the phase of finishing off. By the time this phase is reached, any deviations from the initial plan will have been either accepted or corrected (Keller 2001: 40). If I have kept my saw to the drawn line, then I need have no further concern that it might deviate from it; if I have not, then it is far too late for remedial action. Yet the judgement of when and how to finish can be just as crucial as choosing the moment to set out. To reach this judgement the practitioner must once again focus down on the finer details of the work. Keller's examples are drawn from the crafts of the weaver and the silversmith. The weaver has to decide at what point no more weft strands can be added; the silversmith how many more hammer blows the metal will take without cracking. Likewise in sawing a plank, to obtain a clean cut the final strokes must be finely judged such that one reaches the edge without actually sawing through it. Thus the end of the line is approached as an asymptote: the closer I come to it, the gentler and more delicate my strokes, and the more my attention is focused on the finishing point, until eventually the free end comes loose in my hand.

Finally, journey completed, I put away my saw and place the plank, now cut to the right length, where it will next be needed. Yet this placement of tools and materials is already part of the formation of the umbrella plan for the next operation. Putting things away in the right places is a way of getting ready. Thus in the use of tools, every ending is a new beginning.

The synergy of practitioner, tool and material

What does it mean to say that in carrying out some task, a tool is used? We might suppose that use is what happens when an object, endowed with a certain function, is placed at the disposal of an agent, intent on a certain purpose. I want to cut a plank, and I have a saw. So I use the saw to cut the plank. However, from the account I have already presented it is clear that I need more than the saw to cut wood. I need the trestle to provide support, I need my hands and knees respectively to grip the saw and to hold the plank in place, I need every muscle of my body to deliver the force that drives the saw and to maintain my balance as I work, I need my eyes and ears to monitor progress. Even the plank itself becomes part of the equipment for cutting, in that the evolving groove helps to guide the work. Cutting wood, then, is an effect not of the saw alone but of the entire system of forces and relations set up by the intimate engagement of the saw, the trestle, the workpiece and my own body. What then becomes of our concept of use? To answer this question we need to consider three things. First, what does it take for an object of some kind, such as the saw or trestle, to count as a tool? Secondly, how does the instrumentality of the tool compare with that of the human body with which it is conjoined? And thirdly, can this conjunction be considered apart from the gestural movements in which it is set to work?

No object considered purely in and for itself, in terms of its intrinsic attributes alone, can be a tool. To describe a thing as a tool is to place it in *relation* to other things within a field of activity in which it can exert a certain effect. Indeed we tend to name our tools by the activities in which they are characteristically or normatively engaged, or by the effects they have in them. Thus to call an object a saw is to position it within the context of a story such as the one I have just told, of cutting a plank. To name the tool is to invoke the story. It follows that for an object to count as a tool it must be endowed with a story, which the practitioner should know and understand in order to recognise it as such and use it appropriately. Considered as tools, things *are* their stories. We are of course more accustomed to think of tools as having certain functions. My point, however, is that the functions of things are not attributes but narratives. They are the stories we tell about them. This point, I believe, resolves a paradox that has long bedevilled discussions of the concept of function. The dictionary defines function as 'the special kind of activity proper to anything; the mode of action by which it fulfils its purpose'. Thus the function of the saw is to cut wood: this is the activity traditionally deemed 'proper' to it, and for which it has been expressly designed. Yet as David Pye has observed, nothing we design is ever truly fit for purpose. A saw that really worked would not produce quantities of sawdust. The best we can say of its function is that it is 'what someone has provisionally decided that [it] may reasonably be expected to do at present' (Pye 1978: 11–14). So if we were to decide that the saw should be used, in a quite different context, as a musical instrument, that should count just as well. How can the idea that every tool has a proper function be reconciled with the fact that in practice, nothing ever works except as a component of a system constituted in the present moment (Preston 2000)?

The parallel between tool use and storytelling suggests an answer. As I shall show in Chapter 13 (p. 162), the meanings of stories do not come ready-made from the past, embedded in a static, closed tradition. Nor, however, are they constructed *de novo*, moment by moment, to accord with the ever-changing conditions of the present. They are rather discovered retrospectively, often long after the telling, when listeners – faced with circumstances similar to those recounted in a particular story – find in its unfolding guidance on how to proceed.

Now just as stories do not carry their meanings ready-made into the world so, likewise, the ways in which tools are to be used do not come pre-packaged with the tools themselves. But neither are the uses of tools simply invented on the spot, without regard to any history of past practice. Rather, they are revealed to practitioners when, faced with a recurrent task in which the same devices were known previously to have been employed, they are perceived to afford the wherewithal for its accomplishment. Thus the functions of tools, like the meanings of stories, are recognised through the alignment of present circumstances with the conjunctions of the past. Once recognised, these functions provide the practitioner with the means to keep on going. Every use of a tool, in short, is a remembering of how to use it, which at once picks up the strands of past practice and carries them forward in current contexts. The skilled practitioner is like an accomplished storyteller whose tales are told in the practice of his craft rather than in words. Thus considered as tools, things have the same processional character as the activities they make possible. As we have seen, the activity of cutting a plank is more a walk than a step. Similarly the function of the saw lies more in a story, or perhaps a series of stories, than in a set of attributes. Functionality and narrativity are two sides of the same coin.

Yet although the saw, both in its construction and in its patterns of wear and tear, embodies a history of past use, it remembers nothing of this history. Indeed it remembers nothing at all. And this suggests an answer to our second question. We have already seen that to cut wood, a saw is not enough. At the very least, the saw is gripped by hand and watched by eye. How, then, does the use of these bodily organs compare with the use of extra-somatic equipment such as the saw? In his essay on body techniques, ethnologist Marcel Mauss declared that the body is 'man's first and most natural technical object, and at the same time technical means' (Mauss 1979: 104). But if using the hands to grip and the eyes to watch, and even the brain to think, is tantamount to converting them into objects of my will, then where am *I* the subject, the user of these bodily means? Should we, like Mauss, follow Plato in supposing that the entire body, and not just the tools that serve to extend the range and effectivity of its actions, is the instrument of an intelligence that is necessarily disembodied, and that stands aloof from the world in which it intervenes? Or should we rather find an alternative way of thinking about use that does not presuppose an initial separation between the user and the used, between subject and object? Perhaps it would be better to say that in an activity like cutting wood, my hand is not so much used as brought into use, in the sense that it is guided in its movements by the remembered traces of past performance, already inscribed in an accustomed – that is *usual* – pattern of dextrous activity (Ingold 2000a: 352). But if the hand, as it drives the saw, remembers how to move, the saw it grips does not. For *only the body remembers*. Thus in the relation between hand and saw there lies a fundamental asymmetry. The hand can bring itself into use, and in its practised movements can tell the story of its own life. But the saw relies on the hand for its story to be told. Or more generally, while extra-somatic tools have biographies, the body is both biographer and autobiographer.

If an object such as a saw, however, becomes a tool only through being placed within a field of effective action, then the same goes for the organs of the body. In his massive work, *Gesture and Speech* (*Le Geste et la parole*), André Leroi-Gourhan – himself a student of Mauss – observed that it is in what it makes or does, not in what it is, that the human hand comes into its own (Leroi-Gourhan 1993: 240). Where the tool has its stories, the hand has its gestures. Considered in purely anatomical terms, of course, the hand is merely a complex arrangement of bone and muscle tissue. But the hands I use in sawing are more than that. They are skilled. Concentrated in them are capacities of movement and feeling that have been developed through a life history of past practice. What is a hand if not a compendium of such capacities, particular to the manifold tasks in which it is brought into use, and the gestures they entail? Thus while hands make gestures, gestures also make hands. And of course they make tools too. It follows that gesture is foundational to both toolmaking and tool use. The point would be obvious were it not for a certain conceptual blindness, which causes us to see both bodies and tools out of context, as things-in-themselves (Sigaut 1993: 387). We have therefore to be reminded that 'bringing into use' is a matter not of attaching an object with certain attributes to a body with certain anatomical features, but of joining a story to the appropriate gestures. *The tool, as the epitome of the story, selects from the compendium of the hand the gestures proper to its re-enactment.* Yet the tool has its story only because it is set in a context that includes the trestle, the wood, and all the other paraphernalia of the workshop. And the hand has its gestures only because it has grown and developed within the organic synergy of practitioner, tool and material. The practice of sawing issues as much from the trestle and plank as from the saw, as much from the saw as from the carpenter, as much from the carpenter's eyes and ears as from his hands, as much from his ears and hands as from his mind. You only get sawing when all these things, and more, are bound together and work in unison.

The coupling of perception and action

Close examination of a carpenter at work reveals an apparent paradox. In sawing, as I have already observed, no two strokes are precisely the same. In its oscillations the right hand – alternately driving the saw down and pulling it back up – never follows an identical trajectory. The force, amplitude, speed and torque of the manual gesture vary, albeit almost imperceptibly, from stroke to stroke. So also does the posture of the body, and the muscular–skeletal configurations of tension and compression that keep it in balance. Yet the outcome, in skilled hands, is a perfectly clean, straight cut. How can the regularity of the cut be reconciled with this variability of posture and gesture, given that the body alone imparts movement to the blade of the saw? In a now classic study, the Russian neuroscientist Nicholai Bernstein was confronted with an identical paradox. Bernstein observed the gestures of a skilled blacksmith, hitting the iron on the anvil over and over again with a hammer. He found that although the smith consistently brought the hammer down to the exact same spot on the anvil, the trajectories of individual arm joints varied from stroke to stroke. How, he wondered, can the motion of the hammer be so reliably reproduced, when it is only by way of the inconstant arm that the hammer is contrived to move (Latash 1996: 286)? His answer was that the essence of the smith's dexterity lay not in the constancy of his movements, but in the '*tuning of the movements to an emergent task*' (Bernstein 1996: 23, original emphasis). For the novice every stroke is the same, so that the slightest irregularity throws him irretrievably off course. For the accomplished blacksmith or carpenter, by contrast, every stroke is different. The fine-tuning or 'sensory correction' of the craftsman's movement depends, however, on an intimate coupling of perception and action. Thus in sawing, the visual monitoring of the evolving cut, through eyes positioned above to see the wood on either side, continually corrects the alignment of the blade through subtle adjustments of the index finger along the handle of the saw (Figure 4.1, top). Likewise the right hand responds in its oscillations to the sound and feel of the saw as it bites into the grain. This multisensory coupling establishes the dexterity and control that are the hallmarks of skilled practice.

Dexterity is a necessary accompaniment to what David Pye (1968: 4–5) has called the 'workmanship of risk'. In such workmanship the quality of the outcome depends at every moment on the care and judgement with which the task proceeds. Thus when working with a saw, as with any other hand-held tool, the result is never a foregone conclusion; rather there is an ever-present danger, throughout the work, that it may go awry. The greatest risk is undoubtedly in the phases of setting out, when the first indelible marks are cut in the edge of the plank, and in finishing off, where careless work could lead to splintering. Of course there are ways to reduce risk, as when the carpenter initially steadies the blade against the joint of the thumb. And the phase of carrying on, during which the groove is well advanced and helps to guide the saw, is much less risky than those of setting out and finishing off. As Pye notes, the workmanship of risk is hardly ever seen in a pure form, but is rather combined in various ways with what he calls the 'workmanship of certainty'. If, in the workmanship of risk, the result is always in doubt, in the workmanship of certainty it is already predetermined and unalterable from the outset. For example, in my use of the set square to draw a line across the plank, prior to cutting, the trajectory of the pencil point is pre-set by the straight edge of the square. All I have to do is run my pencil along it, which I can do at speed. But just as every craftsman engaged in the workmanship of risk will seek to reduce it through the use of jigs and templates, so conversely, a degree of risk invariably creeps into the most apparently predetermined of operations. Even when the saw is guided by its own groove, maintaining the uniformity of the line calls for continuous attention and correction.

Earlier I compared sawing a plank to going for a walk. As with the walk, the task has a beginning and an ending. Every ending, however, is potentially a new beginning, marking not a terminus but a pause for rest in an otherwise continuous journey. The carpenter, a workman of risk, is like the wayfarer who travels from place to place, sustaining himself both perceptually and materially through a continual engagement with the field of practice, or what I have elsewhere called the 'taskscape' (Ingold 2000a: 194–200), that opens up along his path. In this respect he is the complete opposite of the machine operative, a workman of certainty, whose activity is constrained by the parameters of a determining system. Here, 'the product is made by a planned series of operations, each of which has to be started and stopped by the operative, but with the result of each one predetermined and outside his control' (Pye 1968: 6). Starting and stopping, as this passage reveals, is not the same as beginning and ending. Between beginning and ending the practitioner's movements are continually and subtly responsive to the ever-changing conditions of the task as it proceeds. Between starting and stopping, by contrast, he has nothing to do but to leave the system to run its course, according to settings determined in advance. Thus whereas for the craftsman the intervals between ending and beginning again are pauses for rest, for the machine operative those between stopping and restarting are when all the significant action takes place: when plans are laid, instruments reset and materials assembled. Like a traveller who goes everywhere by transport rather than on foot, it is only when he reaches successive destinations that the operative gets down to business. His journey is more like a series of interconnected terminals than a walk. The intimate coupling between movement and perception that governs the work of the craftsman is broken.[1]

Now in any episode of tool use, some gestures are performed just once or a few times, others are repeated over and over again. The former typically occur while getting ready, setting out and finishing off; the latter during the intermediate phase of carrying on. In our case of sawing a plank, drawing the line, kneeling down, nicking the edge, and shifting the left hand to hold the cut end exemplify the first, while the regular strokes of the saw exemplify the second. When we speak of the activity of sawing, it is usually these *recurrent* movements that we have in mind, rather than the 'one-off' or *occurrent* movements with which they open and close. In this sense, sawing is one of a suite of commonplace tool-assisted activities, including also hammering, pounding and scraping, that all involve the repetition of manual gesture. Indeed this kind of back-and-forth or 'reciprocating' movement comes naturally to the living body. In a fluent performance, it has a rhythmic quality (Leroi-Gourhan 1993: 309–310). This quality does not, however, lie in the repetitiveness of the movement itself. For there to be rhythm, movement must be *felt*. And feeling lies in the coupling of movement and perception that, as we have seen, is the key to skilled practice. As Leroi-Gourhan clearly recognised, technical activity is conducted not against a static background but in a world whose manifold constituents undergo their own particular cycles. By way of perception, the practitioner's rhythmic gestures are attuned to the multiple rhythms of the environment. Thus any task, itself a movement, unfolds within the 'network of movements' in which the existence of every living being, animal or human, is suspended (ibid.: 282). An operation like sawing a plank, for example, comprises not one movement but an ensemble of concurrent movements, both within and without the body. The carpenter who has a feel for what he is doing is one who can bring these several movements more or less into phase with one another, so that they resonate or are 'in tune'.[2]

Rhythm, then, is not a movement but a dynamic coupling of movements. Every such coupling is a specific resonance, and the synergy of practitioner, tool and raw material establishes an entire field of such resonances. But this field is not monotonous. For every cycle is set not within fixed parameters but within a framework that is itself suspended in movement, in an environment where nothing is quite the same from moment to moment. As the philosopher Henri Lefebvre argued, in his incomplete and posthumously published *Rhythmanalysis* (2004), there is no rhythm in the mechanical oscillations of a determining system such as a pendulum, which periodically returns to its exact starting point. Likewise the mechanically operated, rotary saw feels nothing, and is wholly unresponsive to what is going on while it cuts. It is precisely because no two strokes are identical that the back-and-forth movement of the handsaw, unlike the spinning of the rotary cutter, is rhythmic rather than metronomic. Rhythmicity, Lefebvre maintained (ibid.: 90), implies not just repetition but *differences within repetition*. Or to put it another way, fluent performance is rhythmic only because imperfections in the system call for continual correction. This is why, as ethnoarchaeologist Willeke Wendrich observes in her study of Egyptian basket weaving, which involves techniques that have scarcely changed since pharaonic times, 'working rhythm goes hand in hand with concentration'. Among the contemporary practitioners whose movements she attempted to choreograph, the most skilled were distinguished by a steady working rhythm, intense concentration and a regular appearance of the product. Inexperienced practitioners, by contrast, could not maintain a rhythm; they were easily distracted and their work was irregular in appearance (Wendrich 1999: 390–391). The same, I am sure, applies in the field of carpentry. An arrhythmic and distracted performance with the saw is unlikely to lead to a regular line.

I emphasise this point in order to correct the widespread misapprehension that the training of the body through repetitive exercise – or what Lefebvre (2004: 38–45) calls *dressage* – leads to a progressive loss of conscious awareness or concentration in the task. The social historian Paul Connerton, for example, remarks that the repetition of certain operations leads to their bodily execution becoming increasingly automatic, to the point that 'awareness retreats [and] the movement flows involuntarily' (Connerton 1989: 94). In this view, awareness intervenes only to interrupt the otherwise automatic and involuntary flow of habitual action. I have shown, to the contrary, that the skilled handling of tools is anything but automatic, but is rather rhythmically responsive to ever-changing environmental conditions (see also Ingold 1999: 437). In this responsiveness there lies a form of awareness that does not so much retreat as grow in intensity with the fluency of action. This is not the awareness of a mind that holds itself aloof from the messy, hands-on business of work. It is rather immanent in practical, perceptual activity, reaching out into its surroundings along multiple pathways of sensory participation (Farnell 2000: 409). The retreat of awareness that Connerton takes to be an effect of enskilment in fact results from the very opposite process of deskilling – that is, from the *dissolution* of the link between perception and action that underwrites the skill of the practitioner. Only in a perfect, determining system can concentration be thus banished from practice, so as to intervene solely in the intervals between stopping and starting. The conjunction of rhythmicity and concentration is, as we have seen, characteristic of the workmanship of risk. It is in the workmanship of certainty – in the operation of a determining system – that concentration lapses, movement becomes automatic and rhythm gives way to mechanism.

Technology and the end of skill

Throughout history, at least in the western world, the project of technology has been to capture the skills of craftsmen or artisans, and to reconfigure their practice as the application of rational principles whose specification has no regard for human experience and sensibility. 'At the core of technology', as philosopher Carl Mitcham succinctly puts it, 'there seems to be a desire to transform the heuristics of technique into algorithms of practice' (1978: 252). It is a desire driven by an ideal of mechanical perfection epitomised in the definition of the machine proposed by the engineer–scholar Franz Reuleaux in his classic work of 1876, *The Kinematics of Machinery*: 'a combination of resistant bodies so arranged that by their means the mechanical forces of nature can be compelled to do work accompanied by certain determinate motions' (Reuleaux 1876: 35, 503). So far as Reuleaux was concerned, the body of the human operator, insofar as it delivers a purely physical effort, could be considered a 'force of nature' like any other, and thus an integral part of what he called the 'closed kinematic chain' comprising the machine as a whole (ibid.: 508). Where the artisans of yesteryear had been guided on their way through the taskscape by stories of past use, the operatives of the industrial age seemed – to an engineer like Reuleaux – to be bound to the execution of step-by-step sequences of determinate motions already built into the design and construction of their equipment. In any particular task, then, the flow of action would be broken up into discrete operational steps. Though each operation might differ from the one preceding and the one following, the operation itself would be perfectly monotonous and its repetitive motion – no longer reciprocating but rotary – would be underwritten by sameness rather than difference. Thus the rhythmic pulse of dextrous activity, governed by the coupling of perception and action, would have given way to the metronomic oscillations of mechanically determining systems.

As inhabitants of modern industrial societies, contemporary practitioners find themselves in an environment where the technological project appears to have triumphed, sweeping all else before it. Has this, then, spelled the end of skill? Was American socialist Harry Braverman right to forsee that the increasing mechanisation of industry, driven by the inexorable demands of monopoly capitalism, would inevitably lead to the deskilling of the workforce or – which amounts to the same thing – an impoverished conception of skill (Braverman 1974: 443–444)? I believe the prognosis to be premature, for two reasons. First, no machine can be perfect. Let me return for a moment to my earlier comparisons between the handsaw and the rotary cutter, and between the arm of the carpenter and the pendulum. In order to establish the distinction between rhythmic and metronomic oscillation, I overstated the contrast. In the real world, mechanical contrivances are sensitive to environmental perturbations, just as people are. Even the most finely tuned circular saw, for example, is susceptible to irregularities and imperfections in the wood, while a pendulum may respond in its swing to the contours of the surface on which it is mounted, as well as to air pressure, heat and humidity. Even the metronome may not be truly metronomic. Indeed the philosopher Gilbert Simondon has gone so far as to claim that the perfection of the machine lies in precisely this: that the apparent closure of the kinematic chain conceals a margin of indeterminacy. 'A purely automatic machine closed in on itself in a predetermined operation could only give summary results', says Simondon. 'The machine with superior technicality is an open machine …' (Simondon 1980: 4). And the human practitioner, surrounded by such machines, is *among* them, working with machines that work with him.

Not only, then, are machines open rather than closed, but also the project of technology chases a target that recedes as fast as it is approached. Here lies the second reason why technological advance does not inevitably augur the end of skill. 'The entire history of technics', argues historian François Sigaut, 'might be interpreted as a constantly renewed attempt to build skills into machines by means of algorithms, an attempt constantly foiled because other skills always tend to develop around the new machines' (Sigaut 1994: 446). So generally is this the case that Sigaut feels justified in referring to the 'law of the irreducibility of skills'. To rephrase the law in our terms: at the same time that narratives of use are converted by technology into algorithmic structures, these structures are themselves put to use within the ongoing activities of inhabitants, and through the stories of this use they are reincorporated into the field of effective action within which all life is lived. The essence of skill, then, comes to lie in the improvisational ability with which practitioners are able to disassemble the constructions of technology, and creatively to reincorporate the pieces into their own walks of life. In this ability lies life's power to resist the impositions of regimes of command and control that seek to reduce practitioners to what Karl Marx (1930: 451) once called the 'living appendages' of lifeless mechanism. Thus skill is destined to carry on for as long as life does, along a line of resistance, forever undoing the closures and finalities that mechanisation throws in its path.

PART II

The meshwork

Imagine two intersecting lines, A and B. Their intersection defines a point, P. What difference would it make if we depicted A and B as points, and P as the line of their connection? Mathematically, these alternatives might be regarded as simple transforms of one another. As such, they would be equivalent ways of positing a relation between A and B: either as intersection or as connection. But if we start not with abstract, geometrical lines but with real lines of life – of movement and growth – then the difference is profound. For the operation by which these lines are converted into points is one that puts life on the inside, and the world on the outside, of innumerable compartments or cells. And the places where life lines meet or bind with one another are, by the same token, re-imagined as sites of external contact or adjacency. The lines we might draw to represent this contact are not ones along which anything moves or grows. They are lines not of flight, but of interaction. I use the term *inversion* to refer to the operation that wraps lines of flight into bounded points. The chapters making up this part are dedicated to undoing this inversion, and thereby to revealing, behind the conventional image of a network of interacting entities, what I call the *meshwork* of entangled lines of life, growth and movement. This is the world we inhabit. My contention, throughout, is that what is commonly known as the 'web of life' is precisely that: not a network of connected points, but a meshwork of interwoven lines.

This contention is not far removed from understandings of the lifeworld professed by peoples commonly characterised in ethnographic literature as animists. It has been conventional to describe animism as a system of belief that imputes life to inert objects. But as I show in Chapter 5, such imputation is more typical of people in western societies who dream of finding life on other planets than of indigenous peoples to whom the label of animism has generally been applied. These peoples are united not in their belief but in a way of being that is alive and open to a world in continuous birth. In this animic ontology, beings do not propel themselves across a ready-made world but rather issue forth through a world-in-formation, along the lines of their relationships. To its inhabitants this world, embracing both sky and earth, is a source of astonishment but not surprise. There is a difference, here, between being surprised by things, and being astonished by them. Surprise is the currency of experts who trade in plans and predictions. We are surprised when things do not turn out as predicted, or when their values – as experts are inclined to say – depart from 'what was previously thought'. Only when a result is surprising, or perhaps counterintuitive, are we supposed to take note. What is not surprising is considered of no interest or historical significance. Thus history itself becomes a record of predictive failures. In a world of becoming, however, even the ordinary, the mundane or the intuitive gives cause for astonishment – the kind of astonishment that comes from treasuring every moment, as if, in that moment, we were encountering the world for the first time, sensing its pulse, marvelling at its beauty, and wondering how such a world is possible. Reanimating the western tradition of thought, I argue, means recovering the sense of astonishment banished from official science.

In Chapter 6, I return to the perennial problem of what it means to speak of the *environment* of an animal or, more particularly, of a human being. To avoid the contradictions entailed in assuming that human environmental relations are mediated by systems of symbolic meaning – with its absurd corollary that non-human animals inhabit meaningless worlds – I consider the sources of environmental meaning for non-humans and their possible availability to humans as well. In psychology, James Gibson's theory of affordances offers one possible approach, though it is ultimately found to privilege the environment as a site of meaning vis-à-vis its inhabitants, whether human or non-human. In ethology, Jakob von Uexküll's theory of the *Umwelt* suggests, quite to the contrary, that meaning is bestowed by the organism on its environment. In philosophy, and following von Uexküll's lead, Martin Heidegger drew a sharp distinction between the animal's 'captivation' in its *Umwelt* and the way the world is disclosed, or opened up, to human beings. But the animal's captivation also implies a sense of openness, in the manner in which its life flows along lines comparable – in von Uexküll's terms – to those of polyphonic music. This sense has been taken up in the philosophy of Gilles Deleuze. The living organism, for Deleuze, is a bundle of lines, a haecceity. Critically, these lines do not connect points but pass forever amidst and between. Considering the way in which this idea has been taken up in so-called actor-network theory, particularly associated with the work of Bruno Latour, I return to the importance of distinguishing the network as a set of interconnected points from the meshwork as an interweaving of lines. Every such line describes a flow of material substance in a space that is topologically fluid. I conclude that the organism (animal or human) should be understood not as a bounded entity surrounded by an environment but as an unbounded entanglement of lines in fluid space.

Theorists, the emperors of the academic world, are prone to self-aggrandizement, dressing their disputations in sumptuous verbal apparel the meaning of which neither they nor those who flatter them can see. It takes a fool to recognise that nothing's there. In Chapter 7, the fool's part is played through a dialogue between two lowly characters, ANT and SPIDER, whose disdain for human vanity is matched only by their shared love of philosophy. In relating their dialogue I highlight the similarities and differences between Latourian actor-network theory and my own, 'meshwork' approach to being alive. ANT claims that events are the effects of an agency that is distributed around a far-flung network of act-ants comparable to the spider's web. But the web, as SPIDER explains, is not really a network in this sense. Its lines do not connect; rather, they are the lines along which it perceives and acts. For SPIDER, they are indeed lines of life. Thus whereas ANT conceives of the world as an assemblage of heterogeneous bits and pieces, SPIDER's world is a tangle of threads and pathways; not a network but a meshwork. Action, then, emerges from the interplay of forces conducted along the lines of the meshwork. It is because organisms are immersed in such force fields that they are alive. To cut the spider from its web would be like cutting the bird from the air or the fish from water: removed from these currents they would be dead. Living systems are characterised by a coupling of perception and action that arises within processes of ontogenetic development. This coupling is both a condition for the exercise of agency and the foundation of skill. Where ANT, then, stands for actor-network theory, SPIDER – the epitome of my own position – stands for the proposition that *skilled practice involves developmentally embodied responsiveness*.

5

RETHINKING THE ANIMATE, REANIMATING THOUGHT

The discovery of life

Every so often the media of the western world register a surge of excitement about the imminent prospect of discovering life on the planet Mars. So potent is this expectation that world leaders – albeit of questionable intellectual stature – have been known to stake their reputations upon the promise of its fulfilment. Wily astronomers, beleaguered by chronic lack of funding for their most expensive science, are well aware of the importance of keeping the sense of excitement on the boil. So long as politicians see in it a chance of securing their place in history, they know that the money will keep coming in. For the rest of us, perhaps naively but also less cynically, the thought of life on another planet exerts an enduring fascination. I, too, am fascinated by the idea. I am at a loss to know, however, what it is exactly that scientists hope or expect to find on the surface of the planet. Is life the kind of thing that might be left lying about in the Martian landscape? If so, how would we recognise it when we see it? Perhaps the answer might be that we would identify life on Mars in just the same way that we would identify it on our own earth. But I am not even sure how we would do that. What I *am* sure about, because we know it from ethnography, is that people do not always agree about what is alive and what is not, and that even when they *do* agree it might be for entirely different reasons. I am also sure, again because we know it from ethnography, that people do not universally discriminate between the categories of living and non-living things. This is because for many people, life is not an attribute of things at all.[1] That is to say, it does not emanate from a world that already exists, populated by objects-as-such, but is rather immanent in the very process of that world's continual generation or coming-into-being.

People who have such an understanding of life – and they include many among whom anthropologists have worked, in regions as diverse as Amazonia, Southeast Asia and the circumpolar North – are often described in the literature as animists. According to a long established convention, animism is a system of beliefs that imputes life or spirit to things that are truly inert (see Chapter 2, p. 28). But this convention, as I shall show, is misleading on two counts. First, we are dealing here not with a way of believing *about* the world, but with a condition of being *in* it. This could be described as a condition of being alive to the world, characterised by a heightened sensitivity and responsiveness, in perception and action, to an environment that is always in flux, never the same from one moment to the next. Animacy, then, is not a property of persons imaginatively projected onto the things with which they perceive themselves to be surrounded. Rather – and this is my second point – it is the dynamic, transformative potential of the entire field of relations within which beings of all kinds, more or less person-like or thing-like, continually and reciprocally bring one another into existence. The animacy of the lifeworld, in short, is not the result of an infusion of spirit into substance, or of agency into materiality, but is rather ontologically prior to their differentiation.

I am surely not the first to observe that the real animists, according to the conventional definition of the term, are precisely those who dream of finding life on Mars. They truly believe that there exists an animating principle that may be lodged in the interior of physical objects, causing them to go forth and multiply. It was this same belief that ethnologists of the nineteenth century projected onto the savages of their acquaintance, accusing them nevertheless of applying it far too liberally to cover anything and everything, whether actually alive or not. We should not therefore be surprised by the parallel between the astronomers of the early twenty-first century, who hope to discover life lurking within the matter of other planets, and their ethnological predecessors who set out to discover animistic beliefs lurking within the minds of other cultures. Psychologists have suggested that such beliefs are founded upon the bedrock of an unconscious predisposition that even 'educated adults' share with children and supposedly primitive folk – a predisposition to act as though inanimate objects are actually alive (Brown and Thouless 1965). The argument goes that if you don't know whether something is alive or not, it is a better bet to assume that it is, and reckon with the consequences. The costs of getting it wrong in some instances are outweighed by the benefits of getting it right in others (Guthrie 1993: 41). Those who take rocks to be crocodiles have greater chances of survival than those who mistake crocodiles for rocks. As intuitive non-animists have been selected out, due to unfortunate encounters with things that turned out to be more alive than anticipated, we have all evolved to be closet animists – without of course realising it.

Continuous birth

Such nonsense aside, arguments of this general form follow the same logic. I call it the logic of inversion, and it is deeply sedimented within the canons of western thought (Ingold 1993: 218–219). Through this logic, the field of involvement in the world, of a thing or person, is converted into an interior schema of which its manifest appearance and behaviour are but outward expressions. Thus the organism, moving and growing along lines that bind it into the web of life, is reconfigured as the outward expression of an inner design. Likewise the person, acting and perceiving within a nexus of intertwined relationships, is presumed to behave according to the directions of cultural models or cognitive schemata installed inside his or her head. By way of inversion, beings originally open to the world are closed in upon themselves, sealed by an outer boundary or shell that protects their inner constitution from the traffic of interactions with their surroundings. My purpose in this chapter is to put the logic of inversion into reverse. Life having been, as it were, installed inside things, I want to restore these things to life by returning to the currents of their formation. By doing so I aim to recover that original openness to the world in which the people whom *we* (that is, western-trained ethnologists) call animist find the meaning of life.

One man from among the Wemindji Cree, native hunters of northern Canada, offered the following meaning to the ethnographer Colin Scott. Life, he said, is 'continuous birth' (Scott 1989: 195). I want to nail that to my door! It goes to the heart of the matter. To elaborate: life in the animic ontology is not an emanation but a generation of being, in a world that is not preordained but incipient, forever on the verge of the actual (Ingold 2000a: 113). One is continually present as witness to that moment, always moving like the crest of a wave, at which the world is about to disclose itself for what it is.[2] In his essay on 'Eye and mind' the philosopher Maurice Merleau-Ponty attributed precisely the same kind of sensibility – the same openness to a world-in-formation – to the painter. The painter's relation to the world, Merleau-Ponty writes, is not a simple 'physical–optical' one. That is, he does not gaze upon a world that is finite and complete, and proceed to fashion a representation of it. Rather, the relation is one of 'continued birth' – these are Merleau-Ponty's very words – as though at every moment the painter opened his eyes to the world for the first time (see Chapter 10, p. 128). His vision is not of things in a world, but of things becoming things, and of the world becoming a world (Merleau-Ponty 1964: 167–168, 181).

The relational constitution of being

I want to stress two points about this animic perception of the world. One concerns the relational constitution of being; the other concerns the primacy of movement. I shall deal with each in turn. The first point takes me back to the logic of inversion. Let us imagine an organism. I might depict it like this:

But in this apparently innocent depiction I have already effected an inversion. I have folded the organism in on itself such that it is delineated and contained within a perimeter boundary, set off against a surrounding world – an environment – with which it is destined to interact according to its nature. The organism is 'in here', the environment 'out there'. But instead of drawing a circle, I might just as well have drawn a line. So let us start again. Here is an organism:

In this depiction there is no inside or outside, and no boundary separating the two domains. Rather there is a trail of movement or growth. Every such trail discloses a relation. But the relation is not *between* one thing and another – between the organism 'here' and the environment 'there'. It is rather a trail *along* which life is lived. Neither beginning here and ending there, nor vice versa, the trail winds through or amidst like the root of a plant or a stream between its banks. Each such trail is but one strand in a tissue of trails that together comprise the texture of the lifeworld. This texture is what I mean when I speak of organisms being constituted within a relational field. It is a field not of interconnected points but of interwoven lines; not a network but a *meshwork* (Ingold 2007a: 80).

The distinction is critical. Network images have become commonplace across a broad spectrum of disciplines, from the 'webs of life' of ecology, through the 'social networks' of sociology and social anthropology, to the 'agent–object' networks of material culture studies.[3] Across all these fields, proponents of network thinking argue that it encourages us to focus, in the first place, not on elements but on the connections between them, and thereby to adopt what is often called a relational perspective. Such a perspective allows for the possibility that with any pair of connected elements, each can play an active part in the ongoing formation of the other. By way of their relations, it is supposed, things, organisms or persons may be mutually constitutive. However as Frances Larson, Alison Petch and David Zeitlyn point out in a recent study of connections between museum objects, collectors and curators, the network metaphor logically entails that the elements connected are distinguished from the lines of their connection (Larson et al. 2007: 216–217). Thus there can be no mutuality without the prior separation of the elements whose constitution is at issue. That is to say, the establishment of relations *between* these elements – whether they be organisms, persons or things of any other kind – necessarily requires that each is turned in upon itself prior to its integration into the network. And this presupposes an operation of inversion.

To draw the relation as a trail, as I have done above, is to undo this inversion, and to repudiate the distinction, key to the idea of the network, between things and their relations. Things *are* their relations. As the description of an organism, however, the single line presents a gross oversimplification. No complex organism is like that. Rather, the lives of organisms generally extend along not one but multiple trails, issuing from a source. 'To live', as the philosopher of biology Georges Canguilhem wrote in his *Knowledge of Life* of 1952, 'is to radiate; it is to organise the milieu from and around a centre of reference' (Canguilhem 2008: 113–114, see Figure 5.1). The organism, then, should be depicted something like this:

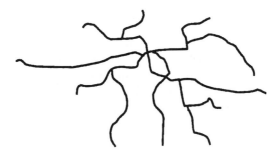

It goes without saying that this depiction would do just as well for persons who, being organisms, likewise extend along the multiple pathways of their involvement in the world.[4] Organisms and persons, then, are not so much nodes in a network as knots in a tissue of knots, whose constituent strands, as they become tied up with other strands, in other knots, comprise the meshwork.

But what, now, has happened to the environment? Literally, of course, an environment is that which *surrounds* the organism. But you cannot surround a bundle without drawing a boundary that would enclose it, and this would immediately be to effect an inversion,

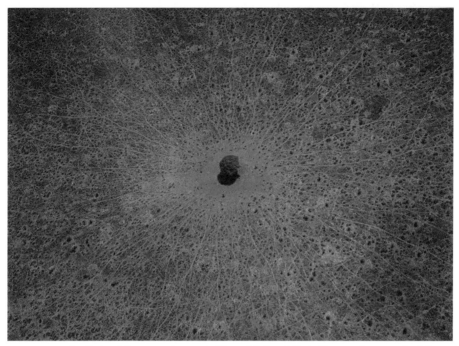

FIGURE 5.1   Radiating life: an acacia tree in Tsavo National Park, Kenya, photographed from the air. Photo: Yann Arthus-Bertrand, courtesy of Agence Altitude.

converting those relations along which a being lives its life in the world into internal properties of which its life is but the outward expression. We can suppose, however, that lines of growth issuing from multiple sources become comprehensively entangled with one another, rather like the vines and creepers of a dense patch of tropical forest, or the tangled root systems that you cut through with your spade every time you dig the garden. What we have been accustomed to calling 'the environment' might, then, be better envisaged as a domain of entanglement. It is within such a tangle of interlaced trails, continually ravelling here and unravelling there, that beings grow or 'issue forth' along the lines of their relationships.

This tangle is the texture of the world. In the animic ontology, beings do not simply occupy the world, they *inhabit* it, and in so doing – in threading their own paths through the meshwork – they contribute to its ever-evolving weave. Thus we must cease regarding the world as an inert substratum, over which living things propel themselves about like counters on a board or actors on a stage, where artefacts and the landscape take the place, respectively, of properties and scenery. By the same token, beings that inhabit the world (or that are truly indigenous in this sense) are not objects that move, undergoing displacement from point to point across the world's surface. Indeed the inhabited world, as such, has no surface. As we saw in Chapter 3 (p. 47), whatever surfaces one encounters, whether of the ground, water, vegetation or buildings, are *in* the world, not *of* it (Ingold 2000a: 241). And woven into their very texture are the lines of growth and movement of its inhabitants. Every such line, in short, is a way *through* rather than *across*. And it is as their lines of movement, not as mobile, self-propelled entities, that beings are instantiated in the world. This brings me to my second point, about the primacy of movement.

The primacy of movement

The animic world is in perpetual flux, as the beings that participate in it go their various ways. These beings do not exist at locations, they occur along paths. Among the Inuit of the Canadian Arctic, for example, as the writer Rudy Wiebe has shown (1989: 15), as soon as a person moves he or she becomes a line. People are known and recognised by the trails they leave behind them (I return to this example in Chapter 12, p. 149). Animals, likewise, are distinguished by characteristic patterns of activity or movement signatures, and to perceive an animal is to witness this activity going on, or to hear it. Thus, to take a couple of illustrations from Richard Nelson's wonderful account of the Koyukon of Alaska, *Make Prayers to the Raven*, you see 'streaking like a flash of fire through the undergrowth', not a fox, and 'perching in the lower branches of spruce trees', not an owl (Nelson 1983: 108, 158). The names of animals are not nouns but verbs.[5]

But it is no different with celestial bodies, such as the sun and the moon. We might think of the sun as a giant disk that is observed to make its way from east to west across the great dome of the sky. It could be depicted like this:

But in the pictographic inscriptions of native peoples of the North American Plains, it is depicted like this:

or this:

where the little nick at the end of the line indicates sunrise or sunset (Farnell 1994: 959). In these depictions the sun is not understood as an object that moves *across* the sky. Rather it is identified as the path of its movement *through* the sky, on its daily journey from the eastern to the western horizon. Just how we are to imagine the sky, and in particular the relation between sky and earth, is a problem to which I shall return below.

Wherever there is life there is movement. Not all movement, however, betokens life. The movement of life is specifically of becoming rather than being, of the incipience of renewal along a path rather than the extensivity of displacement in space (Manning 2009: 5–6). Every creature, as it 'issues forth' and trails behind, moves in its characteristic way. The sun is alive because of the way it moves through the firmament, but so too are the trees because of the particular ways their boughs sway or their leaves flutter in the wind, and because of the sounds they make in doing so. Of course the western scientist would agree that the tree is alive, even though he might have doubts about the sun. But his reasons would be quite different. The tree is alive, he would say, not because of its movement but because it is a cellular organism whose growth is fuelled by photosynthetic reactions and regulated by DNA in the cell nucleus. As for its movements, these are just effects of the wind. But what of the wind itself? Again, the scientist would have his own explanations: the wind is caused by horizontal and vertical differences in atmospheric air pressure. It, too, is an effect. In most animic cosmologies, however, the winds are taken to be alive and to have agentive powers of their own; in many they are important persons that give shape and direction to the world in which people live, just as do the sun, the moon and the stars.

Once we recognise the primacy of movement in the animic cosmos, the inclusion in the pantheon of beings of what modern science would classify as meteorological phenomena – not just the winds but commonly also thunder – becomes readily comprehensible. We are not required to believe that the wind is a being that blows, or that thunder is a being that claps. Rather the wind *is* blowing, and the thunder *is* clapping, just as organisms and persons *are* living in the ways peculiar to each. But I think there is rather more to be said about the prominence accorded to these weather-related manifestations of being, and this brings me back to the relation between earth and sky.

Sky, earth and the weather

I mentioned earlier our propensity to suppose that the inanimate world is presented to life as a surface to be occupied. Life, we say, is lived on the ground, anchored to solid foundations, while the weather swirls about overhead. Beneath this ground surface lies the earth; above it the atmosphere. In the pronouncements of many theorists, however, the ground figures as an interface not merely between earth and atmosphere but much more fundamentally between the domains of *agency* and *materiality*. As we saw in Chapter 2 (p. 23), this has the very peculiar consequence of rendering *immaterial* the medium through which organisms and persons move in the conduct of their activities. Between mind and nature, persons and things, and agency and materiality, no conceptual space remains for those very real phenomena and transformations of the medium that generally go by the name of weather. This, I believe, accounts for the virtual absence of weather from philosophical debates on these matters. It is a result of the logic of inversion – a logic that places occupation before habitation, movement across before movement through, surface before medium. In the terms of this logic, the weather is simply unthinkable.

In the animic ontology, by contrast, what is unthinkable is the very idea that life is played out upon the inanimate surface of a ready-made world. Living beings, according to this ontology, make their way *through* a nascent world rather than *across* its preformed surface. As they do so, and depending on the circumstances, they may experience wind and rain, sunshine and mist, frost and snow, and a host of other weather-related phenomena, all of which fundamentally affect their moods and motivations, their movements and their possibilities of subsistence, even as these phenomena sculpt and erode the plethora of surfaces upon which inhabitants tread. For them, the inhabited world is constituted in the first place by the aerial flux of weather rather than by the grounded fixities of landscape. The weather is dynamic, always unfolding, ever changing in its currents, qualities of light and shade, and colours, alternately damp or dry, warm or cold, and so on. In this world the earth, far from providing a solid foundation for existence, appears to float like a fragile and ephemeral raft, woven from the strands of terrestrial life, and suspended in the great sphere of the sky. This sphere is where all the lofty action is: where the sun shines, the winds blow, the snow falls and storms rage. It is a sphere in which powerful persons seek not to stamp their will upon the earth but to take flight with the birds, soar with the wind and converse with the stars. Their ambitions, we could say, are more celestial than territorial.

This is the point at which to return to the question I posed a moment ago, of the meaning of the sky, and of its relation to the earth. Consider the definition offered by my Chambers dictionary. The sky, the dictionary informs us, is 'the apparent canopy over our heads'. This is revealing in two respects. First, the sky is imagined as a *surface*, just like the surface of the earth except of course a covering overhead rather than a platform underfoot. Secondly, however, unlike the earth's surface, that of the sky is not real but only *apparent*. In reality there is no surface at all. Conceived as such, the sky is a phantasm. It is where angels tread. Following what is by now a familiar line of thought, the surface of the earth has become an interface between the concrete and the imaginary. What lies below (the earth) belongs to the physical world, whereas what arches above (the sky) is sublimated into thought. With their feet on the ground and their heads in the air, human beings appear to be constitutionally split between the material and the mental. Within the animic cosmos, however, the sky is not a surface, real or imaginary, but a medium. Moreover this medium, as we have seen, is inhabited by a variety of beings, including the sun and the moon, the winds, thunder, birds and so on. These beings lay their own trails through the sky, just as terrestrial beings lay their trails through the earth. The example of the sun's path has already been mentioned. But the winds, too, are commonly supposed to make tracks through the sky, coming from the quarters where they reside (Farnell 1994: 943). Nor are the earth and the sky mutually exclusive domains of habitation. Birds routinely move from one domain to the other, as do powerful humans such as shamans. The Yup'ik Eskimos, according to Anne Fienup-Riordan (1994: 80), recognise a class of extraordinary persons who are so fleet of foot that they can literally take off, leaving a trail of wind-blown snow in the trees.

Astonishment and surprise

In short, far from facing each other on either side of an impenetrable division between the real and the immaterial, earth and sky are inextricably linked within one indivisible field, integrated along the tangled lifelines of its inhabitants. Painters know this. They know that to paint what is conventionally called a 'landscape' is to paint both earth and sky, and that earth and sky blend in the perception of a world undergoing continuous birth. They know, too, that the visual perception of this earth–sky, unlike that of objects in the landscape, is in the first place an experience of light. In their painting they aim to recover, behind the mundane ordinariness of the ability to see *things*, the sheer astonishment of that experience, namely, of being able to *see*.[6] Astonishment, I think, is the other side of the coin to the very *openness* to the world that I have shown to be fundamental to the animic way of being. It is the sense of wonder that comes from riding the crest of the world's continued birth. Yet along with openness comes vulnerability. To outsiders unfamiliar with this way of being, it often looks like timidity or weakness, proof of a lack of rigour characteristic of supposedly primitive belief and practice. The way to know the world, they say, is not to open oneself up to it, but rather to 'grasp' it within a grid of concepts and categories. Astonishment has been banished from the protocols of conceptually driven, rational inquiry. It is inimical to science.

Seeking closure rather than openness, scientists are often surprised by what they find, but never astonished. Scientists are surprised when their predictions turn out to be wrong. The very goal of prediction, however, rests upon the conceit that the world can be held to account. But of course the world goes its own way, regardless. What the designer Stewart Brand says about architectural constructions applies equally to the constructions of science: 'All buildings are predictions; all predictions are wrong' (1994: 178). Following the Popperian programme of conjecture and refutation, science has turned surprise into a principle of creative advance, converting its cumulative record of predictive failure into a history of progress. Surprise, however, exists only for those who have forgotten how to be astonished at the birth of the world, who have grown so accustomed to control and predictability that they depend on the unexpected to assure them that events are taking place and that history is being made. By contrast, those who are truly open to the world, though perpetually astonished, are never surprised. If this attitude of unsurprised astonishment leaves then vulnerable, it is also a source of strength, resilience and wisdom. For rather than waiting for the unexpected to occur, and being caught out in consequence, it allows them at every moment to respond to the flux of the world with care, judgement and sensitivity.

Are animism and science therefore irreconcilable? Is an animistic openness to the world the enemy of science? Certainly not. I would not want my remarks to be interpreted as an attack on the whole scientific enterprise. But science as it stands rests upon an impossible foundation, for in order to turn the world into an *object* of concern, it has to place itself above and beyond the very world it claims to understand. The conditions that enable scientists to *know*, at least according to official protocols, are such as to make it impossible for scientists to *be* in the very world of which they seek knowledge. Yet all science depends on observation, and all observation depends on participation – that is, on a close coupling, in perception and action, between the observer and those aspects of the world that are the focus of attention. If science is to be a coherent knowledge practice, it must be rebuilt on the foundation of openness rather than closure, engagement rather than detachment. And this means regaining the sense of astonishment that is so conspicuous by its absence from contemporary scientific work. Knowing must be reconnected with being, epistemology with ontology, thought with life. Thus has our rethinking of indigenous animism led us to propose the reanimation of our own, so-called 'western' tradition of thought.

6

POINT, LINE, COUNTERPOINT

FROM ENVIRONMENT TO FLUID SPACE

Beginning with the environment

This chapter is the latest in my attempts over two decades and more, and that are still ongoing, to figure out what is meant by the environment of an animal. Coming from a background in ecological anthropology, which professes to study the relations between people and their environments, I cannot avoid the questions of what an environment is and, more particularly, what, if anything, is special about the environments of those animals we call human beings. Initially, my inquiries were prompted by a realisation that ecological anthropology appeared to have reached an impasse that was blocking further development in the subject. It lay in the contradictory imperatives, epitomised in the title of a celebrated book by Marshall Sahlins (1976), of *culture* and *practical reason*. Does all meaning and value lie in systems of significant symbols? If so, then the motives and finalities for human action on the environment must lie in what the mind brings to it: in the ideas, concepts and categories of a received cultural tradition. Yet does not culture with its artefacts and organisational arrangements, and the knowledge of how to apply them, provide human beings with the equipment to draw a livelihood from the world around them? Would they not, as Clifford Geertz once remarked (1973: 49–50), be crippled without it? If so, then whence come the ultimate requirements of human practice if not from the environment itself? Precisely where are we to place culture in the nexus of human environmental relations? Does it dictate the terms of adaptation, or is it a means of adaptation on terms dictated by nature, or both at once?

All sorts of ingenious solutions had been proposed to this dilemma, branded with a bewildering array of cumbersome labels – cultural materialism, neofunctionalism, symbolic ecology, structural Marxism – whose very clumsiness was symptomatic of epistemological collapse. None of them offered a satisfactory way out. Searching around for an alternative approach, I began to wonder whether the source of the difficulty might lie in the one assumption that everyone had taken for granted: namely that human relations with the environment are necessarily mediated by culture (Ingold 1992). After all, non-human animals that – with one or two possible exceptions – are not supposed to share the human capacity for symbolic representation are nevertheless quite well able to get along in their environments. Are we really meant to believe, as advocates of cultural reason would have it, that all meaning is symbolic, and therefore that non-humans inhabit meaningless worlds? To my mind, such a conclusion seemed absurd. So to turn the question around, I asked: 'What kind of meaning can there be in the absence of symbolic representation?' If we could only identify the sources of environmental meaning for non-human animals, then we could go on to consider the extent to which such sources are available to human beings as well. Only when these sources are exhausted would we finally need to have resort to the sphere of cultural representation.

Looking for answers to my question, I found none in mainstream psychology, nor any in the ethological study of animal behaviour. For the most part, cognitive psychologists were convinced that there could be no action in the world that was not preceded and determined in its course by an interior mental representation – that is, by an intention conceived in thought. If animals could not think or intend, then neither could they act. All they could do is behave, responding more or less automatically to received stimuli through innate mechanisms loosely known as 'instincts'. No meaning there! The majority of students of animal behaviour took the same view. Admittedly there were mavericks such as Donald Griffin (1984), who surmised that even the lowly insects might be capable of deliberating over the course of action. They too assumed, however, that there could be no action without forethought. Their theory of meaning, which rested on a Cartesian split between the thinking mind and the executive body, diverged not at all from the mainstream; they differed only in where they drew the line, in the animal kingdom, between creatures with minds and creatures without. Yet is it not ironic that we should expect of the ant or bee, as a condition of its finding some meaning in the environment, that it holds before its mind some representation of the world and acts in accordance with it, when this is something we humans so rarely do ourselves? How often, I wonder, do we think before we act? Even when we do, the action hardly follows automatically from the thought, and may often diverge from it in ways never intended. As the philosopher Alfred North Whitehead wisely observed, 'from the moment of birth we are immersed in action, and can only fitfully guide it by taking thought' (Whitehead 1938: 217).

I therefore had to leave the mainstream to find my answers. In psychology I turned to the work of James Gibson, whose ecological approach to perception, developed in 1950s and 1960s, was explicitly opposed to the prevailing paradigm of cognitivism. And in ethology I rediscovered the long neglected, pre-war writings of the Estonian-born pioneer of bio-semiotics, Jakob von Uexküll. Both seemed to offer a radically alternative way of thinking about meaning, finding it not in the correspondence between an external world and its interior representation, but in the immediate coupling of perception and action. Yet, as I also found, behind this commonality lay significant differences.

James Gibson and the concept of affordance

Gibson's first move is to distinguish very clearly between 'the animal environment' and the 'physical world' (Gibson 1979: 8). Physics may strive to comprehend the nature of the world as it really is, pared down to its essential constituents of force, energy and matter. An environment, however, does not exist in and of itself. It exists only *in relation* to the being whose environment it is. Thus, just as there can be no organism without an environment, so also there can be no environment without an organism (see also Lewontin 1982: 160).

Though no less real than the physical world, the environment is reality *for* the organism in question (Ingold 1992: 44; 2000a: 168). Gibson's next step is to show that the fundamental constituents of any environment comprise what he calls *affordances* (Gibson 1979: 127). His argument is that in encountering any particular environmental object, the animal perceives what it facilitates or hinders in the immediate context of its current activity. Perception, then, is not a matter of affixing some meaning to the object – of recognising it as one of a certain kind to which certain uses may be attached – but of discovering meaning in the very process of use.

Despite the clarity of Gibson's reasoning, it is in fact shot through with contradiction. The problem lies in his inability to reconcile his relational understanding of the environment with an older and more conventional view that posits the environment as a set of objective conditions that exist independently and in advance of the creatures that come to inhabit it, and to which they must perforce adapt. His solution is to try to have it both ways, as the following passage reveals:

> An important fact about the affordances of the environment is that they are in a sense objective, real, and physical, unlike values and meanings, which are often supposed to be subjective, phenomenal and mental. But, actually, an affordance is neither an objective property nor a subjective property; or it is both if you like. An affordance cuts across the dichotomy of subjective-objective and helps us to understand its inadequacy. It is equally a fact of the environment and a fact of behavior. It is both physical and psychical, yet neither. An affordance points both ways, to the environment and to the observer.
>
> (ibid.: 129)

Are affordances, then, objectively and physically instantiated in the environment prior to the assignation to them of value and meaning by a perceiving subject? As a matter of fact they are, says Gibson, before immediately qualifying himself. Well, they are 'in a sense'. And *actually*, he goes on to say, that sense rests on the entirely inadequate foundation of a subject–object dualism! For the affordances of things *are* their values and meanings, and what is more, they can be directly perceived (ibid.: 127).

I believe the root source of this contradiction can be found in the very assumption that the environment comprises a world furnished with *objects*. For Gibson this is axiomatic. Without objects, he surmises, an environment would be virtually uninhabitable (ibid.: 78).[1] In practice, however, inhabitants find themselves in a world cluttered with objects of all sorts, like householders in an attic or actors on a stage-set. It is all this furniture that makes it possible for them to get on with the activities of life. From the analogy of the environment to furnished accommodation is drawn the classical ecological concept of the *niche*, a little corner of the world to which an organism has fitted itself through a process of adaptation. Just as, literally, an alcove in the wall provides the perfect place to display a vase of the right size and proportion, so metaphorically, every kind of creature has evolved to fill its particular niche in the environment. A corollary of the metaphor, however, is that as with the dimensions of alcove, the niche is specified by essential properties of the environment, irrespective of the presence and functioning of the organism. Take away the vase, and the alcove is still there; remove the organism and the niche remains. As 'a set of affordances' (ibid.: 128), the niche is already laid out in the furnishing of the environment before any creature arrives to fill it. It sets the conditions to which any occupant must adapt. Moreover every object of furniture, Gibson insists, 'offers what it does because of what it is' (ibid.: 139), whether or not any animal is present to detect it. As properties of the furnished world, the affordances of the environment are there to be discovered and put to use by any creature equipped to do so.

In short, far from inhering in a relation between a living being and its environment, and pointing both ways, it now seems that the affordance rests unequivocally on the side of the environment and that it points in just one way, towards any potential inhabitant. Having begun by assuring us that 'an environment implies an animal (or at least an organism) to be surrounded', Gibson goes on to assert, with equal assurance but quite to the contrary, that 'the environment does *not* depend on the organism for its existence' (ibid.: 8, 129, my emphasis). Indeed he is at pains to distinguish his view of the niche from 'what some animal psychologists have called the *phenomenal environment* of the species', and particularly from any suggestion that such an environment might amount to a 'subjective world' in which it is supposed to live (ibid.: 129). Though he does not name names, he could have been referring to the works, among others, of Jakob von Uexküll.

Jakob von Uexküll and the concept of *Umwelt*

Much as Gibson was later to do, von Uexküll set out to understand how the world exists *for* the animal, given its own particular morphology, sensibilities and action potentials. No more than Gibson, could he accept that animals live in meaningless worlds. One could hardly imagine an animal farther removed from human beings in structure, size and complexity – though not, irritatingly, in proximity – than the humble tick. Yet even for the tick, von Uexküll showed, the environment is imbued with meaning, albeit of only three kinds (Uexküll 1992: 324–325). The first is carried in the smell of sweat common to mammals, the second in characteristics of the host's skin and hair, and the third in the temperature of warm blood. The significance of each lies in the action it prompts: falling (so as to land on the host), burrowing (on a relatively hairless patch of skin) and sucking (from blood vessels close to the surface). For von Uexküll as for Gibson, there is meaning in the animal's world not because it is capable of fashioning an internal representation of an external state of affairs but because its action in the world is so closely and intimately attuned to its perception (ibid.: 320).

That is where the similarity ends, however. For whereas Gibsonian affordances are supposed to exist as the inherent potentials of environmental objects, regardless of whether they are attended to or put to use by any organism, von Uexküll maintained that what he called the 'quality' (*Ton*) of a thing, by virtue of which it has significance for a particular creature, is not intrinsic to the thing itself but is *acquired* by virtue of its having been drawn into that creature's activity (Uexküll 1982: 27–29). The same stone, for example, may function as shelter for the crab that hides beneath it, as an anvil for the thrush that uses it to break open snail shells, and as a missile for an angry human to hurl at an adversary. In Gibson's terms, shelter, anvil and missile are all properties of the stone that are available to be *taken up*. For von Uexküll, by contrast, they are qualities that are *bestowed upon* the stone by the need of the creature in question and in the very act of attending to it. The stone only *becomes* a shelter when the crab scuttles under it, an anvil when the thrush smashes the shell against it, and a missile when the man picks it up to throw. Outside of these activities it was none of these things. Thus, far from fitting into a given corner of the world (a niche), it is the animal that fits the world to itself by ascribing functional qualities to the things it encounters and thereby integrating them into a coherent system of its own (Uexküll 1992: 360–361; see Ingold 1992: 42). To denote this system – the world as it is constituted within the animal's circuit of perception and action – von Uexküll used the term *Umwelt* (1992: 320). The life of every creature, von Uexküll thought, is so wrapped up in its own *Umwelt* that no other worlds are accessible to it. It is as though each one were floating in its own particular 'bubble' of reality (ibid.: 338–339). Though the perceptual and effector organs of different creatures may be perfectly attuned, neither can access what is real for the other. For example the threads of the spider's web, as von Uexküll elegantly showed (1982: 42), are precisely proportioned such that they evade the visual sensors of the fly, yet the spider knows absolutely nothing of the fly's world.

We have seen that the niche, as a set of affordances, is on the side of the environment and points towards the organism. The *Umwelt*, it now seems, is just the opposite: it is on the side of the organism pointing towards the environment. Remove the organism, and the *Umwelt* disappears with it. What then remains? A man may throw a stone in anger, but in more measured circumstances he might ponder its possible uses as a paperweight, pendulum bob or hammer. Whilst he holds the stone in his hand and deliberates on the matter it is not yet any of these things. It is merely an object of a certain shape, size and composition, with certain properties of hardness and durability, which could, in principle, find an almost unlimited range of uses. Regarded as such, the stone is an example of what von Uexküll (ibid.: 27) called 'neutral objects'. No animal, however, or at least no *non-human* animal, is in a position to observe the environment from such a standpoint of neutrality. To live, it must already be immersed in its surroundings and committed to the relationships this entails. And in these relationships, the neutrality of objects is inevitably compromised. The thrush, for example, does not first perceive the stone *as* a stone, and then wonder what to do with it, any more than it wonders what to do with its beak. Rather, using both stone and beak, it smashes shells. But what of the human? In a paper published over twenty years ago, I argued that humans are different. Uniquely among animals, it seemed to me, human beings are capable of making their own life activity the object of their attention, and thus of seeing things *as they are*, as a condition for deliberating about the alternative uses to which they might be put (Ingold 1989: 504–505). For this reason I took exception to the conventional English translation of the German *Umwelt* as 'subjective universe' (e.g., Uexküll 1982: 31). For human beings alone, I thought, can exist as subjects confronting a world of neutral objects. In that very act of standing back and reflecting on the conditions of existence, the human *Umwelt* becomes an *Innenwelt* – literally a 'subjective universe' – an organisation of representations, internal to the mind, which lend meaning to the raw material of experience.

Martin Heidegger on life in the open

It was not until two or three years later, guided by Hubert Dreyfus (1991: 60–87), that I began to engage with the philosophy of Martin Heidegger, and specifically with what he has to say about the ways in which human beings and non-human animals relate to the world around them. Heidegger distinguishes between two ways in which things can show up to a being that is active in the world: Dreyfus renders them as *availableness* and *occurrentness*. To the skilled practitioner absorbed in an activity, the things he uses are available and ready to hand. So long as the activity flows smoothly, their objectness melts into the flow. As the practitioner's awareness becomes one with the activity, he or she does not attend to the objects as such. Hammering, the carpenter does not inspect the hammer; fiddling, the musician does not subject the violin to scrutiny. Only when the instrument fails to respond to the demands of the moment does the practitioner run hard up against it, in its brute facticity. The thing, at this point, is no longer available but occurrent. 'What is this?' curses the carpenter as the hammer misses its mark; or the musician when the violin goes out of tune or a string snaps. This is not the kind of question that a non-human, without the gift of language, would ever ask. In this sense, humans alone are haunted by the spectre of the *loss* of meaning that occurs when action fails. It is not in their construction of meaningful worlds, then, that the singularity of human beings resides, but rather in their occasional glimpses of a world rendered meaningless by its dissociation from action.

Should we infer, from this, that so long as the human practitioner is absorbed without interruption in the task at hand, there is little or nothing to distinguish his or her perception from that of the animal in its *Umwelt*? This was certainly the drift of my own thinking. But it was not so for Heidegger. In a course of lectures delivered in 1929–1930, but which lay unpublished until 1983, Heidegger set out his unequivocal stance on the question of human uniqueness in direct response to the work of von Uexküll, which he much admired. The animal in its *Umwelt*, he argued, may be open to its *environment*, but it is closed to the *world*. The human practitioner is unique in inhabiting the world of the open. To explain what he meant, Heidegger asked his listeners to compare an inanimate object like a stone, an animal and a human being. How do they differ? His answer took the form of three theses: 'The stone … is *worldless*; the animal is *poor in world*; man is *world-forming*' (Heidegger 1995: 263). The stone has no world since it lacks a perceptual apparatus. Suppose that we find a stone lying on our path. 'The stone lies upon the earth', observed Heidegger, 'but does not touch it.' Though it crops up amidst a host of other things, everything around remains inaccessible to the stone itself (ibid.: 197). There is, in short, no reality *for* the stone. What, then, of the animal? Why should its world have the character of poverty? If it is by the potential loss of meaning, and not by its contribution, that humans distinguish themselves from animals, then how come that human worlds are nevertheless more richly endowed?

The world of the animal is poor, Heidegger argued, because it is *captivated* (ibid.: 239). But as Giorgio Agamben has shown through a detailed commentary on Heidegger's text, there are two sides to captivation (Agamben 2004: 49–56). On the one hand, although the animal is encircled within what Heidegger called a 'disinhibiting ring', precisely equivalent to the *Umwelt*, this encirclement is absolutely not an encapsulation (Heidegger 1995: 255, 263). For it is thanks to its ring of disinhibitors that the instinctual drives of the animal can be released and find expression in the presence of appropriate stimuli. The disinhibiting ring is like a ring of keys, each of which opens a door through which the life of the animal spills out into its surroundings. But the animal knows nothing of this. It completely fails to apprehend the things with which its life is mingled, *as things*. For the animal, driven to behave in the way it does, there is no possibility of apprehension (ibid.: 247). Thus the very same encircling ring that opens the animal to its environment also ensures that the world as we humans know it – infinitely extendable in range and possibility – is forever withheld from it (ibid.: 193). This is the other side of captivation. The animal is poor in world, for Heidegger, because it lacks access to the things and beings that comprise it.

Yet if the closure entailed in the animal's captivation implies an openness to its environment so, conversely, the world of the human practitioner can be open only because it can appear closed in a way that the animal's can never do. Since the world cannot be disclosed to the animal there is no possibility, either, of its being *closed off* (ibid.: 248). For human beings, by contrast, the very opening of the world, the *dis*closure of things for what they are, is predicated upon an initial closure. Unlike the animal in its captivation, which finds itself *taken* in an environmental embrace that is as passionate as it is overwhelming, the human being stands before the world, as a domain of things-in-themselves, and has of necessity to take a stance *towards* it. Here, concludes Heidegger,

> we see ... the essential contrast between the animal's being open and the *world-openness* of man. Man's being open is a being held toward ... whereas the animal's being open is a being taken by ... and thereby a being absorbed in its encircling ring.
>
> (ibid.: 343)

The contrast between these contrary understandings of openness and closure is epitomised in what Heidegger has to say, elsewhere, about hands and handiwork. 'The hand exists as a hand', he declares in his lectures on *Parmenides*, 'only where there is disclosure and concealment' (1982: 80). No animal, he thinks, can have a hand or be handy. Animals can have paws, claws and talons, but these are mere conduits for its behaviour. The hand, by contrast, is an instrument of world forming. It is a hand precisely because it is *not* tied to any particular way of working, but delivers an engagement that is both thoughtful and reflexive, guided by consideration. It is, in short, an instrument not of *behaviour* but of *comportment* (Elden 2006: 280; see also Heidegger 1992: 84; 1995: 237).

The peculiar boundedness of Heidegger's notion of the 'open' is evident in his recurrent metaphor of the clearing, imagined as a space for dwelling that is *opened up* (that is, disclosed) from the surrounding forest. Within this space, human existence is reined in and contained, while other creatures meld into the surroundings from which they are deemed incapable of distinguishing themselves, and to which they are therefore unable to relate *as such* (Agamben 2004: 59; Harrison 2007: 634). To be sure, Heidegger is anxious to avoid placing any hierarchical evaluation on the difference between the animal's poverty in world and the human capacity for world formation (Heidegger 1995: 194). That he should characterise the world in terms of what the human *possesses* and the animal *lacks* reveals, nevertheless, where his priorities lie. Poor animals (Elden 2006: 274)! Indeed, in his stress on human uniqueness, Heidegger seems to arrive at a picture of the inhabitant that is, in every respect, the precise inverse of Gibson's. Recall Gibson's contention that what he calls the *open environment* – realised in the limiting case as a perfectly level desert stretching to the horizon under an empty sky – would be practically uninhabitable (Gibson 1979: 33, 78). To create a space for dwelling the open must be furnished with objects. Yet these objects, affording what they do because of what they are, remain indifferent to the presence of the inhabitant. They are supposed to comprise, in themselves, a meaningful world, into which the inhabitant arrives as a kind of interloper, probing this niche and that and picking up their affordances (ibid: 139). For Heidegger, to the contrary, the space of dwelling is one that the inhabitant has formed around himself by clearing the clutter that would otherwise threaten to overwhelm his existence. The world is rendered habitable not as it is for Gibson, by its partial *en*closure in the form of a niche, but by its partial *dis*closure in the form of a clearing.

Gilles Deleuze and life on the line

Can there be any escape from this shuttling back and forth between enclosure and disclosure, between an ecology of the real and a phenomenology of experience? So long as we suppose that life is fully encompassed in the relations *between* one thing and another – between the animal and its environment or the being and its world – we are bound to have to begin with a separation, siding either with the environment vis-à-vis its inhabitants or with the being vis-à-vis its world. A more radical alternative, however, would be to reverse Heidegger's priorities: that is, to celebrate the openness inherent in the animal's very captivation by its environment. This is the openness of a life that *will not be contained*, that overflows any boundaries that might be thrown around it, threading its way like the roots and runners of a rhizome through whatever clefts and fissures leave room for growth and movement (see Chapter 9, p. 124). Once again, we can take our cue from von Uexküll, who compares the world of nature to polyphonic music, in which the life of every creature is equivalent to a melody in counterpoint (Uexküll 1982: 52–54). In the case of musical performance, we may speak of the connection between the player and his instrument, say a violin. Each has a bearing on the other. But the line of the melody does not lie in this connection. On the contrary, it is a line that continually issues forth from that place, in the midst of things, where the fiddler and the violin are conjoined in a passionate embrace. So too, the lifelines of organisms issue from the sites of their symbiotic connection, but in a direction that runs not from one to the other but forever in between, as the river flows between its banks in a direction orthogonal to their transverse connection. The life of the spider thus runs in counterpoint to that of the fly: to the melodic line of the first, the second figures as a refrain (ibid.: 68). To adopt this view is to go with the grain of another of the twentieth century's most influential philosophers, Gilles Deleuze.

Life, for Deleuze, is lived not within a perimeter but along lines. He calls them 'lines of flight', or sometimes 'lines of becoming'. Such lines prise an opening, even as they bind the animal with its world. Every species, indeed every individual has its own particular line, or rather bundle of lines (Deleuze and Guattari 2004: 224–225). Critically, however, these lines do not connect:

> A line of becoming is not defined by the points it connects, or by the points that compose it; on the contrary, it passes between points, it comes up through the middle, it runs … transversally to the localizable relation to distant or contiguous points. A point is always a point of origin. But a line of becoming has neither beginning nor end … [It] has only a middle … A becoming is always in the middle: one can only get it by the middle. A becoming is neither one nor two, nor the relation of the two; it is the in-between, the … line of flight … running perpendicular to both.
>
> (ibid.: 323, see also Figure 6.1)

Thus in life as in music or painting, in the movement of becoming – the growth of the organism, the unfolding of the melody, the motion of the brush and its trace – points are not joined so much as swept aside and rendered indiscernible by the current as it flows through. So it is that the line does not link the spider and the fly, or the wasp and the orchid, but 'passes between them, carrying them away in a shared proximity in which the discernibility of points disappears' (ibid.: 324). Life is open-ended: its impulse is not to reach a terminus but to keep on going. The spider spinning its web or the musician launching into the melody

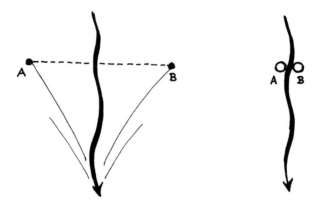

FIGURE 6.1 'A line of becoming, in relation to the localizable connection of A and B (distance), or in relation to their contiguity.' Redrawn after Deleuze and Guattari (2004: 604, fn. 83).

'hazards an improvisation'. But to improvise, Deleuze continues, is 'to join with the World, or meld with it. One ventures from home on the thread of a tune' (ibid.: 343–344).[2]

If the individual organism is to be understood as a bundle of lines, or what Deleuze calls a *haecceity* (ibid.: 290), then what becomes of our original concept of 'the environment'? Let us imagine ourselves, as did Charles Darwin in *The Origin of Species*, standing before 'the plants and bushes clothing an entangled bank' (Darwin 1950: 64). Observe how the fibrous bundles comprising every plant and bush are entwined with one another so as to form a dense mat of vegetation. On the bank, 'the environment' reappears as an immense tangle of lines. Precisely such a view was advanced by geographer Torsten Hägerstrand, who imagined every constituent of the environment – including 'humans, plants, animals and things all at once' – as having a continuous trajectory of becoming. 'Seen from within', wrote Hägerstrand, 'one could think of the tips of trajectories as sometimes being pushed forward by forces behind and besides and sometimes having eyes looking around and arms reaching out, at every moment asking "what shall I do next"?' The entwining of these ever-extending trajectories, in Hägerstrand's terms, comprises the texture of the world – the 'big tapestry of Nature which history is weaving' (Hägerstrand 1976: 332). In this tapestry there are no insides or outsides, no enclosures or disclosures, only openings and ways through. Like Darwin's entangled bank, Hägerstrand's tapestry is a field not of interconnected points but of interwoven lines, not a network but a meshwork.

Bruno Latour and the actor network

I have borrowed the term 'meshwork' from the philosophy of Henri Lefebvre (1991: 117–118). There is something in common, Lefebvre observes, between the way in which words are inscribed upon a page of writing, and the way in which the movements and rhythms of human and non-human activity are registered in lived space, but only if we think of writing not as a verbal composition but as a tissue of lines – not as *text* but as *texture*. 'Practical activity writes on nature', he remarks, 'in a scrawling hand.' Think of the reticular trails left by people and animals as they go about their business around the house, village and town. Caught up in these multiple entanglements, every monument or building, viewed in its context and surroundings, is more 'archi-textural' than architectural (ibid.: 118). It, too, despite its apparent solidity and permanence, is a haecceity, experienced in the opening and occlusion of vistas as inhabitants enter, leave or proceed from one room to another (see Chapter 12, p. 146). Like the environment of which it forms a part, the building neither encloses the inhabitant, nor is it disclosed from within. 'The significant division', as I have argued elsewhere, 'is not so much between inside and outside, as between the movement "from the inside going out", and "from the outside going in"' (Ingold 2004: 239). As the life of inhabitants overflows into gardens and streets, fields and forests, so the world pours into the building, giving rise to characteristic echoes of reverberation and patterns of light and shade. It is in these flows and counter-flows, winding through or amidst without beginning or end, and not as connected entities bounded either from within or without, that living beings are instantiated in the world.

The critical distinction between the lines of flow of the meshwork and the lines of connection of the network (see Chapter 5, p. 70) has been persistently obscured, above all in the recent elaboration of what has come to be known, rather unfortunately, as 'actor-network theory'. The theory has its roots not in thinking about the environment but in the sociological study of science and technology. In this latter field, much of its appeal comes from its promise to describe interactions among people (such as scientists and engineers) and the objects with which they deal (such as in the laboratory) in a way that does not concentrate mind or agency in human hands, but rather takes it to be distributed around all the elements that are connected or mutually implicated in a field of action. The term 'actor-network', however, first entered the Anglophone literature as a translation from the French *acteur réseau*. And as one of its leading proponents – Bruno Latour – has observed in hindsight, the translation gave it a significance that was never intended. In popular usage, inflected by innovations in information and communications technology, the defining attribute of the network is connectivity: 'transport *without* deformation, an instantaneous, unmediated access to every piece of information' (Latour 1999a: 15). But *réseau* can refer just as well to netting as to network – to woven fabric, the tracery of lace, the plexus of the nervous system or the web of the spider. The lines of the spider's web, for example, quite unlike those of the communications network, do not connect points or join things up. Secreted from the body of the spider as it moves, they are the lines *along* which it acts and perceives (see Chapter 7).

The *acteur réseau* was intended by its originators (if not by those who have been beguiled by its translation as 'network') to be comprised of just such lines of becoming. Their inspiration came, in large measure, from the philosophy of Deleuze. As we have already seen, with acknowledgement to Deleuze, the line of the web does not link the spider to the fly, neither does the latter's 'line of flight' link it to the spider. Ensconced at the centre of its web, the spider knows that a fly has landed somewhere on the outer margins, as it sends vibrations down the threads that are picked up by the spider's super-sensitive, spindly legs. And it can then run along the lines of the web to retrieve its prey. Thus the thread-lines of the web lay down the *conditions of possibility* for the spider to interact with the fly. But they are not themselves lines of interaction. If these lines are relations, then they are relations not *between* but *along*. Of course, as with the spider, the lives of organisms generally extend along not one but multiple lines, knotted together at the centre but trailing innumerable 'loose ends' at the periphery. Thus each should be pictured, as Latour has latterly suggested, in the shape of a star 'with a center surrounded by many radiating lines, with all sorts of tiny conduits leading to and fro' (Latour 2005: 177). No longer a self-contained object like a ball that can propel itself from place to place, the organism now appears as an ever ramifying web of lines of growth. This is the Deleuzeian *haecceity*, famously compared to a rhizome (Deleuze and Guattari 2004: 290). I personally prefer the image of the fungal mycelium (Ingold 2003: 302–306). Indeed as the mycologist Alan Rayner (1997) has suggested, the whole of biology would be different had it taken the mycelium as the prototypical exemplar of the living organism. For it could not, then, have been built upon the presumption that life is contained within the absolute bounds of fixed forms. We would rather have a biology that starts from the fluid character of the life process, wherein boundaries are sustained only thanks to the continual flow of materials across them (see also Pearson 1999: 166–168).

Ending with fluid space

In the science of mind, the absoluteness of the boundary between organism and environment has not gone unquestioned. Thus in a lecture delivered in 1970 the anthropologist Gregory Bateson declared that 'the mental world – the mind – the world of information processing – is not limited by the skin' (Bateson 1973: 429). His point was that the processing loops involved in perception and action are not interior to the creature whose mind we are talking about, whether human or non-human, nor can that creature's activity be understood as the merely mechanical output of one or more cognitive devices located in the head. Rather, such activity has to be understood as one aspect of the unfolding of a total system of relations comprised by the creature's embodied presence in a specific environment. Much more recently, in his book *Being There*, Andy Clark has made the same point. The mind, Clark tells us, is a 'leaky organ' that refuses to be confined within the skull but mingles shamelessly with the body and the world in the conduct of its operations (Clark 1997: 53). More strictly, he should have said that the skull is leaky, whereas the mind is what leaks! From Bateson to Clark, however, there remains a presumption that whereas the mind leaks, the organism does not. Whatever we might say about the mind, and about its propensity to mingle with the world along the multiple pathways of sensory engagement with its surroundings, the organism at least remains confined within the envelope of the body. This presumption, along with the division between mental and organic activity on which it rests, seems to me to be unsustainable. For how can there be any sensory engagement that does not also involve a flow of materials within a wider field of forces? For this reason I would like to return to Bateson's declaration and take it one step further. I want to suggest that as a nexus of life and growth within a meshwork of relations, *the organism is not limited by the skin*. It, too, leaks.

Another way to express this is to say that organisms inhabit what Annemarie Mol and John Law (1994) have called 'fluid space'.[3] In fluid space there are no well-defined objects or entities. There are rather substances that flow, mix and mutate, sometimes congealing into more or less ephemeral forms that can nevertheless dissolve or re-form without breach of continuity (ibid.: 659–664). Every line – every relation – in fluid space is a path of flow, like the riverbed or the veins and capillaries of the body. As the sanguinary image suggests, the living organism is not just one but a whole bundle of such lines. In a quite material sense, lines are what organisms are made of. Indeed anatomists have always known this as they have spoken of bodily 'tissues' (Ingold 2007a: 61). For the tissue is a texture formed of a myriad of fine threads tightly interlaced, presenting all the appearance, to a casual observer, of a coherent, continuous surface. To the anatomical gaze, however, the organic tissue becomes – as J. Arthur Thomson wrote in 1911 – 'in a quite remarkable way translucent', resolving into its constituent threads of nerve, muscle, blood vessels and so on (Thomson 1911: 27; see Figure 6.2). What is the nervous system, asked the philosopher Henri Bergson, if not 'an enormous number of threads which stretch from the periphery to the centre, and from the centre to the periphery' (Bergson 1991: 45)? Indeed the skin is not an impermeable boundary but a permeable zone of intermingling and admixture, where traces can reappear as threads and vice versa (Ingold 2007a: 59–61). Thus, as we saw in Chapter 5 (p. 70), instead of thinking of organisms as entangled in relations, we should regard every living thing as itself an entanglement.

To appreciate the distance we have come, let me return in conclusion to Gibson. Recall that for the organism to inhabit the open, in his view, it must find a semi-enclosure – a niche – comprised of objects. It is by their outward surfaces, according to Gibson, where more or less solid substances come up against the volatile medium, that objects are revealed to perception. If the substance of an object is dissolved or evaporates into the medium, then its surface disappears, and the object with it (Gibson 1979: 22–23). Thus the very objectness of things lies in the separation and immiscibility of substance and medium. Remove every object, however, and a surface still remains – for Gibson the most fundamental surface of all – namely the ground, marking the interface between the substance of the earth below and the gaseous medium of the sky above (ibid.: 10, 33). Has the earth, then, turned its back on the sky? If it had, then as Gibson correctly surmised, no life would be possible. The open could not be inhabited. Our conclusion, to the contrary, is that the open *can* be inhabited precisely because, wherever life is going on, the division of earth and sky gives way to flows and counter-flows of materials. As I shall show in Chapter 9, what we call the ground is not really a coherent surface at all but – just like the skin – a zone in which the air and moisture of the sky bind with substances whose source lies in the earth in the germination and growth of living organisms.

Thus, far from inhabiting a sealed ground furnished with objects, the animal lives and breathes in a world of earth and sky – or becoming earth and becoming sky – where to

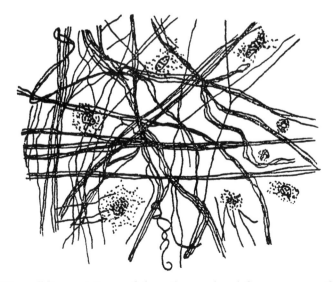

FIGURE 6.2 '"Loose" ligament tissue of the rat', reproduced from an unspecified source in Wassily Kandinsky's essay of 1926, *Point and Line to Plane* (Figure 74).

perceive is to align one's movements in counterpoint to the modulations of day and night, sunlight and shade, wind and weather. It is to feel the currents of air as it infuses the body, and the textures of the earth beneath one's feet. In the open world, to leave the last word to Deleuze, 'there is no line separating earth and sky; there is no intermediate distance, no perspective or contour, visibility is limited; and yet there is an extraordinarily fine topology that relies not on points or objects but rather on haecceities, on sets of relations (winds, undulations of snow or sand, the song of the sand or the creaking of the ice, the tactile qualities of both)' (Deleuze and Guattari 2004: 421). These haecceities are not *what* we perceive, since in the world of fluid space there are no objects of perception. They are rather what we perceive *with*. In short, to perceive the environment is not to look back on the things to be found in it, or to discern their congealed shapes and layouts, but to join with them in the material flows and movements contributing to their – and our – ongoing formation.

7

WHEN *ANT* MEETS *SPIDER*

SOCIAL THEORY FOR ARTHROPODS

Deep in the woods, amidst the undergrowth and detritus of a forest floor, two distinguished arthropods – renowned in the animal kingdom for their ingenuity and technical accomplishments – have struck up a conversation. One is ANT (Figure 7.1), the other is SPIDER (Figure 7.2). Both being philosophically inclined, their concern is to understand the world and their place in it. On this particular occasion, it is ANT's turn to open the debate.

'We ants', he declares, 'are not isolated individuals. Our brains may be no bigger than pinheads, yet we can achieve great things. Our nests are monumental mounds, and our roads are highways through the forest, overrunning everything in their path. We can accomplish these feats because we collaborate. We live together in colonies, many thousand strong, sharing our food and work. In a word, we are the most *social* of insects.'

SPIDER, more solitary by nature, finds the idea of life in a colony hard to grasp. She admits that she would be more inclined to eat others of her kind than to work with them. Curious to know what it means to be social, she resolves to press ANT on the issue. 'In the course of your activities', she remarks, 'you have to deal with all sorts of things. I have seen you dragging worms and bugs that you have killed for food to your nests, along with building materials like twigs, pine needles and leaves, often many times your body size. I

FIGURE 7.1   ANT, the mound builder

FIGURE 7.2 SPIDER, the web weaver

have seen you "touching up" aphids and licking the honeydew from their bodies. And I have seen you picking up and carrying around the larvae of your own kind. Tell me, do you have social relations with these things, or only with mature members of the colony like yourself?'

'Now there, my dear SPIDER', replies ANT, 'you have touched on an issue that has been the source of some controversy in the formicoid world, and I have to confess that my own views on the matter are somewhat unorthodox. To cut a long story short, there have up to now been two schools of thought. According to one school, we should think of the colony as a functioning totality that is more than the sum of its parts – a sort of super-organism – within which the life of every individual is entirely given over to the greater good of the collectivity. According to the other school, what we call "the colony" does not correspond to any real, concrete entity. We merely use the term as shorthand for what, in reality, is a vast aggregation of individuals, each driven by those basic instincts with which it has been innately endowed. My own view, however, is that we should characterise the colony, in the first place, in terms not of its membership or composition but of what is actually going on there. Every colony is abuzz with activity. And if we follow the lines of activity, we find that they can be traced back neither to a single, collective super-organism nor to a plurality of individual organisms. Rather, to trace the lines of activity is to describe a vast network, in which any individual appears as but a particular node. Every ant in the colony is part of the action and carries it forward in its own way; it is, if you will, an *act*-ant.'

'So if you want to assign responsibility for what is going on', interjects SPIDER, 'you could not lay it at the door of the individual or the collectivity. It is rather spread around the entire network.'

ANT waves his antennae in approval. 'Exactly so. That's why I say that the individual act-ant is not an agent. Rather, agency – that is, what makes things happen – is *distributed* throughout the network.'

'That is all very well', retorts SPIDER, 'but you have still not answered my original question. You speak of the colony as a network of *act*-ants. But can the network also include *non*-ants? Can non-ants also have social lives?'

'Absolutely', ANT continues. '*Anything* can belong to the network, whether ant or non-ant. It is on precisely this point that I take issue with my colleagues. They seem to think there is something about being an ant – some essential anthood – that sets them apart from other creatures, in a separate world of *anture* as distinct from the material world of *nature* in which the existence of all other creatures is confined. Social relations, they claim, are not natural but *antural*. But the world I inhabit comprises both act-ants and non-ants, including such things as pine needles, aphids and larvae. I insist that these things are not just passive objects. I am bound up in relations with them, as I am with my fellow ants. They, too, are part of the network. And they are caught up in it just as flies, my dear spider, are caught up in your web.'

'But there you are surely wrong', exclaims SPIDER. 'The lines of my web are not at all like those of your network. In your world there are just bits and pieces of diverse kinds that are brought together or assembled so as to make things happen. Every "relation" in the network, then, is a connection *between* one thing and another. As such, the relation has no material presence. For the materiality of the world, in your view, is fully comprehended in the things connected. The lines of my web, to the contrary, are themselves spun from materials exuded from my own body, and are laid down as I move about. You could even say that they are an extension of my very being as it trails into the environment – they comprise, if you will, my "wideware".[1] They are the lines *along* which I live, and conduct my perception and action in the world. For example, I know when a fly has landed in the web because I can feel the vibrations in the lines through my spindly legs, and it is along these same lines that I run to retrieve it. But the lines of my web do not *connect* me to the fly. Rather, they are already threaded before the fly arrives, and set up through their material presence the conditions of entrapment under which such a connection can potentially be established.'

SPIDER's account reminds ANT of an incident that took place during his winged mating flight, when he very nearly became caught in a spider's trap. It was touch and go, but after a sticky experience he had eventually managed to break free. Was it the web, however, or the spider that had ensnared him? Wondering about this, ANT comes to the conclusion that 'it was, of course, both the spider and the web, or what we might regard as a *hybrid* entity, the "spider–web", formed by their conjunction'. But there is more, as ANT goes on to explain. 'The web cannot function as a trap unless it is supported. In fact it was hung from lines attached to the twigs of bushes and to grass stems. So it was the way in which the spider, the web, the stems and the bushes all came together in the network, at that particular moment, that led to my nearly ending up as the spider's dinner.'

On hearing the word 'hybrid', SPIDER's legs begin to twitch nervously. She dislikes the term, and has reservations about the way it has been bandied about by ANT and his confabulators. 'Your talk of hybridity', she responds tetchily, 'entirely misses the point. You imagine a world of entities – spider, web, stems, twigs and so on – which are assembled to comprise the necessary and sufficient conditions for an event to happen. And you claim that the agency that "causes" this event is distributed throughout the constituents of the assemblage.[2] My point, however, is that *the web is not an entity*. That is to say, it is not a closed-in, self-contained object that is set over against other objects with which it may then be juxtaposed or conjoined. It is rather a bundle or tissue of strands, tightly drawn together here but trailing loose ends there, which tangle with other strands from other bundles. For the twigs or stems to which I attach these trailing ends are themselves but the visible tips of complex underground root systems. Every plant, too, is a living tissue of lines. And so, indeed, am I. It is as though my body were formed through knotting together threads of life that run out through my many legs into the web and thence to the wider environment. The world, for me, is not an assemblage of bits and pieces but a tangle of threads and pathways. Let us call it a *meshwork* (see Figure 7.3), so as to distinguish it from your *network*. My claim, then, is that action is not the result of an agency that is distributed around the network, but rather emerges from the interplay of forces that are conducted along the lines of the meshwork.'

As ANT and SPIDER are conversing on the forest floor – surrounded by what ANT (the network builder) perceives as an assortment of heterogeneous objects and what SPIDER (the web weaver) perceives as a tissue of interlaced threads – something else is going on in the air above their heads. A pair of butterflies are rapt in a courtly dance. 'Observe', says ANT, 'how in its fluttering, each butterfly responds to the movements of the other. We might even call it a "dance of agency".[3] Clearly, the butterflies are interacting in the air, just as we act-ants interact on the ground in the acrobatics of our collaboration.'

'But have you', asks SPIDER, 'given any thought to the air itself? The butterfly's flight is made possible thanks to air currents and vortices partly set up by the movement of its wings. Similarly, the fish in the river is able to swim, sometimes at remarkable speed, because of the way it creates eddies and vortices in the water through the swishing of its tail and fins.[4] But what sense would it make to say that the air, in the first case, is a participant in the network, with which the butterflies dance as they do with one another; or, in the second case, that the fish dances with water as it might with other fish in the shoal? Indeed it would make no sense at all. Air and water are not entities that act. They are material media in which living things are immersed, and are experienced by way of their currents, forces and pressure gradients. True, it is not the butterfly alone that flies but butterfly-in-air, and not the fish alone that swims but fish-in-water. But that no more makes the butterfly a fly–air

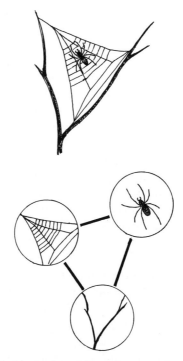

FIGURE 7.3 The meshwork (spider/web/twig) and the network of relations between spider, web and twig

hybrid than it makes the fish a fish–water hybrid. It is simply to recognise that for things to interact they must be immersed in a kind of force field set up by the currents of the media that surround them. Cut out from these currents – that is, reduced to objects – they would be *dead*. Having deadened the meshwork by cutting its lines of force, thus breaking it into a thousand pieces, you cannot pretend to bring it back to life by sprinkling a magical dust of "agency" around the fragments.[5] If it is to live, then the butterfly must be returned to the air and the fish to the water.

'And I', SPIDER goes on, 'must return to my web. For I have to say that what air is for the butterfly and water is for the fish, my web is for me. I cannot fly or swim, but I can weave a web and exploit its properties of stickiness, tensile strength and so on to run around and catch flies. I may dance the tarantella with the fly that alights on my web, but the web itself is not a dancing partner. It is not an object that I interact with, but the ground upon which the possibility of interaction is based. The web, in short, is the very condition of my agency. But it is not, in itself, an agent.'

'That, if I may say so', interjects ANT, 'is a very arachnocentric viewpoint. Presumably, by your same argument, if you were a fly you could also claim to be an agent and, if you were an ant like me, you could claim to be an agent too. How many legs, I wonder, do you need to qualify as an agent: six, eight, a hundred? Our mutual acquaintance the centipede would indeed do very well. With so many legs he must be a truly powerful agent.'

'You jest of course, my dear ANT', responds SPIDER. 'Nevertheless to your question – how many legs do you need to be an agent? – I would answer: at least four! For although I would be prepared to admit to the agency of our four-footed friends, the rat and the mouse, I would draw the line at bipedal humans. You may be an agent from your formicoid perspective, and I from my arachnid one, but from the perspective by which humans distinguish themselves from all other creatures, it is impossible to see how they could exercise any agency at all. On one occasion I dangled inconspicuously from the ceiling of one of their so-called "classrooms", and overheard a human philosopher lecturing to others of his number.

> "I am a human subject", the man intoned. "*I know, therefore I am.* I know, and am, because I have a mind. That is what makes me human. And it is this, too, that enables me to act. Of course I have a body too, like every other creature. The spider has a body; so does the ant. But the spider and the ant are all body; there is no more to them than that. Though we may observe their behaviour, they cannot act. But *I* am not my body. I am a body *plus*.[6] It is by the measure that I am *more* than my body that my humanity – along with the scope of my action – is defined."

'"Well", thought I silently to myself, as I swung from the end of my thread, "if that's where you imagine the essence of your humanity lies, then it is certainly not to be found in what you humans do. What you have been talking about is intelligence, a cognitive capacity to work things out in advance, in the head, prior to their implementation in the world. But *intelligence* is one thing, *agency* quite another. It is a serious mistake to confuse the two". And I remembered the story of the apocryphal centipede who, when asked how he managed to coordinate the movements of his hundred legs, found himself paralysed and starved to death. So long as he had acted unthinkingly, leaving his legs to look after themselves, there had been no problem. But as soon as he stopped to think intelligently about what he did, he could no longer act. His agency was thwarted. More generally, a creature that could do nothing that had not been fully thought out in advance could never, in practice, do anything at all.'

'We all know about the arrogance and stupidity of humans', laughs ANT in response, 'especially the philosophers among them who have nothing else to do in life than to think. If we could only reduce them in scale and put them to work in one of our nests, they would learn a thing or two! They would soon discover, as I have explained already, that agency is not exclusive either to ants or to non-ants but is distributed throughout the network formed by their collaboration. We need, in short, to establish a principle of symmetry, by which neither side of the ant/non-ant dichotomy is privileged over the other.'

'I do not want to accord a special privilege to ants or to spiders', responds SPIDER, 'let alone to human beings. Yet I cannot accept your principle of symmetry. The problem lies in your blanket category of the "non-ant", which includes everything from grains of sand and dead leaf matter to aphids and butterflies – and even humans! Our concept of agency must make allowance for the real complexity of living organisms, as opposed to inert matter. It is simply absurd to place a grain of sand and an aphid on the scales of a balance and to claim that they are equivalent. They may weigh the same amount, but in terms of complexity they are poles apart. The key difference is that the aphid, animal that it is, has a nervous system – just as you and I do. When I crouch at the centre of my web, I am all a-quiver, just like the leaf of a tree in the summer breeze. I am sensitive to the slightest movement or vibration. What makes the difference between me and the leaf, however, is that every movement I make is also a movement of my *attention*. It is the attentiveness of this movement that qualifies it as an instance of *action* and, by the same token, qualifies me as an *agent*. To put it another way, the essence of action lies not in aforethought (as our human philosopher would claim) but in the close coupling of bodily movement and perception. But that is also to say that all action is, to varying degrees, *skilled*. The skilled practitioner is one who can continually attune his or her movements to perturbations in the perceived environment without ever interrupting the flow of action. But such skill does not come ready-made. Rather, it *develops*, as part and parcel of the organism's own growth and development in an environment. Since agency calls for skill, and since skill arises through development, it follows that the process of development is a *sine qua non* for the exercise of agency. To attribute agency to objects that do not grow or develop, that consequently embody no skill, and whose movement is not therefore coupled to their perception, is ludicrous.'

Listening to this, ANT remains unimpressed. 'Well, you would say that, wouldn't you?' he remarked caustically. 'You are SPIDER, and you stand for the proposition that *S*killed *P*ractice *I*nvolves *D*evelopmentally *E*mbodied *R*esponsiveness. I appreciate your views; they are indeed worth their weight IN GOLD (which is very little, I might add, since you are such a lightweight creature). But I am ANT. I stand for *A*ctor-*N*etwork *T*heory. Not for nothing am I known as THE TOWER among arthropods.[7] For my philosophy towers over yours.'

'You are indeed a master of lofty thoughts', admits SPIDER wearily. 'But I cannot, for the most part, understand a word of what you say.' And with that, she scuttles off.

PART III

Earth and sky

We are, these days, increasingly bombarded with information about what is known as 'the environment'. Seated in our homes, in classrooms or in conference theatres, this environment is flashed before our eyes in images of landscapes, wildlife and peoples from around the globe, often to the accompaniment of facts and figures assembled to deliver a compelling message of change. Indeed, so accustomed are we to viewing images of this kind that we are, I think, inclined to forget that the environment is, in the first place, a world we live in, and not a world we look at. We *inhabit* our environment: we are part of it; and through this practice of habitation it becomes part of us too. We see with eyes trained by our experience of watching what is going on around us, hear with ears tuned by the sounds that matter to us, and touch with bodies that have become accustomed, by the lives we lead, to certain kinds of movement. Smells, too, excite memories and anticipations. This inhabited world – the world of our perception – includes the earth beneath our feet, the sky arching above our heads, the air we breathe, not to mention the profusion of vegetation, powered by the light of the sun, and all the animals that depend on it, busily absorbed in their own lives as are we in ours. To remind yourself of this, I would like you to take a walk outside, in the open air. For so long as you are sitting indoors, as you probably are while you read these lines, the world of earth and sky is one you can only imagine. It is, moreover, such a fragile imagining that it is all too readily crushed by the high-powered impact of a global science more intent on establishing the authority of its own particular view of the environment, and of what human beings are doing to it, than on enhancing our own awareness or powers of observation.

What this science is telling us in conference rooms around the world – furnished with exactly the same equipment of projection, with blinds drawn to cut out the light, and populated by globetrotting international experts – is that if you thought the environment was as you found it when you took your stroll out of doors, you were wrong, or at least childishly naive. You were as wrong as were some of the young participants in a recent study conducted by researchers in developmental psychology, on which I report in Chapter 8. The researchers wanted to know how children acquire their knowledge of the shape of the earth. Many of the children recruited for the study, when asked to depict the earth, drew it as a roughly level ground with people and buildings standing on it. And when asked to depict the sky, they described it as a region above the earth, with a shining sun and floating clouds. Others, however, depicted the earth in the form of a circle, adding some stick figures around the circumference. These latter children, according to the experimenters, had got it right. They had acquired what was supposed to be the scientifically correct view, which is that contrary to intuition, people actually live *all around on the outside* of a spherical earth. But when the experimenters then requested that the children add the sky to their pictures, they were flummoxed. 'You mean space', one queried. It was not of course the children who were confused. They understood perfectly well that it is one thing to comprehend the environment from the point of view of an inhabitant, and quite another to adopt an imaginary viewpoint that could only be obtained from outer space.

From the former perspective, the environment might indeed be conceived as the world around us, extending from where we are to the horizon, with the earth below and the sky above. But from the latter perspective, the relation between people and the world seems to be turned inside out. When scientists speak of the 'global environment', they have in mind a world that we humans have ourselves surrounded. Expelled to its outer surface, we have become exhabitants rather than inhabitants. Indeed this global environment is not one to which you or I or anyone else can relate. It is too big. I can relate to the model globe that usually stands on a shelf in my house. Along with the books, family photos and potted plants placed beside it, this globe is a familiar item of my environment. But I cannot relate to the globe *as* an environment. Whereas the globe is measured and recorded, the environment is experienced. One has climate, the other has weather. One has its atmosphere, the other includes the sky. And it is on this environment of earth and sky that I focus in Chapter 9. To inhabit the earth–sky world, I argue, is to live life in the open. Yet philosophical attempts to characterise the open lead to paradox. Do we follow Martin Heidegger in treating the open as an enclosed space cleared from within, or Immanuel Kant (and, following his lead, mainstream science) in placing the open all around on the outside? One possible solution is offered by James Gibson in his ecological approach to perception. The Gibsonian perceiver is supported on the ground, with the sky above and the earth below. In this view, however, the world is habitable only to the extent that it is furnished with objects. These objects, for Gibson, are laid out upon the ground like models on a baseboard, or scenery on a stage. Yet in such a world, how could anything live or breathe?

There could be no terrestrial life were it not for the processes of respiration, by which living organisms bind air with rainwater and nutrients drawn from the soil, in the presence of sunlight, in forging their own growth and movement. Crucially, these processes continually disrupt any interface between earth and sky. Thus to inhabit the open is not to be stranded on the outer surface of the earth but to be caught up in the substantial flows and aerial fluxes of what I call the *weather-world*. While much has been written on how we see the landscape, there is virtually no literature on the relation between visual perception and the weather. Chapter 10 is an attempt to take the study of vision out of doors. I argue that weather enters visual awareness not as a scenic panorama but as an experience of *light*. Rather than placing sight and light on opposite sides of a boundary between the mind and the physical world, I follow Maurice Merleau-Ponty in claiming that light is fundamentally an experience of being *in* the world that is ontologically prior to the sight of things. Though we do not see light, we do see *in* light. Since weather, as a phenomenon of the medium, is an experience of light, to see in the light is to see in the weather. In the canons of modern thought, however, the surfaces of the landscape are identified with the limits of materiality. This, in turn, renders immaterial the medium through which persons and organisms move in perception and action. Thus while the landscape appears to be real, the weather can only be imagined. Overturning this ontology, I show that in the perception of the weather-world, earth and sky are not opposed as real to immaterial, but inextricably linked within one indivisible field.

Clearly, light is essential to organic growth; there would be no life without it. But it is also essential to vision: we could not see without it. Yet the experience of light has been marginalised by parallel reductions on the sides of both bioscience and visual studies. Where does the discourse of contemporary bioscience find the key to life? Not in the photosynthetic reactions that bind earth, air and water in the light, but secreted away in the nucleus of the cell, in the DNA of the genome. On its own, of course, the DNA molecule is remarkably inert, which is precisely why it has proved such a powerful tool of forensic analysis. Only in the biochemical environment of multicellular organisms, themselves enmeshed in exchanges of substance along the lines of flow comprising the wider environment, do molecules of DNA have the effects they do. What logic, then, leads scientists – or perhaps more accurately, those who speak for science – to attribute life to the agency of genes? It is of course the logic of inversion, which we have already encountered in the second part of this book. The life of the organism, having been read into its genes, is recast by this logic as the outward, phenotypic expression of an inner design, the genotype. Exactly the same inversion, however, is at work in studies of visual culture, where the image has been made to do the same work as the genome in bioscience: just as the genome codifies the process of life so that it can be 'played back' to science, so the image captures the process of vision and renders it back to the analyst. Where the bioscientist looks to recover life from the genome, the visual analyst seeks to recover vision from the image.

The visual, in brief, is shorthand for *vision relayed in the visible*. That is to say, it is produced through an operation of playback, by which we are allowed to see and to interpret our own visual experience only as this experience is encoded in objects of sight. It is precisely this logic that underwrites the notion of landscape as a primarily visual phenomenon. In Chapter 11, which is really just a postscript to the tenth chapter, I apply the same argument in a critique of the concept of soundscape. Just as the idea of the visual rests on the playback functions of images, so, I argue, does the idea of the aural rest on the playback functions of recordings. As the visual is to light, and the aural to sound, so the landscape is to the weather-world. To regain the currents of life, and of sensory awareness, we need to join in the movements that give rise to things rather than casting our attention back upon their objective and objectified forms. We need, in a word, to undo the operation of inversion, abandoning the fixities of genes, images, recordings and landscapes for the generative movements, respectively, of life, light, sound and weather.

8

THE SHAPE OF THE EARTH

Round, not flat

As every educated grown-up knows, the earth is round and not flat. Though much remains contentious in physics and astronomy, the truth of this proposition appears beyond dispute. Yet it took centuries of painstaking observation, measurement, calculation and deduction to establish what most of us now take for granted. The idea that the earth is spherical in form is generally credited to Pythagoras and his school, in the sixth century BC, though it was the mystical perfection of the form rather than any empirical evidence that led them to it. Two centuries later, in his *On the Heavens* (350 BC), Aristotle marshalled a series of physical arguments to prove why the earth must be round, and adduced as evidence both the curved shadow cast by the earth during a lunar eclipse and the changing inclination of the stars to the horizon as one travels northwards or southwards. It was left to Ptolemy of Alexandria, in the second century AD, to establish the earth's place within the system of known planets, and to Copernicus in the sixteenth century – building on the work of Islamic astronomers such as the ninth-century Al Balkhi and the eleventh-century Al Biruni – to recognise that far from being the immoveable centre around which all else turns, it is in truth the earth itself that revolves around the sun. Today this heliocentric model, updated in the light of more recent discoveries, is impressed on every schoolchild through the cosmic maps and charts that adorn the walls of classrooms.

It is one thing to be familiar with a model, however; quite another for this model to be so internalised as to structure one's very thinking about the world. There is no reason to suppose that children are born with the knowledge that the earth is round, let alone that it revolves around the sun. If this is something that every adult knows, then it must somehow be learned. Just how children learn the shape of the earth is, however, a matter of some controversy in cognitive and developmental psychology. A number of studies suggest that a correct understanding of the earth, as a solid sphere surrounded by space, challenges fundamental presuppositions that children everywhere, regardless of cultural background, initially bring to their reasoning. These presuppositions are, first, that the ground is flat, and, secondly, that unless supported, things fall. To grasp such a counter-intuitive understanding that the earth is round like a ball and that people can live anywhere without falling off calls, it is argued, for nothing less than a complete conceptual restructuring of the child's mind, comparable to a paradigm shift in the history of science. What took centuries for our predecessors, as flat-earth gave way to round-earth thinking, and as geocentrism gave way to heliocentrism, has to be recapitulated by every child in the space of a few short years. How does this come about?

Experimenting with schoolchildren aged between six and eleven years, from the State of Illinois, psychologists Stella Vosniadou and William F. Brewer claim to have identified a developmental sequence in thinking about the earth, running from an initial mental model of an earth that is flat like a pancake[1] to a final model of a spherical earth, by way of various intermediate models in which children attempt to synthesise their initial presuppositions with information supplied by their teachers, or gleaned from books, charts or other sources (Vosniadou and Brewer 1992; Vosniadou 1994; see Figure 8.1). One such model is what they call 'hollow sphere'; another is 'dual earth'. Each looks like a peculiar hybrid of flat-earth and round-earth thinking. I shall begin by describing these models, and the kinds of reasoning in which the children alleged to hold them engage. My ultimate aim in doing so, however, is to show that their hybrid character, and the internal contradictions to which it gives rise, is not a symptom of their transitional status between

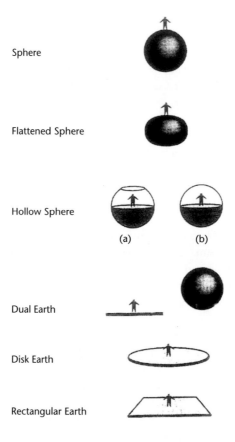

Sphere

Flattened Sphere

Hollow Sphere

(a)   (b)

Dual Earth

Disk Earth

Rectangular Earth

FIGURE 8.1 Mental models of the earth. Reproduced from Vosniadou and Brewer (1992: 549). Reprinted by permission of Elsevier.

the naive intuition that the earth is flat and the informed knowledge that it is really a sphere. It is rather indicative of a more fundamental existential dilemma, as pressing for adults as it is for children, and indeed for philosophers as it is for laypersons, that arises when access to what passes for certain knowledge – in this case of the shape of the earth – is predicated upon the renunciation of the very experience, of *inhabiting* the earth, that makes such knowledge possible.

Mental models of the earth

In their experiment, Vosniadou and Brewer (1992: 543–545) presented each of the children interviewed with a series of questions. These questions were deliberately open-ended, requiring the child to work out a response by drawing on whatever conceptual resources they could muster, rather than simply to choose between ready-made options. The experimenters began by asking 'What is the shape of the earth?' To this, most answered 'round' or 'like a ball'. They then asked which way you would look to see the earth, and what is above, below and to the sides of it. At this point, the child was instructed to draw a picture of the earth and to indicate on the picture where the moon and stars would go. Having done that, the child was told to draw in the sky and to show on the drawing where people live. To respondents who had begun by claiming that the earth was round, and had drawn it as a rough circle, the experimenters then revealed a picture of a house on an apparently flat landscape. A dialogue of the following kind would then ensue:

> *Experimenter:* The house is on the earth, isn't it?
> *Child:* Yes, the house is on the earth.
> *Experimenter:* How come here the earth is flat but before you made it round?

The child was then asked where they would end up if they walked for many days in a straight line. If they answered 'somewhere else', 'in another country' or 'on the coast', they were told to keep on going, in the mind's eye, helped along if necessary by cars, trains and boats. Would they eventually reach the ends of the earth, or would they find themselves back where they started? And if they were to reach the ends of the earth, would they be at risk of falling off? 'Now tell me', pressed the experimenters, in reference to the drawing, 'what is down here below the earth?'

Seven-year-old Mathew accepted that if you just kept walking and walking, and had a never-ending supply of provisions, you might reach the end of the earth, but that there would be no danger of falling off. 'If we were outside the earth', he explained, 'we could probably fall off, but if we were inside the earth we couldn't fall off' (ibid.: 548). Mathew's logic, according to Vosniadou and Brewer, is precisely what is to be expected from a 'hollow sphere' model of the earth. The children alleged to reason in terms of this model were in no doubt that the earth is spherical in form, but most envisaged the sphere as comprising two hemispheres, solid below and hollow above, with people living on the flat interface between the two (ibid.: 549–550). Ten-year-old Venica, for example, insisted that the real shape of the earth is 'round like a ball'; however, it looks flat to its inhabitants because they live 'inside the ball … in the middle of it' (ibid.: 563–564). Like Mathew, Venica was convinced that there was no danger for the inhabitant of falling off the edge of the earth; interestingly, however, she also observed that to perceive the earth as the sphere it really is one would have to be in a spaceship. Since spaceships are seen from an earthbound perspective to rise into the heavens, she concluded that the edge or circumference of the earth is perceptible 'only if you go up'.

High in her spaceship, Venica would look *down* to see the earth as a ball. Other children, however, said that to see the earth one would definitely have to look *up*. These children maintained that the earth is not only round, but also completely solid. They would draw the earth as a circle. But when asked to show on their drawings where people live, far from locating their figures inside the circle or around its circumference, they would either place them on a horizontal line drawn beneath their depiction of the earth-ball or use the lower edge of the paper itself as a baseline, and place their figures on the border. At first, the experimenters were perplexed by this, as the following exchange with nine-year-old Darcy reveals. In response to initial requests, Darcy has drawn a round earth, and has added the moon and some stars. When the experimenter asks where people live, Darcy draws a house whose base lies along the lower border of the paper. The experimenter asks again, and Darcy draws another house. On the third request, Darcy eventually gives in to the experimenter's implicit demands, rubs out one of her houses, and draws a stick figure upon her round earth (Figure 8.2b). This, however, only sparks off a further round of interrogation. 'This house is on the earth isn't it?' says the experimenter, pointing to the sketch of the house that remains after the other was erased. 'How come the earth here is flat but before you made it round?' The following dialogue ensues:

> *Darcy:* I don't know.
> *Experimenter:* Is the earth really round?
> *Darcy:* No.
> *Experimenter:* It's not really round. Well, what shape is it?
> *Darcy:* Yaa, it's round.
> *Experimenter:* Then how come it looks flat here?
> *Darcy:* Because it's on the ground.
> *Experimenter:* But why does that make it look flat?
> *Darcy:* Because the ground's flat.
> *Experimenter:* But the shape of the earth is…
> *Darcy:* Round.
>
> (ibid.: 570)

To the experimenter it seemed that Darcy was being wilfully inconsistent, wavering between conceptions of the earth's surface as round and flat. But it was in fact the experimenter who had thrown the whole exercise into confusion by insisting on using the word 'earth' for what Darcy clearly and consistently distinguished as the ground. Faced with this confusion, Darcy does not at first know how to respond. Then she admits that if the earth is understood in the specific sense in which the experimenter had just used the term, that is to denote the ground, then of course it is not round. Appearing to contradict herself, however, she actually regains her footing, reasserting that the earth is indeed round, by contrast to the flat ground. On her own terms she is, indeed, being thoroughly consistent. Along with other children who responded along similar lines, Darcy's reasoning appears to be structured by what Vosniadou and Brewer call a 'dual earth model'. According to this model there are two earths, 'a round one which is up in the sky and a flat one where people live' (ibid.: 550). Adherents of this model, like Darcy, generally use the word 'earth' only for

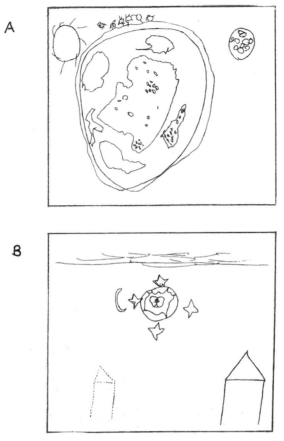

FIGURE 8.2   (a) Ethan's drawing of the spherical earth surrounded by the 'sky'; (b) Darcy's drawing of the sky, the ground (with houses) and the spherical earth. Reproduced from Vosniadou and Brewer (1992: 558). Reprinted by permission of Elsevier.

the former and 'ground' for the latter. Thus whereas adherents of the hollow earth reconcile their experience of living on the flat with their knowledge that the earth is round by putting the one inside the other, dual earthers keep the two strictly separate.

It was not only by mixing up earth and ground that the experimenters confused their research subjects. Another layer of confusion was introduced in their request to the children to add the sky to their drawings of the earth, moon and stars. Even adults, as Vosniadou and Brewer admit (ibid.: 544), might find the idea of drawing the sky a little strange, and it is not obvious how one should go about it. For hollow earthers who identify the sky with the dome-like canopy of the earth's upper hemisphere, it is hard to see how the sky can be added to a drawing that already depicts the spherical earth. Since the moon and stars are in the sky, hollow earthers could just as well place them within the circumference of the earth as around on the outside. Dual earthers were equally puzzled. When Darcy, for example, drew her round earth, she logically placed the moon and the stars around it on the outside, since this earth was supposed to be solid. Asked to add the sky to the picture, however, Darcy was confounded. 'It's icky', she says (ibid.: 570). Draw the sky she must, however, and she does so by sketching some roughly horizontal lines, looking much like a cloud base, near the top of the paper, above her drawing of the earth, moon and stars. This sky, however, is positioned not in relation to her drawing of the earth, but in relation to the ground that is supposed to coincide with the lower edge of the paper, and on which she drew her houses.

The absurdity of asking children to add the sky to a drawing of the round earth is most starkly revealed in the case of those children who appeared to have fully grasped the 'scientifically correct' model of the earth as a sphere, and to have laid their naive intuitions to rest. One such was six-year-old Ethan. In response to the experimenter's questions, Ethan has already explained that the earth is round like a ball, that to see it one has to look downwards, and that above, below and all around it is just space. To the question about walking on and on in a straight line, he will confidently go on to respond that you would end up where you started. There is no end to the earth, he will say, and wherever you are on its surface, gravity pulls you down. The precocious Ethan, it seems, ticks all the scientific boxes. But at the point in the interview when the experimenter asks him to add the sky to his picture of the earth, even he is momentarily stuck. How can you add the sky to a picture of the earth in space? From the vantage of space there is no sky (Berleant 2010: 138). Scientifically speaking, what surrounds the earth is its atmosphere, understood as a gaseous envelope that peters out with increasing distance from the earth's surface. We do not know whether Ethan had any knowledge of the atmosphere in the strict scientific sense,[2] but, even if he did, this was not what he was asked to draw. He was asked to draw the sky. And the sky no more belongs within a picture of the earth as a solid sphere than does the ground on which people live. To see the sky, you have to be on the ground. Like the ground, the sky pertains to the phenomenal rather than the physical order of reality.

In the event, Ethan duly obliged the experimenter, delivering what was taken to be the 'correct' response by drawing a ring around his earth-circle, but not without first having challenged her with the withering rebuke: 'The sky has no shape, you mean space' (Vosniadou and Brewer 1992: 557; see Figure 8.2a). Whatever the experimenter might have taken his outer ring to mean, so far as Ethan was concerned it was not the sky. Rather, his circumferential gesture, and the trace it left, was his way of saying that the earth is surrounded by space. Darcy, for her part, realised – as the experimenter apparently did not – that the sky can only be described within a picture of the earth conceived as the ground of human habitation, and that in relation to such habitation, it can only be 'on top'. Revealing, too, was the fact that of those children credited with a spherical model of the earth, a substantial proportion confounded expectations by insisting that to see the earth one must look up, not down. Vosniadou and Brewer attempt to account for this anomaly by suggesting that children may use the phrase 'look up' in ways their teachers do, when they tell their pupils to look up to a chart on the classroom wall or to look something up in a book (ibid.: 555). This explanation could hardly be less convincing. As Ethan himself pointed out, with his characteristic erudition, the reason why the earth looks flat to those who live on it is because they are so close to the ground, and the earth itself is so big, that they are unaware of its curvature (ibid.: 557). So while the terrestrial earth may literally be beneath one's feet, its spherical form can only be revealed through its projection as a heavenly body, and to see the heavens one must look up.

This, of course, is precisely what happens in a lunar eclipse. The astronomer, supported on level ground, looks up and sees the shadow of the spherical earth silhouetted against the moon. Recall that no less a figure than Aristotle appealed to the eclipse, as proving beyond doubt that the earth is round. Had Aristotle been a subject of the Vosniadou and Brewer experiment, he might well have come out as a dual earther. Is the dualism of the dual earth, then, a stage to be overcome in the transition from childish naivety to mature knowledge, or intrinsic to the project of scientific thought itself? This is a question to which I shall return. In the meantime, I want to turn to an alternative set of experiments that lead to very different conclusions about how children – and indeed adults – learn the shape of the earth.

Mental models or methodological artefacts?

Interpreting children's drawings is notoriously tricky. Both the technical constraints of working with pencil on paper and the orientational biases that come from using rectangular sheets with top, bottom and sides can strongly influence the ways a drawing is composed. How, for example, do you render, by means of a continuous line, a three-dimensional body like a sphere that has no lines at all? Most children drew what they took to be an earth-ball by drawing a rough circle. Asked to draw the people, even those credited with a 'spherical' model tended to draw them inside the sphere rather than all around the circumference, on the outside. To have drawn them on the outside, Vosniadou and Brewer admit (ibid.: 556), would have been difficult, particularly as it would have meant drawing some of them on their side, or upside down, relative to the axes of the paper. But it is not obvious, from a drawing of a circle with figures inside, whether the child imagines the people to be inside the earth or stuck to its outer surface. Some children may have simply found it easier to draw figures upright on a horizontal baseline, with results that make it look as though they hold to a model of a hollow or dual earth. It is moreover doubtful whether the drawings of younger children, who have yet to be introduced to adult pictorial conventions, can be taken as representations of what they consider to be the real world. Thus the ring that Ethan drew around his earth did not represent the sky, or even space. It was simply the trace left by a gestural movement through which he performed his understanding that space is all around the earth.

It is also difficult to be sure to what extent the answers the children came up with, under interrogation, reflect their own processes of independent reasoning. They could just as well have been improvised in order to satisfy their expectations of what the experimenter wanted. From the children's point of view, as we have seen, the experimenters were manifestly inconsistent, for example in using the word 'earth' to refer at one moment to the planet, and at another to the ground, forcing ostensibly contradictory responses. Yet it may well be that the children felt under some pressure, in the experimental situation, to be consistent in their answers. It could be, too, that having produced their drawings as instructed, their responses to subsequent questioning were more about justifying the drawings than justifying the models that are alleged to have given rise to them. For all these reasons, the results of Vosniadou and Brewer's experiment cannot necessarily be taken at face value. An alternative experimental procedure, which would get around the problems raised by asking children to draw things and subjecting them to open-ended questioning, would be to ask them to choose between, or to rank in order of veracity, a series of ready-depicted options. Just such a procedure was adopted in a more recent study by Gavin Nobes, Alan E. Martin and Georgia Panagiotaki (2005), and it led to quite contrary results.

In this study the experimenters prepared a set of picture cards, each of which showed the earth, people and sky in one of sixteen possible combinations of the following alternatives:

earth a solid sphere, flattened sphere, hollow sphere or disk; people all around or only on top; sky all around or only on top (Figure 8.3). Participants, who included both children (aged five to ten) and adults, were individually asked first to select the card they thought looked most like the real earth and then to repeat the procedure with all the others so as to yield a ranking from 'most' to 'least like the Earth' (Nobes et al. 2005: 52–54). Some two thirds of the participants in the study selected the combination of solid sphere with both people and sky all around. On the card depicting this combination, the earth figures as a greeny-brown ball, with rigid, lego-like people standing around its circumference and set against a light blue background flecked with fluffy white patches resembling clouds. The selection of this card by the majority of participants, according to Nobes and his collaborators, 'indicated a scientific understanding of the Earth' (ibid.: 55–57). The picture is, however, strangely paradoxical. On the one hand, it depicts people distributed around the outer surface of a solidly spherical earth, but on the other hand, it depicts the sky in a form that would only be apparent to someone lying on their back on the earth's surface, gazing upwards!

Had any child in the Vosniadou and Brewer study produced a picture like this, they would undoubtedly have been credited with a dual earth model. For only a dual earther could stand or lie on the ground, looking up at the sky, and see there not just the clouds but another earth with its inhabitants all around on the surface. Yet not only do Nobes and his colleagues identify this picture card with a correct scientific understanding, it also seems to have caused no particular problem or cognitive dissonance for those participants who selected it. Most likely they treated the sky design as a kind of wallpaper, characterised by shapes and colours drawn from everyday experience, upon which is mounted a quite separate image of the earth, modelled perhaps on the familiar classroom globe. In other words, in this card we have not just one picture but two, the first of which (the earth-ball) is superimposed upon the background of the second (the sky). Might not the same, then, be said of the drawings that, in the Vosniadou and Brewer study, were supposed to have indicated the presence of hollow earth or dual earth models in the minds of the children who drew them? They, too, could be composite pictures. What if Darcy, for example, in response to the experimenter's shifting notions of the earth, has drawn, on the same sheet of paper, one picture of the earth, moon and stars, and then another of the ground (with houses) and sky (Figure 8.2b)? What reason would we then have to doubt Darcy's comprehension of the true shape of the earth?

FIGURE 8.3 Examples of the picture cards used in the experiment by Nobes, Martin and Panagiotaki: flat earth with people around and sky on top; hollow earth with people supported and sky inside; spherical earth with people and sky around. Reproduced from Nobes et al. (2005: 54). Reprinted with permission from the *British Journal of Developmental Psychology* © The British Psychological Society.

In a more recent study, Nobes and Panagiotaki (2007) have gone on to address precisely these questions. They did so by applying a similar experimental protocol to that used by Vosniadou and Brewer with children, to a sample of adults: 350 college and university students from East London ranging in age from 17 to 69. The students were instructed to draw the earth, to draw where the sky and clouds go, and to draw some people to show where they lived. Then they were asked about the shape of the earth, where the sky is, where people live, where they would end up if they walked for days in a straight line, whether the earth ends anywhere and what lies beneath it (ibid.: 650). The drawing tasks in this experiment threw up all the main kinds of pictures identified in the Vosniadou and Brewer study, including hollow earth and dual earth varieties. In written comments on their experience, respondents spelled out explicitly many of the problems that must have been faced by the children tested by Vosniadou and Brewer. One complained, for example, that when instructed to draw the earth, he did not know whether this meant earth the planet, or just the ground. 'If you draw the earth', observed this respondent, 'you can't draw the sky or the people' (ibid.: 654). And vice versa, of course: if you draw the sky and the people, you cannot draw the earth – for reasons of both scale and perspective. He solved the problem by drawing two pictures – one of the planet, the other of people on the ground with the sky above – conspicuously separating the two pictures with the word 'or' (Figure 8.4a). Another respondent drew three separate pictures: of the planetary earth, of a little house on the ground beneath the sky (with clouds), and of the same house on a much larger scale showing the people inside (ibid.: 652; Figure 8.4b).

If the meaning of 'earth' was ambiguous, the meaning of 'sky' was still more so. These adult respondents were familiar with the scientific concept of the atmosphere, but they were not sure whether, when asked to draw the sky, they were supposed to draw the atmosphere, as it surrounds the planet, or the sky and clouds that we ordinarily see above our heads. 'I have never really thought about where the sky and the clouds are in relation to the whole world', mused one respondent, 'the sky and clouds are always above.' Another asked: 'Sky meaning what we see – blue above + clouds – or sky everywhere – e.g. outer space surrounding

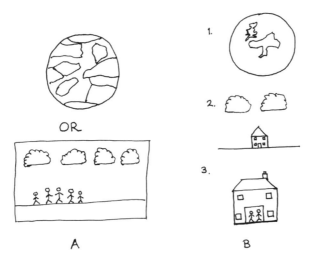

FIGURE 8.4 Adults' drawings of the earth (examples redrawn after Nobes and Panagiotaki 2007: 652). (a): two pictures with 'or'; (b) three pictures.

Earth?' (ibid.: 656). If the sky is the atmosphere, some reasoned, and if the atmosphere is an integral part of planet earth, then perhaps the sky should be inside the earth rather than outside of it. And by the same token, so should the people. Many respondents accordingly rejected the 'scientifically correct' view that people live all around on the outside of the earth. Outside, they argued, is space, and you cannot live in space. To live, there must be ground to walk on and air to breathe. Thus, people must live inside the earth (ibid.: 657). But perhaps the most perplexing question of all was the last: what is below the earth? The 'correct' scientific answer should have been either 'sky' or 'space'. Yet a little reflection shows the question to be absurd. 'Above' and 'below' can only be established in relation to a base or ground. So what is below the ground? Earth! As one respondent commented, in conclusion, 'these questions are not easy for adults to answer. For young people this would be difficult, confusing and probably quite upsetting for many!' (ibid.: 658).

To clinch their argument, that depictions deviating from the 'scientifically correct' ideal tell us more about ambiguities in the questions asked than about the mental models of respondents, Nobes and Panagiotaki have carried out one further study, again with university students from East London of all ages (Nobes and Panagiotaki 2009). In this they reformulated the original questions so as to make it absolutely plain that by 'the earth' is meant our planet, and not the ground underfoot. 'Imagine you are an astronaut in space', the new instruction read. 'You look out of the window of your spaceship and you see the earth. Please draw a picture of the earth as you think you would see it from your spaceship' (ibid.: 353). The results were unequivocal. All dual earth and other multiple drawings were eliminated. Overall, the proportion of pictures classified as 'scientific' increased substantially, while the proportion of those that depicted the earth as it might be seen from the ground was markedly reduced. The problem with the Vosniadou and Brewer experiment, conclude Nobes and Panagiotaki, was that it prompted respondents to take first a panoptic, global perspective and then a grounded, local one, and proceeded to attribute the consequences of this perspectival double take, in fact built into the experimental design, to structures of reasoning in the minds of the children interviewed. Thus the dual earth drawings, far from depicting two earths – a round one up in sky and a flat one where people live – in fact depict the *same* earth from two different perspectives (ibid.: 359). So too do the hollow earth drawings, which differ only in that the order of enframing is reversed. In dual earth drawings a picture of the round earth is framed within one of the ground and the sky; in hollow earth drawings a picture of the ground and sky is framed within one of the earth.

Vosniadou and her colleagues have yet to respond to this latest study by Nobes and Panagiotaki. They have, however, responded to the earlier experiment with the picture cards (Vosniadou et al. 2004). It comes as no surprise that they are unimpressed. Requiring respondents to choose among ready-depicted options, they note, tells us nothing about how they think. The majority who selected the 'scientifically correct' spherical earth, with people all around on the outside, may have done so because they had been told, by people in authority, that this is what the earth is like. This does not mean, however, that they have understood what they have been told, to the extent of being able to think through it to other domains of experience (ibid.: 206). Anyone can tell you that the earth is round, but how many can use this knowledge to explain, with the lucidity of an Ethan, why it appears flat to someone on the ground? If the studies by Nobes and Panagiotaki have proved anything, it is that this is as much of a puzzle for many adults as it is for many children, calling as it does for a sophisticated grasp of scale and proportion. But by doing everything possible to remove the ambiguities from the original questions, their latest study comes close to providing the answers in advance, absolving respondents of any need to think them through. How, after all, could you imagine yourself to be an astronaut in space, looking at the earth through the window of your spaceship, if you had not already been provided with the clues to deliver the 'correct' answer of what it would look like?

Behind this controversy lies a well rehearsed debate in psychology about whether knowledge acquisition is strongly constrained by internal mental structures or more fundamentally dependent on sociocultural contexts of learning. Ranged on one side are the so-called 'theory theorists'. Following in the footsteps of the great Swiss pioneer of developmental psychology, Jean Piaget, they imagine that inside every child is a miniature scientist. It is supposed that children, independently of one another, draw on native intuition, the evidence of direct observation and their developing powers of reason to build their own theories to explain the shape of the earth and why it appears to them in the way it does. On the other side are those, influenced more by Piaget's Russian contemporary, Lev Vygotsky, who compare every child to a novice apprentice. Setting out with open minds, children are said to acquire their knowledge piecemeal, in loosely connected fragments, through participation in a social and cultural environment scaffolded by knowledgeable adults such as teachers, but also by artefacts such as the ubiquitous globes of school classrooms. Since, according to this latter approach, there is no initial conceptual barrier to be overcome, and given adequate scaffolding, children have little difficulty in acquiring a 'scientific' picture of the earth. In the design of their respective experiments, both sides have chosen methods to suit their approaches. These methods build in, from the start, precisely what the experiments purport to show: on the one side, that to know the earth is round is to have a theory and to think in terms of it; on the other, that to know it is round is to be able to repeat what you have been told. It is no wonder that each side has accused the other of circularity (Vosniadou et al. 2004: 205; Nobes and Panagiotaki 2009: 349–350). This is perhaps the point, then, at which to leave our psychologists in the pit they have dug for themselves, and to cast a more philosophical eye on the question of the shape of the earth.

What is the earth anyway?

In what follows I would like to try an experiment of my own. It is certainly not one that would meet with the approval of psychologists, since it yields no data for analysis. My research subjects are not even alive, and cannot therefore be tested directly. But they have left rich testimony to their thinking in their writings. What would happen if we put some of the tasks that Vosniadou and Brewer, and subsequently Nobes and Panagiotaki, put to their research subjects – respectively children from Illinois and students from East London – to a cast of dead philosophers? Let us ask them: what is the shape of the earth, where is the sky, and where do people live? How would they reply? My cast, in order of appearance, includes Saint Augustine, Immanuel Kant, James Gibson and Martin Heidegger.

Let us first despatch our team of experimenters far into the past, to the turn of the fifth century AD, to interview Saint Augustine. They command him to describe the earth. He replies that the earth is the entirety of the visible world, of God's creation. It encompasses all that one can see. 'Tell us, then', press our experimenters, 'what can you see?' 'We see *heaven* and *earth*', responds Augustine, 'that is, the upper and lower parts of the material world. We see that space of air, likewise called heaven, through which the birds take their wandering flight. We see the plains of the sea; and the dry land, the mother of plants and trees. We see the great lights shining above, the sun sufficing to the day, moon and stars comforting the night. We see water spread around us and swarming with fish. We see the face of the earth diversified with land-animals. And we see man…' (1943: 108; XIII, xxxii).[3] The experimenters, however, scent a contradiction. 'You said that all we see is but earth, but now you say that the earth is only one part of this totality – the lower part – as distinct from the upper part of sky or heaven. Is the sky, then, above the earth or encompassed within it?' Augustine patiently explains that 'earth' can be understood in two senses, to each of which there corresponds a certain sense of 'heaven'. There is, on the one hand, the heaven that God created when he made 'heaven and earth'. This is a material heaven, the heaven we can see, in relation to which the earth – in Augustine's words – is 'the earth I tread, the earth of which is made the body I bear' (ibid.: 289; XII, ii). On the other hand, there is what Augustine calls the 'heaven of heaven', the abode of a transcendental intellect. To such an intellect, the material world is revealed in its entirety in one act, rather than piecemeal, one thing at a time, as it is to ordinary mortals destined to dwell within it and to draw together, in memory, the images to which their experiences give rise (ibid.: 219; X, viii; 294; XII, ix). 'Compared to that heaven of heaven', Augustine concludes, 'the heaven above our earth is but earth. Thus it is not absurd to call each of these two great bodies "earth" in comparison to that mysterious heaven which is the Lord's, and not for the children of men' (ibid.: 289; XII, ii).

Our experimenters might well come away from this encounter convinced that Saint Augustine is committed to a model of the hollow earth, placing man in the midst of a world comprising the solid earth below and the aerial heaven above, while yet conceiving of the earth, from a God's-eye perspective, as a totality comprising the two. Returning to their time machine, they fix its coordinates to the town of Königsberg, in Germany, towards the end of the eighteenth century. They are on their way to interview its most celebrated citizen, Immanuel Kant. Asked to describe the shape of the earth, Kant replies without hesitation that it is spherical. Yet, anticipating the experimenters' next question, he hastens to admit that to his senses, the earth appears to be flat (Kant 1933: 606). 'Then how do you know', ask the experimenters, 'that the earth is round?' Kant, who scarcely ever ventured beyond his home town, responds that from the evidence of his senses alone, he would have no way of knowing this. The spherical form of the earth, he points out, is not an *object* of geographical knowledge. It is rather an idea that the mind brings to experience, a priori, in order to establish the *possibility* of such knowledge. Supposing that he lacked this idea, then, positioned at a particular point on the earth's surface – such as his home of Königsberg – he would be able to acquire at most a knowledge of things lying within the circle of the horizon. He could further expand this knowledge by reading the reports of travellers relayed from other parts of the world. Indeed, Kant was an avid collector of such reports. But irrespective of the amount of information at his disposal, the one thing he could never know would be how much more there is still to be known. 'I would know', he explains, 'the limits of my actual knowledge of the earth at any given time, but not the limits of all possible geography' (ibid.: 606). In such a situation there could be no possibility of systematic knowledge, no way of fitting what is known so far within an overall conception of the whole.

But if, says Kant, 'I have got so far as to know that the earth is a sphere and its surface is spherical', then the situation is transformed. For, as the extent of the surface is finite and potentially calculable, he can estimate not only the limits of his present knowledge but also the limits of the entire, potentially knowable world. And if the knowable world is spherical, Kant argued, so likewise is the world of knowledge.

> Our reason is not like a plane indefinitely far extended, the limits of which we know in a general way only; but must rather be compared to a sphere, the radius of which can be determined from the curvature of the arc of its surface – that is to say, from the nature of synthetic *a priori* propositions – and whereby we can likewise specify with certainty its volume and its limits.
>
> (ibid.: 607–608)

Knowledge is thus arrayed upon the spherical surface of the mind, just as the objects of knowledge are arrayed upon the spherical surface of the earth. The global topology of the earth's surface here comes to stand for the fundamental idea, which the mind is said to contribute to experience, of the unity, completeness and continuity of nature. It is at this surface – conceived as an interface not just between the solid substance of the earth and its gaseous atmosphere but between matter and mind, and between sensation and cognition – that all knowledge is constituted (Richards 1974; Ingold 2000a: 212). The 'scientifically correct' view, that people live all around on the outside of a solidly spherical earth, has its source in this Kantian cosmology. As human reason takes the place of Augustine's 'heaven of heaven', the earth itself becomes external to man. People, according to this view, do not find themselves within a world of heaven and earth but on the outside of a material world-sphere that is already closed up. In the words of Kant himself, 'the world is the substratum and the stage on which the play of our skills proceeds' (1970: 257). Life is played out upon this stage. People do not then live *within* the world, but *upon* its outer surface. They are no longer inhabitants but exhabitants.

Taking their leave of Kant, our experimental team now makes an appointment with one of the leading but also most heterodox thinkers of twentieth-century psychology, namely James Gibson. Reacting against the Kantian agenda, by now well established in mainstream theories of perception and cognition, Gibson was anxious to restore the perceiver to a world that is 'all around' rather than 'out there', or in a word to the *environment* as distinct from the physical world. In relation to the environment, perceivers are inhabitants. Gibson positions the inhabitant not on the outer surface of a solid sphere but at the very core of what he calls 'an unbounded spherical field' (Gibson 1979: 66). This field comprises two hemispheres: of the sky above and of the earth below. At the interface between upper and lower hemispheres, and stretching out to the 'great circle' of the horizon, lies the ground upon which the inhabitant stands (ibid.: 162). The ground is a surface; indeed for terrestrial animals it is the most important of surfaces, since it provides their basic support (ibid.: 10, 33). But it is a surface *in* the world, not *of* it. With their feet planted in the ground and their lungs inhaling the air, inhabitants straddle a division not between the material world and the world of ideas, but between the more or less solid *substances* of the earth and the ambient, volatile *medium* in which they are immersed (ibid.: 16–22).

Indeed to our experimenters, Gibson's depiction of the environment immediately brings to mind the 'hollow earth' model that they had also found to underwrite the reasoning of Augustine. In order to ascertain whether this is indeed the case, they ask him to draw in outline the earth–sky world that he has described. But Gibson refuses. The very practice of outline drawing, he maintains, introduces a false notion of confinement (ibid.: 66). It leads us to imagine that earth and sky are enclosed within a shell. But for Gibson, the 'spherical field' of the inhabitant's perception is unbounded. The horizon is not a boundary because it moves with the inhabitant. It cannot be reached or crossed. Things do not break through a barrier when they come into view. And when you look upwards, you do not see yourself surrounded by a closed surface. Life under the sky is lived *in the open*, not within the confines of a hollow hemisphere with a flat base and a domed top. Thus the sky has no outline, and you cannot draw it. All you can draw are the shapes of things *in* the sky, or silhouetted *against* it. Indeed whilst Gibson objects to drawing the earth and the sky, he has no such scruples about drawing what is *on* the earth and *in* the sky. When the experimenters ask him to draw people and houses on a baseline that depicts the ground, and to add clouds, the sun and moon and stars to the space above it, he is ready and willing to oblige.

In the interpretation of these drawings, however, Gibson is unequivocally at odds with our experimenters. For he will not accept them as evidence for the conceptual ordering of experience, or as revealing anything about the way he thinks. No more than the drawings of children, he says, do they give visible form to mental models inside his head. It is not as though, when you are about to draw, you first look at an object so as to obtain a mental image of it, and then, projecting the image 'back' onto your drawing pad, trace its outline on the page. You may draw a person, a house, or the sun in the sky, making marks on a surface that record the movements of the pencil in your hand. What these marks delineate, however, are not images but what Gibson calls 'invariants' (ibid.: 278–279). Invariants emerge as parametric constants underlying the continuous flow of perspective structure as one moves along a path of observation. Unlike perspective structure, which is unique to every point of observation, invariant structure is common to all points and therefore discloses 'the rigid layout of environmental surfaces' (ibid.: 73–74). To draw, then, is not to render the likeness of a thing, but to extract its rigidity. The result, however, is peculiarly static. As a rigid layout, Gibson's 'environment' seems locked solid. It is as though the people, the houses, the clouds and the sun were turned to stone. Admittedly, by comparison to the Kantian exhabitant who roams the outer surface of the globe, the Gibsonian inhabitant finds himself at the centre of a spherical world. But though exquisitely realistic and fully furnished, it is a world that turns out to harbour no life at all.

After their appointment with Gibson, our intrepid experimenters head off, rucksacks on their backs, into the Black Forest of Germany. They are making for the mountain hut that the philosopher Martin Heidegger has turned into a retreat for meditation. In preparation for their trip, they had read one of Heidegger's earlier essays, on the origin of the work of art.[4] In this essay, he insists that the earth, 'that on which and in which man bases his dwelling', is not a material mass, and absolutely not a planet. It is rather the ground on which – or better, *in* which – we dwell (Heidegger 1971: 42). For the earth–ground does not just support its inhabitants. In an important sense it nourishes and shelters them. It is the very matrix of their dwelling. People are *of* the earth, they do not just live *on* it. Here, Heidegger recognises, as Augustine also did, that human bodies are as earthly as is the earth of the ground they tread, being of the same substance. So too are the plants that grow there, and the animals that are nourished by this growth. Likewise, clouds, sunsets and stars are phenomena *of* the sky, rather than – as Gibson thought – objects *in* it. '"On the earth"', wrote Heidegger in his much later essay *Building Dwelling Thinking*, 'already means "under the sky"' (ibid.: 149). Earth and sky, then, are not two separate halves of the world that, if put together, add up to a unity. Each, rather, enfolds the other in its own becoming: the earth the sky in becoming earth; the sky the earth in becoming sky. The earth binds the sky in the tissues of the plants and animals it supports and nourishes; the sky sweeps the earth in its currents of wind and weather. One is unthinkable without the other (ibid.: 149, 178).

Now in Heidegger's terms, if you were to go up in a spaceship and look out of the window, the one thing you would *not* see is the earth. When, in 1966, the first photographic images of the earth as seen from space were beamed from the satellite *Lunar Orbiter 1*, Heidegger reacted with unbridled hostility. 'I do not know whether you were frightened', he remarked to an interviewer, 'but I at any rate was frightened when I saw pictures coming from the moon to the earth … This is no longer the earth on which man lives' (in Wolin 1993: 103). Perhaps it should have come as no surprise to our experimenters, then, that on putting their questions to Heidegger, he responds with equal if not greater hostility. He refuses, point blank, to admit that the earth is round. The *planet* is round, he says, but not the ground, and before all else, the earth is the ground. 'Well, draw the planet, then', our experimenters say, in exasperation. Heidegger draws the planet. 'Now show where the people live.' Heidegger explodes. 'There is no place for *Dasein* on the planet', he fumes. This is not just a problem of scale – that on any drawing of the earth, the people would be too small to see, just as they were invisible in the shots from *Lunar Orbiter*. More importantly, in an earth conceived as a solid sphere, there is nowhere for a person to *be*. For Heidegger, as Benjamin Lazier observes, 'the rise of the planetary in the modern imagination was synonymous … with the demise of the earthly' (Lazier n.d.: 10). It signified the displacement of human indebtedness to the earth by a technologically induced alienation. As Augustine's 'heaven of heaven' has been replaced by a spaceship, humans have been expelled from the earth. The space station, as the contemporary philosopher Peter Sloterdijk has put it (2005: 236), represents a model for being in the world condemned to artificiality.

Round, flat and much else

What is a human being? What does it mean to be human? On the face of it, these questions seem to call for entirely different answers. To the first, we might respond that human beings collectively comprise a species of nature. They are terrestrial animals whose lives and livelihoods are necessarily bound to the potentials and constraints of the material world. As living organisms they are made of the same earthly stuff of this world, tread the same ground and breathe the same air. But to the second question, we are inclined to respond that to be human is to rise above and beyond the confines of nature within which the lives of all other creatures are bound. It is through the power of reason and its eventual triumph over both our own inner nature and the nature that surrounds us, we say, that the essence of our humanity is realised. It is realised historically, in the rise of civilisation and the concomitant advance of science. And it is recapitulated in the intellectual development of every modern individual from childhood to maturity. This claim to the transcendence of reason over nature provides science with the platform of supremacy from which, with no little hubris and profound contradiction, it asserts that human beings are part and parcel of the natural world. Are not scientists, and all who think like them, also human beings? How, then, can they be both *of* nature and *beyond* it at the same time? On further reflection, however, it seems that the very meaning of 'human' epitomises this contradiction. Referring neither to a species of nature nor to a condition of being that transcends nature, but rather to both simultaneously, 'human' is a word that points to the existential dilemma of a creature that can know itself and the world of which it is a part only through the renunciation of its very being in that world.

If the experiments – both actual and fictional – that I have set out above prove anything, it is that precisely the same dualism, intrinsic to the concept of the 'human', is also responsible for the duplicity, in the western intellectual tradition, in understandings of the earth. For the human being, the earth is the ground, from which it derives both nourishment and support. This ground, argues philosopher Alphonso Lingis, 'is not – save for astronauts and for the imagination of astronomers – the planet, an object which viewed from a distance is spherical. We do not feel ourselves on a platform … but feel a reservoir of support extending indefinitely in depth' (Lingis 1998: 14). To be human, by contrast, means projecting ourselves to a beyond – whether it be Augustine's intellectual heaven or Sloterdijk's imaginary space station – that lies on the 'far side' of nature, and from there to look back on the earth as a planet. Historically, the 'heaven of heaven' that Augustine thought to be the preserve of God rather than man has been usurped by space scientists and astronauts. Only by going *beyond* the earth, it seems, can we see ourselves as *of* the earth. The ubiquity of what look like hybrid models in our experimental results is symptomatic not so much of a halfway stage in the development of scientific reason, as of the contradictory foundations of science itself, and of its enforced separation of knowing from being.

This separation has, I think, led us to an impasse. To find a way forward, we have to recognise that our humanity is neither something that comes with the territory, with our species-specific nature, nor an imagined condition that places the territory outside ourselves, but rather the ongoing historical process of our mutual and collective self-creation. What we are, or what we can be, is something that we continually shape through our actions – which we have constantly to work at, and for which we alone must bear the responsibility. But in shaping one another we also shape the earth, for which, too, we are responsible. This shaping is not a matter of imposing form on the formless substance of the material world. Rather, the shape of the earth emerges, whether in the imagination or on the ground, or both simultaneously, through our very practices of habitation. The earth is neither an object in space nor a space for objects; neither a round ball nor a flat base. Or if you will, it is both of these and much else besides. For the earth is 'earthing', continually growing and sprouting as a melange of material flows, practical activities, perceptive observations and personal stories, and its shape is woven from all of these. The drawings elicited in the experiments I have described, for example, are not representations but little pictograms by means of which we tell particular stories about ourselves and about our understanding of the world we inhabit. Yet just as the child draws the sky, the ground and the planet, so too, the river draws the valley, the plough the field, the ship the ocean and the surveyor the map. Every time – and in whatever way – we draw the earth we add a new line to the melange. In short, drawing shapes the world in which we dwell, at the same time as it shapes our own humanity.

9

EARTH, SKY, WIND AND WEATHER

So there I lie on the plateau, under me the central core of fire from which was thrust this grumbling, grinding mass of plutonic rock, over me blue air, and between the fire of the rock and the fire of the sun, scree, soil and water, moss, grass, flower and tree, insect, bird and beast, rain and snow – the total mountain. Slowly I have found my way in.

Nan Shepherd (1977: 93)

'To be alive', writes Alphonso Lingis, 'is to enjoy the light, enjoy the support of the ground, the open paths and the buoyancy of the air' (1998: 17). Knowing what it feels like to be out for a walk in the open air, we readily concur. Yet once we try to pin it down within established categories and conventions of thought, no feeling could be more elusive. Where is the ground? What is the air? How can we inhabit the open? If we can do so only by containing it, then how can the wind still blow? In what follows I seek to establish what it means to be 'in the open'. Instead of thinking of the inhabited world as composed of mutually exclusive hemispheres of sky and earth, separated by the ground, we need to attend, as I shall show, to the fluxes of wind and weather. To feel the air and walk on the ground is not to make external, tactile contact with our surroundings but to mingle with them. In this mingling, as we live and breathe, the wind, light and moisture of the sky bind with the substances of the earth in the continual forging of a way through the tangle of lifelines that comprise the land.

To reach this conclusion I shall proceed in three stages. I show, first, that a ground populated solely by people and objects, and a sky that is empty but for birds and clouds, can exist only within a simulacrum of the world, modelled in an interior space. The second stage of the argument is to show that in the open world, beings relate not as closed, objective forms but by virtue of their common immersion in the fluxes of the medium. The process of respiration, by which air is taken in by organisms from the medium and in turn surrendered to it, is fundamental to all life. Thus, finally, to inhabit the open is to dwell within a weather-world in which every being is destined to combine wind, rain, sunshine and earth in the continuation of its own existence. I conclude with some remarks on how, in modern western societies, the environment has been engineered, or 'built', to conform to expectations of closure, but how life always, and inevitably, breaks through the bounds of the objective forms in which we have sought to contain it.

Earth and sky

Where should we begin? For initial inspiration, I went back to the writings of the pioneer of ecological psychology, James Gibson. You will recall from the last chapter his telling our imaginary team of experimenters that the living being is positioned not on the external surface of a solid globe, as Immanuel Kant had imagined, but rather at the centre of a spherical field comprising the two hemispheres of sky and earth, with the ground as the interface between them. Supported by the ground, the inhabitants of Gibson's account are not so much composites of mind and body, participating at once in the material world and the world of ideas, as immersed in a world of materials comprising earthly substances and the aerial medium.[1] Like surfaces of all sorts, the ground has a characteristic, non-homogeneous texture that enables us to tell what it is a surface *of*: whether, for example, it is of bare rock, sand, soil or concrete (Gibson 1979: 16–22). We can recognise the texture visually because of the characteristic scatter pattern in the light reflected from the surface. Conversely, however, if there is no discernible pattern in the ambient light, then there is no identifiable texture, and instead of perceiving a surface we see an empty void (ibid.: 51–52).

The perception of the sky offers a case in point. Suppose that we cast our eyes upwards, from the ground on which we stand to the clear blue sky of a summer's day. As our gaze rises above the line of the horizon, it is not as though another surface comes into view. Rather, the textureless blue of the sky signifies boundless emptiness. Nothing is there. Amidst this void, of course, there may exist textured regions that specify the surfaces, for example, of clouds *in* the sky. From a shower cloud, rain falls, leaving puddles on the ground. When the sun comes out again and the puddle dries up, the surface of water gives way to reveal another, of dry mud, in its place. But when the cloud, drained of moisture, eventually disperses, it vanishes to leave no surface at all (ibid.: 106). For the sky has no surface. It is open. But having said that, Gibson goes on to acknowledge that 'an open environment is seldom or never realised' and that life within such an environment would be all but impossible. Imagine an absolutely level earth, extending in all directions to the horizon without any obstruction, under a cloudless sky. It would be a desolate place indeed! 'It would not be quite as lifeless as geometrical space', Gibson admits, 'but almost.' You could stand up in it, walk and breathe, but not much else (ibid.: 78).

No ordinary environment is like that, however. Rather, it is 'cluttered' with every kind of thing, from hills and mountains to animals and plants, objects and artefacts. Or to put it another way, the environment is *furnished*. 'The furniture of the earth', Gibson continues, 'like the furnishings of a room, is what makes it liveable.' A cloudless sky, in these terms, would be uninhabitable, and could not therefore form any part of the environment for a living being. Birds could not fly in it. And an empty earth provides a terrestrial animal with nothing more than basic support; 'the furniture of the earth', as Gibson puts it, 'affords all the rest of behaviour' (ibid.: 78). Like actors on the stage, Gibsonian perceivers can only make their entrance once the surface has been furnished with the properties and scenery that make it possible for the play to proceed. Roaming around as on a set, they are fated to pick their way amidst the clutter of the world. It seems that for all his efforts to describe the world from an inhabitant's point of view, Gibson is drawn to the conclusion that the terrestrial environment becomes habitable only to the extent that it is no longer open but enclosed. Such enclosure may never be more than partial, but for just that reason the inhabitant inevitably remains, to an extent, an exile.[2]

A world without objects

Gibson is adamant that the inhabited environment does not *just* comprise the furniture of the world, any more than it comprises *just* earth and sky, empty of content. It must rather comprise both together, consisting – in his words – 'of the earth and the sky with objects *on* the earth and *in* the sky, of mountains and clouds, fires and sunsets, pebbles and stars' (ibid.: 66, original emphasis). It is worth pausing to consider some of the things he takes to be objects: on the earth there are mountains, pebbles and fires; in the sky there are clouds, sunsets and stars. Now of the things on the earth, perhaps only pebbles can be regarded as objects in any ordinary sense and, even then, only if we consider each individual stone in isolation from its neighbours, from the ground on which it lies and from the processes that brought it there. The hill is not an object on the earth's surface but a formation of that surface, which can only appear as an object through its artificial excision from the landscape of which it is an integral part. And the fire is not an object but a manifestation of the process of combustion. Turning to the sky: stars, whatever their astronomical significance, are perceived not as objects but as points of light, and sunsets as the momentary glow of the sky as the sun vanishes beneath the horizon. Nor are clouds objects. Each is rather an incoherent, vaporous tumescence that swells and is carried along in the currents of the medium. To observe the clouds is not to view the furniture of the sky but to catch a fleeting glimpse of a sky-in-formation, never the same from one moment to the next.

Indeed in a world that is truly open there are no objects as such. For the object, having closed in on itself, has turned its back on the world, cutting itself off from the paths along which it came into being, and presenting only its congealed, outer surfaces for inspection. That is to say, the 'objectness' of things, their 'over-againstness' (Heidegger 1971: 167), is the result of an inversion[3] that turns the lines of their generation into boundaries of exclusion. The open world, however, has no such boundaries, no insides or outsides, only comings and goings. Such productive movements may generate formations, swellings, growths, protuberances and occurrences, but not objects. Thus in the open world hills rise up, as can be experienced by climbing them or, from a distance, by following the contours with one's eyes.[4] Fires burn, as we know from their flickering flames, the swirling of smoke and the warming of the body. And pebbles grate. It is of course this grating that gives rise to their rounded forms; tread on them, and that is what you hear underfoot. In the sky, the sun shines by day and the moon and stars by night, and clouds billow. They *are*, respectively, their shining and billowing, just as the hills *are* their rising, the fire *is* its burning and the pebbles *are* their grating.

In short, and contrary to Gibson's contention, it is not through being furnished with objects that the open sphere of sky and earth is turned into a habitable environment. The furnished world is a full-scale model – a world brought indoors and reconstructed within a dedicated, enclosed space (see Figure 9.1). As in a stage set, hills are placed on the ground, while stars, clouds and the sun and moon are hung from the sky. In this *as if* world hills do not rise, nor do fires burn or pebbles grate, nor do the sun, moon and stars shine or the clouds billow. They may be made to look as though they do, but the appearance is an illusion. Absolutely nothing is going on. Only once the stage is set, and everything made ready, can the action begin. But the open world that creatures inhabit is not prepared for them in advance. It is continually coming into being around them. It is a world, that is, of formative and transformative *processes*. If such processes are of the essence of perception, then they are also of the essence of what is perceived. To understand how beings can inhabit this world

FIGURE 9.1 The world brought indoors. In this painting by René Magritte, entitled *Poison* (1939), a cloud is shown entering a room, where it will become an object of furniture. The world of ocean and sky, whence it came, can be glimpsed through the open door. © ADAGP, Paris and DACS, London 2010.

means attending to the dynamic processes of world-formation in which both perceivers and the phenomena they perceive are necessarily immersed. And to achieve this, we must think again about the relations between surfaces, substances and the medium.

Contending with the weather

To make a start, let me return to the metaphysical reflections of Martin Heidegger that I introduced towards the end of the last chapter. Like Gibson, Heidegger also recognises that people live 'on the earth' and 'under the sky'. But his description of earth and sky could hardly be more different from Gibson's. In place of nouns describing objects of furniture, Heidegger's description is replete with verbs of growth and motion. 'Earth', writes Heidegger, 'is the serving bearer, blossoming and fruiting, spreading out in rock and water, rising up into plant and animal' (1971: 149). And of the sky, he writes that it 'is the vaulting path of the sun, the course of the changing moon, the wandering glitter of the stars, the year's seasons and their changes, the light and dusk of the day, the gloom and glow of the night, the clemency and inclemency of the weather, the drifting clouds and blue depth of the ether' (ibid.: 149). Moreover one cannot speak of the earth without already thinking also of the sky, and vice versa. But if we are to think of earth and sky thus, not as mutually exclusive domains but as manifolds of movement that are directly implicated in one another, then how should we go about it? How can we progress beyond the idea that life is played out upon the surface of a world already furnished with objects? It is perhaps because we are so used to thinking and writing indoors that we find it so difficult to imagine the inhabited environment as anything other than an enclosed, interior space. What would happen if, instead, we were to take our inquiry out of doors?

First and foremost, we would have to contend with those fluxes of the medium that we call weather (Ingold 2005a). For Gibson (1979: 19), the weather is simply what is going on in the medium, and beyond noting that it calls for various kinds of adaptation or behavioural adjustment on the part of inhabitants, he has no more to say about it. For the substances of the earth, in his view, are impervious to these goings-on. The terrestrial surface, which is taken to be relatively rigid and non-porous, ensures that aerial medium and earthly substances keep to their respective domains and do not mix. It is as though in the forms of the land, the earth had turned its back on the sky, refusing further intercourse with it. Thus the weather swirls about *on top* of the land, but does not participate further in its formation. Yet as every inhabitant knows, rainfall can turn a ploughed field into a sea of mud, frost can shatter solid rocks, lightning can ignite forest fires on land parched by summer heat, and the wind can whip sand into dunes, snow into drifts and the water of lakes and oceans into waves. In his study of how Koyukon people in Alaska perceive their surroundings, anthropologist Richard Nelson declares that 'weather is the hammer and the land is the anvil' (Nelson 1983: 33). But there are other, more subtle and delicate ways in which the land responds to fluxes in the medium. Think of the pearls of dew that pick out the tendrils of plants and spiders' webs on a cool summer's morning, or of the little trails left by a passing gust of wind in the dry leaves and broken twigs of a woodland floor.

Living in the land

Seasoned inhabitants know how to read the land as an intimate register of wind and weather.[5] Like the Koyukon, they can sense the approach of a storm in the sudden burst of flame in a campfire, or – as the Yup'ik elder Fred George explains – they can read the direction of the prevailing wind in the orientation of tufts of frozen grass sticking out from the snow (Figure 9.4), or of snow 'waves' on ice-bound lakes (Nelson 1983: 41; Bradley 2002: 249). Yet the more one reads into the land, the more difficult it becomes to ascertain with any certainty where substances end and where the medium begins. For it is precisely through the *binding* of medium and substances that wind and weather leave their mark. Thus the land itself no longer appears as an interface separating the two, but as a vaguely defined zone of admixture and intermingling. Indeed anyone who has walked through the boreal forest in summer knows that the 'ground' is not really a coherent surface at all but a more or less impenetrable mass of tangled undergrowth, leaf litter and detritus, mosses and lichens, stones and boulders, split by cracks and crevasses, threaded by tree roots, and interspersed with swamps and marshes overgrown with rafts of vegetation that are liable to give way underfoot. Likewise, teacher, writer and hillwalker Nan Shepherd, describing her sojourn in the Cairngorm Mountains of north-east Scotland in an evocative passage that I have selected to head this chapter, finds herself *between* the solid rock beneath and the clear sky above. Here, in this intermediate zone, are 'soil and water, moss, grass, flower and tree, insect, bird and beast'. It is in this zone that life is lived, at depths depending upon the scale of the creature and its capacity to penetrate an environment that is ever more tightly woven. 'Slowly', Shepherd says, 'I have found my way in' (Shepherd 1977: 93).

This is the sense in which creatures live *in* the land and not *on* it (Figure 9.2). There could be no life in a world where medium and substances do not mix, or where the earth is locked inside – and the sky locked out – of a solid sphere. Wherever there is life and habitation, the interfacial separation of substance and medium is disrupted to give way to mutual permeability and binding. For it is in the nature of living beings themselves that, by way of their own processes of respiration, of breathing in and out, they bind the medium with substances in forging their own growth and movement through the world. Of a seed that has fallen to the ground, the painter Paul Klee writes that 'the relation to earth and atmosphere begets the capacity to grow… The seed strikes root, initially the line is directed earthwards, though not to dwell there, only to draw energy thence for reaching up into the air' (Klee 1973: 29). In growth, the point becomes a line, but the line, far from being mounted upon the pre-prepared surface of the ground, contributes to its ever-evolving weave. As Heidegger noted in his description of the earth, to which I have already referred, earthly substances 'rise up' into the forms of plants and animals (1971: 149). The land, we could say, is continually *growing over*, which is why archaeologists have to dig to recover the traces of past lives. And what hold it all together are the tangled and tangible lifelines of its inhabitants (Ingold 2007a: 80–81).

The wind, too, mingles with substances as it blows through the land, leaving traces of its passing in tracks or trails. 'Around, up, above, what wind-walks!', exclaimed Gerard Manley

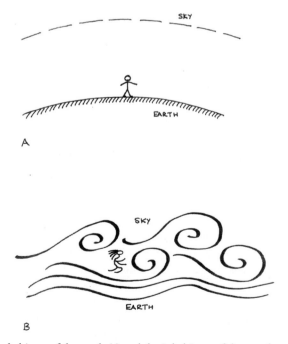

FIGURE 9.2 The exhabitant of the earth (a) and the inhabitant of the weather-world (b)

Hopkins in his poem *Hurrahing in Harvest* (Hopkins 1972: 27). We could say of the wind that 'it winds', wending its way along twisted paths as do terrestrial travellers. These paths are often likened to ropes. There is an old tradition among Sámi people that by tying the ropes into knots the wind may be stopped, and that by untying them they are once more unleashed (Helander and Mustonen 2004: 537). Precisely because of the indeterminacy of the interface between substances and the medium, the same line of movement can register concurrently on the ground as a trace and in the air as a thread, such as when an animal is linked to the hunter by both its track and its scent. In his ethnographic account of the significance of wind among Khoisan hunter-gatherers of southern Africa, Chris Low (2008: 68) tells how, for the Khoisan, 'wind connects the hunter with the prey like a thread leading from one body to another'. As every animal has its distinctive smell, the whole environment is riddled with such scent threads, binding its human and non-human inhabitants into an intricate mesh and percolating the very depths of their awareness. People even spoke of the threads as vibrating inside them, making a ringing sound.

Binding life

To inhabit the open is not, then, to be stranded on a closed surface but to be immersed in the incessant movements of wind and weather, in a zone wherein substances and medium are brought together in the constitution of beings that, by way of their activity, participate in stitching the textures of the land. 'The first track', explains the American tracker Tom Brown, 'is the end of a string' (1978: 1; see Ingold 2007a: 50–51). As this powerful metaphor suggests, the relation between land and weather does not cut across an impermeable interface between earth and sky but is rather one *between the binding and unbinding of the world*. Nowhere has this binding and unbinding been more vividly brought to life than in the drawings of Vincent van Gogh, of which art historian Philip Rawson writes: 'the urgent movements of the clusters of lines show us how … the weather is *weathering*, the field *fielding* …' (Rawson 1979: 23). The very ground appears to be bursting with life and movement (see Figure 9.3). In the open world that van Gogh reveals to us, the task of habitation is to bind substances and the medium into living forms. But bindings are not boundaries, and they no more contain the world, or enclose it, than does a knot contain the threads from which it is tied. They rather gather it up. And as Heidegger showed (1971: 181), every being, as it inhabits the world, gathers it up in its own particular way.

   The Koyukon of Alaska often invoke the beings that inhabit their world by means of riddles (see Chapter 14). Taking up the subject position of the being to which he refers, the riddler describes its characteristic movements as though he were carrying them out himself, by means of an analogy with familiar human gestures. Like gusts of wind, these are fugitive movements in a weather-world in which all are immersed, and in which nothing ever stands still. In one such riddle, recorded by the Jesuit priest Julius Jetté at the beginning of the twentieth century, the riddler imagines himself as a tuft of grass. The literal translation runs as follows:

>   *over-there around I-sweep-with-my-body*
> (Jetté 1913: 199–200)[6]

The riddler is a broom, and the broom *is* its sweeping. He sweeps the place around him, just like the withered grasses that still poke out above the first snows of winter. In the wind the blades of grass bend over so as to touch the snow, still soft and loose from recent falls, sweeping

FIGURE 9.3 A pencil sketch by Vincent van Gogh, dating from summer 1889, of a wheat field with cypress trees. Reproduced courtesy of the Van Gogh Museum, Amsterdam (Vincent van Gogh Foundation).

a small circular patch around the place where they stand. With a vivacity and lightness of touch that trumps the writings of any western philosopher, the Koyukon riddler captures, in miniature, the way in which the manifold of earth, sky, wind and weather is concentrated in the experience of an inhabitant tasked with binding substances and medium. Here, the whole world is in a tuft of grass. Grown from the earth under the summer sunshine, now frozen in place by winter frost and blown by the wind, the grass makes a place for itself in the world by creating a patch in the snow (Figure 9.4). It is by such movements that every living being inhabits the world of the open.

But if life binds, then fire unbinds. Rather than binding the medium with substances, in the smoke of the hearth we find the reverse transformation, a release of substances to the medium in volatile form. As it rises, smoke mingles with circulations of air in the weather-world, and can even condense into clouds. In northern Finland, where I have carried out fieldwork, every dwelling was traditionally known as a 'smoke' since it could be recognised, even from some distance, by the white column rising vertically into the sky on a still, frosty day. However, the dwelling, with the hearth at its centre, still pertains to the world of the open, as does the life that goes on within it. Just as the living body is sustained by the rhythmic movement of breathing in and out, so the dwelling is sustained by the continual coming and going of its inhabitants. Thus it is important to distinguish between the 'indoors' of the dwelling that is wrapped around its inhabitants like a warm coat, and the 'indoors' of the *as if* world, of which I have already spoken, that has been reconstructed in an enclosed

FIGURE 9.4 Withered grasses in frozen snow, Goodnews Bay, Lower Kuskokwim District, Alaska. Reproduced courtesy of the Lower Kuskokwim School District, Alaska.

space. In the traditional dwelling, earth and sky are unified at the centre, where the smoke from the hearth rises to meet the sky; in the modern residence, by contrast, they are divided at the horizon, viewed through a vertical 'picture window' that frames the land as a backdrop. Whereas the dwelling is a place holder for life, the residence is a container.

Breaking through the surface

It has, of course, long been the ambition of modernist architecture and urban planning to bring closure to life, or to 'put it inside', by means of projects of construction that would seek to convert the world we inhabit into furnished accommodation, made ready to be occupied. Part of this containment entails creating the illusion of an absolute division between earth and sky, in part by hiding from view those disruptions of the surface that are necessary for the bubble to be sustained. It is in this light that we can interpret the progressive banishment of the hearth, in the architecture of modernity, from the centre to the periphery of the dwelling, along with the confinement of smoke within ever-lengthening chimneys. The tall factory chimney, belching smoke, proclaims the absolute separation of earth and sky at the same time as it hides away the points of disruption where fires actually burn. Likewise, paving the

FIGURE 9.5 Fungi breaking through asphalt, from an installation by Klaus Weber. Photo courtesy of the artist.

streets of the modern city, as we saw in Chapter 3, makes it possible for inhabitants to sustain an illusion of groundlessness, as though they could traverse the pavements without making any contact with, or impression in, the earth. Under the rubric of the 'built environment', human industry has created an infrastructure of hard surfaces, fitted out with objects of all sorts, upon which the play of life is supposed to be enacted. Thus the rigid separation of substances from the medium that Gibson took to be a natural state of affairs has in fact been engineered in an attempt to get the world to conform to our expectations of it, and to provide it with the coherent surface we always thought it had.

Yet while designed to ease the transport of occupants across it, the hard surfacing of the earth actually blocks the very intermingling of substances with the medium that is essential to life, growth and habitation. Earth that has been surfaced cannot 'rise up', as Heidegger put it, into the plant or animal. Every paved road and every concrete foundation is a desert: nothing can grow there. The blockage is only provisional, however. Theodosius Dobzhansky (1965), one of the architects of the so-called new synthesis of twentieth-century evolutionary biology, liked to describe life as a process of 'groping'. Literally 'pervading everything so as to try everything, and trying everything so as to find everything' (ibid.: 214), life will not be confined within bounded forms but rather threads its way through the world along the myriad of lines of its relations, probing every crack or crevice that might potentially afford growth and movement. Nothing, it seems, escapes its tentacles. Thus wherever anything lives the infrastructure of the occupied world is breaking up or wearing away, ceaselessly eroded by the disorderly groping of inhabitants, both human and non-human, as they reincorporate and rearrange its crumbling fragments into their own ways of life (Ingold 2007a: 103).

For me, not only the futility of hard surfacing but also the sheer irrepressibility of life have been nowhere better dramatised than in a recent work by the German artist Klaus Weber (2004: 45–63). Having acquired an allotment in Berlin, Weber persuaded the Roads Department to coat it in a thick layer of motorway-grade asphalt. But before the machines rolled in, he sprinkled the area with the spores of a certain fungus. Once the asphalt had been laid he built a shed on one side of the plot, in which he lived as he watched what happened. After a while, bell-shaped bumps appeared, the asphalt began to crack and eventually fungi burst forth in great white blobs (Figure 9.5). Weber collected the fungus and fried it in his shed; apparently it tasted delicious! The mycelium had triumphed. And so too, in an open world, the creeping entanglements of life will always and inevitably triumph over our attempts to box them in.

10

LANDSCAPE OR WEATHER-WORLD?

The scope of the land

Theories of how people perceive the world around them – including theories that I have put forward myself (Ingold 2000a) – generally work from the assumption that this world is terrestrial. It is a world in which we can expect to find formations of the land such as hills and valleys, mountains and plains, interspersed with settlements such as villages and towns and threaded by paths, roads and waterways. To describe such a world, it is customary to use the word 'landscape'. The word has a chequered history. Of early medieval provenance, it referred originally to an area of land bound into the everyday practices and customary usages of an agrarian community. However, its subsequent incorporation into the language of painterly depiction – above all through the tradition of Dutch art that developed in the seventeenth century (Alpers 1983) – has led generations of scholars to mistake the connotations of the suffix -scape for a particular 'scopic regime' of detailed and disinterested observation (Jay 1988). They have, it seems, been fooled by a superficial resemblance between scape and scope that is, in fact, entirely fortuitous and has no foundation in etymology. 'Scope' comes from the classical Greek skopos – literally 'the target of the bowman, the mark towards which he gazes as he aims' (Carruthers 1998: 79), – from which is derived the verb skopein, 'to look'. 'Scape', quite to the contrary, comes from Old English sceppan or skyppan, meaning 'to shape' (Olwig 2008).

Medieval shapers of the land were not painters but farmers, whose purpose was not to render the material world in appearance rather than substance, but to wrest a living from the earth. Shape, for them, was as intrinsic to the constitution of the land as is weave to the constitution of cloth. Just as cloth is woven from the intertwined threads of warp and weft, so, in medieval times, the land was scaped by the people who, with foot, axe and plough, and with the assistance of their domestic animals, trod, hacked and scratched their lines into the earth, and thereby created its ever-evolving texture. This was work done close-up, in an immediate, muscular and visceral engagement with wood, grass and soil – the very opposite of the distanced, contemplative and panoramic optic that the word 'landscape' conjures up in many minds today. Nevertheless, the equation of the shape of the land with its look – of the *scaped* with the *scopic* – has become firmly lodged in the vocabulary of modernist art history. Landscape has thus come to be identified with scenery and with an art of description that would see the world spread out on a canvas, much as in the subsequent development of both cartography and photography, it would come to be projected onto a plate or screen, or the pages of an atlas.

In a landscape painting, however, and by contrast to a map, a large part of the picture often consists of sky. The painter is depicting a world of both earth and sky, recognising full well that in the play of colour, light and shade, one could not exist without the other. Painters such as John Constable devoted a great deal of attention to the sky, making detailed studies of clouds and cloud formation that were as rigorous as the science of the day would allow (Thornes 1999). Yet the sky has been almost universally ignored by art historians and others who have taken it upon themselves to comment on the paintings.[1] Assuming that to depict a landscape is to render on canvas a particular portion of the earth's surface and what lies upon it, the sky recedes in their attention to an unnoticed and taken-for-granted background. It might as well not be there. And it leads me to propose the following, as a kind of thought experiment (not to be repeated in the gallery). Suppose that we take a masterpiece of landscape art and cut the canvas along the horizon or skyline. Discarding the upper part, we then paste the lower part onto light blue or light grey wallpaper. Would it make any difference? Of course it would. But in all the writings on landscape art, I would challenge anyone to find some explanation as to what the difference is.

Looking up at the sky

The question comes down to this: is the sky a part of the landscape or is it not? If it is, then can we any more suppose that to perceive the landscape is to observe the surfaces of the earth, or of things on the earth? If it is not, then what are we to make of our perception of the sky? Does it float *above* the landscape? Or is it all just an illusion? In the psychology of visual perception, as we saw in the last chapter, the ecological approach pioneered by James Gibson is almost unique in offering some account of the sky. Yet it is an account shot through with paradox and contradiction. Reacting against the idea that what we see is a picture of the world, projected onto the retina as if on a screen, Gibson places perceivers right at the centre of a world that is all around them rather than passing by in front of their eyes. But he also insists that what we perceive are surfaces, both *of* the ground and of more or less solid objects *on* the ground. How, then, do we perceive the sky? Is the sky a surface – an interface between an aerial medium and a solid substance? If it were, then air travel would be hazardous, to say the least! Or is the sky, rather, the epitome of emptiness? If so, then how can it be inhabited? And what should we make of the clouds?

Imagine yourself in the woods, looking up toward the canopy of leaves overhead. Amidst the leafy texture, there are gaps or spaces that remain open to the sky. It is as though the canopy had holes in it. Birds fly into these holes, Gibson says, as they take wing from the treetops (Gibson 1979: 106). But can an environment really have holes in it? Do birds fly into holes? Can clouds cover them over? Does the sky have a surface, on an overcast day, which melts away on a clear one? Are isolated clouds objects suspended in the void? To answer in the affirmative would be to side with Winnie-the-Pooh, who famously hoped that by hanging from a balloon he might trick the bees into thinking that he, too, was a passing cloud when he was actually after their honey. The bees, of course, were not that stupid! But from Gibson's account, Pooh might just have got away with it. Indeed Gibson has a particular problem with the sky, and with clouds. It stems from his insistence that while we see by means of light, the one thing we do not see is light itself. Rather, he claims, we see the surfaces of things, by way of their illumination.

I would like to digress for a moment to compare vision and hearing in this regard. We often think of sight as an objectifying sense. Standing here we look and see that cloud there, or that tree, or that bird, each as an object that is set over against us, at a distance. But with hearing it seems to be different. We say we hear sounds, as though we were bathed in them. They get inside us, and shake us up. Indeed, hearing and the experience of sound appear to be one and the same. But if that is so, why cannot vision equally be an experience of *light*? Can we not be bathed in the fluxes of light just as much as we are in those of sound? 'Visual space', writes Alphonso Lingis, 'is not pure transparency; it is filled with light... Our gaze is immersed in it and sees with its cast' (Lingis 1998: 13). Why then, against the evidence of such immersion, are sight and light so generally opposed rather than identified? The answer, I believe, lies in a peculiar set of beliefs that have long held sway in the western tradition, concerning the topology of the human head. In this topology, the ears are imagined as holes that let the sound in, whereas the eyes are likened to screens that let no light through. Inside the head, then, it is noisy but dark. As sound penetrates the inner sanctum of being, mingling with the soul, it merges with hearing. But light is shut out. It is left to vision to reconstruct, on the inside, a picture of what the world 'out there' might be like. These pictures, of course, can be wrong – which is why psychologists of perception have devoted so much attention to optical illusions, compared with little or no attention to aural ones (Rée 1999: 46).

The light of being

Now it is obvious enough that when we look around we see things of all sorts. This is so obvious, indeed, that we tend to forget that we could see nothing unless we first could *see*. Behind the mere ordinariness of the sight of things lies the sheer astonishment of being able to see. This is what the philosopher Maurice Merleau-Ponty, in his celebrated essay on 'Eye and mind', called the magic – or the delirium (Merleau-Ponty 1964: 162) – of vision: the sense that at every moment one is opening one's eyes upon a world-in-formation. For formerly blind persons whose sight has been restored by a surgical operation, and doubtless for the newborn opening their eyes for the first time, the delirium can be overwhelming. 'The first time we see light', wrote William James, 'we *are* it rather than see it' (James 1892: 14). Light, I contend, is another way of saying 'I can see'. It is not merely a phenomenon of the physical world (whether treated as photons or radiant energy), nor is it a phenomenon of the interior mind. It is neither on the far side nor on the near side of the retinal surface. Rather, light is an *experience*. For sighted persons, it is the experience of inhabiting the world of the visible, and its qualities – of brilliance and shade, tint and colour, and saturation – are variations on this experience.

Let me present an imaginary scenario, nevertheless scripted with actual words. So far as I know, Gibson and Merleau-Ponty never met. But let us suppose that they did, on a fine summer's day. There they are, stretched out on the grass, looking up into the sky. 'What do you see?' Gibson asks Merleau-Ponty. To which the latter dreamily replies: 'I am the sky itself as it is drawn together and unified, and as it begins to exist for itself; my consciousness is saturated with this limitless blue' (1962: 214). Gibson is unimpressed. Why, he wonders, will this Frenchman not answer the question? He had asked what his companion can *see*, not what he *is*. And in any case, how can he claim to be the sky when he is stretched out here on the ground? Eventually, Gibson responds, 'To me it seems that I see the sky, not the luminosity as such' (1979: 54). Gibson's problem, however, was that he could never figure out *how* the sky should be distinguished from its luminosity. This was not a problem, however, for Merleau-Ponty, who could readily respond that the sky is no less than the world of light itself, to which we open ourselves up in vision. 'As I contemplate the blue of the sky', Merleau-Ponty insists, 'I am not *set over against* it as an acosmic subject …' (1962: 214). To see the sky is to *be* the sky, since the sky *is* luminosity and the visual perception of the sky *is* an experience of light.

The sky, then, is not an object of perception. It is not so much what we see as what we see *in*. We see in the sky as we see in the light, because the sky *is* light. Indeed painters have always known this, as on their canvases they have attempted to convey the experience of the world's coming to light. For them, as for us, the sky is not illuminated, it is luminosity itself. Moreover it is sonority too, as the musicologist Victor Zuckerkandl explained. In the experience of looking up into the sky, according to Zuckerkandl (1956: 344), lies the essence of what it means to hear, to which I would add that in this experience also lies the ecstasy of feeling. Thus what goes for vision goes for auditory and tactile perception as well. If we can see things because we first can see, so too, we can hear things because we first can hear, and touch things because we first can feel. The sight, hearing and touch of things are grounded in the experience, respectively, of light, sound and feeling. And if the former force us to attend to the surfaces of things, the latter, by contrast, redirect our attention to the medium in which things take shape and in which they may also be dissolved. Rather than thinking of ourselves only as observers, picking our way around the objects lying about on the ground of a ready-formed world, we must imagine ourselves in the first place as participants, each immersed with the whole of our being in the currents of a world-in-formation: in the sunlight we see in, the rain we hear in and the wind we feel in. Participation is not opposed to observation but is a condition for it, just as light is a condition for seeing things, sound for hearing them, and feeling for touching them.

In the mist

With these thoughts in mind, I would now like you to accompany me – at least in your imagination – to the seashore. On a wet and stormy February day I walked with a group of anthropology students from Aberdeen University the short distance from the classroom to the beach. There we stood, battered by rain and wind, while we continued (having to shout to make ourselves heard above the din) a conversation we had begun indoors concerning the perception of the landscape. Among other things, we had been reading the explorations of the archaeologist Christopher Tilley (1994, 2004) on the theme of landscape phenomenology. Tilley is rightly insistent that the landscape is not a physical constant that is simply given to empirical observation, description and measurement. It is rather given only in relation to its inhabitants, to their lives, movements and purposes, and the places where they dwell, and draws its meanings from these relations. Thus people and landscape – to recycle an overused anthropological formula – are 'mutually constituted'. Landscapes take on meanings and appearances in relation to people, and people develop skills, knowledge and identities in relation to the landscapes in which they find themselves.

We had been puzzled, however, by a passing remark in one of Tilley's texts. To prove his point that landscapes are not constant but vary according to the multiple perspectives of their inhabitants, he invites us to compare the view on a clear day with a view from the same spot on a misty day. Everything looks different. Yet we would be quite wrong, Tilley argues, to conclude that the clear view discloses a reality of the landscape that is obscured when it is shrouded in the mist. Neither view is any more real than the other. To claim otherwise would be 'to abstract that landscape from the person who perceives it' (Tilley 2004: 12). The difference between clarity and mistiness, he seems to be saying, is to be found not in the landscape itself but in the ways people relate to it in acts of perception. And here's the puzzle. For if that were really so, then it would take only a change in the ways people comport themselves in relation to the landscape to turn a clear prospect into a misty one, or vice versa. As we huddled together on Aberdeen beach, in the drenching rain and howling wind, the claim that it was all down to *us* rang a little hollow! Try as we might, we could not calm the storm by any ploy of perception.

Further consideration of the matter revealed that for all his insistence on both doing and writing archaeology out of doors, the weather is conspicuous by its absence from Tilley's account. More remarkably, it is absent from the accounts of practically every author, in anthropology and archaeology, who has set out to investigate the engagements between people and what is conventionally known as the 'material world'. In these accounts, as we have already seen in Chapter 2, materiality is identified with everything that has – so to speak – precipitated out from the medium, with the result that the medium itself is rendered immaterial. Rainwater enters the material world only when it accumulates in puddles on the ground, and snow only when it settles. The wind can figure only as a figment of the imagination, leading armchair theorists to suppose that boats sail, kites fly and trees flex their limbs on account of some animating force – an agency – lodged within the things themselves, as solid objects. Suffused in sunlight, even the sky becomes an imaginary realm that we can inhabit only in our thoughts and dreams, while the air we breathe is dematerialised into a spiritual ether that sustains the soul, but not the material body.

In reality, of course, the landscape has *not* already congealed from the medium. It is undergoing continuous formation, above all thanks to the immersion of its manifold surfaces in those fluxes of the medium that we call weather – in sunshine, rain, wind and so on. The ground is not the surface of materiality itself, but a textured composite of diverse materials that are grown, deposited and woven together through a dynamic interplay across the permeable interface between the medium and the substances with which it comes into contact. And so, to return to Tilley, we can see that in his passing reference to a landscape in the mist – one of those rare moments when the weather makes an appearance – he presents us with a topsy-turvy world in which the weather (in this case, mist) is an emergent outcome of the mutual constitution of people and landscape, when in truth, it is the condition for such constitution. It is only because of their common immersion in the fluxes of the medium that people and landscape can engage at all. As an experience of light, sound and feeling that suffuses our awareness, the weather is not so much an *object* of perception as what we perceive *in*, underwriting our very capacities to see, to hear and to touch. As the weather changes, so these capacities vary, leading us not to perceive different things, but to perceive the same things differently. The weather, in short, is the 'world's worlding' – to adopt Heidegger's (1971: 181) expression – and as such it is not a figment of the imagination but the very *temperament* of being (Ingold 2010: S133).

On the beach

As the students and I gathered on the beach, on that stormy day, we looked first towards the land. Then we turned and looked out to sea. What did we see there? Before attempting an answer, let me recall Gibson's characterisation of the terrestrial environment as comprising neither objects alone, nor only earth and sky, but 'the earth and the sky with objects *on* the earth and *in* the sky' (Gibson 1979: 66, see Chapter 9, p. 117). We, of course, were standing onshore. Glancing down, we saw the pebbles of the shingle on which we stood. Are pebbles, then 'objects *on* the earth'? Gibson would say so, and so would we, were each of us to stoop to pick one up and, having examined it, to replace it where it lay. Yet every pebble rested upon others, which in turn rested on others beneath them. If they, too, are *on* the earth, then where is the earth itself? Would removing layer after layer of pebbles take us any closer to it? Or should we think of the relation between pebbles and the earth in terms of the history of their formation? After all, it is only because of their incessant pounding and grating as they are washed by the surf at high tide that pebbles have gained their rounded forms. To think of a pebble as an object is to imagine it cut off from this formative process, as though it had been placed there, already shaped, like a piece of sculpture on a plinth. Yet as a stone, ground down from a piece that must once have broken off from solid rock, does not the pebble retain a connection to the earth as intrinsic as that of a seed to its parent body? Who is to say whether it is *on* the earth or *of* it?

Standing on the shingle, it was not in practice possible to draw any kind of line between these contrary conditions. We had rather to recognise that the ground on which we stood was not really a supporting platform upon which things rest but a zone of formative and transformative processes set in train through the interplay of wind, water and stone, within a field of cosmic forces such as those responsible for the tides. This became even more apparent as we lifted our glance to the surging breakers collapsing on the shore. What we saw were not objects and surfaces, but materials in motion. Raising our eyes still further we saw waves upon waves capped with foam, gradually panning out to the level expanse of the ocean, which in turn gave way to the unrelenting grey of the sky. Against this background, we could dimly make out the wheeling forms of seabirds, but we recognised them not as objects that moved, but as movements – oftentimes accompanied by sounds – that only resolved themselves into objective forms when they came to rest, perched on one of the many breakwaters that section the beach. In short, looking out to sea we saw a world in movement, in flux and becoming, a world of ocean and sky, a weather–world. We saw a *world without objects*.

Sea-ing the land

Armed with this perspective, we then turned our sights back on the land. Our question was: what happens if we regard the land from the point of view of the sea? What if, instead of land-ing the sea, we try sea-ing the land? It has been conventional to assimilate the ocean to a land-based perspective, and one moreover that focuses, under the rubric of 'landscape', on its more solid formations and their surface configurations. Looking seawards with such a perspective, we think that we are gazing upon a *seascape*, conferring on waves and troughs, or on becalmed or turbulent waters, a permanence and solidity that they lack in reality (Cooney 2003). In sea-ing the land, by contrast, it is the solidity of the ground itself that is thrown into doubt. That it is also restless, in ceaseless motion and change, is – writes sailor and philosopher Martin Dillon – 'a lesson the sea can teach us about the earth' (2007: 267). As we already found in the case of the shingle beach, seen from the perspective of the sea the ground is much more complex and dynamic than we might have thought. Far from being the hard surface of materiality that we had imagined, upon which all else rests, it reappears as a congeries of heterogeneous materials, thrown together by the vicissitudes of life in the weather-world. Indeed wherever we look, the ground bears witness to the liveliness of the processes that have gone on or are going into its formation – to the effects of rain, wind, frost and so on.

In a study of the ways in which perceptual experience underlies aesthetic sensibility, philosopher Arnold Berleant observes that the prevailing restlessness of the fluid environment profoundly affects 'all the parameters that ordinarily delimit one's terrestrial existence and, on a larger scale, even our understanding of metaphysical being'. Berleant, too, casts his eye from the ocean towards the land, and finds not only that the land undergoes continual change – 'slow, to be sure, but nevertheless incessant' – but also that fluidity does not end there.'The atmosphere is itself a fluid medium' (Berleant 2010: 139). Thus to sea the land, in our terms, is to disclose a world without objects whose solid forms are, to varying degrees, overwhelmed by the fluxes of this atmospheric medium. Rather than being opposed, sea and land, along with the littoral that marks their perpetual dialogue, appear to be engulfed in the wider sphere of forces and relations comprising the weather-world, together subsumed under the great dome of the sky. It is in this dome, where the sun shines, storms rage and the wind blows – and not, as Gibson surmised, at the surfaces of solid objects and the ground they rest on – that 'all the action is' (Gibson 1979: 23). To perceive and to act in the weather-world is to align one's own conduct to the celestial movements of sun, moon and stars, to the rhythmic alternations of night and day and of the seasons, to rain and shine, sunlight and shade. For the weather engulfs the landscape just as the sight of things is engulfed by the experience of light, the hearing of things by the experience of sound, and the touch of things by the experience of feeling.

The change in perspective from land-ing the sea to sea-ing the land corresponds rather precisely to the contrast drawn by the philosophers Gilles Deleuze and Félix Guattari between *striated* and *smooth* space (2004: 408, 524–525). Striated space, they say, is homogeneous and volumetric: in it, diverse things are laid out, each in its assigned location. To look around in striated space is, as the original meaning of *skopos* implies, to shoot visual arrows at their targets. Smooth space, to the contrary, has no layout. It presents, rather, a patchwork of continuous variation, extending without limit in all directions. It is an atmospheric space of movement and flux, stirred up by wind and weather, and suffused with light, sound and feeling. The eye, in smooth space, does not look *at* things but roams *among* them, finding a way through rather than aiming for a fixed target. It is an eye that is tuned not to the discrimination and identification of individual objects but to the registration of subtle variations of light and shade, and the surface textures they reveal. Whereas the landscape of striated space, closed off and apportioned, has turned against the sky, in smooth space the surfaces of the land – like those of the sea – open up to the sky and embrace it. In their ever-changing colours, and patterns of illumination and shade, they reflect its light; they resonate in their sounds to the passing winds, and in their feel they respond to the dryness or humidity of the air, depending on heat or rainfall. In smooth space, to continue with Deleuze and Guattari, 'there is no line separating earth and sky' (ibid.: 421). One could not exist without the other.

The haptic and the optical

In short, where landscape belongs to the order of the striated, the weather-world belongs to the order of the smooth. For Deleuze and Guattari, the archetypal denizens of smooth space were pastoral nomads who, with their herds, rode the pastures as mariners rode the waves, carried along on the windswept surfaces of sand, steppe and snow, and responding in their movements, at every moment, to real and imaginary forces, both celestial and subterranean. If, in the experience of the mariner, the world was a blend of sky and ocean, then for the nomad it was a blend of sky and earth. In this regard, the nomads' relation to the land was quite unlike that of their agrarian counterparts amongst whom the concept of landscape first took hold. The original architects of striated space were farmers who literally shaped the land by straking it with rigs and furrows. Far from going with the flow, life for them was a matter of counteracting the friction of an immobile and often unyielding earth. Deleuze and Guattari (ibid.: 524–525) compare the difference to that between felt and linen, the one matted from a swirling morass of fibres that have no consistent direction, the other woven through the regular intertwining of warp and weft. However, the modern identification of *scape* with the *scopic* – that is, of the shape of the land with its look, with form, as opposed to substance – has realigned the difference along quite another axis of contrast. This is between the *haptic* and the *optical*.

Haptic engagement is close range and hands on. It is the engagement of a mindful body at work with materials and with the land, 'sewing itself in' to the textures of the world along the pathways of sensory involvement. An optical relation between mind and world, by contrast, is founded on distance and detachment. Here, the shape of the land inheres no longer in its weave, nor would one find it by following the striations of its texture, as does the ploughman as he cuts the earth of his fields, or the journeyman as he wends his way, most likely by foot, along its tracks and trails. It is found, rather, by a kind of back-projection by which the world is cast as though fully formed, in appearance but not substance – that is, as an image – upon the surface of the mind. It is doubtless because the association between *scape* and the *scopic* implies such an optical projection that the modern concept of landscape (unlike its medieval precursor) is so often assumed to be tainted with visualist bias. In principle, however, this kind of projection could be mediated just as well by manual touch as by vision. This, for example, is how Descartes thought of blind touch, in his *Optics* of 1637. The blind, he thought, could use straight sticks to perceive the forms of objects at a distance, just as the sighted use light rays (Descartes 1988: 67). Likewise the gloved hand of the clinician, detective or curator, who handles possibly invisible objects in order to extract their form while ensuring that there should be no contact or exchange of materials across the surface of the skin, exerts an optical touch.

Conversely, haptic engagement may run along the pathways of vision as well as touch. In close-up work, the eye can be as myopically entwined in the fine grain of the world as the hand. Think of the seamstress, peering at her fabric as she draws in the threads, or the medieval scribe whose eye is caught up in the inky traces of his writing (Ingold 2007a: 92). So too, the eyes of the ploughman are close to the ground, as they line up the share with the furrow. Deleuze and Guattari are thus quite right to point out (2004: 543–544) that the opposition between the optical and the haptic cross-cuts that between eye and hand: besides optical vision and haptic touch we have optical touch as well as haptic vision. But they are wrong to assume a correspondence between the haptic/optical distinction and that between the smooth and the striated. Between the haptic and the optical lies all the difference between the perspective of the farmer who shapes the land close-up and that of the painter who views the resulting scene from a distance, or – as Deleuze and Guattari themselves observe – between 'the ground-level plane of the Gothic journeyman' and 'the metric plane of the architect, which is on paper and off site' (ibid.: 406).[2] But that does not, as they seem to think, make the farmer or the journeyman a nomad! To the contrary, the division between the haptic and the optical is a division *within* the striated, and distinguishes the medieval sense of landscape from its modern derivative. This conclusion, however, leaves us with an unresolved question. If the experience of smooth space is given neither in optical projection nor in haptic engagement, then how should we describe it?

The atmosphere

For a possible answer, we can return to the imaginary conversation, recounted above, between Gibson and Merleau-Ponty. For it comes down, once again, to the question of how we perceive the sky. Gibson thought he was looking *at* the sky; Merleau-Ponty insisted, to the contrary, that he was looking *with* it. Eyes that are open to the sky, wrote Merleau-Ponty (1962: 317), and that know moonlight and sunlight, bring these qualities of light into their own ways of perceiving. When they look, the sun and the moon look, since these celestial bodies, in their luminosity, have already invaded the perceiver's visual awareness. Similarly, when the body feels, the wind feels, since the wind, in its currents, has already invaded the body's tactile awareness. And when we gathered on the beach, the students and I found that the noise of the breakers, as they crashed on the shingle, had likewise invaded our auditory awareness: we did not just hear them; we heard *with* them. Far from being disclosed to us as targets of perception, waves, wind and sky were present as an all-enveloping experience of sound, light and feeling – that is, an *atmosphere* (Böhme 1993). The breaking waves *were* their sound, not objects that make a sound; the wind *was* its feel, not an object touched; the sky *was* light, not something seen in the light. Thus in its atmospheric manifestation, smooth space is not set over against perceivers but commingles with, and saturates, their consciousness, wherein it is generative of their own capacity to perceive. In short, the experience of smooth space *is* light, sound and feeling, not something that we obtain by their means. It is neither optical nor haptic but atmospheric.

This leads me to two points in conclusion. The first is that we would be ill-advised to assimilate the experience of light, sound or feeling to a landscape perspective by coining such compound terms as lightscape (Bille and Sorensen 2007), soundscape (Schafer 1994) or even feelingscape. These qualities of sensory experience, as I have shown, are phenomena of the weather-world. They belong to the fluxes of the medium, not to the conformation of surfaces. Indeed, there is something oxymoronic about compounds that couple the currents of sensory awareness with a regime, implicit in the modernist equation of *scape* with the *scopic*, which reduces such currents to vectors of projection in the conversion of objects into images.[3] Secondly, and following from this, we would be wrong to suppose that sensory experience is embodied, or that through it, people are tied to place (Feld and Basso 1996). We may, in practice, be anchored to the ground, but it is not light, sound or feeling that holds us down. On the contrary, they contrive to sweep us off our feet. Light floods, sound drowns out (as we found when we tried to converse on the beach) and feeling carries us away. Light, sound and feeling tear at our moorings, just like the wind tears at the limbs of trees rooted to the earth. Far from being enfolded into the body – as the concept of embodiment would imply[4] – they take possession of it, sweeping the body up into their own currents. Thus, as it is immersed in the fluxes of the medium, the body is enlightened, ensounded and enraptured. Conversely, a body confined to a place in the landscape, and that did not equally inhabit the sky, would be blind, deaf and unfeeling. In the words of the environmental philosopher David Macauley (2005: 307), 'we breathe, think and dream in the regions of the air': not on the fixed surface of the landscape but in the swirling midst of the weather-world.

I close with a brief ethnographic vignette. Nicole Revel (2005) has described how Palawan Highlanders of the Philippines have a very special relationship with birds, considering them to be their close yet ephemeral companions. Their understanding of this relationship is epitomised in the practice of flying kites. Constructed of leaves or paper with split bamboo struts, kites are regarded as the copies of birds. Flying a kite is as close as terrestrial humans can get to sharing in the experience of their avian companions. Playing the wind, flyers can feel with their hands, holding the connecting strings, what birds might feel with their wings. 'Anchored to the earth', as Revel puts it, Palawan kite flyers 'dream in the air, their thrill equal to the splendour of the whirling of their ephemeral creations' (ibid.: 407). Becoming like birds, their consciousness is launched on the same aerial currents that animate their kites, and is subject to the same turbulence. Armed with their kites, the Palawans have achieved the precise reverse of what modern art historians have achieved with the concept of landscape. Where the latter have confined the world within the ambit of its surfaces, the former, reaching out from these surfaces, have regained the openness of the atmosphere.

11

FOUR OBJECTIONS TO THE CONCEPT OF SOUNDSCAPE

I very much welcome the recent growth of interest in sound, the impact of which is being felt not only in my own discipline of anthropology, but also in the related fields of art, architecture and archaeology, to name just a few. But I am also concerned lest we repeat mistakes that have already befallen studies in visual culture. The 'visual', in these studies, appears to have little or nothing to do with what it means to be able to see. That is to say, it scarcely deals with the phenomenon of light. It is rather about the relations between objects, images and their interpretations. A study of aural culture, built along the same lines, would be about the interpretation of a world of things rendered in their acoustic forms. It has become conventional to describe such a world by means of the concept of soundscape.[1] Undoubtedly when it was first introduced, the concept served a useful rhetorical purpose in drawing attention to a sensory register that had been neglected relative to sight. I believe, however, that it has now outlived its usefulness. More to the point, it carries the risk that we might lose touch with sound in just the same way that visual studies have lost touch with light. In what follows I will set out four reasons why I think the concept of soundscape would be better abandoned.

First, the environment that we experience, know and move around in is not sliced up along the lines of the sensory pathways by which we enter into it. The world we perceive is the *same* world, whatever path we take, and in perceiving it, each of us acts as an undivided centre of movement and awareness. For this reason, I deplore the fashion for multiplying *scapes* of every possible kind. The power of the prototypical concept of landscape lies precisely in the fact that it is not tied to any specific sensory register – whether of vision, hearing, touch, taste or smell. In ordinary perceptual practice these registers cooperate so closely, and with such overlap of function, that their respective contributions are impossible to tease apart. The landscape is of course *visible*, but it only becomes *visual* when it has been rendered by some technique, such as of painting or photography, which then allows it to be viewed indirectly, by way of the resulting image, which, as it were, returns the landscape back to the viewer in an artificially purified form, shorn of all other sensory dimensions. Likewise, a landscape may be *audible*,[2] but to be *aural* it would have to have been first rendered by a technique of sound art or recording, such that it can be *played back* within an environment (such as a darkened room) in which we are otherwise deprived of sensory stimulus.

We should not be fooled by art historians and other students of visual culture who write books about the history of seeing that are entirely about the contemplation of images. Their conceit is to imagine that the eyes are not so much organs of observation as instruments of playback, lodged in the image rather than the body of the observer. It is as though the eyes did our seeing for us, leaving us to (re)view the images they relay to our consciousness. For the active looking and watching that people do as they go about their business, visual theorists have substituted regimes of the 'scopic', defined and distinguished by the recording and playback functions of these allegorical eyes. Although, as we saw in the last chapter, the apparent etymological kinship between the scopic and the 'scapes' of our perception is spurious, such a connection is commonly presumed. Thus in resorting to the notion of soundscape, we run the risk of subjecting the ears, in studies of the aural, to the same fate as the eyes in visual studies. This is my second objection to the concept. We need to avoid the trap, analogous to thinking that the power of sight inheres in images, of supposing that the power of hearing inheres in recordings. For the ears, just like the eyes, are organs of observation, not instruments of playback. Just as we use our eyes to watch and look, so we use our ears to listen as we go forth in the world.

It is of course to light, and not to vision, that sound should be compared. The fact, however, that sound is so often and apparently unproblematically compared to *sight* rather than light reveals much about our implicit assumptions regarding vision and hearing, which, as I have already explained (p. 128), rest on the curious idea that the eyes are screens that block out the light, leaving us to reconstruct the world inside our heads, whereas the ears are holes in the skull that let the sound in so that it can mingle with the soul. One result of this idea is that the vast psychological literature on optical illusions is unmatched by anything on the deceptions of the ear. Another is that studies of visual perception have had virtually nothing to say about the phenomenon of light. It would be unfortunate if studies of auditory perception were to follow suit, and to lose touch with sound just as visual studies have lost touch with light. Far better, by placing the phenomenon of sound at the heart of our inquiries, we might be able to point to parallel ways in which light could be restored to the central place it deserves in understanding visual perception. To do this, however, we have first to address the awkward question: what *is* sound? This question is a version of the old philosophical conundrum: does the tree falling in a storm make any sound if there is no creature present with ears to hear it? Does sound consist of mechanical vibrations in the medium? Or is it something we register only inside our heads? Is it a phenomenon of the material world or of the mind? Is it 'out there' or 'in here'? Can we dream it?

It seems to me that such questions are wrongly posed, in so far as they set up a rigid division between two worlds, of mind and matter – a division that is reproduced every time that appeal is made to the *materiality* of sound. Sound, in my view, is neither mental nor material, but a phenomenon of *experience* – that is, of our immersion in, and commingling with, the world in which we find ourselves. Such immersion, as the philosopher Maurice Merleau-Ponty (1964) insisted, is an existential precondition for the isolation both of minds to perceive and of things in the world to be perceived. To put it another way, just as light is another way of saying 'I can see' (see Chapter 10, p. 128), so sound is another way of saying 'I can hear'. If this is so, then neither sound nor light, strictly speaking, can be an *object* of our perception. Sound is not *what* we hear, any more than light is what we see. Herein lies my third objection to the concept of soundscape. It does not make sense for the same reason that a concept of 'lightscape' would not make sense.[3] The scaping of things – that is, their surface conformation – is revealed to us thanks to their illumination. When we look around on a fine day, we see a landscape bathed in sunlight, not a lightscape. Likewise, listening to our surroundings, we do not hear a soundscape. For sound, I would argue, is not the object but the medium of our perception. It is what we hear *in*. Similarly, we do not see light but see *in* it (Ingold 2000a: 265).

Once light and sound are understood in these terms, it becomes immediately apparent that in our ordinary experience, the two are so closely involved with one another as to be virtually inseparable. This involvement, however, raises interesting questions that we are only beginning to address. How, for example, does the contrast between light and darkness compare with that between sound and silence? It is fairly obvious that the experience of sound is quite different in the dark than in the light. Does the experience of light likewise depend on whether we are simultaneously drowned in sound or cocooned in silence? These kinds of questions bring me to my fourth objection to the concept of soundscape. Since it is modelled on the concept of landscape, soundscape places the emphasis on the *surfaces* of the world in which we live. Sound and light, however, are infusions of the *medium* in which we find our being and through which we move. Traditionally, both in my own discipline of anthropology and more widely in fields such as cultural geography, art history and material culture studies, scholars have focused on the fixities of surface conformation rather than the fluxes of the medium. They have, in other words, imagined a world of persons and objects that has already precipitated out, or solidified, from these fluxes (see Chapter 2, p. 26). Going on to equate the solidity of things with their materiality, they have contrived to dematerialise the medium in which they are primordially immersed. Even the air we breathe, and on which life depends, becomes a figment of the imagination.

Now the mundane term for what I have called the fluxes of the medium is *weather*. So long as we are – as we say – 'out in the open', the weather is no mere phantasm, the stuff of dreams. It is, to the contrary, fundamental to perception. We do not perceive it; we perceive *in* it (Ingold 2005a). We do not touch the wind, but touch in it; we do not see sunshine, but see in it; we do not hear rain, but hear in it. Thus wind, sunshine and rain, experienced as feeling, light and sound, are essential to our capacities, respectively, to touch, to see and to hear (see Chapter 10, p. 130). In order to understand the phenomenon of sound (as indeed those of light and feeling), we should therefore turn our attention skywards, to the realm of the birds, rather than towards the solid earth beneath our feet. The sky, as we saw in the last chapter, is not an object of perception, any more than sound is. It is not a thing we see. It is rather luminosity itself. But it is sonority too. Recall the argument of the musicologist Victor Zuckerkandl (1956: 344), that if we really want to know what it means to hear, we should gaze into the sky. If he is right, then perhaps our metaphors for describing auditory space should be derived not from landscape studies but from meteorology.

Let me conclude with a couple of points that address not the concept of soundscape itself but rather its implied emphasis on, first, *embodiment*, and second, *emplacement*. I have mentioned the wind, and the fact that to live we must be able to breathe. Wind and breath are intimately related in the continuous movement of inhalation and exhalation that is fundamental to life and being. Inhalation is wind becoming breath, exhalation is breath becoming wind. At a recent anthropological conference on *Wind, Life, Health* (Low and Hsu 2008), the issue came up of how the wind is embodied in the constitution of persons affected by it. For my part, I felt uneasy about applying the concept of embodiment in this context. It made breathing seem like a process of coagulation, in which air was somehow sedimented into the body as it solidified. Acknowledging that the living body, as it breathes, is necessarily swept up in the currents of the medium, I suggested that the wind is not so much embodied as the body *enwinded* (Ingold 2007b: S32). It seems to me, moreover, that what applies to wind also applies to sound. After all, the wind whistles, and people hum or murmur as they breathe. Sound, like breath, is experienced as a movement of coming and going, inspiration and expiration. If that is so, then we should say of the body, as it sings, hums, whistles or speaks, that it is *ensounded*. It is like setting sail, launching the body *into* sound like a boat on the waves or, perhaps more appropriately, like a kite in the sky.

Finally, if sound is like the wind, then it will not stay put, nor does it put persons or things in their place. Sound flows, as wind blows, along irregular, winding paths, and the places it describes are like eddies, formed by a circular movement *around* rather than a fixed location *within*. To follow sound, that is to *listen*, is to wander the same paths. Attentive listening, as opposed to passive hearing, surely entails the very opposite of emplacement. Again the analogy with flying a kite is apposite. Though the flyer's feet may be firmly planted on the spot, it is not the wind that keeps them there. Likewise, the sweep of sound continually endeavours to tear listeners away, causing them to surrender to its movement. It requires an effort to stay in place. And this effort pulls *against* sound rather than harmonising *with* it. Place confinement, in short, is a form of deafness.

PART IV

A storied world

My earliest attempt to write the first essay of this part, Chapter 12, goes back a long way. It was for a conference on *Space, Culture, Power*, held at the University of Aberdeen in April 2001 (Kirby 2009). I remember remarking, at the time, on how in the work of geographers, place and space always seem to be rolled together, as though one could no more exist without the other than a door knocker could exist without a door. And I wondered how much this had to do with the fortunate circumstance that the words place and space happened to rhyme. Spelled backwards, space becomes 'ecaps', and place 'ecalp'. How many books and articles, I asked, would have been published with *ecaps and ecalp* in the title? Not many, I thought. Only later, thanks to the timely intervention of historical geographer Kenneth Olwig, did I become aware of the real reason for the coupling of space with place, which lies in the problem of translation from the Germano-Scandinavian *raum* or *rum*. What I did not know however, as I worked further on the essay, was that all the while, another distinguished geographer, Doreen Massey, was hard at work on a parallel endeavour, albeit of much greater scope and ambition. Whereas for my essay I had selected the title *Against Space*, Massey called her book, published in 2005, *For Space*. With such diametrically opposed titles, I anticipated that we would be in fundamental disagreement. But when I eventually had an opportunity to read the book, I was surprised and gratified to discover that, to the contrary, we were largely of one mind! Both of us imagine a world of incessant movement and becoming, one that is never complete but continually under construction, woven from the countless lifelines of its manifold human and non-human constituents as they thread their ways through the tangle of relationships in which they are comprehensively enmeshed. In such a world, persons and things do not so much exist as occur, and are identified not by any fixed, essential attributes laid down in advance or transmitted ready-made from the past, but by the very pathways (or trajectories, or stories) along which they have previously come and are presently going.

Why then, despite our agreement, did we end up arguing from what, ostensibly, were opposite sides of the ring? Massey is *for* space, I am *against* it. Clearly we mean different things by the term. Indeed Massey, too, is against a certain conception of space. This conception is resolutely flat or two-dimensional: it pictures an isotropic surface upon which all things are wrapped up in themselves, fixed in their respective places, broken off from the movements that brought them there, and caught in a finite, closed and all-encompassing network of synchronic connections. Such space is lifeless. Nothing is going on there. No wonder that legions of philosophers have protested against the 'spatialisation' inherent in endeavours, especially in fields of natural science and cartography, to pin the world down in terms of stable conceptual representations. To bring it back to life they have celebrated time, not as a fourth dimension to be added to the three of space, as in the physicists' space–time continuum, but as the very movement of creative becoming that ensures that for so long as life goes on, it will always forge ahead of our systematic and systemising attempts to hold it to account. Thus time is to space as dynamic is to static, lively to lifeless, open to closed, becoming to being and so on.

Now in arguing *for* space, Massey does not dispute such philosophies of time. On the contrary, she is with them all the way, and so am I. What she rejects is the kind of dichotomisation that leaves space as an empty shell, as the negative of time. She wants us to think of space positively, as just as dynamic, lively and open-ended as time. Space, for her, is a domain of co-presence, of relationships-in-practice, of the entanglement of multiple lifelines as they become caught up with one another in going their respective ways. It is, to cite just two of her many formulations, a 'sphere of … contemporaneous multiplicity' and the 'simultaneity of stories-so-far' (Massey 2005: 10–12, 148, 183). Indeed the very multiplicity of trajectories, in her argument, *requires* space. In other words, when we say that life is not just one story but a host of different stories, we are asserting the possibility that these multiple stories can run alongside one another. Space establishes this possibility. If time is the guarantor of life, space is the guarantor that heterogeneous lives proceed concurrently. Perhaps, then, the only difference between Massey and myself is that like the philosophers to whom she refers, I remain a flat-earther when it comes to space. Yet I do not deny that the world is teeming with multiple forms of life whose entanglements comprise an ever-ravelling and unravelling relational meshwork. What I am quite unable to do, however, is to bring myself to describe this world as one of *space*. I just cannot get out of my head the idea of space as a void, as non-world, as absence rather than co-presence. To my mind the world is a world, not space; and what is going on in it – the processes wherein its manifold forms arise and are held in place – are processes of life, not time. Massey's time–space is, for me, the lifeworld.

'Space', of course, is just a word, and you can use it to mean what you like. But more than just a semantic issue is at stake here. As a geographer, Massey cannot simply sidestep the concept of space, as I am tempted to do, and use a word like 'world' instead. We anthropologists have had similar problems with our key concept, of 'culture'. As Massey the geographer seeks to breathe life into space, many anthropologists have likewise sought to enliven culture by stressing its creativity and open-endedness, and its relational constitution as an interweaving of stories rather than a received and totalising system of classification. I attempt to do just this myself, in Chapter 13, through a critique of the metaphor of *transmission*, so commonly used to characterise the twin processes of biological and cultural reproduction. Behind this metaphor lies the founding axiom of what I call the *genealogical model*, namely, that individuals are specified in their genetic and cultural constitution independently and in advance of their life in the world, through the bestowal of attributes from ancestors. So far as cultural transmission is concerned, the model implies that knowledge already acquired is imported into contexts of practical engagement with the environment, and therefore that this knowledge is, in itself, context independent. I show that an organisation of context independent knowledge can only take the form of a classification. Thus, claims that knowledge universally takes a classificatory form are circular: they follow from the initial assumptions of the genealogical model. They are also invalidated by what we have learned, from many anthropological studies, of how people actually come to know what they do. This is by *going around* in an environment. The knowledge they acquire, I argue, is integrated not *up* the levels of a classification but *along* paths of movement, and people grow into it by following trails through a meshwork. I call this trail-following *wayfaring*, and conclude that it is through wayfaring and not transmission that knowledge is carried on.

This argument is fleshed out ethnographically in Chapter 14, drawing on material from the Koyukon people, indigenous hunters of Alaska. The argument turns on the practices of naming. In the modern western imagination, to be properly human is to possess a unique named identity and to occupy a specific named address. In between persons and places, however, there lies a universe of things that are known only by appellatives or common nouns. Behind the conventional grammatical distinction between proper names and appellatives, I argue, lies a more fundamental distinction between the networked knowledge of persons and places and the classificatory knowledge of things. The network singles out persons on the plane of humanity, and places on the surface of the earth; the classification groups things on the basis of their intrinsic attributes, irrespective of where they stand. There is nothing absolute, however, about this tripartite division between places, things and persons. For the Koyukon, names are not nouns but verbs, and knowing is akin to storytelling. The names that Koyukon people give to animals may be based on descriptions of their behaviour, or Distant Time stories of world creation, or riddles. In each case, to name the animal is not to affix a label to it but to tell its story. Animals do not exist for the Koyukon; rather, they *occur*, and life activity of the animal and the telling of its story are alternative manifestations of the same occurrence.

12

AGAINST SPACE

PLACE, MOVEMENT, KNOWLEDGE

I wish to argue, in this chapter, against the notion of space. Of all the terms we use to describe the world we inhabit, it is the most abstract, the most empty, the most detached from the realities of life and experience. Consider the alternatives. Biologists say that living organisms inhabit *environments*, not space, and whatever else they may be, human beings are certainly organisms. Throughout history, whether as hunters and gatherers, farmers or herders of livestock, people have drawn a living from the *land*, not from space. Farmers plant their crops in the *earth*, not in space, and harvest them from *fields*, not from space. Their animals graze *pastures*, not space. Travellers make their way through the *country*, not through space, and as they walk or stand they plant their feet on the *ground*, not in space. Painters set up their easels in the *landscape*, not in space. When we are at home, we are *indoors*, not in space, and when we go outdoors we are in the *open*, not in space. Casting our eyes upwards, we see the *sky*, not space, and on a windy day we feel the *air*, not space. Space is nothing, and because it is nothing it cannot truly be inhabited at all.

How have we arrived at such an abstract and rarified concept to describe the world in which we live? My contention is that it results from the operation of what I have called the logic of inversion. I have already introduced this logic in Chapter 5 (p. 68). In a nutshell, inversion turns the pathways along which life is lived into boundaries within which it is enclosed. Life, according to this logic, is reduced to an internal property of things that *occupy* the world but do not, strictly speaking, *inhabit* it. A world that is occupied but not inhabited, that is filled with existing things rather than woven from the strands of their coming-into-being, is a world of space. In what follows I shall show how the logic of inversion transforms our understanding, first, of place, second, of movement, and third, of knowledge. Emplacement becomes enclosure, travelling becomes transport, and ways of knowing become transmitted culture. Putting all these together, we are led to that peculiarly *modular* conception of being that is such a striking feature of modernity, and of which the concept of space is the logical corollary.

Place

I have nothing against the idea of place. I do, however, think there is something wrong with the notion that places exist *in space*. The persistent habit of counterposing space and place, as Doreen Massey complains, leads us to imagine that life is lived at the base of a vortex, from which the only escape is to lift off from the ground of real experience, upwards and outwards, towards ever higher levels of abstraction (Massey 2005: 183). Time and again, philosophers have assured us that, as earthbound beings, we can only live, and know, *in* places (e.g. Casey 1996: 18). I do not live, however, in the sitting room of my house. Any ordinary day sees me wandering around between the sitting room, dining room, kitchen, bathroom, bedroom, study and so on, as well as in the garden. Nor am I housebound, as I travel daily to my place of work, to the shops and to other places of business, while my children go to school. To this, philosophers of place respond that of course, places exist like Russian dolls on many levels in a nested series, and that at whatever level we may select, a place is liable both to contain a number of lower-level places and to be contained, alongside other places at that level, within a higher-level one. Thus my house, as a place, contains the smaller places comprised of the rooms and garden, and is contained within the larger places of my neighbourhood and home town. As J. E. Malpas writes, 'places always open up to disclose other places within them ... while from within any particular place one can always look outwards to find oneself within some much larger expanse (as one can look from the room in which one sits to the house in which one lives)' (1999: 170–171).

Only a philosopher could look from his sitting room and see his whole house! For its ordinary residents, the house or apartment is disclosed processionally, as a temporal series of vistas, occlusions and transitions unfolding along the myriad of pathways they take, from room to room and in and out of doors, as they go about their daily tasks. Malpas, however, writes of leaving his room for his apartment, his apartment for the building, and the building for the neighbourhood and city in which he lives, as though each step along the way were a movement not along but *upwards*, from level to level, from smaller, more exclusive places to larger, more inclusive ones. And the higher he climbs, the further removed he feels from the groundedness of *place*, and the more drawn to an abstract sense of *space*. Conversely, the return trip homeward takes him on a downward movement, through the levels, from space back to place (ibid.: 171). Each level, here, is like one line on an address that enables the postman eventually to deliver the letter into the lowest-level container within which the recipient is supposed to lie ensconced. When the letter drops through the philosopher's front door it is as if it also drops *down* one level, from street to house. And when he picks it up and takes it through to his living room (rather than, say, the kitchen), it drops one level still. Although in reality, the letter comes into his hands through having been relayed along a number of paths that have touched one another at various places along the way, such as the letterbox, the sorting office and so on, the impression is conveyed that it has come 'down' to him through a progressive refinement of spatial scale, from everywhere to somewhere, or from space to place.

Opening the letter in his living room, he might pause to reflect on how the concepts of 'life' and 'room' have come to be conjoined in the denomination of this area of his house. In vernacular English the word 'room', in this context, simply means an interior part of the building enclosed by walls, floor and ceiling. And 'living' covers a suite of common indoor activities that would be undertaken by the occupants of this particular room. But, as Kenneth Olwig has pointed out, when 'life' and 'room' are joined in German they yield an entirely different concept, namely *lebensraum* (2002: 3). Here the meaning of life comes closer to what Martin Heidegger identified as the foundational sense of dwelling: not the occupation of a world already built, but the very process of inhabiting the earth. Life, in this sense, is lived in the open, rather than being contained within the structures of the built environment (Heidegger 1971). Hence, too, the 'room' of *lebensraum* is not an enclosure but an opening, one that affords scope for growth and movement. It has no walls, only the horizons progressively disclosed to the traveller as he passes along a trail; no floor, only the ground beneath his feet; no ceiling, only the sky arching overhead.

My reason for digressing on the significance of room is to address a peculiar problem of translation. The German *raum*, or its cognate *rum* in the Scandinavian languages, is nowadays the accepted equivalent of the Anglo-American concept of *space*. Yet their connotations are far from identical. In English, 'space' and 'room' are quite distinct, with room conceived as a highly localised, life-containing compartment within the boundless totality of space. It appears, however, that in its translation as 'space', *raum/rum* never entirely lost the sense of containment or enclosure that currently attaches to the notion of place. Perhaps that is why, as Olwig suggests, a geography that has its roots in the intellectual traditions of Germany and the Nordic countries so often rolls together space and place. For in the modern concept of *raum/rum* it seems that the two contradictory connotations of openness and closure, of 'absolute space and confined room' (Olwig 2002: 7), are conflated. It was this duplicity that allowed Nazi propagandists, in the run-up to the Second World War, to seize upon the notion of *lebensraum* as justification at once for the unlimited expansion and bounded self-sufficiency of the German nation.

Even Heidegger, himself somewhat complicit in this enterprise, thought of *raum* as a clearing for life that was nevertheless bounded.[1] But he promptly went on to explain that this boundary was not a border but a *horizon*, 'not that at which something stops but … that from which something *begins its presencing*' (Heidegger 1971: 154). It seems that in the transition from its ancient sense of a clearing, opening or 'way through' to the modern oxymoron of 'space and place', the concept of room has been called upon to perform the trick of inversion, turning the affordances for dwelling opened up along a path of movement into an enclosed capsule for life suspended in the void. The idea that places are situated in space is the *product* of this inversion, and is not given prior to it. In other words, far from being applied to two opposed yet complementary aspects of reality, space and place, the concept of room is centrally implicated in setting up the distinction between them. It is not a distinction that is immediately given to our experience, which, as I shall now argue, is drawn from lives that are never exclusively here or there, lived *in* this place or that, but always on the way from one place to another.

Let me introduce the argument by way of a simple experiment. Take a sheet of plain paper and a pencil, and draw a rough circle. It might look something like this:

How should we interpret this line? Strictly speaking, it is the trace left by the gesture of your hand as, holding the pencil, it alighted on the paper and took a turn around before continuing on its way to wherever it would go and whatever it would do next. However, viewing the line as a totality, ready-drawn on the page, we might be inclined to interpret it quite differently – not as a trajectory of movement but as a static perimeter, delineating the figure of the circle against the ground of an otherwise empty plane. In just the same way we tend to identify traces of the circumambulatory movements that bring a place into being as boundaries that demarcate the place from its surrounding space. Whether on paper or on the ground, the pathways or trails *along* which movement proceeds are perceived as limits *within* which it is contained. Both cases exemplify the logic of inversion at work, turning the 'way through' of the trail into the containment of the place-in-space. This is illustrated below.

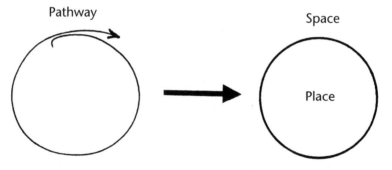

Pathway

Space

Place

My contention is that lives are led not inside places but through, around, to and from them, from and to places elsewhere (Ingold 2000a: 229). I use the term *wayfaring* to describe the embodied experience of this perambulatory movement. It is as wayfarers, then, that human beings inhabit the earth (Ingold 2007a: 75–84). But by the same token, human existence is not fundamentally place-*bound*, as Christopher Tilley (2004: 25) maintains, but place-*binding*. It unfolds not in places but along paths. Proceeding along a path, every inhabitant lays a trail. Where inhabitants meet, trails are entwined, as the life of each becomes bound up with the other. Every entwining is a knot, and the more that lifelines are entwined, the greater the density of the knot.

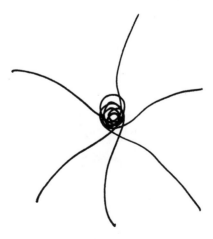

Places, then, are like knots, and the threads from which they are tied are lines of wayfaring. A house, for example, is a place where the lines of its residents are tightly knotted together. But these lines are no more contained within the house than are threads contained within a knot. Rather, they trail beyond it, only to become caught up with other lines in other places, as are threads in other knots. Together they make up what I have called the *meshwork* (Ingold 2007a: 80).

Places, in short, are delineated by movement, not by the outer limits to movement. Indeed it is for just this reason that I have chosen to refer to people who frequent places as 'inhabitants' rather than 'locals'. For it would be quite wrong to suppose that such people are confined within a particular place, or that their experience is circumscribed by the restricted horizons of a life lived only there (Ingold 2007a: 100–101). Inhabitants can indeed be widely travelled, as David Anderson, for example, found during fieldwork among Evenki reindeer herders in Siberia. When he questioned his hosts about the location of their original clan lands, he was told that in the past people travelled – and lived – not somewhere but *everywhere* (Anderson 2000: 133–135). This 'everywhere', however, is not 'nowhere'. Evenki herders did not formerly live in space rather than place. The illusion that they did is a product of our own cartographic conventions that lead us to imagine the surface of the earth divided into a mosaic of areas, each occupied by a named nation or ethnic group. On a map drawn according to these conventions, the few thousand Evenki appear to occupy an area almost twice the size of Europe! The Evenki people, however, did not occupy their country, they inhabited it. And whereas occupation is areal, habitation is lineal. That is to say, it takes people not *across* the land surface but *along* the paths that lead from place to place. From the perspective of inhabitants, therefore, 'everywhere' is not space. It is the entire meshwork of intertwined trails along which people carry on their lives. While on the trail one is always somewhere. But every 'somewhere' is on the way to somewhere else (Ingold 2007a: 81). This is an appropriate moment, therefore, to turn from place to movement. How has our understanding of movement been transformed by the logic of inversion?

Movement[2]

In his contemplation on the Arctic, *Playing Dead* (1989), the Canadian writer Rudy Wiebe compares native Inuit understandings of movement and travel over land or sea ice with those of the sailors of the Royal Navy in their maritime search for the elusive Northwest Passage to the Orient. For the Inuit, *as soon as a person moves he becomes a line*. To hunt for an animal, or to find another human being who may be lost, you lay one line of tracks across the expanse, looking for signs of another line of motion that would lead to your objective. Thus the entire country is perceived as a mesh of lines rather than a continuous surface. The British sailors, however, 'accustomed to the fluid, trackless seas, moved in terms of area' (ibid.: 16). The vessel, supplied for the voyage before setting sail, was conceived as a moving dot upon the surface of the sea, its position always located by latitude and longitude. We have already encountered this difference, between lineal movement *along* paths of travel and lateral movement *across* a surface, in our comparison of the respective 'everywheres' of habitation and occupation. I have referred to movement of the former kind as *wayfaring*. Movement of the latter kind, I call *transport*. I shall now show that the inversion that renders the inhabited world as space, also converts wayfaring into transport.

The wayfarer is continually on the move. More strictly, he *is* his movement. As with the Inuit in the example presented above, the wayfarer is instantiated in the world as a line of travel. It is a line that advances from the tip as he presses on, in an ongoing process of growth and development, or self-renewal. As he proceeds, however, the wayfarer has to sustain himself, both perceptually and materially, through an active engagement with the country that opens up along his path.[3] Though from time to time he must pause for rest, and may even return repeatedly to the same place to do so, each pause is a moment of tension that – like holding one's breath – becomes ever more intense and less sustainable the longer it lasts. Indeed the wayfarer has no final destination, for wherever he is, and so long as life goes on, there is somewhere further he can go.

Transport, by contrast, is essentially destination-oriented (Wallace 1993: 65–66). It is not so much a development *along* a way of life as a carrying *across*, from location to location, of people and goods in such a way as to leave their basic natures unaffected. For in transport, the traveller does not himself move. Rather he is moved, becoming a passenger in his own body, if not in some vessel that can extend or replace the body's powers of propulsion. While in transit he remains encased within his vessel, drawing for sustenance on his own supplies and holding a predetermined course. Only upon reaching his destination, and when his means of transport comes to a halt, does the traveller begin to move. But this movement, confined within a place, is concentrated on one spot. Thus the very places where the wayfaring inhabitant pauses for rest are, for the transported passenger, sites of occupation. In between sites, he barely skims the surface of the world.

To highlight the contrast, let me suggest a second experiment. Take up your pencil once again, but this time draw a continuous freehand line. Like the circle you drew before, the line remains as the trace of your manual gesture. In the memorable phrase of the painter, Paul Klee, your line has gone out for a walk (1961: 105).

But now I want you to draw a dotted line. To do this you have to bring the tip of your pencil into contact with the paper at a predetermined point, and then cause it to perform a little pirouette on that point so as to form a dot. All the energy, and all the movement, is focused down on the point, almost as though you were drilling a hole. Then you have to lift your pencil from the paper and carry it across to the next point where you do the same, and so on until you have marked the paper with a series of dots.

Where, in this series, is the line? It is not generated as a movement, or even as the trace of a movement, since all the movement is in the dots. Whatever movements you might make between drawing each dot serve merely to carry the pencil tip from one point to the next, and are entirely incidental to the line itself. During these intervals the pencil is inactive, out of use. Indeed you could even rest it on your desk for any length of time before picking it up again and returning it to the paper surface.

The dotted line, in short, is defined not by a gesture but as a connected sequence of fixed points. Now just as in drawing, the line is traced by a movement of your hands, so the wayfarer in his perambulations lays a trail on the ground in the form of footprints, paths and tracks. Thus, writing of the Walbiri, an Aboriginal people of the Australian Central Desert, Roy Wagner notes that 'the life of a person is the sum of his tracks, the total inscription of his movements, something that can be traced out along the ground' (1986: 21). The logic of inversion, however, converts every track or trail into the equivalent of a dotted line, first by dividing it into stages,

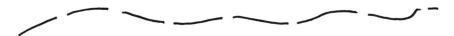

and then by rolling and packing each stage into the confines of a destination.

The lines linking these destinations, like those of an air or rail traffic map, are not traces of movement but point-to-point connectors. These are the lines of transport. And whereas the wayfarer signs his presence on the land as the ever-growing sum of his trails, the passenger carries his signature about with him as he is transported from place to place. Wherever he may be, he should be able to replicate this highly condensed, miniature gesture as a mark of his unique and unchanging identity (Ingold 2007a: 94). Once again we find the logic of inversion at work here, turning the paths along which people lead their lives into internal properties of self-contained, bounded individuals. Whenever the individual is required to sign on the dotted line, this inversion is re-enacted. An occupant of everywhere and an inhabitant of nowhere, the signatory declares by this act his allegiance to space.

As I have already suggested, occupation is areal whereas habitation is lineal. The various destinations to be linked in a system of transport are conceived to be laid out upon an isotropic surface, each at a location specified by global coordinates. The lines connecting these destinations comprise a network that is spread across the surface, and 'pinned down' at each of its nodes. To the wayfarer, however, the world is not presented as a surface to be traversed. In his movements he threads his way *through* this world rather than routing *across* it from point to point. Of course the wayfarer is a terrestrial being, and must perforce travel over the land.[4] The surfaces of the land, however, are *in* and not *of* the world, woven from the lines of growth and movement of inhabitants (Ingold 2000a: 241, and see Chapter 5, p. 71). What they form, as we have already seen, is not a network of point-to-point connections, but a tangled mesh of interwoven and complexly knotted strands. Every strand is a way of life, and every knot a place. Indeed the mesh is something like a net in its original sense of an open-work fabric of interlaced or knotted cords. But through its metaphorical extension to the realms of modern transport and communications, and especially information technology, the meaning of 'the net' has changed.[5] We are now more inclined to think of it as a complex of interconnected points than of interwoven lines. For this reason I have found it necessary to distinguish between the *network* of transport and the *meshwork* of wayfaring. The key to this distinction is the recognition that the lines of the meshwork are not connectors. They are the paths *along* which life is lived.

And it is in the binding together of lines, not in the connecting of points, that the mesh is constituted.

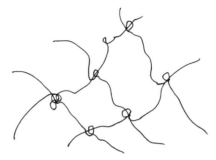

I have argued that wayfaring is our most fundamental mode of being in the world. Does this mean that the possibility of genuine transport is but a dream, on a par with the illusion that the places it connects are fixed in space? If so, then we must also acknowledge that modern metropolitan societies have done much to turn the dream into reality (Ingold 2007a: 102). They have created transport systems that span the globe in a vast network of destination-to-destination connections. And they have converted travel from an experience of movement in which action and perception are intimately coupled into one of enforced immobility and sensory deprivation. The passenger, strapped in his seat, no longer has the 'all around' perception of a land that stretches without interruption from the ground beneath his feet towards the horizon. It rather appears as so much scenery projected onto vertical screens, more or less distant, that seem to slide past one another due to the operation of parallax. This flattening and layering of the landscape, as ethnologist Orvar Löfgren has observed (2000: 24), may have more to do with the effects of travel at speed than with the anchoring of vision to a fixed location. Indeed the essence of speed may lie less in the actual ratio of distance travelled to elapsed time than in the decoupling, in transport, of perception and motility.

Once this decoupling has been effected – once, that is, movement is reduced to sheer mechanical displacement, thereby establishing the possibility of speed – then the actual speed of transport can, in principle, be increased indefinitely. Ideally it should take no time at all. This is because the lines of the transport network, criss-crossing the continuum of space, lack duration. By connecting points on a network, or 'joining the dots', the prospective traveller can *virtually* reach his destination even before setting out. As a cognitive artefact or assembly, the route plan pre-exists its physical enactment. Yet in practice it takes time to get there, even by the fastest means. Perfect transport is impossible for the same reason that one cannot be in two places, nor indeed everywhere, simultaneously. As all travel is movement in real time, a person can never be quite the same, on arrival at a place, as when he set out: some memory of the journey will remain, however attenuated, and will in turn condition his knowledge of the place. We might wish it were otherwise: thus scientific researchers are routinely advised not to allow the travails of gaining access to field sites to intrude upon their observations, lest this might distort the data collected and compromise their objectivity.[6] But total objectivity is as impossible an ideal as is perfect transport, or indeed the perfect machine (see Chapter 4, p. 62). We cannot get from one place to another by leap-frogging the world. Or in the wise words of the nursery rhyme, *We're Going on a Bear Hunt*:

We can't go over it.
We can't go under it.
Oh no!
We've got to go through it! [7]

Knowledge

A team of scientists has set out to investigate changes in the ecology and hydrology of the Arctic tundra in a particular region of the Russian North.[8] They wish to ascertain the major drivers of these changes, including global warming and industrial pollution. On a map of the region they have drawn a straight line of twenty dots, spaced out at equal intervals of one centimetre (corresponding to fifty kilometres on the map). Each of these dots marks a site where the team intends to collect soil and water samples, to record the vegetation, and to take any necessary measurements, for example of the acidity of the soil or of background radiation. As overland travel is slow and hazardous in this region, which in summer is a maze of mosquito-infested swamps, aimlessly meandering rivers and stagnant pools, the team will hire a helicopter to transport themselves and their equipment from one location to the next. In effect, these airborne trips, re-enact at full scale, the drawing of the dotted line on the map. Just as the tip of the pencil had been lowered at a succession of points in order to mark the paper surface of the map, so the helicopter with its burden of scientists and instruments will 'drop down' at site after site, enabling them to take their readings from the actual surface of the tundra. Though it might be otherwise for the pilot, who has to guide his machine to the right place and find a suitable spot to land, so far as the scientists are concerned their helicopter transport is wholly ancillary to the primary task of data collection. Indeed while the pilot, an inhabitant of the region, is preoccupied with finding the way to the next landing place, the scientists have little to do but admire the view from the windows. Only when the pilot takes a break can the scientists get on with the job of making their observations.

In this example, data are being collected from a series of fixed locations. For the scientific team these locations comprise a thousand-kilometre transect that cuts across the surface of the earth. But the transect is not a pathway: it is not the trace of a movement but a chain of point-to-point connections. Held together by these connections, the constituent locations of the transect are – we could say – *laterally* integrated. But what of the data obtained from them? Every datum is a 'thing given', a fact. Though discovered among the contents of a site, *where* it is, or how it came to be there, forms no part of *what* it is. As a sample or specimen, each fact is deemed to be one of a kind. And its significance lies not in the story of its discovery but in its juxtaposition and comparison with facts of similar kind – or whose intrinsic properties can be measured by the same yardstick – collected from other sites. Thus once the season's fieldwork is completed, members of the team will send the data they have collected back to their respective laboratories, where it will be fed into a database that will, in turn, allow them to search for systematic correlations upon which could be built predictive models of ecosystemic and climatic change. The data, in effect, are passed 'upwards' for analysis, as they are fed into frameworks of progressively wider and ultimately universal scope. In the construction of the database, in their classification and tabulation, the scientists' findings – we could say – are *vertically* integrated. Through this process of integration, knowledge is produced.

In short, to the laterally integrated geography of locations there corresponds a vertically integrated classification of the things found in them. The former is held together by chains or networks of point-to-point connections, the latter by the taxonomic aggregations and divisions of the database. But what of the knowledge of inhabitants? How is *that* integrated? Consider the helicopter pilot in our example. He has accumulated a good deal of experience of flying in these parts. Unlike the visiting scientists, he knows the terrain, and how to find his way under variable weather conditions. But this knowledge is not derived from locations. It is rather comes from a history of previous flights, of take-offs and landings, and of incidents and encounters en route. In other words it is forged in *movement*, 'in the passage from place to place and the changing horizons along the way' (Ingold 2000a: 227). Thus the geographic knowledge of the pilot, as an inhabitant, is not laterally integrated, since places for him are not spatial locations, nor are they held together by point-to-point connections. They are rather *topics*, joined in stories of journeys actually made.[9] Nor is his knowledge of things vertically integrated. For the things the inhabitant knows are not facts. A fact simply exists. But for inhabitants, things do not so much exist as *occur*. Lying at the confluence of actions and responses, they are identified not by their intrinsic attributes but by the memories they call up. Thus things are not classified like facts, or tabulated like data, but narrated like stories. And every place, as a gathering of things, is a knot of stories.

Inhabitants, then, know as they go, as they journey *through* the world *along* paths of travel. Far from being ancillary to the point-to-point collection of data to be passed up for subsequent processing into knowledge, movement is itself the inhabitant's way of knowing. I have trawled the vocabulary of English to find a word, grammatically equivalent to 'laterally' and 'vertically', that would convey this sense of knowing 'along', rather than 'across' or 'up'. But I have found nothing. I have therefore had to resort to an awkward neologism. Inhabitant knowledge – we could say – is integrated *alongly*. Thus instead of the complementarity of a vertically integrated science of nature and a laterally integrated geography of location, wayfaring yields an alongly integrated, practical understanding of the lifeworld. Such knowledge is neither classified nor networked but *meshworked*.[10]

In reality, of course, scientists are human like everyone else. And so, like everyone else, they are also wayfarers. Thus the picture of scientific practice presented in the example above is somewhat idealised. It corresponds, if you will, to the 'official' view of what is supposed to happen. In the actual conduct of scientific investigation materials collected in the field are sent not 'up' but 'along' to the laboratory, which is, after all, just another place where the work goes on. Moreover, there is no unified framework within which observations of all kinds, from all contexts, can be accommodated. Much of the labour of science, it seems, lies in attempts to establish the commensurability and connectivity that would render procedures developed and results obtained in one place applicable in another. As the sociologist David Turnbull (1991) has shown, scientific knowledge is not integrated into one grand edifice but rather grows in a field of practices constituted by the movements of practitioners, devices, measures and results from one laboratory to another. Thus, contrary to the official view, what goes for inhabitant knowledge also goes for science. In both cases, knowledge is integrated not through fitting local particulars into global abstractions, but in the movement from place to place, in wayfaring. Scientific practices have the same place-binding (but not place-bound) character as the practices of inhabitants. Science, too, is meshworked.

It is of course the logic of inversion that lays the epistemological foundations for official science, by turning occurrences into discrete, self-contained facts and their taking place into the occupation of enclosed sites. The same logic, moreover, also underlies the orthodox view of inhabitant knowledge as a kind of 'upside down' science that works not through the *export*, from specific locales, of observational data for processing at higher levels, but through the *import*, into them, of systems of concepts and categories for ordering the data of experience. These concepts and categories, it is supposed, are not so much 'built up' as 'passed down', ready-made, as part of a received tradition. Thus, as places are construed as containers for people, so these people – or rather their minds – come to be seen as containers for the elements of tradition that are passed on to them from their ancestors, and that they in turn will pass on to their descendants. That is why traditional knowledge is so often assumed to be local. It is knowledge in the heads of local – and hence *localised* – people (Ingold and Kurttila 2000: 194). Conventionally, this knowledge has gone by the name of culture. It has been conventional, too, to contrast culture to science, which – since it is founded on the export of data rather than the import of schemata for organising them – claims a global reach, and appeals to principles of rational analysis of universal scope. Thus cultures appear to be in place, science in space. The same logical operation that bifurcates room into place and space also bifurcates knowledge into culture and science.

This operation, to conclude, converts the growth of inhabitants' knowledge along the manifold ways of the meshwork into a gradual filling up of the capacities of the mind with cultural content. The conversion is effected through the twin processes of what anthropologist Paul Nadasdy (1999) has called 'distillation' and 'compartmentalisation'. Distillation severs the links that bind every occurrence to its narrative context, compartmentalisation inserts the entities and events thus isolated into the several divisions of a classification. In this way, the alongly integrated knowledge of the wayfarer is forced into the mould of a vertically integrated system, turning the ways along which life is lived into categorical boundaries within which it is constrained. Stories become repositories of classified information; wayfaring becomes the application of a naive science. I have argued, to the contrary, that inhabitant knowledge is forged not by fitting the data of observation into the compartments of a received classification but through histories of wayfaring. To unravel the meshwork, and to reassemble the resulting fragments on the basis of their intrinsic similarities and differences, is to destroy its very meaning and coherence. Rather than treating science and culture as equal and opposite, ranged on either side of an arbitrary division between space and place, and between reason and tradition, a better way forward – I suggest – would be to acknowledge that scientific knowledge, as much as the knowledge of inhabitants, is generated within the practices of wayfaring. For scientists are people too, and inhabit the same world as the rest of us.

13

STORIES AGAINST CLASSIFICATION

TRANSPORT, WAYFARING AND THE INTEGRATION OF KNOWLEDGE

The genealogy and the classification

Human beings are supremely knowledgeable creatures. That much is obvious. It is not so obvious, however, how they come to know what they do. By all accounts, without such knowledge they would be helpless. Non-human animals seem to know instinctively what to do in any circumstances they would normally encounter. But human beings are apparently born with a deficit, a gap – as Clifford Geertz once put it – 'between what our body tells us and what we have to know in order to function' (1973: 50). This gap, Geertz goes on to tell us, is filled by *culture*, a corpus of information containing all the essential guidelines for a certain way to live, and distinguished by the fact that it is passed on from one generation to the next by some mechanism other than genetic replication. It is, in other words, acquired rather than innate. This is not to say that by comparison with its human cousins, the non-human animal learns nothing. Every organism lives and grows in an environment, and, at any stage of development, environmental impacts can prompt it to follow one course rather than another. The animal's learning could be described as the developmental outcome of a series of responses to such prompts. It is in this sense – to adopt Peter Medawar's terms (1960: 90–94) – an 'elective' process. The acquisition of culture, by contrast, is 'instructive'. That is to say, it is a matter not of the environmental steering of development along one of a number of possible routes, but of the installation of those programmes without which normal development could not take place at all (Ingold 1986: 357–359).

The picture I have just presented is widely accepted in mainstream science. Though debates continue about whether cultural learning is truly unique to humans or more widely distributed in the animal kingdom, few doubt that its overwhelming importance for humans is unmatched in any other species. There are debates, too, about the extent to which the forms of acquired culture are constrained by the psychological mechanisms, presumed innate, that make this acquisition possible (Sperber 1996). But again, these debates have no bearing on the fundamental logic of the argument. This is that human beings are universally equipped, thanks to their evolutionary heritage, with a suite of *capacities* – for language, for reasoning, for symbolic imagination – which are then filled in the lifetime of every individual, especially during the early years, with variable cultural *content*. Since the capacities have to be in place in advance of the content to be received into them, they must be built according to specifications that are transmitted genetically, as must all those other characteristics that make us creatures of a manifestly human kind. Cultural content, on the other hand, is said to be transmitted by *non-genetic means*, by which is usually meant some form of observational learning that leads to the replication, in the minds of novices, of representations guiding the conduct of already knowledgeable practitioners. Equipped with these representations, freshly enculturated individuals can go forth into the world where they will encounter diverse environmental conditions, causing their knowledge to be 'expressed' in one way or another, in the subtle variations and idiosyncrasies of observed behaviour.

One basic premise, however, underlies this argument. It is embedded in the very metaphor of *transmission* by which we so readily describe the twin processes of biological and cultural reproduction. The metaphor implies that information is being 'passed along' (D'Andrade 1981: 179) the lines of descent linking successive generations. It is supposed that in biological reproduction this information is encoded in genetic material, whereas in cultural reproduction it is encoded in words and symbols. In both cases, however, we are required to assume that the information can be 'read off' from the materials by which it is conveyed, by means of decoding rules that are independent of the specific environmental contexts in which it is applied. In biology this assumption underwrites the distinction between *genotype* and *phenotype*. The genotype is imagined as the covert specification of an organism-to-be, built out of elements passed down the line from ancestors and installed through genetic replication at its point of inception; the phenotype is the manifest form of the organism as it is subsequently realised through a life history of growth and development within a particular environment. Drawing on precisely the same logic, anthropologists Peter Richerson and Robert Boyd distinguish between the 'phenotype of a cultural organism … and its "culture-type", the cultural message that the organism received from individuals of the same species' (1978: 128). The culture-type is established through a process of instruction, which ensures that the informational content of the message is copied into the heads of novices. The phenotype, in turn, is the outcome of an elective process: it is the manifest behaviour that results when already copied representations are applied in specific environmental circumstances (see Figure 13.1). This is where 'knowledge', in Geertz's terms, gives way to 'functioning'. The assumption, then, is that individuals are specified in their essential genetic and cultural constitution – as genotype and culture-type – independently and in advance of their life in the world, through the bestowal of attributes from ancestors.[1] This assumption is the defining feature of what can be called the *genealogical model* (Ingold 2000a: 134–139).

Let us, for the moment, accept this model, in order to follow through its implications. My concern, in particular, is with what it implies about the nature of cultural knowledge. Evidently, to the extent that knowledge is passed down the line from ancestors, it *cannot* have its immediate source in the knower's experience of inhabiting particular places or their surroundings. An individual's genealogical position, after all, is fixed from the start, without regard for where he lives or what he does in life. One implication of the genealogical model, therefore, is that knowledge already acquired is *imported* into the contexts of practical engagement with the environment (see Chapter 12, p. 155). What kind of knowledge of the environment, then, can pre-exist such engagement? It must, in essence, be categorical. That

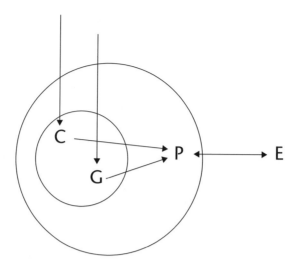

FIGURE 13.1 The dual inheritance model of genetic and cultural transmission. Both the genotype (G) and the 'culture-type' (C) are established through the replication of elements handed down from previous generations. Together they specify the individual in its essential constitution (inner circle). The phenotype (P, outer circle) is then the expression of this constitution within an environment (E). Adapted from Diener et al. (1980: 12).

is to say, it must permit the isolation of discrete phenomena as objects of attention from the contexts in which they occur, and the identification of these objects as of a certain kind on the basis of intrinsic attributes that are invariant across contexts. In short, the content of the message that is supposedly transmitted across generations by non-genetic means is tantamount to a system of classification. To function in the world (or so the argument goes), you have first to know what you are dealing with; and to know what you are dealing with you have to be able to assimilate every object you encounter to the idea of a class of objects sharing the same characteristics. This idea is a concept. Thus conceptual knowledge is classificatory knowledge. It operates by fitting particulars encountered at 'ground level' into classes of progressively higher order, working 'upwards' from the most specific to the most general. Such knowledge, as I suggested in Chapter 19 (p. 153), could be described as *vertically* integrated.

But if the genealogical model implies a transmission of vertically integrated, classificatory knowledge, the reverse also holds. That is, the project of classification, combined with a principle of transmission by descent, generates the genealogical model. Common to both are the familiar tree diagrams of taxonomy, with higher order categories at the top splitting up at lower levels into ever finer divisions. In both, things are identified on the basis of specifications that are intrinsic and invariant to each. Where it is further supposed, as in the case of living things, that every individual derives the essential specifications of its constitution by *descent*, the taxonomic tree – for example of orders, genera and species – readily translates into a genealogical one (Ingold 2000a: 138–139). In sum, the genealogical model and the classificatory project are mutually reinforcing: each entails the other. One holds that the knowledge we receive from our ancestors, and that enables us to function, comprises a system of concepts for classifying the objects we encounter in the world. The other, in seeking to classify living things (including human beings) in terms of transmitted attributes, converts the resulting taxonomy into a genealogy. Indeed, whether we start with the one or the other, it seems that we are caught in a loop from which there is no escape. In what follows, however, I want to suggest a way out. I shall argue that the genealogical model offers an inadequate and unrealistic account of how human beings come to know what they do. And by the same token, I contend, that knowledge is not classificatory. It is rather *storied*.

Classificatory knowledge and storied knowledge

This contrast can best be introduced by way of a distinction, proposed by David Rubin (1988), between what he calls 'complex-structure' and 'complex-process' metaphors. Rubin is specifically concerned with the ways we talk about memory, but his argument applies more generally to the understanding of knowledge and its formation. Adopting the complex-structure metaphor, we could say that knowledge takes the form of a comprehensive configuration of mental representations that has been copied into the mind of the individual, through some mechanism of replication, even before he or she steps forth into the environment. The application of this knowledge in practice is, then, a simple and straightforward process of sorting and matching, so as to establish a homology between structures in the mind and structures in the world. A complex-process metaphor, on the other hand, would lead us to prioritise the practice of knowing over the property of knowledge. Rather than supposing that people apply their knowledge in practice, we would be more inclined to say that they know *by way of* their practice (Ingold and Kurttila 2000: 191–192) – that is, through an ongoing engagement, in perception and action, with the constituents of their environment. Thus, far from being copied, ready-made, into the mind in advance of its encounter with the world, knowledge is perpetually 'under construction' within the field of relations established through the immersion of the actor–perceiver in a certain environmental context. Knowledge, in this view, is not transmitted as a complex structure but is the ever-emergent product of a complex process. It is not so much *replicated* as *reproduced*.[2]

With its presumptions about the replication and transmission of complex, classified information, the genealogical model is clearly locked into a metaphorical frame of the complex-structure kind. Yet as Rubin (1988: 375) shows, whatever can be explained through a complex-structure approach can, in principle, be just as well explained through an approach that emphasises the complexity of process. Were we to adopt such an approach, what could be said about knowledge and its integration? The answer hinges on how the idea of *process* is itself to be understood. In the language of complex structure, typical of mainstream cognitive psychology, the verb 'to process' is generally used in a transitive sense to refer to what the mind is supposed to do to the raw material of bodily sensation. Thus the cognitive 'processing' of sensory data is equivalent to their sorting by the categories of a received classification. In every case it begins with an object in the world and ends with its representation in the mind. In terms of the complex process metaphor, however, knowing does not lie in the establishment of a correspondence between the world and its representation, but is rather immanent in the life and consciousness of the knower as it unfolds within the field of practice set up through his or her presence as a being-in-the-world (Ingold 2001a: 143). This unfolding is the complex process to which the metaphor refers. Here, 'to process' is understood in an intransitive sense. Like life itself, it does not begin here or end there, but is *continually going on*. It is equivalent to the very movement – the *processing* – of the whole person, indivisibly body and mind, through the lifeworld.

The point that processing involves movement is critical (Ingold 2000a: 18). It implies that knowledge is integrated not by fitting isolated particulars encountered here and there into categorical frameworks of ever wider generality, but by going around in an environment. The point has been well made by David Turnbull. 'All knowing', he writes, 'is like travelling, like a journey between the parts of a matrix' (Turnbull 1991: 35). That matrix is, in effect, a tangled mesh of paths of coming and going, laid down by people as they make their way from place to place. Not even the advocates of a complex-structure approach, of course, would deny that people move about. But from their point of view, these movements are ancillary to the process by which knowledge is integrated. They serve merely to transport the individual from one stationary locus of observation to another. It is then supposed that the data collected and extracted from each locus are inputted to higher processing centres in the mind, where they are sorted and assembled within an overarching system of classification that is indifferent to the contexts in which they were encountered. From a complex-process perspective, by contrast, movement *is* knowing. The integration of knowledge, in short, does not take place 'up' the levels of a classificatory hierarchy, but 'along' the paths that take people from place to place within the matrix of their travelling. Accordingly, as I suggested in Chapter 19 (p. 154), we should say that for the inhabitants of the lifeworld, knowledge is not vertically but *alongly* integrated.[3] I have already shown that the epitome of vertically integrated knowledge is the classification. Our next step is to show that the epitome of alongly integrated knowledge is the story.

In a classification, as we have seen, every element is slotted into place on the basis of intrinsic characteristics that are given quite independently of the context in which it is encountered, and of its relations with the things that presently surround it, that preceded its appearance, or that follow it into the world. In a story, by contrast, it is precisely by this context and these relations that every element is identified and positioned (Ingold 2007a: 90). Thus *stories always, and inevitably, draw together what classifications split apart.* Another way of expressing the same contrast would be in terms of a distinction suggested by the physicist David Bohm (1980). The world according to classification is what Bohm would call an *explicate* order, in which every thing is what it is due to its own given nature, and is connected to other things only through an external contact that leaves this nature unaffected. Thus we do not have to attend to their relations to know what things are. For what they are is specified independently of what they do, and only in what they do – in their functioning – do things connect. In the genealogical model, this same principle is extended to living things, in the distinction between genotype and phenotype, and to persons, in the distinction between transmitted culture and manifest behaviour. The storied world, by contrast, is an *implicate* order in Bohm's terms. It is a world of movement and becoming, in which any thing – caught at a particular place and moment – enfolds within its constitution the history of relations that have brought it there. In such a world, we can understand the nature of things only by attending to their relations, or in other words, by telling their stories.

For the things of this world *are* their stories, identified not by fixed attributes but by their paths of movement in an unfolding field of relations. Each is the focus of ongoing activity. Thus in the storied world, as we have already seen (Chapter 12, p. 154), things do not exist, they occur. Where things meet, occurrences intertwine, as each becomes bound up in the other's story. Every such binding is a place or topic. It is in this binding that knowledge is generated. To know someone or something is to know their story, and

FIGURE 13.2 Story and life. In storytelling, past occurrences are drawn into present experience. The lived present, however, is not set off from the past of the story. Rather, past and present are continuous (redrawn from Ingold 2007a: 90).

to be able to join that story to one's own. Yet, of course, people grow in knowledge not only through direct encounters with others, but also through hearing their stories told. To tell a story is to *relate*, in narrative, the occurrences of the past, bringing them to life in the vivid present of listeners as if they were going on here and now. Here, and as we saw in Chapter 5 (p. 69), the meaning of the 'relation' has to be understood quite literally, not as a connection between predetermined entities, but as the retracing of a path through the terrain of lived experience.[4] Making their way from place to place in the company of others more knowledgeable than themselves, and hearing their stories, novices learn to connect the events and experiences of their own lives to the lives of predecessors, recursively picking up the strands of these past lives in the process of spinning out their own. But rather as in looping or knitting, the strand being spun now and the strand picked up from the past are both of the same yarn (Figure 13.2). There is no point at which the story ends and life begins. Stories should not end for the same reason that life should not. And in the story, as in life, it is in the movement from place to place – or from topic to topic – that knowledge is integrated.

Transport and wayfaring

But precisely because knowledge in this sense is open-ended rather than closed off, because it merges into life in an active process of remembering rather than being set aside as a passive object of memory, *it is not transmitted*. That is to say, it is not passed on as a compendium of information from one generation to the next, but rather subsists in the current of life and consciousness. No one has put this better than V. N. Vološinov, in his masterpiece of 1929, *Marxism and the Philosophy of Language*. Language, Vološinov argued, is not tossed like a ball from generation to generation. It endures, 'but it endures as a continuous process of becoming. Individuals do not receive a ready-made language at all, rather they enter upon the stream of verbal communication; indeed, only in this stream does their consciousness first begin to operate' (Vološinov 1973: 81). As with language in particular, so with knowledge in general, what is carried on is the process and not its (more or less ephemeral) products. We cannot therefore regard knowledge, along the lines of the genealogical model, as a kind of heritable property that comes into the possession of an individual as a legacy from his or her ancestors. To be sure, the expert is more knowledgeable than the novice. What distinguishes them, however, is not a greater accumulation of mental content – as though with every increment of learning yet more representations were packed inside the head – but a greater sensitivity to cues in the environment and a greater capacity to respond to these cues with judgement and precision. The difference, if you will, is not one of how *much* you know but of how *well* you know.

Someone who knows well is able to *tell*. They can tell not only in the sense of being able to recount the stories of the world, but also in the sense of having a finely tuned perceptual awareness of their surroundings. Thus knowing *is* relating the world around you, and the better you know, the greater the clarity and depth of your perception. To tell, in short, is not to represent the world but to trace a path through it that others can follow. Of course, anthropologists have long-recognised the educative functions of storytelling among people the world over. But they have been wrong to treat stories as vehicles for the intergenerational transmission of encoded messages that, once deciphered, would reveal an all-embracing system of conceptual categories. For stories do not, as a rule, come with their meanings already attached, nor do they mean the same for different people. What they mean is rather something that listeners have to discover for themselves, by placing them in the context of their own life histories.[5] Indeed it may not be until long after a story has been told that its meaning is revealed, when you find yourself retracing the very same path that the story relates. Then, and only then, does the story offer guidance on how to proceed. Evidently, as Vološinov said of language, people do not acquire their knowledge ready-made, but rather *grow into it*, through a process of what might best be called 'guided rediscovery'. The process is rather like that of following trails through a landscape: each story will take you so far, until you come across another that will take you further. This trail-following is what I call *wayfaring* (see Chapter 12, p. 148). And my thesis, in a nutshell, is that it is through wayfaring, not transmission, that knowledge is carried on.

It is usual to say of the people of a culture that they follow a 'way of life'. More often than not, this is taken to mean a prescribed code of conduct, sanctioned by tradition, that individuals are bound to observe in their day-to-day behaviour. The task of the wayfarer, however, is not to act out a script received from predecessors but literally to negotiate a path through the world (Ingold 2000a: 146–147; Ingold and Kurttila 2000: 192). Thus the way of life is a path to be followed, along which one can keep on going rather than reaching a dead end or getting caught in a loop of ever-repeating cycles. Indeed 'keeping going' may involve a good measure of creative improvisation. It is in following this path – *in their movement along a way of life* – that people grow into knowledge. Perhaps an analogy might be drawn in the plant world, with the growth of roots and runners that trail behind their ever-advancing tips as the latter grope for a path through the tangle of vegetation above or below the soil. Following the argument set out in the last chapter (pp. 149–52), I draw on this analogy to make an emphatic distinction between wayfaring and transport (Figure 13.3). By transport, I mean the displacement or carrying across of an already constituted, self-contained entity from one location to another, rather like the 'move', in draughts or chess, of a piece across the board. This is how all movement is understood in the terms of the genealogical model. In wayfaring, by contrast, things are instantiated in the world as their paths of movement, not as objects located in space. They *are* their stories. Here it is the movement itself that counts, not the destinations it connects. Indeed wayfaring always overshoots its destinations, since wherever you may be at any particular moment, you are already on your way somewhere else (Ingold 2007: 78–81).

To this distinction between wayfaring and transport there corresponds an important difference in our understanding of the world in which movement occurs. The definitive feature of the genealogical model, as I have shown, is that every living thing is specified in its essential nature through the bestowal of attributes passed down along lines of descent, independently and in advance of its placement in the world. To life excised from the world,

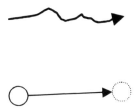

FIGURE 13.3 Wayfaring (top) and transport (bottom). In transport, a pre-constituted entity is displaced laterally across a surface, from one location to another. In wayfaring, the thing is a movement alongly in the world, creating itself endlessly in the process.

the world presents itself not as a field of habitation but as a surface to be occupied. Where things are classified according to their natures, on this surface they are indexed according to their locations. Each such location is specified independently of the things that are found there, just as each thing is specified independently of where it has been or where it is currently found. Thus while classification arranges things vertically into a hierarchy of taxonomic categories, transport links locations laterally in a network of point-to-point connections. To the classificatory knowledge of things (building from the particular to the general) there corresponds, therefore, a networked knowledge of locations (extending from the local to the global). But the storied knowledge of the wayfarer is neither vertically nor laterally integrated. It is not hierarchical, like a classification, nor is it 'flat' or planar, like a network. In the last chapter I argued that the paths of wayfaring, as they thread their way through the inhabited world rather than routing across it from point to point, comprise a meshwork. Storied knowledge, then, is neither classificatory nor networked. It is meshworked.

The tree and the globe

The conception of the unity of life, in mainstream biology, is overwhelmingly a genealogical one. It is said that we share our world with other creatures because – or to the extent that – we are related to them along lines of descent from putative common ancestors. When primatologist Jane Goodall shook hands with the chimpanzee David Graybeard, the popular press proclaimed it as 'the handshake that spanned five million years' (Goodall 1990). I wonder how many million years you span, quite unremarkably, every time you stroke your cat! The answer, of course, is irrelevant. The degree of relatedness, or genetic connection, has no bearing whatever upon our material involvements with fellow constituents of the lifeworld, including not only non-human animals of all sorts but also things like trees, rivers, mountains and earth. An understanding of the unity of life in terms of genealogical relatedness is bought at the cost of cutting out every single organism from the relational matrix in which it lives and grows. In this understanding, life presents itself to our awareness not as the interlaced meshwork, famously invoked by Charles Darwin in his image of the 'entangled bank' (Darwin 1950: 64, see Chapter 6, p. 84), but rather as an immense scheme of classification – nowadays going by the name of 'biodiversity' – in which every individual is assigned to a specific taxon (species, genus) on the basis of covert attributes, comprising the genotype, that it is deemed to possess in advance of their phenotypic expression in a real-world environment (Ingold 2000a: 217).

If the unity of life can thus be understood in genealogical terms only by treating every living thing as a virtual object, abstracted from the world it inhabits, then how does modern thought understand the unity of the world? Introducing his text of 1802 on *Physical Geography*,[6] Immanuel Kant argued that while the mind identifies all possible objects by fitting them within the compartments of an overarching classification, it identifies all possible locations by fitting them into what he called 'an extended concept of the whole surface of the earth' (Kant 1970: 262), which assumes this surface to be *spherical* in form. Characteristically, as we saw in Chapter 8 (p. 110), this spherical surface – at once continuous, homogeneous and finite in extent – is imagined as that of a globe (Richards 1974: 11; Ingold 2000a: 212). Thus to the genealogically arrayed, tree diagrams of evolutionary phylogeny, depicting the vertical unification of life on the axis of time, there correspond the global images of physical geography, depicting the lateral integration of locations as they are arrayed in space. The first, as we have seen, give us the opposition between the particular and the general; the second the opposition between the local and the global. There is, then, an essential correspondence between the biological modelling of life as a tree and the geographical modelling of the world as a globe, and it is no surprise that the two so regularly occur together in the canons of modern thought. Tree and globe are complementary images: each, indeed, presupposes the other.

I began with the distinction between innate and acquired knowledge. Recall that according to the genealogical model, a suite of genetically transmitted capacities conditions the acquisition, by non-genetic means, of cultural content. I have shown, however, that stories cannot serve as vehicles for the transmission of knowledge – that is, for its importation into contexts of development – for the simple reason that there is no way of 'reading' them that is not dependent on these contexts. Precisely the same objection can be levelled against the notion of genetic transmission. For such transmission to occur, information specifying the genotype would have to be copied into the incipient organism in advance of its growth within an environment. To date, however, no mechanism has been demonstrated that is capable of bringing this about. In reality, the 'reading' of stories, as of the genome, is tantamount to the process of development itself, of which embodied knowledge is the ever-emergent outcome. I have shown that people grow into knowledge rather than having it literally passed down to them. That growth, however, is part and parcel of the total process of development of the human organism–person in his or her environment. Like the powers of the human body, the capabilities of the mind are not given in advance but are emergent within this process. If there is a difference in this regard between humans beings and non-human animals, it lies not in the extent to which, in humans, genetic pre-programming facilitates the instructional acquisition of a complementary corpus of conceptual categories, but in that peculiarly human ability to weave stories from the past into the texture of present lives. It is in the art of storytelling, not in the power of classification, that the key to human knowledgeability – and therefore to culture – ultimately resides.

14

NAMING AS STORYTELLING

SPEAKING OF ANIMALS AMONG THE KOYUKON OF ALASKA

Say the soft bird's name, but do not be surprised to see it fall
headlong, struck skyless, into its pigeonhole –
columba palumbus and you have it dead,
wedged, neat, unwinged in your head.
                                    Alastair Reid (1978: 3)

Names and appellatives

According to the rules of grammar I was taught at school, all words of the sort we call
nouns are of two kinds: 'common' nouns or appellatives and 'proper' nouns or names. An
appellative refers to all or any number of members of a certain class of entities; a name
singles out a particular, individual referent. For the most part the distinction does not
trouble us in the course of ordinary speech, but it can become an issue for the makers of
dictionaries, which are supposed to include only common nouns, for players of Scrabble
among whom proper nouns are disallowed, and for writers who are trying to decide
whether or not to begin a word with a capital letter. Their decisions can sometimes have
political consequences, especially when what is at stake is the denomination of human
groups. Words like native, aboriginal or black, used as common nouns, seem derogatory and
almost to deny the humanity of their referents. Capitalised, however, they can designate
a singular and valued identity in the exclusive possession of a particular, named group.
Indeed there appears to be a widespread presumption in modern western societies that
to have a name is to be human. The fact that we often give names to domestic animals, or
to animal characters in children's stories, only lends support to this presumption, for these
are commonly understood as cases of anthropomorphism – that is, of our tendency to
treat certain animals *as if* they were human. But why should words that confer singularity
on their referents be considered especially appropriate for humans or for quasi-humans
such as pets?[1] And why, conversely, should words that designate membership of a class be
considered appropriate for everything else, from wild animals to all kinds of inanimate

objects? To answer this question calls for a brief excursion into western ideas concerning persons, places and things.

I want to draw attention, in particular, to two canonical features of the western tradition of thought. The first is the doctrine of the uniqueness of the individual; the second lies in the separation of human society from the domain of nature. The two are connected, since it is as social beings – that is, as persons – that humans are supposed to realise their self-identity as unique individuals. The personal name is, of course, a marker of this identity. But it is more than that, for it also indexes what is thought to be a distinctive capacity of human beings *qua* persons to intervene in nature and, through their labour, to make their mark upon the earth. Laying hold of particular portions of the earth's surface and transforming them according to their purpose, human beings are deemed to have made them into places. And every place bears the stamp of its creator in the name that has been bestowed upon it. Thus place names bear witness, in the western imagination, to the history of humanity's colonisation and appropriation of nature. Non-human animals, by contrast, are deemed incapable of creating places. Their lives, unlike those of human beings, are wholly wrapped up within the world of nature; they cannot therefore take possession of this world in the way that humans can. Thus to the wild animal, according to western juridical precepts, the surface of the earth presents itself as *terra nullius*, empty space, over which no claim can be established. Animals are destined to roam over this surface without making any part of it their own. During the heyday of colonialism this same logic was extended to populations of human hunters and gatherers. Imagined to be living like wild animals in a state of nature, these populations were construed as placeless, wandering nomads, with no greater claim to the lands they inhabited than other species of wildlife.

To be properly human, in western eyes, is thus to be a person with a unique, named identity and to occupy a specific, named place in accordance with certain principles of tenure. It is, in short, to have a name and an address. A human being without name or address is a vagrant or fugitive, a 'wild man', excluded from society and reduced in effect to an animal existence. Conversely, by attributing names and addresses to animals we introduce them into our homes as quasi-human companions. Outside of the domestic domain, in the wild, animals are but 'living things'. Sandwiched *in between* persons and places, between the plane of humanity and the surface of the earth, there lies a whole universe of things, both animate and inanimate, which are distinguished neither by name nor by address. My body, for example, is considered a thing, which both divides the person-I-am (corresponding to my interior self) from the place where I reside, and mediates the relations between them. I and the place have names, but my body does not. Nor do the clothes I wear, the tools I use, or the furnishings of my house. But when it comes to the house itself, though it is – in one sense – a house like any other, it is also my home. Thus it is one thing to say 'I live in a house'; quite another to say 'I live at Number Eighteen'. As a place, the house is uniquely specified by a number, which functions in just the same way as a proper name and forms part of my address. But as a thing, it is just a building of a particular kind. As with buildings, so with artefacts or organisms: things are invariably identified as belonging to one or another category, or species, each known by an appellative or 'common' noun. Thus it seems that the designation of things, unlike that of persons and places, is governed by a logic of classification. And this logic, in turn, rests on an order of knowledge entirely contrary to that underlying the name and address. My hypothesis is that the grammatical distinction between proper and common nouns is based, more fundamentally, on a distinction between these orders of knowledge. Let me spell this distinction out more precisely.

The network and the taxonomy

Consider an address book, in which you keep contact details of your personal acquaintances. It may be that the entries are arranged alphabetically, but this arrangement is a classification of names, not of the persons listed. That is, it has nothing to do with any resemblances among these persons, nor with their residential proximity. Equipped with my address book, however, I can *reach* anyone in my circle of contacts. And if they, too, have address books of their own – which would presumably include my details – then they in turn can reach their contacts, and so on. In effect, a collection of address books comprises a *network*, and since each address establishes an association between a specific person and a specific place, the network of connections between persons is also a network of connections between places. One could indeed imagine the entire network mapped out on a plane, corresponding to the earth's surface. Starting from any point on the plane, knowledge of persons and places expands laterally as the circle widens to embrace an ever greater field. Crucially, everyone and everywhere in this system of networked knowledge has a name.

But now, consider a field identification guide, of the kind used by naturalists to recognise different species of animals and plants. The guide does not single out particular individuals, nor does it tell you how to reach any of them, or exactly where they live. At most it may give a general description of the habitat in which animals or plants of such-and-such a *kind* are to be found. What the guide does enable you to do is assign an individual, on the basis of observations of its distinguishing features, to a certain class. The task of recognition, here, is quite different from that entailed in the recognition of persons. To identify another person is to *acknowledge* their uniqueness, to pick them out from the crowd on the grounds of a familiar face, voice or gesture. To identify an animal or plant, to the contrary, is to *deny* its uniqueness, to set aside any individual idiosyncrasies in order to highlight characteristics shared with others of the same or similar kind. In this process of identification, knowledge does not extend *outwards* along chains of connection, but is rather built *upwards*, incorporating particulars observed at ground level into ever higher levels of categorical inclusion. Or to put it another way – drawing on a distinction introduced and elaborated in the last two chapters – such knowledge is not laterally but vertically integrated. To establish a relation between particulars is not to go *across*, tracing a connecting line from one to the other, but to go *up*, to a level at which their particularity is filtered out such that each may be considered an exemplar of the same class. Conversely, to recover the particularity of things is not to connect but to divide, focusing on difference rather than similarity.

In short, vertically integrated knowledge – such as the authoritative knowledge of natural history presented in the field guide – takes the form of a taxonomy. And in this system of classificatory knowledge, *there are no proper nouns*. Everything is identified as one of a class. We have, then, a networked knowledge of persons-in-places, in which everyone and everywhere is named, and a classification of things known only by common nouns. The network *singles out* persons on the plane of humanity as it does places on the surface of the earth; the classification *groups* things on the basis of their intrinsic attributes, irrespective of where they stand. In the first case – as we saw in the last chapter (p. 164), where the distinction was traced to the philosophy of Immanuel Kant – the relation of part to whole is of the local to the global; in the second it is of the particular to the universal. The network indexes positionality by means of names; the classification indexes diversity by means of appellatives. The distinction between these two orders of knowledge is embedded in a discourse that resolutely divides persons from things and that, by the same token, orders things without regard to the places in which they are found. There is nothing absolute, however, about this tripartite ontological division between the surface of the earth, the universe of things and the society of persons. What if we were to think of the earth's surface not as already laid out, only awaiting discovery and occupation, but rather as continually unfolding in the course of life itself, through the movements of people and animals, wind and currents, celestial bodies and so on? And what if we were to think of persons not as individuals whose identity is fixed in advance of their life in the world, but as loci of ongoing activity without beginning or end?

Every place, in such a world, would come into being as a particular enfoldment of the lives of persons, a nexus in the perpetual current of comings and goings in which their life activity consists. And conversely, every person would come into being as an enfoldment of the experience of the places they have inhabited, and of the journeys between them. I purposefully use the word 'inhabit' here, rather than 'occupy', since, as we saw in Chapter 12, it is this mutual constitution of persons and places that distinguishes the process of habitation from mere occupation. The occupant takes up a position in a ready-made world; the inhabitant contributes through his or her activity to the world's ongoing regeneration (Ingold 2000a: 149). But now that we have closed the gap between persons and places, so that each is intrinsically bound up with the other rather than externally linked, is there any longer room for things? If nothing exists in and for itself, but is only the more or less ephemeral embodiment of activity-in-relation-to-others, then the whole project of classification – which groups and divides things according to fixed attributes – becomes impossible. There can be no common nouns. Nor, moreover, can there be proper nouns in anything like the conventional sense. For persons are not beings that move, they *are* their movements. It is in their very patterns of activity that their presence lies. And places are not so much locations to be connected as formations that arise within the process of movement, like eddies in a river current. In short, in such a world names are not nouns but verbs: each one describes a going on.

So what kind of knowledge do these words convey? It cannot be classified knowledge, since they do not refer to classes of things. Nor can it be networked knowledge, since they do not refer exclusively to individuals or their addresses. In the construction of a network we begin with an array of points, denoting persons or places. We then draw lines to connect them up. But in the world I am asking you to imagine, we begin with the lines themselves. The life of every being, like the rhizome of a plant, issues forth into the world as it proceeds. These lifelines are not traced, as we might trace lines on a cartographic map, *across* a world already laid out, but *through* a world in perpetual formation. In Chapter 19, I argued that every such line is a *story*. Every name, then, is a condensation of that story. Thus the knowledge that names convey is storied knowledge. This kind of knowledge is neither vertically integrated like a classification, nor laterally integrated like a network. The division between vertical and horizontal axes of integration itself belongs to a colonial imaginary that sees the world spread out before it like a surface to be occupied, and whose contents are to be collected, inventoried and classified. The lives of inhabitants, however, are not inscribed upon the surface of the world but woven into its very fabric. As they meet up with one another and go their various ways, their paths converge and diverge to form an ever-extending, reticulate meshwork. This is the meshwork of storied knowledge.

Koyukon animal names

So far I have left it to your imagination to conjure up a world suspended in movement, in which names are verbs, and in which knowing is akin to storytelling. Trying to imagine such a world in the abstract is not easy. Fortunately, however, we can call ethnography to our aid. For there *are* societies that perceive the world in this way, and they have been well documented.[2] I refer in particular to societies of people whom western observers have traditionally called hunters and gatherers – descendants of the supposedly nameless, nomadic savages of early anthropological literature. The ethnography I know best is of northern circumpolar hunters, and I want to present material from one such hunting people – the Koyukon of Alaska – to illustrate my arguments. I have chosen to focus on the Koyukon because they have been the subject of a wonderful study, by anthropologist Richard Nelson (1983), which has much to say about the names of animals. Moreover like Nelson, I have been able to draw on the rich corpus of material collected among the same people by the Jesuit priest Julius Jetté in the first decades of the twentieth century (Jetté 1908–1909, 1911, 1913). Jetté, however, calls these people the Ten'a.

Koyukon animal names appear to draw on three sources. First, there are straightforward descriptions of the animal's observed behaviour. Second, there are the Distant Time stories, tales from the era of world creation when the beings that were to become animals had yet to assume permanently their animal forms. Third, there are riddles, which describe the impression left by an animal in such an oblique or metaphorical form that the listener is left to guess at its identity. These sources are not mutually exclusive, and it is possible for a name to be a behavioural descriptor, to call up a Distant Time story, and to be posed as a riddle, all at once. Let me begin, then, with names of the first kind.

Descriptive names

Here are a few examples from the world of insects. The name of what we call a gnat translates as 'it gnaws', while the maggot's name is 'comes to life' (referring to the moment when the larva is transformed into a fly). A butterfly or moth is called 'flutters here and there', and the sort that eats clothing is called 'eats clothing' (Nelson 1983: 61, 64). Similar examples can be adduced from the world of birds. The diving bird that we call the grebe is called by a name that translates as 'its feet work only in water', referring to the bird's clumsiness on land (ibid.: 87). The spotted sandpiper's name is 'flutters around the shore', the osprey's is 'stares into the water', the boreal owl's is 'perches in the lower part of spruce trees', and the savanna sparrow's is 'sits on a stalk of grass' (ibid.: 101, 104, 108, 119). Among mammals, the mink is called 'bites things in water', and the flying squirrel 'glides down' (ibid.: 143,127). Obviously a list of names of this kind could be extended almost indefinitely. Indeed, although not explicitly stated in the ethnography, one gets the impression that there is a certain arbitrariness in the nomenclature, in the sense that people are free to devise what names they will, by highlighting any aspect of an animal's behaviour that is especially salient to the narrative of their encounter with it, and to leave their interlocutors to draw on their own experience to guess at the identity of the animal in question. Thus the borderline between names of this kind and riddles is a fuzzy one. The meaning of 'it gnaws' may be obvious to anyone who has been bitten by a gnat, but you may not immediately understand what is meant by 'flies up, ringing the bell' (ibid.: 60; Jetté 1913: 189). Having once heard this name, however, next time you share a confined space with a mosquito you will know what the riddler meant!

Whatever its name may be, in every case the animal *is* what it *does*, and is known by the signature of its activity. Many animals of the boreal forest are reclusive creatures, and it is rare to catch more than a fleeting glance of them: the flick of a tail in the undergrowth, darting shadows in a tree, the streak of wings in the sky, a splash in the water. Animals are otherwise revealed by their prints or tracks, and of course by their calls or cries, or the sounds they make as they move. Thus for the Koyukon, to behold an animal is not to observe an object that is then perceived to act. It is rather to glimpse a moment of activity that may subsequently be resolved – for example if the animal is hunted and killed – into an objective form. In the west we are accustomed to thinking of animals as 'living things', as though life were an interior property of a class of objects deemed 'animate' and that causes them to act in particular ways. In Koyukon ontology, by contrast, each animal is the instantiation of a particular way of being alive – a concentration of potential and a locus of growth in that entire field of relations that is life itself (Ingold 2000a: 95–98).

The names of animals, then, do not refer to classes of objects, for in the Koyukon world there are no objects *as such* to classify. They refer, rather, to ways of living. For example, 'perches in the lower part of spruce trees' tells us something about how the boreal owl lives. The name describes a pattern of activity that may then resolve itself into the form of an owl. This helps to explain what would otherwise be a very puzzling ethnographic fact. With one exception the names of animals never take a plural form (Nelson 1983: 191). We ourselves might speak of having seen an owl, or several owls. But the Koyukon name does not really refer to the owl as an object, but to what we might call the activity of 'owling'. With every sighting of an owl this activity is seen to be going on in the woods. It is the same, moreover, for every other creature, with the singular exception of the dog. If dogs are different it is because, as the only domestic animal of the Koyukon, each is known individually, just as a grandfather knows his grandchildren. The owner of dogs is indeed called their 'grandfather', and the dogs his 'grandchildren' (loc. cit.).

Story names

However, there is another reason why animal names generally take the singular form, and it brings me to the second source on which they draw – the stories from the Distant Time. In this era, while the world was still taking shape, it was inhabited by beings with a variety of personalities, characters and dispositions, none of whom, however, was unequivocally human or animal. The stories recount their various deeds and adventures, but invariably end with the principal protagonists being turned, once and for all, into the animal forms in which they can be seen today. In their appearance and behaviour, these animals bear all the hallmarks of their previous lives. For example, one of the stories recorded by Jetté features 'gull man', a lewd, dishevelled and disgusting character whose house is a mess, and who regards the slimy mucus that collects on the skin of fish as the most delicious fat. Indeed it is not hard for listeners to guess from the story, as it unfolds, that the dirty old man is a gull, for his present-day incarnations are said to display the same bad habits: they are regarded as unclean, unkempt gluttons who relish rotten food (Jetté 1908–1909: 331–332). Another story tells of a man whose jealous wife would drag him around by the hair. He became the songbird whose common name, in English, is the waxwing. All that hair-pulling has left its mark in the crest that crowns the bird's head, and the pitiful cries that waxwing–man let out as his wife dragged him about are preserved in its call, which sounds like a shrill squeak. The

Koyukon name for the waxwing, which literally translates as 'it squeaks', simultaneously describes this aspect of its behaviour and refers back to the Distant Time story of its origin (Nelson 1983: 116).

Now there is, of course, no limit to how many gulls and waxwings there are in the world. But each is nevertheless destined to re-enact, in its life history, the character of the original Distant Time story. Just as the same story can be told over and over again, so these enactments can be reproduced indefinitely. Thus every bird that flies is like every telling of the story: the character endures in its living enactments as the story endures in its retellings. This correspondence between the life lived and the story told is most compellingly exemplified in those cases where creatures tell their own stories. One such creature is the fox sparrow, a regular and conspicuous visitor to Koyukon country. The bird is known only by its song: 'It says *sitsoo sidziy huldaghudla gheeyits*.' This translates as 'grandmother poked a bone awl into my ear'. In the Distant Time, fox sparrow had been a beautiful woman, who lived with her husband and grandmother. But the grandmother, jealous for the husband's favours, had killed the young wife with an awl and – by donning her scalp – had tried to fool the husband into thinking she was his wife. Naturally the ruse failed, and when the husband found the body of his wife in the woods it became a little bird that flew off. Ever since, the bird has continued to sing of what happened (Nelson 1983: 119).

Yet however many fox sparrows there are, or however many waxwings or gulls, there was but one fox-sparrow woman, one waxwing man and one gull man. And when the animal's name is drawn from a story, it is to the singular character that it refers. For example, the name of another common sparrow, the white-crowned sparrow, translates as 'dentalium shell man'. In the Distant Time story, the man who became a sparrow was making for a spring camp with a cord of dentalium shells, but died of starvation before reaching it. Turned into a sparrow, he flew the rest of the way, but on reaching camp he could only sing *dzo do'o sik'its'eetee tl'ot*, 'here is Tse'eetee tl'ot, but it's too late'. Today the bird still sings these words, while the cord of dentalium shells it was carrying are preserved as white marks on its head (Nelson 1983: 119–120). Another example of a bird name drawn from the Distant Time is 'knocked the swan down'. The name refers to a small duck, the green-winged teal, much prized by the Koyukon for its delicious flavour. In the story, the duck defeated its much larger adversary, the swan, in a wrestling match. The teal is more often known, however, by another name which translates as 'whips around', referring to a characteristic of the bird's movement in the water (ibid.: 94). In this case the name that serves as a behavioural descriptor is quite different from that drawn from the story, for the teal – in ordinary life – is not always fighting with the swan!

I would like to introduce one further example to demonstrate how closely the stories of animals are bound into the lives and experiences of Koyukon people themselves. This time it concerns a fish, the longnose sucker. Its Koyukon name is 'bad man in the water'. Once again, the name comes from a story of the Distant Time, when sucker-man was a thief who went around stealing a motley assortment of things. He stole a pair of moose antlers, two duck's feet, two little combs and a tree stump, packing away all the loot into his head. But there was no room left for a bunch of needles that he had also stolen. So when sucker-man became a fish, the needles became the bones of his tail fin. All the other objects, however, were turned into the odd collection of bones that are still to be found in the sucker's skull. As people eat the boiled fish, an elder will pick out the skull bones, finding each of the items that sucker-man stole, and telling the story as he proceeds. It is a moral tale, about the impropriety of taking other people's things. Sucker was a bad man. Indeed for this very reason some people prefer not to eat the fish, concerned lest they should acquire something of its thieving personality (ibid. 75–76). Once we recall that in the world of the Koyukon, beings – whether human or non-human – do not come into the world with their essential attributes already predetermined but rather enfold, at any moment in time, a past history of growth and movement within a field of relationships with others, this kind of concern, of which there are numerous examples, becomes much easier to understand. Eating an animal contributes directly to the growth of the person; through this act the animal's story, indeed the very trajectory of its life, merges into and becomes one with the life of the eater. So when you eat a longnose sucker, the sucker's story becomes your own as well. Its thieving past becomes part of your own past, and as such is liable to affect your future development. On the same grounds, people will not eat gulls for fear of taking on their unclean habits, nor do they eat grebes since to do so is to run the risk of developing the extreme clumsiness so characteristic of the bird's movements on land. On the other hand, they are keen to eat light-bodied geese and ducks that walk easily on land, in the hope of becoming as agile and fleet of foot themselves (Nelson 1983: 99, 84, 88–89).

Whether or not it is consummated by killing and consumption, every encounter with an animal is, as we have seen, equivalent to hearing its story retold. Thus as people go about their business in the woods, they are continually connecting stories of other lives to their own. It is in these connections that the meanings of stories are found, and from them people draw both moral and practical guidance on how to carry on. Now if the names of animals, as I have suggested, are miniature stories, or episodes of stories, then again, one discovers what each name means only at the point when it is confirmed by experience, in a subsequent encounter with the animal in question. Attending to the very features of its appearance and behaviour that the name had served to highlight, one also comes to reflect on them, and on their significance for one's own life. This characteristic of story-based names – that their meanings do not come encrypted within the words themselves but are recursively revealed by direct observation of aspects of the world to which they direct attention – is common also to simple descriptive names of the kind I have already discussed. Suppose, for example, that I report having seen 'flutters around the shore'. You want to know what I am talking about? Go down to the water's edge, watch and find out for yourself! When you notice fluttering going on, only then will you know what I meant (the spotted sandpiper, see Nelson 1983: 101). I could, however, have described the bird's activity more obliquely, perhaps through the use of a metaphor that would invite comparison with some other phenomenon of familiar experience. Had I done so I would have had resort to the third source of names in the Koyukon repertoire: the language of riddles.

Riddles

Koyukon people, it appears, take a certain delight in speaking in riddles, and the names of animals, plants and artefacts can often take this form. As I have already observed, the distinction between simple descriptors and riddles is not clear-cut. With both, meaning is confirmed by experience, in the ephemeral trace of a passing encounter left in the eye of the beholder. For what they describe, more or less figuratively, are the barest glimpses of movement or activity. Thus for the red fox as it streaks through brushwood: 'far away yonder there appears a flash of fire' (Jetté 1913: 190). By convention, however, riddles such as this are distinguished by being prefaced with the enigmatic phrase *tla-dzor-karas'ana*. Jetté was unable to obtain any clues from his informants as to the original meaning of this phrase, and simply translates it by analogy with customary usage in European folklore, as 'riddle-me' (ibid.: 183). Nelson perhaps comes closer to Koyukon understanding in translating the same phrase as 'Wait, I see something' (e.g., Nelson 1983: 158). The riddler, in short, uses his words and his imagination not to describe a static scene spread out before him like a spectacle, but to catch a fugitive moment in a world in which all are immersed, and in which nothing ever stands still. This world waits for no one. It cannot be halted to allow closer inspection, and the image the riddler conjures up is one that vanishes as fast as it appears. It is, moreover, a visual image. Thus riddles, as Jetté puts it, 'are kith and kin to the light'. They are proposed and resolved in daylight hours and their season is the spring, as the days lengthen and people are cheered by the approach of summer. In this they contrast with stories of the Distant Time, which are always told in the dark, as the nights draw in towards midwinter, and which – though not without humour – are somewhat sombre in tone (Jetté 1913: 181).

Very often in the telling of a riddle, the narrator takes up the subject position of the animal, describing its movements as though he were carrying them out himself. Thus the beaver, 'I drag my shovel along the trail', and the rabbit, 'I carry my hook behind me on the trail'. The shovel, of course, is the beaver's broad, bare tail, and the hook is the curved tail bone or coccyx of the rabbit (Jetté 1913: 187–188, 195). Salmon are imagined as people travelling by canoe, thus 'we come upstream in red canoes'. The riddle refers to the breeding colours of the fish, and to its annual migration to the spawning grounds (ibid.: 196). Sometimes the riddler assumes the position of an animal that is itself posing as something else that it resembles. Thus the grey owl: 'the ends of my spruce-branches are round and shiny'. Here, speaking as an owl, the narrator compares his feathery legs, ending in horned feet, to the downward sloping and densely foliated boughs of the Alaska spruce (ibid.: 192). Another case of double substitution can be found in the riddle for the stag beetle. 'In a small hole in the ground, it drags its ears across each other.' This, in itself, is a pretty accurate description of the way the beetle, which often occupies small hollows, carries its long, horny antennae. But when the riddler speaks of ears, it is by comparison not with the beetle's antennae but with the antlers of the caribou, for the analogy of antlers to antennae is already implicit in the regular name for the stag beetle, which is 'caribou-picture' (Jetté 1913: 188; Nelson 1983: 63).

These riddles, and many more,[3] attest to an astonishingly precise observational knowledge of the non-human world. Together they amount to something akin to a comprehensive natural history. But unlike our western natural history, this knowledge comprises an unfolding tapestry of interrelated stories rather than an all-embracing classification. One of the ways in which personal names differ from common nouns, according to western convention, is that persons know their names, can pronounce them themselves, and will respond to them when summoned. By contrast, an object that is classified as a member of a category designated by a common noun is entirely insensible to what it is called. Koyukon people, however, do not *occupy* a world of immobile and insensate objects; they *inhabit* a world of mobile and sensate beings, which are not only forever watching and being watched, but listening out for one another as well. Animals know their names, and when these names are uttered they, as well as other people, can hear. There are times, however, when for fear of courting danger or causing offence, it would be better if the animals did *not* hear what was being said about them. On these occasions, Koyukon have recourse to circumlocutions.

The red fox, which in the riddle glints like a flash of fire in the undergrowth, is usually known as 'twisted eyes'. But in its presence, when the dead fox is brought inside the house for skinning, it is called 'many tracks' (Nelson 1983: 156). That most powerful and dangerous of animals, the bear, is also the most hedged around by circumlocutions. The brown bear, for example, is normally known by a term that translates as 'bad animal', but the bear would be angered to hear a woman describe it thus. So women call brown bears 'big animals' or 'those who are in the mountains', or even 'keep out of their way' (ibid.: 185). Likewise they will call the black bear 'that black thing' or 'black place' (ibid.: 174). Jetté notes that women are forbidden to pronounce any place names including syllables that might sound like the bear's 'real' name, and that might lead the animal to think that it is being spoken of with disrespect (Jetté 1911: 605). But if the animals are alert to the utterances of humans, whether names, stories or songs, so humans, conversely, listen out for what the animals have to say. No animal is more communicative, or more intently listened to, than the horned owl (Jetté 1911: 247–248). One name for the owl is *nodneeya*, meaning 'tells you things'. You can ask the owl questions, to which it responds by hooting, *hoo … hoo*, a sound taken to be the word for 'yes' (*oho*). But owls also hoot in tone-patterns that can be interpreted as utterances in the native language, boding good or ill. Since most auguries are inauspicious, the hooting of the owl is a sound that Koyukon people would prefer not to hear (Nelson 1983: 105–106). Other animals may be less knowledgeable, and less informative, than the horned owl. Nevertheless the general point remains. If humans respond to the calls of animals in the same way that animals respond to their vocal invocation by humans, then there can be no absolute difference between animal vocalisation and human name calling.

Conclusion: on languaging animaling

There are three kinds of animals, explain Gilles Deleuze and Félix Guattari (2004: 265) – or rather, three ways of regarding any animal. One way, to paraphrase their argument in our terms, is to treat it as a family pet, to anthropomorphise it, to sentimentalise it and to mark its subjectivity with a name. A second way is to see it as the living embodiment of certain attributes or characteristics by which it may be classed, as of one sort or another. This is to make an object of the animal, and to group it under the anonymity of an appellative. Such is the way of science and the State, inseparable partners in the colonial project of control by classification. The third way is to regard the animal as a going on: not as a living thing of a certain kind but as the manifestation of a process of becoming, of continuous creation, or simply of *being alive*. From this perspective the wolf, for example, 'is not fundamentally a characteristic or a certain number of characteristics; it is a wolfing' (ibid.: 265). To say that the wolf is a pack animal, argue Deleuze and Guattari, is not to suppose that it lives in packs, or to enumerate the individuals of which each pack is comprised. Rather, it is to say that the wolf *is itself* a pack. It is, in other words, the 'going on' of wolfing, seen now here, now there, in its multiple instantiations. To speak thus of animals animaling is, as we have seen, to follow the way of the Koyukon of Alaska. And it also takes us back to the lines with which I opened this chapter.

They are from a poem by the Scottish writer and translator Alastair Reid, entitled *Growing, Flying, Happening*. The bird he describes,

> straking the harbour water and then plummeting
> down, to come up, sleek head-a-cock,
> a minted herring shining in its beak

is what we call a *guillemot*. Yet merely to speak the name, Reid declares, is to strike it lifeless. No longer glimpsed as a streak of vital activity, the bird is reduced to an object of classification, locked in a grid of cognitive categories, 'wedged, neat, unwinged in your head'. The point, for Reid, is that truly to witness a bird on the wing is to see beyond recognition: it is not to identify *what* grows and flies but to open our eyes to growing, flying, happening – that is, to life – 'beyond the range of language, beyond its noun' (Reid 1978: 3).

Now if the names of animals were nouns, and if the nature of language required that this be so, then seeing would indeed take us beyond naming, and beyond language. It is fundamental to language as we know it – that is, to what most of us reared in the western tradition axiomatically take language to be – that subjects (who possess and use language) and objects (which do not, but about which subjects speak and write) are known respectively by proper and common nouns. The former are singled out as the nodes of a network; the latter are grouped into the compartments of a classification. However, the naming of animals among the Koyukon shows us how it is possible to go beyond nouns *without* going beyond language. To speak of an animal among the Koyukon is not – as Reid would say – to 'have it dead'. It is, on the contrary, to enter into the process of its life. Rather than killing off the animal, speaking its name is part of the process whereby language itself is brought to life: the animal can be animaling in a language that is languaging. Long ago, the father of anthropological linguistics, Edward Sapir (1944: 94), introduced a distinction between words he called *existents* (such as the noun, *house*) and those he called *occurrents* (such as the verb, *run*). In a languaging language – one not semantically locked into a categorical frame but creating itself endlessly in the inventive telling of its speakers – animals do not exist, either as subjects or objects; rather they *occur*.[4] The name of an animal as it is uttered, the animal's story as it is told, and the creature itself in its life activity are all forms of this occurrence. Animals happen, they carry on, they *are* their stories, and their names – to repeat – are not nouns but verbs.

PART V

Drawing making writing

Drawing is fundamental to being human – as fundamental as are walking and talking. For whenever we walk or talk we gesture with our bodies, and insofar as these gestures leave traces or trails, on the ground or some other surface, lines have been, or are being, drawn. Yet contemporary western society attaches little value to drawing, and those who have been educated into its values are happy to admit not only that they 'can't draw' (even though they can and do) but also that there is no particular reason why they should. For all but the practitioners of a few specialist disciplines including art, architecture and archaeology, but curiously not anthropology, drawing is regarded as a practice left behind at primary school. It is a childish thing to do. With writing, of course, it is the other way about, since the inability to write – so-called illiteracy – is considered a shameful deficit that should at all costs be rectified. Moreover the underestimation of drawing exists side by side with what appears to be a gross overestimation of the importance of images of one kind and another. It seems that an exhaustive division between the visual image and the written text has squeezed drawing out from most fields of contemporary endeavour. Why draw, indeed? If your purpose is to describe or explain, you can do it better with words. If your purpose is to represent, illustrate or display, you can do it more quickly and accurately by photographic means. Drawing, to the extent that it persists at all, looks like a survival, rendered more or less obsolete by the keyboard and the camera.

In the chapters comprising this part I show how the expulsion of drawing and writing from the field of their original convergence to opposite poles of a dichotomy between image and text is a consequence of the encompassment of both within a certain generic view of making, which, while characteristic of the modern era, has its roots in antiquity. It is a view that understands making as a *project*, by which an idea, already framed within the imagination, is realised in a material substrate pre-prepared to receive it. Thus in drawing, we suppose that the mind projects an image onto paper, which the draughtsman then 'pencils in' by tracing its outlines. As he does so, the image slides like a transfer from mind to page. If that were indeed the point of drawing, then it is not hard to see why people should easily become frustrated by their efforts to emulate the images they see projected all around them, and would willingly resort, when they can, to alternative representational media. Likewise, if the point of writing were to project upon the page, in visible form, thoughts already conceived in words, then it is equally easy to understand why the keyboard should serve as well as the pen, if not better. The modern understanding of the text, as a verbal composition, is one that attaches no particular significance to the inscriptive work of the hand. Nothing is lost, and much is gained – in terms of speed and legibility – by dispensing with it.

This view of making as projection, however, does not resonate well with what makers actually do. In Chapter 17, I argue that in practice, making is less a matter of projection than one of *gathering*, more analogous, perhaps, to sewing or weaving than to shooting arrows at a target. As they make things, practitioners bind their own pathways or lines of becoming into the texture of the world. It is a question not of imposing form on matter, as in the so-called *hylomorphic model* of creation, but of intervening in the fields of force and flows of material wherein the forms of things arise and are sustained. Thus the creativity of making lies in the practice itself, in an improvisatory movement that works things out as it goes along. Against the background of this latter view of making, the practices of drawing and writing take on a quite different significance.

On the side of writing we recover the original meaning of the text: not a networked assembly of printed words but a meshwork of interwoven lines inscribed through gestural movements of the hand. To be sure, the line of handwriting traces individual letters in sequence. Yet it lends to the words that these letters spell out an expressive depth and resonance equivalent to what melody and rhythm lend to the words of song. This point is demonstrated in Chapter 15 through a series of experiments with the letter **A**. Though we have been taught since Roman times to treat letters (especially capitals) as the building blocks of words, and although every letter we write is a copy of letters written before – themselves copies of precursors and so on back into the mists of time – in a cursive script letters are not objects but gatherings, moments of poise or of doubling back in an ongoing flow. Unlike letters that have been typed or printed, they are not strung together on the page but carry on through their iterations. Understood as a weaving of threads rather than a hammering of keys, as melodic rather than percussive, writing is readily comparable to stitching or embroidery, and the idea of the text as something woven is revealed to be not a loose metaphor but an accurate description of what goes on.

On the side of drawing, too, we realise that whatever theorists and historians of art may have to say about it, the practice of drawing has little or nothing to do with the projection of images and everything to do with wayfaring – with breaking a path through a terrain and leaving a trace, at once in the imagination and on the ground, in a manner very similar to what happens as one walks along in a world of earth and sky. Indeed in the art of the scribe, as I show in Chapter 16, writing and drawing, and even painting, become all but indistinguishable. The medieval scribe was a painter of manuscripts, on the pages of which pictures and words intermingled in easy companionship. There was no radical opposition, here, between text and image. Comparing the monastic practices of early medieval Europe, the painting tradition of the Yolngu, an Aboriginal people of north-east Arnhem Land, Australia, and the writings of the great pioneer of modern abstract art, Wassily Kandinsky, I show that, in every case, the purpose of art is not to mediate a shuttling back and forth between radically opposed and mutually exclusive domains of mind and world, inhabited respectively by images and objects, but rather to bind mind and world in an ongoing movement. That movement is nothing less than life itself, and it is the impulse of life that gives rise to the forms we see. Art, then, does not imitate nature, for at root, art and nature spring from the same source.

Returning to this theme in Chapter 17, I compare drawing with carpentry. A task such as sawing through a plank of wood, which I have already described and analysed in detail in Chapter 4, entails a generative movement that is at once itinerant, improvisatory and rhythmic. It is just the same with drawing. The same could not be said, however, of the tradition of oil painting that reigned in the west from the Renaissance until the modernist revolution instigated by Kandinsky and his contemporaries. As I show in Chapter 18, this tradition of painting appeals to an ideal of 'thick description', or of all-over coverage, that is entirely at odds with the openness of the drawn line. This ideal is based on a logic of holism as totalisation. Its aim is to wrap things up, to enframe, and thereby to enforce a kind of closure. Drawing's aim, by contrast, is always to prise an opening, to find a way through. It is in this sense anti-totalising, and appeals to a holism of process rather than structure. In this spirit, I advance a proposal in Chapter 18 for a *graphic anthropology* – or 'anthropography' – centred on the drawn line. Coupling the movements of doing, observing and describing, this anthropology calls on us to do three things: to follow the materials, copy the gestures and draw the lines.

To *follow the materials*, as I show in Chapter 17, means shifting the focus from ready-made objects to processes of generation and dissolution. In other words, harking back to the argument already advanced in Chapter 2, it means attending not to the materiality of things but to materials-becoming-things. This is to call into question, rather than to assume, their 'objectness' – an argument I demonstrate through the experiment of making and flying a kite. Assembled indoors from bits and pieces, the kite might seem like an inert object, but as soon as it is carried outside and caught up in the currents of air that swirl around us, it becomes a lively thing. To *copy the gestures* is to follow the same advice that would be given to a novice practitioner in the performing arts as in any craft. Novices learn through repetitive practice in which they are required to copy exemplars shown to them. This is not, however, like running off identical copies from a template. It is not an iteration. To copy from a master means aligning observation of the master's performance with actions in a world that is itself suspended on movement. And this alignment calls for a good measure of creative improvisation. There is creativity, therefore, even (and perhaps especially) in the maintenance of an established tradition.

It is one thing, however, to observe what is going on; quite another to describe it. In the practice of ethnography, observation and description have become disconnected: the ethnographer *turns away* in order to write. Returning to the idea of writing as a species of gathering rather than projection, I suggest that a possible way to reconnect description with observation might be to think of it primarily as a process not of verbal composition but of line-making. This, finally, is what I mean by my third rule for a graphic anthropology, to *draw the lines*. As a technique of observation, drawing is unrivalled. Yet its potential to couple observation with description has been largely eclipsed on account of its having fallen between the two stools of image and text – a dichotomy that remains as pervasive in recent anthropology as in studies of art history and visual culture. By the same token that the text is conceived to be 'non-visual', the exercise of vision is identified not with observational practice but with the habitation of a domain of images. By replacing the opposition between visual anthropology and written ethnography with a graphic anthropology that embraces all forms of line-making from handwriting to the drawn sketch, I propose that we can escape from the polarity of image and text, and once again restore the discipline of anthropology to life.

15

SEVEN VARIATIONS ON THE LETTER A

In 2005 I was invited to contribute to a small exhibition entitled *Fieldnotes and Sketchbooks: Challenging the Boundaries Between Descriptions and Processes of Describing.*[1] The aim of the exhibition was to explore commonalities and contrasts in the inscriptive practices of artists, architects and anthropologists. The eleven contributors were drawn from all three disciplines, and, like my co-exhibitors, I was tasked with creating a display to fit within a large, wall-mounted and glass-fronted cabinet. For my exhibit, I divided the area framed by the cabinet into twelve panels, each roughly of the size of an A4 sheet of paper, and marked out by wooden battens in a grid of three across and four down. In each panel I placed a little display designed to reveal one of the many possible answers to the question: What is an **A**?

I am fascinated by the letter **A**. Indeed I am fascinated by letters in general, and in principle, any other could have served my purposes just as well. However, as one letter that the words 'art', 'architecture' and 'anthropology' share in common, **A** has come to stand in my imagination for what is also shared by the disciplines named by these words. The idea behind my contribution to the exhibition was that an exploration of the forms, functions and properties of this letter would throw light on a series of issues concerning the relation between surface, line, inscription and notation that are of equal concern to all three disciplines. Some of these are as follows:

- What are the differences between an object, an image, a drawing and an element of notation?
- Lines can appear as traces or threads. How do these different kinds of line relate to surface?
- What is the relation between lines and shapes?
- How, if at all, can we distinguish between drawing letters and writing?
- In drawing and writing, what is the relation between the manual gesture and the inscribed trace?
- What is a line of writing? What is the difference between a handwritten line and a typed one? Do typists write?
- If letters stand for sounds, what is the relation between verbal sound and musical pitch?

Of the twelve original panels comprising the exhibit, I have selected seven on which to focus in this chapter. These include: a silhouette made in the shadow of a cut-out **A** shape; a series of **A**s from a set of letters of the alphabet in moulded plastic designed for pre-school children; a diagram illustrating the evolution of the letter **A** from the Egyptian ox-head hieroglyph; an **A** inscribed in a Gothic hand with a quill pen; a line of typed **A**s compared with a line in cursive script; a phonetic **A** (with corresponding tongue and lip positions) and a musical **A** (with tuning fork); and an embroidered **A** threaded with a needle.[2] I have ordered the paragraphs in a way that I think best brings out the connections between them. It is possible, however, to draw connections between any panels in any order, and one of my purposes in laying out the panels in a grid was to encourage viewers to do so. The text of this chapter should be approached in the same spirit.

This is not an **A**

I made this panel by cutting out a capital letter **A** from thin card, placing it upon a paper surface, and then spraying the surface with red cosmetic dye. Underneath, in a direct allusion to a celebrated painting by René Magritte, I wrote the words *This is not an A*. The original card cut-out, now red-tinted, has slipped away and is now propped up against the lower batten of the panel frame (Figure 15.1).

The paradox of Magritte's painting, which features a picture of a tobacco pipe with the words 'This is not a pipe' (*Ceci n'est pas une pipe*) written beneath it, is that while the words are incorporated into the painting, on the *same* canvas within the *same* picture frame, they tell a literal truth only if it is supposed that they are *not* – that is, if we take them at face value as words rather than as pictures of words. No one in their right mind would confuse the

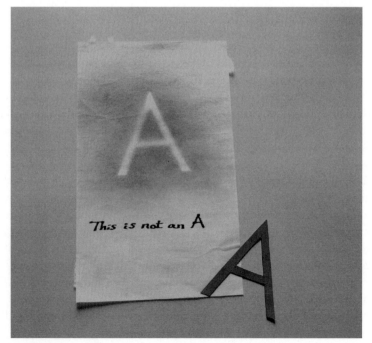

FIGURE 15.1 'This is not an **A**': card, paper, ink and red cosmetic dye

painted image of the pipe with the real artefact as it might be showcased in a shop window or museum cabinet. You cannot stuff the image with tobacco, let alone pick it up and smoke it. Let us imagine, however, that a real, stuffable and smokeable pipe is on display in a cabinet, accompanied by a written label saying what it is: 'This is a pipe'. And suppose, then, that we make a cannily realistic, painterly representation of this display, on canvas. Our painted pipe depicts the pipe in the display; the painted words depict the writing on the label. Yet these words proclaim the very opposite of those in Magritte's picture!

Following in the footsteps of Michel Foucault (1973), philosophers have tangled themselves up in ever more complicated knots in their attempts to unravel the picture's significance (or insignificance). But in fact, Magritte confounds the viewer by playing a trick of the utmost simplicity. You cannot smoke a painted pipe, however realistically it may be depicted, but you *can* read painted words. Had Magritte been a sculptor, and had he carved the pipe from wood or moulded it in clay, it could perfectly well have been stuffed and smoked. The pipe would have been as real, in every sense, as the one he had copied. He could not, then, have played the same trick that he does with his painting. In just the same way, painted words are as real as the words painted. We cannot distinguish between them in the way that we can distinguish the artefactual pipe from its painted image. That is why, had Magritte chosen to depict a letter such as an **A**, instead of an artefact such as a pipe, his trick could not have worked. For the painted **A** would have been every bit as 'real' as the carved pipe. Indeed it *would be* an **A**.

I wondered, therefore, whether the trick might be played in another way. How could I still paint an **A** and write beneath it *This is not an A*? In the panel, I tried to do this by painting the card that had been pre-cut in the shape of the letter. Since I used a spray, I could not prevent the colour spreading all over the backing paper. Once the card cut-out was removed, the letter was revealed as a silhouette. We see it only in the shape of its absence. It is *not* an **A** in the sense that the **A** that it is not (the painted cut-out) has fallen away from the picture. What remains is the *negative* of an **A**. Thus the relation between the cut-out and its silhouette is not one between the 'real thing' and its image or between truth and illusion, but – as in engraving, printing and photography – between positive and negative.

As in plastic

In this panel I mounted four **A**s from a set of moulded plastic letters designed for nursery children (Figure 15.2). The set includes several exemplars of every letter of the alphabet, and they come in a range of primary colours. The letters are large and chunky, making them easy for the child to pick up and hold. Children who play with these letters, although not yet of an age when they can read or write, are already learning to identify individual letters by their shapes. Their design is informed by the pedagogical principle that children need to be able to recognise letters by shape or outline before they can begin to assemble them into words. This principle is not new. On the contrary, it has been around in the western tradition of literacy for the past two millennia. In Book 1 of *The Orator's Education*, compiled in the first century AD, the Roman rhetorician and advocate Marcus Fabius Quintilianus wrote approvingly of 'the well-known practice of giving ivory letter-shapes to play with, so as to stimulate little children to learn … and which they enjoy handling, looking at, or naming' (Quintilian 2001: 77). Replace ivory with plastic, and these words could have been delivered by any modern pedagogue! Like his modern counterparts, Quintilian was

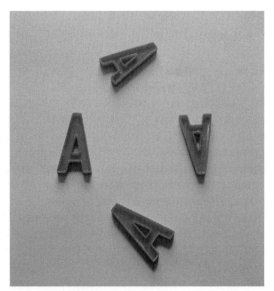

FIGURE 15.2 As in plastic, from an alphabet set for pre-school children

especially concerned that learning sequences of letters before their shapes could actually obstruct the development of children's ability to write. Even once children had reached the stage of tracing the outlines of letters in their own hand, he recommended that they should practise on tablets already inscribed with grooves, so that the stylus – and the hand that held it – would be forced to follow the predetermined letter shapes (ibid.: 77–78).

For today's children undergoing schooling in the western tradition, just as for their predecessors in Roman Antiquity, the first experience of letters is very often as objects they can handle, and the first experience of words is as assemblies of such objects. Equipped with ivory letter sets of the sort recommended by Quintilian, or the plastic equivalents that I used for this panel, children have been turning letters over in their hands – and thereby gaining an appreciation of their form that is at once visual and tactile – long before they begin to copy them on paper, and have been assembling letters into words long before they begin to write. In themselves, whether of carved ivory or moulded plastic, these letters reveal no trace of movement. They are absolutely static. When, later on, children are drilled in the gestures required to form letters and words, the object of these exercises is not to reproduce the gestures but to copy the forms as neatly as possible on the page. Thus the shapes of letters precede and prescribe the manual gestures needed to trace them with pen or pencil, and their sequential juxtaposition precedes the gestural continuity of the handwritten script.

In this regard the experience of western children is precisely the opposite of their Chinese counterparts, who, before they can write, learn and name each element of a character as a sweeping gesture of the arm or hand, and whole characters as a gestural ensemble. Thus characters are learned, remembered and reproduced as movements or sequences of movements, not as shapes. That is why it is easy for literate people in China to communicate by 'writing in the air', but well-nigh impossible for those schooled in the west. Whereas for western readers, movement is tantamount to 'noise' that interferes with the perception of literate form, in the calligraphic tradition of China, a character without movement is literally illegible (Ingold 2007a: 135). Yuehping Yen has described how, in the experience of Chinese readers, if you stare at a character for too long, thus immobilising it, then the character appears to disintegrate before your very eyes (Yen 2005: 110).

Our plastic **A**s, however, are paradoxical objects. Magritte could have had a lot of fun with them. He might, for example, have tried painting them as he did his famous pipe, but from a range of different angles. Under each image he might have written *This is not an A*. Just as you cannot stuff and smoke the picture of a pipe, he might have observed, so the painted **A** – from whatever angle it depicts the model – is not something you can actually turn over in your hands, explore with your fingers, or examine from front, back, sides, top and bottom. Nor is such examination possible, however, with any **A** that has ever been written on the page. Are we, then, to dismiss every **A** of writing as an illusion? Is the **A** we read but an image of the 'real thing' that is held as an object in the child's hands? Surely not. Perhaps, reversing the argument, the plastic **A** would be better regarded as a three-dimensional projection of a two-dimensional reality (which could, in turn, be projected in two dimensions, as in some decorative shadow fonts). In the panel, I mounted one **A** with the acute angle pointing up, another with it pointing down, and the remaining two tilted to one side and the other. As objects they are identical. But as figures positioned on the paper surface they are not. Only the one standing up, on the left, qualifies as a 'true' **A**. Though it is easy to map this figure onto the others, through a simple operation of mental rotation, this very operation requires that we imagine the letter *as if* it were a solid object like the plastic model, which could be turned this way and that. And such an imaginative transformation is the precise equivalent, yet in the reverse direction, of that which transforms the solid pipe into its pictorial representation.

Ox-head to capital **A**

This panel tells the history of the letter **A** (Figure 15.3). It is extraordinary to realise that every time we casually write this letter – or for that matter any other letter of the alphabet – our little gesture and the graphic mark it leaves drag behind them a weight of historical precedent stretching over many millennia. Think back through the many thousands of generations that in copying the marks of their predecessors, just as you do today, have contributed to the letter forms that now lie sedimented in your hand and brain. Imagine medieval European scribes writing letters on vellum with a quill pen, Roman stonemasons cutting them with a chisel on the capitals of monuments, Greek writers scratching with a stylus on waxed tablets, and Phoenician traders recording their wares by means of marks – including one known as *'alef*, from the Canaanite word *'alp* (corresponding to the Hebrew *'aluf*) meaning 'ox'. The latter were merely copying a figure depicting the ox's head that had already been in use among the people of the Sinai Peninsula since the middle of the second millennium BC (Naveh 1975: 63–65). And although the trail runs a little cold before that, there is evidence to suggest a direct line of continuity from these Proto-Sinaitic depictions to the ox-head hieroglyph by means of which the scribes and officials of ancient Egypt would record wealth in cattle.

For the background to this panel I have reproduced a detail from an agricultural scene painted on the wall of the chapel of Djar, in the ancient Egyptian city of Thebes. A pair of oxen is yoked to a plough that is guided by the hands of the ploughman, while a second man cajoles the beasts by tugging on their tails and whipping their buttocks with a switch. The head of the ox, in this as in other Egyptian paintings, is depicted in a characteristic

FIGURE 15.3 Ox-head **A** and a scene painted on the wall of the chapel of Djar in the city of Thebes (from Ingold 2007a: 126)

form that includes a pronounced, rounded snout, a large eye and massive, sweeping horns. The hieroglyph denoting the ox, which I have reproduced on an overlay in the centre of the panel, is a fairly exact copy of the pictured head, with all these features in place. By the time it reappears in the Proto-Sinaitic period, however, it has been somewhat simplified, although the three basic elements (snout, eye, horns) are still there. This simplified depiction appears in the next diagram on the panel, to the left and below the hieroglyph.

The following diagrams, situated along the path of a spiral, indicate the subsequent evolution of the letter. First the eye disappears, while the line that once depicted the horns is both straightened and displaced so that it intersects the curved, U-shaped line of the snout. Then the horn line is further rotated from the horizontal to an almost vertical inclination. But the continuous U-shape is awkward to scratch in hard material. It is more easily done in two sharp movements, meeting at a point. It became a V-shape, lying on its side and intersected by the vertical line. This was the form of the Phoenician 'alef. In archaic Greek inscriptions from the eighth and seventh centuries BC the orientation of this form had still to be standardised. Sometimes it appears reversed, with the point tilted towards the right rather than the left; sometimes the point sticks up with the bar line on a slant, and sometimes it appears in an orientation that – to us – seems completely upside down. This uncertainty did not mean that the Greeks were thinking of the letter as an abstract shape that could be rotated in any direction. It was rather because there was not yet any established convention for the direction of writing. One could write from right to left (as in Egyptian hieratic and Etruscan scripts), or from left to right, or even round and round in a spiral. The apparent rotation of the letter was probably a result of maintaining the same posture and gesture in writing while changing its direction.[3] It was the Romans who finally established the **A** in its 'correct' orientation, as we know it today. They did so because of their transference of lettering to architectural structures. The natural habitat of the Roman capital was the monument, not the page. And like the monument, it had literally to stand upright, on solid foundations. It was the Romans too, as we have seen from the writings of Quintilian, who began to think of letters, in the first place, as building blocks, and of words as buildings.

Nowadays when we write an **A**, we are unaware that that the crossbar can be traced to the horns of an ox, or the slanting sides to its snout. Nevertheless the form of the letter is an outcome of a continuous series of co-options by which, for example, depictions of animals or parts of animals were made to stand for sounds (as in the transition from Egyptian to Sinaitic), and signs for consonantal sounds in one language were made to stand for vowels in another (as in that from Phoenician to Greek). The modern capital **A**, however, is in no sense an *advance* on its predecessors. That is why I have purposefully drawn the evolution of the letter as a spiral.

Gothic **A** with quill

For this panel I copied three versions of the letter **A** in a Gothic book hand, from published examples, using a quill pen (Figure 15.4). The drawing of the hand holding the pen is reproduced from a sixteenth-century manual, and illustrates the recommended penhold. This is worthy of note, as it is very different from the one to which we have become

FIGURE 15.4 Gothic **A** and quill, showing approved penhold

accustomed ever since the replacement, in the nineteenth century, of the quill with the metal-tipped nib. Since the ink flows best when the quill is oriented almost orthogonally to the paper surface, the hand itself does not rest on the page but is raised above it. Thus writing involves considerable dextrous control of the wrist and forearm as well as the fingers (Ingold 2007a: 144–145). As our drawing shows, the index and middle finger, which hold the shaft against the thumb in a precision grip, are somewhat extended along the shaft in order to lend greater fluidity to the motion of writing. As for the pen itself, what appears as a static and detached object when laid down becomes, in the writer's hand, an extension of his very person as its spills forth upon the page. The feather that had once graced a bird in flight, now plucked and sharpened, prolongs or 'draws out' a human hand in motion.

By placing the drawing of the penhold so that the tip of the pen almost touches the end of the last line of the last **A** to be completed, I have endeavoured to show how the precisely controlled movement of the forearm and hand is conveyed without interruption, through the pen, into the curves of the letter-line. Thus in the flow of ink, the *ductus* of the hand finds its way onto the page. The closest parallel is with playing a stringed instrument such as a violin, where the movement of the bowing arm issues, by way of the bowhairs' contact with the strings, into the stream of melodic sound. As the pressure on the bow is mirrored in the amplitude of sound, so the pressure of the writer's pen is reflected in the thickness of his lines (Kandinsky 1982: 612). Though bowing calls for the same dexterity of wrist and arm as writing with a quill, there is, however, one key difference. Unlike the bow, which can be moved both 'up' towards the heel and 'down' towards the tip, the pen can only be drawn in one direction. Quill writing is like playing with a series of down-bows, with a retake between each.

The calligraphic **A**s that I created for this panel could hardly be more different from the plastic **A**s, described above, from the child's play set. Drawn rather than moulded, their lines are sinuous, not straight, and each is the trace of a graceful, manual gesture. The hand, here, feels the letter forms in the very process of their production rather than as finished objects, and remembers them as gestures, not as shapes. This is to think of the hand not as an anatomical structure of flesh and bone but rather as a compendium of gestures,[4] embodied through past practice, upon which the writer draws to form the various letters of his or her script. Indeed in the craft of the scribe, writing and drawing are truly inseparable. The writer's art, here, is not compositional but performative: it lies not in the assembly of letters and words but in the inscription of beautiful lines.

This is no less the case in the script of the contemporary handwriter, done with a metal-tipped or ballpoint pen. At the same time as allowing a greater freedom of manoeuvre, however, the modern pen is held in a hand that – resting on a paper surface – concentrates movement to the fingertips. This, in turn, induces a certain miniaturisation of the gestures involved. To see them, the traces have to be enlarged. The artist Miranda Creswell has experimented with taking small samples of handwriting and magnifying them. At a certain degree of magnification, any distinction between writing and drawing is dissolved, revealing instead a line that twists and twirls with a melodic inflection and rhythmic pulse that is almost musical in its intensity and expressive force. You can try the experiment yourself, as I have also done. Below, much enlarged, is a part of the word 'abrac*adab*raca', which I wrote in my usual cursive hand, on plain paper, with a cheap ballpoint pen:

The modulations of the line revealed at this scale were, to me, a revelation. Yet it is thanks to these modulations, of which both writer and reader are normally unaware, that handwriting not only speaks but sings.

A line of writing

What then do we mean by a line of writing? Is the line a continuous trace or a succession of discrete marks? In this panel I show how the answer depends, at least in part, on whether we are writing by hand or with a keyboard (Figure 15.5). First I wrote the words *I am not typing*

FIGURE 15.5   A line of writing: typed and handwritten on ruled paper

but writing by hand. I wrote on lined paper with a left-hand margin, but these ruled lines – like those that, in the past, were scored into the pages of manuscripts – guided my hand as it formed the letters. They were not what I wrote. The line I wrote, the letter-line, oscillates up and down within the 'band' marked out by adjacent rules, at the same time gradually shifting from left to right (Ingold 2007a: 70). This line is the trace of a gestural movement of my right hand. From time to time I had to lift the tip of my pen from the paper surface, for example, to dot **i**s, cross **t**s and leave spaces between words. This did not interrupt the movement of my hand, however, which was continuous. Likewise the movement of walking is continuous despite the gaps between footprints, as is the movement of rowing even when the oars, on the backstroke, are lifted from the water.

Next, using an old manual typewriter, I tapped out the words 'I am not writing but typing'. What appeared on the page was a sequence of discrete, equidistant marks. Each of these marks can be identified by its characteristic shape as a particular letter. Every typed letter, however, is complete in itself: it does not, as in a cursive script, grow out of the one preceding and into the one following. Here there is nothing corresponding to the letter-line. The letter shapes, moreover, bear no relation to the gestures of my hand in typing them. These gestures were percussive, and although they involved different fingers on different keys, they were basically the same for each letter. This was the gist of Martin Heidegger's diatribe against the typewriter, in his lectures on *Parmenides*, where he claimed that the machine 'tears writing from the essential realm of the hand' (Heidegger 1992: 81). Though manually operated, the typewriter severs the link between gesture and trace.[5] In typing a letter, all the movement and all the energy is concentrated in one spot, at the point where the type bar hammers down onto the page. Moreover the lateral shift from one letter to the next is not motioned by my hand but effected by the mechanics of the carriage, which, powered by muscular fingers, displace the paper one notch to the left with each stroke.

Not only typed letters are self-contained. Handwritten letters can be too, especially in the kind of handwriting that imitates print, as is often required, for example, in the completion of bureaucratic forms (Ingold 2007a: 93). On such forms, each successive letter has often to be placed in a separate box, or the instruction may be to 'print in block capitals'. Here again, the letter-line is broken up into separate pieces, as I found when I tried writing, by hand, *I am writing TYPE*. When I switched over from cursive to capitals, I found that my hand, rather than tracing a continuous line, made a series of quite separate movements, each confined within an imaginary block containing the letter. Just as when I was using the typewriter, the lateral displacement from block to block formed no part of the act of writing itself. But when, instead, I typed the words 'I am typing WRITE', the shift from lower to upper case, effected by pressing a lever, made no difference whatever to my action. To type an **a** you press the same key, with the same force, in the same way, as in typing an **A**. However, with an old machine such as the one I used, the appearance of the letters is not wholly devoid of expression. As in playing the piano, the force with which keys are struck is reflected in the volume of the sound, so on the typewriter, the harder the key is struck, the blacker and heavier the mark it leaves. Nevertheless, the same effect can be attributed to variations in the wear of the ribbon. And with the replacement of manual with electronic keyboards, even this possibility of expression has been withdrawn. The typist's fingers may dance, skilfully and expressively, on the space of the keyboard, but on the hard keys this dance leaves no trace at all, nor does it register on the paper.

The letter-line of handwriting is an example of the type of line that, as the painter Paul Klee said of lines of drawing, 'goes out for a walk' (Klee 1961: 105).[6] Just as the walker signs his presence on the land in the ever-growing sum of his trails, so the hand writer signs his presence on the page in his ever-extending letter-line. The line carries on, going where it will, never straight and often looping around, without any definite point of origin or ultimate destination. A line of type, however, does not go out for a walk. Indeed it does not go out at all. Its essence lies in that epitome of modern bureaucracy, the dotted line (Ingold 2007a: 94). On this line that is not a line, the very movement of life is collapsed into a series of instants. Such a line neither moves nor speaks. It is dead. Yet when we imagine a line of writing, it is often this type of line – namely, the line of type – that we have in mind. To highlight the difference, I wrote one line of **a**s by hand, and typed another. The handwritten letter-line looks like a file of people passing by, every one with their hand on the shoulder of the one in front. Thus the reader has the impression of viewing the letters from the side, as one would view the figures of such a file as they go on their way (Ingold 2007a: 134). These **a**s are itinerants, wayfarers. Each is a carrying on: an **a**-*ing*, if you will. The typewritten **A**s, however, are going nowhere. Rather, each stands stock still. Whereas the handwritten **a**s *occur* along a path of movement, one of the meshwork of paths comprising a woven text, the typed **A**s *exist* upon the blank space of the page, confronting the reader, motionless and face on. To read, then, is not to relive a movement but to identify particulate elements in succession, and the structures assembled from them.

In a delightful mini-essay entitled 'Why do typewriters go "click"?', the eccentric philosopher of design, Vilém Flusser, compares handwriting with numerical calculation:

> In the days when one still wrote by hand, one made a line going from left to right (that is, if one lived in the West) that wound its way from one side of the paper to the other with occasional breaks. This was a linear movement. When one calculates, one picks up little bits out of a large heap and assembles them in little heaps. This is a punctuated movement. First, one calculates (picks out) and then one computes (assembles). One analyses in order to synthesize. This is the radical difference between writing and calculation: Calculation is directed towards synthesis, but writing is not.
>
> (Flusser 1999: 64)

What, then, of typists? Do they write? Do they calculate? If by writing we refer to the kind of skilled line-making that distinguished the craft of the scribe, then they do not write. If by calculation, we mean the arithmetic operations of adding, subtracting, dividing and multiplying, then neither do they calculate. Yet in a sense they do both. In operation, the typewriter is an instrument in which the writerly continuity of the linear walk comes hard up against the calculative discontinuity of the punctual assembly. That, for Flusser, is why it goes 'click' – to which we could add that it is also why the clock or watch goes 'tick'. Every successive click or tick registers the kink, if you will, between the intransitive flow of animate movement and the transitivity of its digital reconstruction. Each momentarily resolves the tension, only for it to build up again. Thus the machine stutters along, in a stuttering world (Flusser 1999: 62).

The sound of **A**

Franz Schubert began one of his last piano sonatas (D. 959), composed in September 1828, with a line of five bars in which the keynote **A**, in the middle of the stave of the treble clef, is boldly repeated no fewer than thirteen times as the harmonies vary beneath. It is as though he wants to drill this **A** into our heads, as the anchor around which the entire sonata revolves. In this panel (Figure 15.6) I mounted a copy of the first line of the score together with a treble clef **A**, written in standard musical notation, and the metal tuning fork I use to obtain a sound of identical pitch in tuning my cello. Taken together, these establish a relation between the printed capital A in the title of Schubert's work (Sonata in A), the pitch notated by an oval placed between the second and third line up on the stave, and the sound emitted by the tuning fork when struck.

However, I have also included in the panel a short extract copied from a book that was required reading for the linguistics course that I took as an undergraduate student at Cambridge in the late 1960s. The book, by Daniel Jones, was entitled *An Outline of English Phonetics*, and it featured a large number of photographs of Dr Jones's elegantly moustached mouth, illustrating the lip and tongue positions for forming the various sounds of English. The extract I copied shows this mouth uttering the vowelic /a/ as it would be pronounced by a middle-class southern Englishman in such words as *bath*, *art* and *grass*. The photo is accompanied by a text explaining precisely how the sound should be formed: with the tongue very low in the mouth (its highest point in advance of the centre of the 'back') and

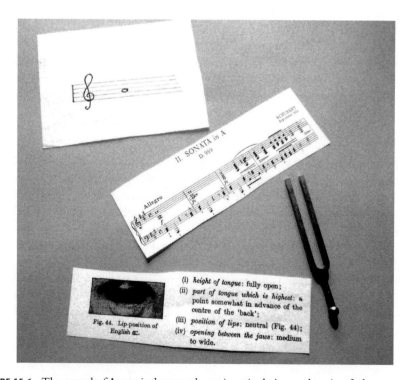

FIGURE 15.6   The sound of A: musical score, phonetic articulation and tuning fork

its tip somewhat retracted from the lower teeth, the lips in a 'neutral' position – neither pursed nor stretched, and the jaws opened fairly wide (Jones 1964: §285).

Now in both writing and musical notation, an **A** can stand for a sound. Indeed if you were to ask a singer to 'sing an **A**', she might well ask whether what is wanted is a particular vowel sound (as distinct from those conventionally denoted by the letters **E**, **I**, **O** and **U**, alone or in various combinations), or a sound of a certain pitch (as distinct from those denoted by the letters **B**, **C**, **D** etc., within the range of an octave), or both at once. Apparently, we have here two parallel but quite independent notational systems – the one linguistic, the other musical – that happen to use the same repertoire of notational elements drawn from the alphabet. One could sing an entire scale of vowelic **A**s while holding the lips and tongue in the recommended position described by Jones. But then again, you could sing a continuous pitched **A** while continually moving the lips and tongue to form the entire gamut of vowel sounds.

The separation of voice and pitch, however, along with the writing of song in two parallel registers, respectively verbal and melodic, is peculiar to modern western notation. Even in the western world, it is the provisional outcome of a long historical process that began with the prosodic annotation of lyric poetry and liturgical chants in order to assist orators with their delivery. These annotations served a largely mnemonic purpose, reminding performers of appropriate inflections of the voice. They were not essential to the song, any more than fingerings on a modern stave score are essential to the music. Ever since the principle was enunciated by Plato in *The Republic*, through to the dawn of the modern era, it has been supposed that the musical essence of any song lies in the sonority of its words (Strunk 1950). Indeed there are remarkable historical parallels here between East and West. In the traditional *noh* theatre of Japan, chants were notated by means of characters drawn from the *katakana* syllabary denoting vowel sounds. The chant, in essence, comprises a flow of vowelic onomatopoeia. The melodic sounds that ensue when, for example, a flute is held to the mouth and played with a certain fingering, merely embellish the music without fundamentally altering it (Iguchi 2008: 258–259).

Most people in contemporary western societies, by contrast, are accustomed to subordinating the words of a song to its melody, and to locating its musicality in the latter. They think of music, ideally, as song *without* words, stripped of its verbal component. And so, when considering a letter as denoting a sound, their first thought is likely to be to music and not to phonetics. For in societies dominated by the printed word, letters do not so much call up specific sounds as mark the differences between them. Phonetics has been sidelined by phonemics. And by the same token, language – envisaged as a system of differences that exists in the minds of speakers quite independently of its manifestation in acts of speech – has been silenced. As a phonemic marker, or an element of language, the letter conveys no sound at all, only a difference that may be registered just as well by graphic as by vocal means. In short, the same process of purification that has removed from the sound of **A** any contamination by speech has also left the **A** of language entirely mute.

An embroidered **A**

We usually think of writing as something we do with an inscribing implement upon a ready-made surface. And we think of the written line as a trace upon that surface. My final panel aimed to challenge these assumptions. As inscriptions on a surface, traces are just one of many different kinds of line. Other kinds include cuts, cracks and creases and – most

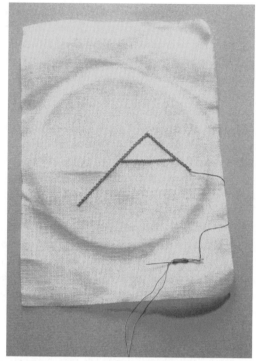

FIGURE 15.7   An embroidered A with needle and thread in fabric

importantly – threads. Can a written line be created from a thread? Indeed it can, if the line is embroidered as on a tapestry. For this panel I asked Susanne Holland, research assistant to the Creativity and Practice Research Group at the University of Dundee, to embroider an **A** with red cotton in a sheet of white fabric. To work on the material she stretched it over a circular frame. However, the work is not quite finished, as the right-hand slant has yet to reach its full length. The loose cotton, still threaded to the needle, hangs from the unfinished slant (Figure 15.7).

How, then, does the thread-line differ from the trace? One obvious difference is that the thread has already been spun along its entire length before the work of embroidery begins. The line itself issues from the spindle, not from the needle. As it rotates, the spindle gathers and twists the fibres comprising the thread. Thus if our concern be with the *generation* of the line, then writing as trace-making should perhaps be compared to the spinning of thread, rather than its subsequent use in embroidery (Mitchell 2006). A line that has been spun instead of traced, however, is not initially bound to any surface. You can knot it, or wind it up on a reel. If it lies on a surface, then you can move it around in any way you want. But you cannot erase it. A traced line, by contrast, cannot be moved but can usually be rubbed out by a smoothing action on the surface. If you want to change the line, there is no alternative but to rub it out and trace it again.

Turning our attention to the needle, its proper function is clearly very different from that of an inscribing tool like a pen or pencil. You could of course use the sharp point of a needle to scratch marks in a surface, but that is not the purpose for which it has been designed. To grasp this purpose, the point must be considered in relation to the eye. By means of the needle, the line – threaded at the eye – is drawn not *across* the surface but *through* it, pulled behind the point. Thus the surface figures not as a solid substrate but as a permeable membrane, itself woven as a mesh or lattice of fine threads, through the interstices of which the needle passes without damage to its integrity. In the formation of a stitch, the needle point is reinserted into the fabric at or close to where the thread-line emerges from it. The line is threaded through the eye, however, some way further along its length. Between point and eye, therefore, the thread forms a loop. As the needle is pulled through to the other side of the material surface the loop is tightened to form a stitch, binding the thread-line to the warp and weft of the fabric itself. The iteration of this looping and stitching forms the embroidered line.

In short, whereas in the action of a pen or pencil the inscribed line grows from the point as the work proceeds, in the action of the needle, the embroidered line grows through the repeated looping back of the trailing thread-line between where the point meets the surface and where the thread meets the eye. Telling stories involves a similar looping back of present experience to connect with that of the past (see Chapter 13, p. 161). I wonder whether the relation between life as it is lived, and its narrative re-enactment, is similar to that between inscribing and embroidering.

Retrospect and prospect

Letters are protean things. Endlessly copied in ever varying forms, they are the currency or small change of written language. Where once they represented objects – as the earliest **A** depicted an ox's head – they are now more likely to be represented *by* objects such as the plastic **A**s of the child's set. But between its representation *of* an object and *by* an object, every letter is but a representation of itself. As such it may be both drawn and written: indeed so long as writing is understood as a handicraft, it cannot be clearly distinguished from the art of drawing letters such as the calligraphic **A**s of Gothic script. And at an appropriate scale of magnification, even the letter-line of an ordinary cursive hand reappears as a line of drawing. We may use letters to notate the human voice, yet the more they come to index pure sounds divorced from words, such as that of the **A** produced by a tuning fork, the more – in language – they come to index the silent meaning that supposedly lies *behind* spoken sound. Letters can be drawn as traces, embroidered as threads, and hammered as keys. That letters can take so many different forms, be made in so many different ways, and used to do so many different things, should be a matter not for concern but for celebration. For it shows that there is much more we can do with them than might be supposed within the narrow conventions of the printed text. Indeed we have hardly begun to explore their descriptive and expressive potential beyond the bounds of these textual conventions. If we could dare to be as inventive with letters as were our predecessors of medieval times and Antiquity, and perhaps as cartoonists and graffiti artists are today, the possibilities before us are immense.

16

WAYS OF MIND-WALKING

READING, WRITING, PAINTING

Questions of walking and seeing

In her history of walking, *Wanderlust*, Rebecca Solnit compares writing to path-making, and reading to travelling. 'To write', she suggests, 'is to carve a new path through the terrain of the imagination … To read is to travel through that terrain with the author as guide' (Solnit 2001: 72). Clearly, both carving paths and guided travel entail the exercise of eyesight. As they proceed on their way, both the path-breaker and the traveller must watch their step and look where they are going, the former to lay the trail, the latter to keep their footing while monitoring features of the terrain as they are pointed out. But what of the writer and reader? If Solnit's analogy holds, then writing and reading, too, should be visual practices. The inquiry that follows is prompted in part by my puzzlement concerning the inclination of many visual anthropologists, and indeed students of visual culture more generally, to describe the written text as a *non*-visual medium, by contrast to the medium of the image.[1] For example, in his introduction to visual methods in social research, anthropologist Marcus Banks assures his novice readers that the materials of visual research are images of various kinds that are made to be looked at, and that it is precisely in looking at these images that people engage in visual practices (Banks 2001). Irit Rogoff maintains, apparently to the contrary, that the study of 'visual culture' is by no means limited to images, but also encompasses sounds, spatial delineations and much else besides. Yet in the same breath, she equates what is specifically *visual* in visual culture with the concern with images. To the extent that visual culture studies encompass more than images, they go beyond vision itself (Rogoff 2002: 24).

What goes on, then, when we walk? In watching our step, we train our eyes on the ground, not on a virtual simulation of the earth's surface based on optical information already relayed to the eyes. In looking where we are going, we scan the horizons of the world around us, and not their imagistic or pictorial representations. Indeed a pedestrian overly engrossed in the perusal of images is most likely to trip or go astray. Are we to conclude that walking, to the extent that it does *not* depend on the enrolment of images, is not really a visual practice after all? Or is some distinction to be made between the observational acuity of eyesight in watching and looking, and the interpretative visuality of seeing? It might be suggested, for example, that the pedestrian certainly watches and looks, but only *sees* when the results of this watching and looking, somehow fixed in the forms of images, are subjected to a subsequent process of interpretation. This seems to be what visual theorist James Elkins has in mind when he argues that we are all blind to a degree – even when our eyesight is functioning perfectly – because so much of what passes before our eyes yields up no images that can be called to mind (Elkins 1996: 203–224). The implications of this argument, however, are bizarre. Consider the cautious pedestrian who looks left, right and left again before crossing the road. Having no recollection of what they looked like, we would have to conclude that he was blind to the cars that would otherwise have run him down!

Once we return from walking to reading, further questions arise. For Solnit, readers and writers walk in the terrain of the imagination. What is the difference, then, between the watching and looking that go on as one walks, respectively, in the terrain of the imagination and in that of real life? Can these terrains even be distinguished at all? If, on the one hand, and as Elkins has it, the imagination 'is a place inhabited by images' (ibid.: 224), then perhaps reading and writing engage with images in a way that walking normally does not. But in that case, it seems all the more peculiar that students of visual culture should oppose reading and writing to practices that are properly visual. On the other hand, the letters and words inscribed on the page of a manuscript have just as much of a material presence as do footprints and tracks impressed on the ground, and both prompt the question of the relation between the observation of marks and traces inscribed or impressed in surfaces in the world and the imagining that is carried on, as it were, on the hither side of eyesight, 'in the mind'. Reading and writing surely involve the exercise of both eye and mind, and the same must be true of walking. Is it possible, then, to find a way of describing the imaginative activity that goes on as one walks, reads or writes, without having to suppose that it involves the perusal of images? Perhaps it is the very notion of the image that has to be rethought, away from the idea that images represent, on another plane, the forms of things in the world to the idea that they are place holders for these things, which travellers watch out for, and from which they take their direction. Could it be that images do not stand for things but rather help you find them?

These general questions can of course be asked of the imaginative work not only of walking, writing and reading but also of such activities as drawing and painting and of the ways of seeing they entail on the part of viewers. Should the drawing or painting be understood as a final image to be inspected and interpreted, as is conventional in studies of visual culture, or should we rather think of it as a node in a matrix of trails to be followed by observant eyes? Are drawings or paintings *of* things in the world, or are they *like* things in the world, in the sense that we have to find our ways through and among them, inhabiting them as we do the world itself? I do not pretend that there are final, correct answers to any of these questions. To an anthropologist like myself, however, one way to approach such intractable problems is through a comparative analysis of the answers that people of radically different provenance have come up with. In what follows I shall explore four such sources. The first lies in the Christian monastic practices of early medieval Europe, the second in the painting tradition of the Yolngu, an Aboriginal people of north-east Arnhem Land, Australia, the third in the work of the great pioneer of modern abstract art, Wassily Kandinsky, and the fourth in a treatise by the tenth-century Chinese landscape painter, Ching Hao.[2]

I had been reading about medieval monasticism because of an interest in the crafts of writing and masonry, and had been especially enthralled by the two magnificent books of historian Mary Carruthers: *The Book of Memory* and *The Craft of Thought* (Carruthers 1990, 1998). This put me in mind of my much earlier reading on Australian Aboriginal art, at a time when I was principally interested in how the differences between ontologies of animism and totemism were reflected in ways of depicting (Ingold 2000a: 111–131). The monks of medieval Europe were neither animists nor totemists, yet it struck me that in the way they enrolled both manuscripts and landscapes on their perambulatory meditations on the presence of God, there were great similarities with Australian Aboriginal meditations on the Dreaming, which likewise enrol both landscapes and paintings in similarly ambulatory endeavours. These meditations are grounded in a fundamental division between 'inside' and 'outside' forms of knowledge, a division that is also prominent in Kandinsky's reflections on the nature of art. My interest in Kandinsky's art was rekindled by a recent opportunity to visit a major exhibition of his paintings at the Pompidou Centre in Paris. At the exhibition I purchased a book on Kandinsky by the philosopher Michel Henry, which I read alongside the two-volume collection of his own writings (Kandinsky 1982). These include his most famous essay, *Point and Line to Plane*, which I had already studied while researching for my book on the history of the line (Ingold 2007a). But now I found more inspiration in his earlier essay, *On the Spiritual in Art*.

Through my work on lines I had become interested in the graphic arts of ancient China, and on a recent visit to the Metropolitan Museum of Art in New York, I happened to pick up a book of texts by Chinese painter-critics from the Han through to the Ch'ing dynasties, originally compiled by the Swedish sinologist Osvald Sirén. Ever since I bought it, the book had lain unopened on my shelf, until I chanced to come across it one day and it literally fell open at the pages devoted to Ching Hao, whose *Notes on Brushwork* are reproduced as Appendix IV of the book (Sirén 2005: 234–238). And it was an observation by Ching Hao, in these notes, that held the key to the grail I was looking for, around which all four sources seemed to converge. This is that the mental and the material, or the terrains of the imagination and the physical environment, run into one another to the extent of being barely distinguishable. They are like countries whose borders are thrown wide open to two-way traffic that, in passing from one country to the other, has to cross no ontological barrier. Such free passage is an offence to modern thought, which insists that what it calls 'figments' of the imagination can have no truck with the world of our corporeal existence. What joins medieval monasticism, Australian Aboriginal Dreaming, Kandinsky's spiritualism and Ching Hao's painterly aesthetic, to the contrary, is the premise that the phenomenal world itself, to use Carruthers's term, is 'figmented' (Carruthers 1998: 187). Whether encountered through a written text, a painting or drawing, or a walk in the landscape, or interchangeably in all these ways, every figment has as good a right to exist as any other. This is not all, however, for our sources converge on a still more fundamental insight, namely, that these figments are but outward, sensible forms that give shape to the inner generative impulse that is life itself.

Walking through the scriptures

There is nothing new in Solnit's idea of reading and writing as modalities of travel. This is precisely what the monastic practitioners of medieval times thought they were doing. They regarded themselves as wayfarers, travelling in their minds from place to place, and composing their thoughts as they went along by drawing on, or 'pulling in', ideas lodged in places previously visited. The word in Latin for this drawing on or pulling was *tractare*, from which is derived the English 'treatise', in the sense of a written composition. And the flow of the thinking mind, as it proceeded along the trails of the written text, was known as its *ductus*. Like water in an aqueduct, thought flows from a source towards a goal. But while the flow is irreversible (the current cannot be contrived to run backwards), it is by no means uniform. It is rather divided – literally punctuated, by pricking the surface of the parchment – into passages of different mood and colour. In a treatise entitled *On Affliction and Reading*, the twelfth-century Benedictine Peter of Celle advises readers of the scriptures to proceed as though walking through a landscape, and draws attention to significant sites along the way, the events that happened there, and the vistas they afford, almost as though he were presenting a guidebook. One's mood, he tells us, should always be responsive to these events and panoramas: now light-stepped and joyous; now more ponderous, with a heavy and grieving heart. Thus the reader, 'seeing' his reading as he 'walks' through it, 'is constantly in motion, all senses continually in play, slowing down and speeding up, like a craftsman using his various instruments' (Carruthers 1998: 109–110).

But if one could walk through the scripture as a landscape, so conversely, as typically in the liturgical procession or pilgrimage, one could walk through a landscape as scripture. In this the physical activity, according to Carruthers, 'exactly mirrors the mental activity in which the participants were engaged' (ibid.: 44). For the wayfarer in the landscape, as in the scriptural text, particular sites marked by recognisable features would serve as place holders for Biblical characters and stories – for the characters, in effect, *were* their stories (see Chapter 13, p. 160). By visiting these sites one would recall the stories and meet the characters as though they were alive and present, harnessing their wisdom and powers to the task of crafting one's own thought and experience, and of giving it sense and direction. Not only were text and landscape ontologically equivalent in this regard, so too were both to buildings, which were also designed and constructed, quite deliberately, as instruments of meditation (ibid.: 254–261). In the building, every stair, arch or cloister – like every feature of the landscape or every word of text – offered a depository for thought. The controlled, manual movements – the *ductus* – of the scribe as he paints letters or figures on the page have their precise counterparts in the purposeful movement through a devotional building expressly designed to channel and focus the restless churning of the human mind (ibid.: 258). The building, however, need not have been built, and many medieval buildings were not, existing only as plans, diagrams or architectural *picturae* that, in themselves, laid down routes and trails for meditative composition. Far from taking in the entire picture at a glance, as we moderns are inclined to do, the viewer was required to move around in it – to perform a 'mnemotechnical perambulation about the picture space' (ibid.: 251, 354 fn. 77) – just as one would move around in an actual building.

The architectural picture was an instance of what medieval thinkers took to be a map (*mappa*). Crucially, however, the map was arrived at not by any process of observation and measurement but through a visionary experience of revelation. Rather than surveying the opaque, outer surfaces of the world, the visionary – in whose eyes these surfaces were rendered transparent – would see *into* it, whereupon was revealed to his mind an inner reality of which the world's outward, visible forms were but appearances. One rendering of this all-encompassing vision was the *mappa mundi* or world map. Far from being the crude effort at cartographic representation that we take it for today, the *mappa mundi* was a model *for* (not *of*) the phenomenal world, the purpose of which was not so much descriptive as prescriptive: to establish a foundational template for the ordered disposition of figurative elements – images, if you will – that marked out places along ways of thought, and that could be actualised just as well in the forms of depictions, landscape features or the components of buildings as they could in words. Conventionally, the capacity of words to evoke images has been known as *ekphrasis*, a term derived from the rhetoric of classical Greece. But as Carruthers shows, for medieval rhetoricians, buildings and landscapes as well as texts could summon up the structures for inventive meditation: they, too, offered varieties of *ekphrasis* (ibid.: 222–223). How, then, did they do this? For an answer, we can turn to the writings of Richart de Fournival, canon of Amiens cathedral in the mid-thirteenth century and author of a popular bestiary, *Li Bestiaires d'Amours.*

In the preface to this work, Richart explained that knowledge can enter the human soul by way of two gates, of sight and hearing, through each of which passes a road. These roads were *painture* and *parole*, painting and speech. With more than 70 drawings of animals, Richart's bestiary was a compendium of words and pictures. But the distinctions, on the one hand, between painting and speech, and on the other, between picturing and writing, are not congruent. Rather, they cross-cut. When writing was read aloud, as it often was in the Middle Ages, it was apprehended acoustically in the sounds of speech: the task of the readers and audiences was then to listen to the 'voices of the pages' (ibid.: 169–170). These voices entered the mind along the road of *parole*, through the gate of hearing. However, the letters of writing only exist because they have been painted (or drawn) on the page. Indeed as Carruthers notes (1990: 225), the scribe who wrote out the letters was often identified as the 'painter' of the manuscript. And when writing was read in silence it would enter the mind along the other road, of *painture*, through the gate of sight. Moreover written words, even if read aloud as *parole*, paint pictures in the listener's mind – pictures that, according to Richart, are seen with the mind's eye. Thus writing both paints and is painted, and both speaks and is spoken. Conversely, pictures are painted on the page just as letters are and, entering through the gate of sight, they paint themselves in the minds of viewer–readers. But pictures also speak and are spoken, they have *parole*. In many texts their speech is actually written out, in the form of scrolls shown issuing from a figure's mouth, rather as in contemporary cartoons (ibid.: 229–230).

Medieval writers, in short, did not subscribe to the modern ontological distinction between words and pictures, or between text and image (Carruthers 1998: 212–213). In their manuscripts, pictures and words were strictly equivalent and even interchangeable. Pictures were no more 'visual' than words; words no less so than pictures (Figure 16.1). Both were accessed through the twin gates of sight and hearing, along the roads of painting and speech. There was nothing incongruous, then, about the juxtaposition, on the pages of the bestiary, of what look to us like fanciful depictions alongside a miscellany of allegorical stories in which the depicted creatures feature in a variety of morally charged situations. Medieval bestiaries, as Willene Clark has stressed, have to be understood 'as spiritual literature, not as degraded natural history' (Clark 2006: 7). The scenes and stories they presented furnished the mind with images that provided sense and direction to currents of experience. To these scenes and stories, moreover, were added sightings of the creatures themselves, and observations of their behaviour, in contexts of everyday life such as agriculture and hunting. 'The animal' was, in effect, a node or knot in a skein of interwoven depictions, stories, sightings and observations, no one of which was ontologically prior to any other, and all of which – taken together – opened up pathways to the experience of God.[3] Thus the traveller in the landscape, meeting with 'real life' creatures on his way, encountered them

FIGURE 16.1 Words in pictures and pictures in words: a page from the Aberdeen Bestiary, written and illuminated in England around the beginning of the thirteenth century. The text at the top of the page tells of various kinds of frogs, including a saying that dogs will not bark if given live frogs to eat. The initial 'A', which binds a number of frogs into its foliage, and whose stem is formed by a sweeping dragon's tail, marks the beginning of a new section on trees and plants.

through the gates of sight and hearing just as he would on the pages of the bestiary, where they figured in writing and depiction. How, then, does reading differ from walking in the landscape? Not at all. To walk is to journey in the mind as much as on the land: it is a deeply meditative practice. And to read is to journey on the page as much as in the mind. Far from being rigidly partitioned, there is constant traffic between these terrains, respectively mental and material, through the gateways of the senses.

Walking through the Dreaming

Let me turn, now, to the Yolngu of north-east Arnhem Land. The Yolngu have no tradition of writing as such, but they do paint, primarily on the surfaces of bark, but also on human bodies. Their ethnographer, Howard Morphy, distinguishes between two kinds – or rather levels – of painting, respectively 'figurative' and 'geometric' (Morphy 1991: 150). Figurative painting is unmistakably iconic, including forms that are readily recognisable as human beings, animals of various sorts, equipment such as spears and digging sticks, and surface features such as trees and rocks. The painting invariably tells a story of how ancestral beings, in the era of world formation known as the Dreaming, made their way from place to place, creating the country as they went along, and peopling it with the clans that would inhabit each respective place. One would 'read' the painting as a story, moving around the picture space as the events of the narrative unfold. Indeed, Yolngu people would inhabit their paintings much as the monastic practitioners of medieval Europe would inhabit the scriptures, walking in their minds the original, creative walk of the ancestors and, in so doing, bringing it forward into the present so as to give sense and direction to their own lives (ibid.: 114). Similarly, just as in the case of the medieval text, painting was a way of walking and walking a way of painting. Travelling from place to place, one finds in each place, and recalls to memory, particular ancestral beings and their stories (and as with Biblical characters, the ancestral beings *are* their stories).

There is a difference, however. One can turn the pages of a manuscript and read something new on each page. Likewise, every Yolngu figurative painting exists as one of a set, telling in its own way some aspect of the story connected with the country, and the novice, as he is introduced to one painting after another in the set, draws on what he has learned from each in 'reading' the next (ibid.: 217). But if the set of paintings were compared to a book, then it would be one whose leaves, as they are superimposed, fold in upon one another. As they do, the figurative diacritica that mark each character as appropriate to a particular reading are absorbed into an underlying generative schema or template from which all are ultimately derived. Paintings of the kind that Morphy calls 'geometric' depict this template. Thus the geometric painting is like a book, the pages of which have folded or melded into one. Such a painting can be pondered again and again, and read differently each time. To the untutored eye, 'geometric' seems an entirely apt designation for paintings of this kind, for at face value they appear to be as devoid of significant content as a mathematical design. What could be more abstract, for example, than an oblong shape with a straight line down the middle (Figure 16.2)? Yet initiated Yolngu would ask: what could be more dense? It can be read in so many ways. In one reading, the oblong is the boulders the kangaroo hopped over when it was chased by the ancestral woman Ganydjalala into rocky country, in another it is the body of the kangaroo itself (with the dividing line as the backbone), and in yet another – referring to the kangaroo's invention of stone spearheads – it is the blocks of stone, split

FIGURE 16.2 Figurative and geometric motifs in Yolngu art. This painting by Welwi of the Marrakulu clan depicts the ancestral woman Ganydjalala hunting a kangaroo through forested uplands. Reproduced from Morphy (1991: 192), courtesy of the Buku-Larrnggay Mulka Centre (on behalf of the Marrakulu clan) and by permission of the University of Chicago Press.

asunder down the midline, from which fragments were struck in the manufacture of spears (ibid.: 191–193, 207).

Thus in the motif of the divided oblong, land, animal and artefact are forged into a unity that resembles none of them but underwrites them all. It is not that the motif has too little content. It has rather too much – more, at least, than can be grasped all at once. For this reason, the novice who would enrol the paintings in his meditative quest for ancestral knowledge and wisdom has to undergo a lengthy induction, starting from the relatively superficial, *outside* knowledge enshrined in the figurative paintings, and gradually working his way down towards the more fundamental, *inside* knowledge of the kind that is concentrated in the geometric art. For Yolngu people, everything has an inside and an outside, though these are relative terms, since what is on the inside of more superficial forms remains on the outside of things that are more deep-seated (ibid.: 78–80). The progressive infolding of outward appearances into inner necessities, in the course of a novice's induction, concentrates the powers of multiple readings of the phenomenal world into a unitary attention that strains ever deeper, striving to know a reality more real than that which can be gleaned from the surface of things. It is a progression that condenses, into geometric forms, knowledge that is revealed only piecemeal, one slice at a time, in the figurative depictions. In essence, inside knowledge consists in an understanding of the underlying unity and coherence of different orders of experience. That unity lies in the Dreaming. The paradox of Yolngu art, as Morphy shows, is that while on the one hand the significance of figurative designs is relatively transparent, whereas that of geometric designs is obscure; on the other hand the geometric designs render transparent the fundamental ordering of things that is obscured, in figurative painting, by its exclusive concentration on one thing rather than another (ibid.: 296).

Morphy's analysis of Yolngu art is somewhat hamstrung by his unwavering commitment to a Saussurian semiotics according to which paintings are systems of signs whose meanings lie in the minds of knowledgeable elders as a set of shared understandings or 'intersubjective cultural structures' (ibid.: 143–144, 292). These meanings, Morphy repeatedly insists, are *encoded* in the paintings, which serve primarily as vehicles for the transmission of ancestral knowledge from elders to novices, thereby ensuring its reproduction across generations. The effect of this logic, however, is to turn the relation between art and its meaning inside out. It is to say that meaning, rather than being immanent in the art, is something external that has been implanted into it and that can – by a reverse process of decoding – be extracted from it. Yet the Yolngu themselves, by Morphy's own account, are saying the very opposite, namely, that paintings do not encode but reveal. So far as they are concerned, he admits, paintings *are* the beings of the ancestral past, brought forward and disclosed in the present (ibid.: 102, 292). Everything stems from this past, just as every surface form arises from what is already there on the inside. Yet painting is only one of many ways in which ancestral beings can reveal themselves, or make their presence felt. Consider for example the crocodile ancestor, who was burned when his bark hut caught fire and dived into the sea to quench the flames. Still burning beneath the waves, the fire scarred the crocodile's back with scales. In painting, he is revealed in the patterns of diamonds distinctive to the designs of the clans that have sprung from him. He may reveal himself in similar patterns of ripples on the surface of the water. But he – that is, his story – may just as well show up in the scaly pattern on the back of the living crocodile (ibid.: 176–177).

Indeed there is a remarkable parallel between the ways in which the Dreaming is rendered manifest to Yolngu initiates through paintings, stories and experiences of living creatures, and the ways in which the hand of God was similarly revealed to the readers of medieval bestiaries. The archetypal beings of their world, too, showed up as clusters of depictions, narratives and direct observations. In Yolngu as in medieval monastic lore, the being *is* the entwining of its manifestations, which together reveal its inner essence, and the appearance of the living animal as a creature of nature is just one of these manifestations, ontologically equivalent to its figurative depictions and the stories that are told about it. Moreover this equivalence, as we have already seen, extends to the relations between paintings and landscape. In earlier work I took exception to Morphy's characterisation of the painting as a *map* of the landscape (ibid.: 221–225). While there is certainly a correspondence between the form of the painting and the morphology of the landscape, I argued, 'it would not be right to suppose that the one *represents* the other. Rather, both landscape and painting exist on the same ontological level, as alternative ways in which an underlying ancestral order is revealed to human experience' (Ingold 2000a: 118). In hindsight, however, and in the light of what we have learned of medieval monastic practice, I would be prepared to accept that Yolngu paintings are maps, but only on condition that the map is understood in its original, pre-cartographic sense, that is as an instrument for revealing the inner reality of the world, and not as a representation of its outer surface. For the Yolngu, as Morphy acknowledges, both the landscape as it is outwardly observed and the corresponding figurative paintings have their source in the same basic template (Morphy 1991: 237). As a depiction of this template, the geometric painting is the precise counterpart of the medieval *mappa mundi* and serves the same purpose, namely to summon up the themes of meditative recollection.

Far from reflecting, on the level of mind, an objectively given reality, and thus reinforcing the division between the mental and the material, both the geometric painting and the *mappa* offer a place where mind and world can merge in forging an inner experience of the unity of life. The same, as I shall now show, can be said of the nominally 'abstract' paintings of Wassily Kandinsky.

Walking through an exhibition

Introducing his essay *On the Spiritual in Art*, Kandinsky presents a captivating parody of pictures at an exhibition:

> Imagine a large, very large, small or medium-sized building, divided up into various rooms. All the walls of the rooms are hung with small, large, and medium-sized canvases. Often several thousand canvases. On them, by means of the application of paint, pieces of 'nature' are portrayed: animals in light and shadow, standing at the edge of the water, drinking the water, lying in the grass, next to them a crucifixion of Christ, portrayed by a painter who does not believe in Christ, flowers, human forms sitting, standing, walking, often naked, many naked women (often seen in foreshortening from behind), apples, and silver dishes, a portrait of Privy Counsellor So-and-so, the evening sun, a woman in pink, flying ducks, a portrait of Baroness X, flying geese, a woman in white, calves in shadow dappled with bright yellow sunlight, a portrait of His Excellency Y, a woman in green. All this is carefully printed in a book; names of the artists, titles of the pictures. People holding these books in their hands go from canvas to canvas, leaf through and read the names. And then they leave, just as rich or poor as when they came in, immediately absorbed again by their own interests, which have nothing whatever to do with art. Why ever did they go?
>
> (Kandinsky 1982: 129–30)

They go, presumably, to see the paintings, and so that they can say that they have seen them. They think that artists are people who paint things, anything. And they suppose that once they have ascertained what a painting is *of*, and perhaps the intention of the artist in painting it, then they have seen it. They might perhaps admire the facility with which the subject matter has been rendered by the artist, or even seek to place the work in a social, cultural or historical context. Yet having accomplished all this, Kandinsky is telling us, they are no closer to experiencing the work of art as a *painting* than they were at the outset (see Henry 2009: 73–74).

To discover what Kandinsky meant by painting, let me turn to another example of an imaginary exhibition. In this case the pictures, including watercolours and drawings, really existed, although most have now been lost. They were produced by the Russian artist and architect Victor Hartmann. It was after Hartmann's premature death in 1873 that his close friend, the composer Modest Mussorsky, wrote his celebrated suite of pieces for piano, *Pictures at an Exhibition*. Each of the ten pieces refers to one of Hartmann's pictures, which Mussorsky imagined hanging in a gallery. They are linked by intervening *promenades* that walk the listener musically from picture to picture. Now for Kandinsky, the music of Mussorsky spoke directly to what painting really is. It appeals not to outward appearances, whether real or imaginary, but to an inner life – to emotion, feeling and the pulsations of the soul. Consider the piece in the suite entitled 'The Old Castle'. This piece does not pretend to depict the castle in sound – it is not programme music, for which Kandinsky had nothing but contempt (1982: 155). It seeks rather to evoke a feeling comparable to what one might experience in the presence of an ancient ruin set in the landscape. With its slow, monotonous pulse in the lower register of the keyboard, the music of 'The Old Castle' conveys an aura that is grey, heavy and brooding. So too, we may suppose, did Hartmann's painting of the same name. Though ostensibly, the painting was *of* the castle, it resonated internally with precisely the same aura as that evoked in the music. But what the composer achieves by means of rhythm and tone, the painter achieves with form and colour. Comparing the painter with the composer–pianist, Kandinsky declares that for the former: 'Colour is the keyboard. The eye is the hammer. The soul is the piano with its many strings. The artist is the hand that purposefully sets the soul vibrating by means of this or that key' (ibid.: 160).

In 1928, Kandinsky staged Mussorsky's *Pictures at an Exhibition* at the Friedrich Theatre in Dessau, transforming the ten 'pictures' into sixteen scenes combining music, stage movement, lighting and decoration. His aim in doing so was to render the forms and colours, as he put it, 'that swam before my eyes in listening to the music' (ibid.: 750). 'The Old Castle', for example, began in pitch darkness save for three long stripes, which vanish to give way to a large red patch on the right, then a green patch on the left. As the light fades towards the end, only the three original stripes remain visible, and these in turn disappear, quite suddenly, with the final *forte* of the piece. The staging, on Kandinsky's insistence, was unequivocally 'abstract'. This is not to say, however, that it was devoid of content. Quite to the contrary, by abstraction Kandinsky meant the removal from the work of art of all those figurative elements that otherwise imprison it or conceal its true nature from us, and that are incidental to its existence *as* art, so as to release it into the fullness of being. In music, this means removing any sounds that could be construed as imitative or programmatic; in painting it means casting aside the illusion that to see a painting is to see what it is a painting *of*. If anything is empty of content, it is the image that serves only to represent an external object but that lacks any life of its own. Such an image depends for its existence on the world of objects. But painting, properly speaking, does not. Nor does music. Together, they open the mind to inner truths that are ontologically prior to the outward forms of things. By a principle that Kandinsky called 'inner necessity' (ibid.: 160), these truths – the 'abstract content' of the work of art – directly touch the soul and set it in motion. This principle corresponds, of course, to what Yolngu people call the Dreaming, and to what medieval monastic thinkers saw as the hand of God.

Like Yolngu painters, Kandinsky continually stressed the distinction between the inside and the outside, between the internal and external aspects of things. He began his essay *Point and Line to Plane* with the enunciation: 'Every phenomenon can be experienced in two ways … External – Internal.' One can look at it as if through a pane, or one can plunge into it, become an active part of it, and 'experience its pulsation with all our senses' (ibid.: 532). This is the difference between the experience of visitors to the exhibition satirised in Kandinsky's opening parody, who look at one canvas after another but are moved by none, and that of the viewer–listener whose *promenade* is evoked in Mussorsky's music. This person, who could have been Mussorsky himself, is profoundly moved by what he sees. The *promenade* sections of the music render in sound his changing moods as he goes from canvas to canvas: now confident, now hesitant, now mournful, now quivering with anticipation, and finally exultant. He is moved precisely because what he sees are not paintings of things, or images in the modern sense, but things that are painted. And he inhabits these things as he inhabits the world, by moving through and among them, and by participating with his entire being in the generative movement of their formation – that is, in what Michel Henry, in his commentary on Kandinsky's writings, calls 'the becoming of our life' (Henry 2009: 83). Indeed our walk through the exhibition, as we listen to Mussorsky's *Pictures*, is not unlike a monastic walk through the scriptures. It relives the history of our feelings, as Henry continues, in 'the eternal movement in the passage from Suffering to Joy' (ibid.: 122). Recall the advice of Peter of Celle, that readers should be ever responsive in mood to the vistas opened up by letters, words and pictures. On the page of a manuscript, as we have already seen, even the painted letter could be understood as a thing in its own right, with both internal and external aspects. In his commentary on the theory of elements that Kandinsky proposed in his *Point and Line to Plane*, Henry explains why (ibid.: 34–35).

Take any letter of the alphabet – let us say an 'o'. Ordinarily, the letter designates a phoneme, and serves its purpose in allowing us to distinguish, in both speech and writing, between one word and another. That, we say, is what letters are *for*, and very useful they are too. But what if we set this practical purpose to one side and concentrate our attention on the letter in itself? There it is, a thing with a life of its own, proudly painted on the page. All at once it stands out as a form, one that we had scarcely noticed before, so accustomed had we been to the practicalities of its everyday use. And as a form, it evokes a certain affective tonality, comparable to that evoked by a tonal pattern in music. It has, then, an internal and external aspect: the pictorial form, which can be seen, and the affective tonality, which can only be inwardly felt. As this example shows, and as Henry points out, the 'external' can be understood in two, quite different senses. On the one hand, it refers to the externality of the world of objects, including tools, letters and words in their ordinary uses. The 'o' to which we are accustomed is external in this sense. On the other hand, it refers to the externality of an element as pure pictorial form, abstracted from any cognitive or practical meaning. Set aside from its regular business in working with words, the 'o' on the page is still visible. It has the essential qualities of form and colour. Relative to ordinary use, it is internal, but relative to the affect it evokes, it is external. Kandinsky was aware of the ambiguity, and attempted to deal with it through the rather clumsy device of distinguishing between elements and 'elements' (Kandinsky 1982: 548; Henry 2009: 36). The 'element' is simply an object or an image in a world of objects and images. The element, on the other hand, is a visible form that vibrates with inner life. For example the point or *punctus*, so long as it functions as the familiar full stop of punctuation, is an 'element'. But the point that stands on its own, 'wrenched free from its habitual state and … emancipated from the tyranny of the practical-purposive', has a life of its own, an inner tension, and it is in this capacity – as an element – that it enters the world of painting (Kandinsky 1982: 541–542).

Though cumbersome, this distinction between 'element' and element should not be hard for us to grasp. For it corresponds quite precisely to that between figurative and geometric elements in Morphy's analysis of Yolngu art. Let me clinch the argument with one more example. In 1935, Kandinsky published a charming little essay, of less than a page, entitled

Line and Fish (ibid.: 774–775). In one sense, he tells us, there is no essential difference between a line and a fish. Evidently, what he had in mind was not just any kind of line. He is not, for instance, thinking of the figurative line that would merely imitate or mark the contour of an object (Henry 2009: 53). The sort of line he has in mind embodies the force of its production; it lives and grows. So, of course, does the fish. Their equivalence lies in the fact that they are both living beings, animated by forces internal to them that find expression in trajectories of movement. Thus the fish may be observed as a line streaking through the water, and the line as a moving point that could assume the guise of a fish. Nevertheless, despite this equivalence, Kandinsky acknowledges that in a more fundamental sense, fish and line are quite different. For the fish, *as a fish*, is a creature of the phenomenal world and depends on this world to exist. It needs an environment. It can swim, but only in a river; it can be cooked and eaten, but only in the kitchen and off a plate. The line, by contrast, lacks the capacities to swim, eat and be eaten. But then, it does not need them. The capacities that are critical to the existence of the fish are superfluous to the existence of the line. And it is for precisely this reason that the line can serve as an abstract element in art, whereas the fish cannot. The fish is destined to remain an 'element' in the outside world of organisms and their environments. 'That is why', Kandinsky confessed, 'I like the line better than the fish – at least in my painting' (1982: 775).[4]

Walking through the woods

Returning, at length, to our original question of the relation between the terrains of the imagination and of 'real life', we can draw two conclusions. First, we must dispense, once and for all, with the convention that the imagination consists in the power to produce images, or to represent things in their absence. It is not, as Henry puts it, about giving us 'decoys to contemplate' (2009: 108). For even if they existed only as pictures in the mind, such decoys would belong – together with the missing things they stand for – in the same outside world of appearances, of 'elements', of programme music, of the figurative. Rather – and this is our second conclusion – we must recognise in the power of the imagination the creative impulse of life itself in continually bringing forth the forms we encounter, whether in art, through reading, writing or painting, or in nature, through walking in the landscape. Remember: the line does not *represent* the fish. But the fish-in-the-water can be understood as but one of many possible emanations of line, of which others would include the words and pictures painted or inscribed upon the surfaces of paper, bark or canvas. Does this not then mean, asks Henry rhetorically, that ultimately, '*the structure of art and the structure of the world are the same*?' (2009: 134). Turning finally to our last source, the *Notes on Brushwork* of Ching Hao, we find this question answered resoundingly in the affirmative.

One day, Ching Hao recounts, he was walking in the T'ai-hang Mountains when he came upon an opening between two steep cliffs that afforded a passage into a place overgrown with old pine trees. One tree stood above the rest, rising to the sky like a dragon, while others were bent around it, their roots coiling and winding in the moss and crumbling stones. The next day, he returned with his brushes to paint the scene. The following spring, as he walked among the cliffs, he chanced to meet an old man, who asked him what he had been doing. Ching Hao explained that he had been painting, but taking his interlocutor for an 'uncouth rustic', he did not expect much by way of a reply. He was therefore taken aback when the ancient challenged him on his knowledge of painting. There are six essentials of painting, said he, namely spirit, resonance, thoughts, motif, brush and ink. To this, Ching Hao remarked: 'Painting is to make beautiful things, and the important point is to obtain their true likeness, is it not?' The old man answered, 'It is not':

> Painting is to paint, to estimate the shapes of things and really obtain them, to estimate the beauty of things and reach it, to estimate the reality of things and grasp it. One should not take outward beauty for reality; he who does not understand this mystery, will not obtain the truth, even though his pictures may contain likeness.

What then, asked Ching Hao, is likeness and what is truth? 'Likeness', responded the old man, 'can be obtained by shapes without spirit, but when truth is revealed, spirit and substance are both fully expressed' (Sirén 2005: 234–235). I believe that not only the monks of medieval Europe but also the Yolngu elders of north-east Arnhem Land would have agreed with this old man. So, indeed, would have Wassily Kandinsky. And so, on reflection, do I.

17

THE TEXTILITY OF MAKING

The hylomorphic model

In his notebooks, the painter Paul Klee repeatedly insisted that the processes of genesis and growth that give rise to forms in the world we inhabit are more important than the forms themselves. 'Form is the end, death', he wrote. 'Form-giving is life' (Klee 1973: 269). This, in turn, lay at the heart of his celebrated *Creative Credo* of 1920: 'Art does not reproduce the visible but makes visible' (Klee 1961: 76). It does not, in other words, seek to replicate finished forms that are already settled, whether as images in the mind or as objects in the world. It seeks, rather, to join with those very forces that bring form into being. Thus the line grows from a point that has been set in motion, as the plant grows from its seed. Taking their cue from Klee, philosophers Gilles Deleuze and Félix Guattari argue that the essential relation, in a world of life, is not between matter and form but between *materials* and *forces* (Deleuze and Guattari 2004: 377). It is about the way in which heterogeneous materials, enlivened by forces of tension and compression and with variable properties, mix and meld with one another in the generation of things. And what they seek to overcome in their rhetoric is the lingering influence of a way of thinking about things, and about how they are made and used, that has been around in the western world for the past two millennia and more. It goes back to Aristotle.

To create any thing, Aristotle reasoned, you have to bring together form (*morphe*) and matter (*hyle*). In the subsequent history of western thought, this hylomorphic model of creation became ever more deeply embedded. But it also became increasingly unbalanced. Form came to be seen as imposed by an agent with a particular design in mind, while matter, thus rendered passive and inert, became that which was imposed upon. My critical argument in this chapter is that contemporary discussions of art and technology, and of what it means to make things, continue to reproduce the underlying assumptions of the hylomorphic model, even as they seek to restore the balance between its terms. My ultimate aim, however, is more radical: with Deleuze and Guattari, it is to overthrow the model itself, and to replace it with an ontology that assigns primacy to the processes of formation as against their final products, and to the flows and transformations of materials as against states of matter. Form, to recall Klee's words, is death; form-giving is life. I want to argue that what Klee said of art is true of skilled practice in general, namely that it is a question not of imposing preconceived forms on inert matter but of intervening in the fields of force and currents of material wherein forms are generated. Practitioners, I contend, are wanderers, wayfarers, whose skill lies in their ability to find the grain of the world's becoming and to follow its course while bending it to their evolving purpose.

Consider, for example, the operation of splitting timber with an axe. The practised woodsman brings down the axe so that its blade enters the grain and follows a line already incorporated into the timber through its previous history of growth, when it was part of a living tree. 'It is a question', write Deleuze and Guattari, 'of surrendering to the wood, and following where it leads' (ibid.: 451). Perhaps it is no accident that the word used in Greek Antiquity to describe the skill of the practitioner, *tekhne*, is derived from the Sanskrit words for axe, *tasha*, and the carpenter, *taksan*. The carpenter is 'one who fashions' (Sanskrit, *taksati*), a shaper or maker. Yet the Latin verb for 'to weave', *texere*, comes from precisely the same root (Mitchell 1997: 330). The carpenter, it seems, was as much a weaver as a maker. Or more precisely, his making was itself a practice of weaving: not the imposition of form on pliant substance but the slicing and binding of fibrous material (Ingold 2000b: 64–65). His axe, as it finds its way through the wood, splitting it as it goes, is guided – as Deleuze and Guattari say – by 'the variable undulations and torsions of the fibres' (2004: 450). As for the axe itself, let us suppose that the blade has been knapped from stone. The skilled knapper works by detaching long, thin flakes from a core, exploiting the property of conchoidal fracture taken on by the lithic material through its history of geological compression (Pelegrin 2005: 25). Before each blow of the hammer, he locates or prepares a suitable striking platform, whence, on impact, the line of fracture ripples through the material like a wave. The wrought surface of knapped stone, at least until it has been ground smooth, bears the scars of multiple, overlapping fractures.[1]

In the history of the western world, however, the tactile and sensuous knowledge of line and surface that had guided practitioners through their varied and heterogeneous materials, like wayfarers through the terrain, gave way to an eye for geometrical form, conceived in the abstract in advance of its realisation in a now homogenised material medium. What we could call the *textility* of making has been progressively devalued, while the hylomorphic model has gained in strength.[2] The architectural writings of Leon Battista Alberti, in the mid-fifteenth century, mark a turning point in this development. Until then, as David Turnbull (2000: 53–87) has shown in the case of the great medieval cathedral of Chartres, the architect was literally a master among builders, who worked on site, coordinating teams of masons whose task was to cut stones by following the curves of wooden templates and to lay the blocks along lines marked out with string. There was no plan, and the outcome – far from conforming to the dictates of a prior design – better resembled a patchwork quilt (Harvey 1974: 33).

For Alberti, to the contrary, architecture was a concern of the mind. 'It is quite possible', he wrote, 'to project whole forms in the mind without any recourse to the material, by designating and determining a fixed orientation and conjunction for the various lines and angles' (Alberti 1988: 7). Such lines and angles together comprise what Alberti called the 'lineaments' of the building. These lineaments have a quite different status from the lines that masons cut from templates or laid with string. They comprise a precise and complete specification for the form and appearance of the building, as conceived by the intellect, independently and in advance of the work of construction. On paper, the lineaments would have been inscribed as drawn lines, which could be either straight or curved. Indeed, Alberti's lines have their source in the formal geometry of Euclid. 'The straight line', he explains, 'is the shortest possible line that may be drawn between two points', while 'the curved line is part of a circle' (ibid.: 19). What art historian Jean-François Billeter writes of the line of Euclidean geometry applies with equal force to the Albertian lineament: it 'has neither body nor colour nor texture, nor any other tangible quality: its nature is abstract, conceptual, rational' (Billeter 1990: 47).

Following materials

Thus the textility of building gave way to an architectonics of pure form. And from that point on, despite their common etymological origin, the technical and the textilic were set on radically divergent paths. While the former was elevated into a system of operational principles, a *technology*, the latter was debased as mere craft, revealing the almost residual or interstitial 'feel' of a world engineered in the light of reason. Embodied within the very concept of technology was an ontological claim, namely, that things are constituted in the rational and rule-governed transposition of preconceived form onto inert substance, rather than in a weaving of, and through, active materials (Ingold 2000a: 312).[3] 'Technology', in other words, is one answer to the question, 'What does it mean to make things?' It is an answer, however, that does not readily stand up in the theatre of practice. For makers have to work in a world that does not keep still until the job is completed, and with materials that have properties of their own and are not necessarily predisposed to fall into the shapes required of them, let alone to stay in them indefinitely (Ingold and Hallam 2007: 3–4). Building contractors, tasked with the implementation of architectural design, know this all too well – as Matisse Enzer, a contractor with long experience of working with architects, explains:

> Architects think of a building as a complete *thing*, while builders think of it and know it as a *sequence* – hole, then foundation, framing, roof, etc. The separation of design from making has resulted in a built environment that has no 'flow' to it. You simply cannot design an improvisation or an adaptation. It's dead.
>
> (cited in Brand 1994: 64)

Or as Stewart Brand puts it (ibid.: 2), there is a kink between the world and the architect's idea of it: 'The idea is crystalline, the fact fluid.' Builders inhabit that kink.

Contemporary architecture is not, however, universally blind to the disjunction between theory and practice. The distinguished Portuguese architect Alvaro Siza, for example, admits that while he can build and design houses, he has never been able to build a *real* house, by which he means 'a complicated machine in which every day something breaks down' (Siza 1997: 47). Besides builders and repairmen of diverse trades – bricklayers, joiners, slaters, plasterers, plumbers and so on – the real heroes of house building, according to Siza, are the people who live in them who, through unremitting effort, shore them up and maintain their integrity in the face of sunshine, wind and rain, the wear and tear inflicted by human occupancy, and the invasions of birds, rodents, insects, arachnids and fungi (ibid.: 48). Like life itself, a real house is always work in progress, and the best that inhabitants can do is to steer it in the desired direction. Likewise the gardener, armed with spade, fork and trowel, has to struggle to prevent the garden from turning into a jungle. More generally, whenever we encounter matter, as Deleuze and Guattari insist, 'it is matter in movement, in flux, in variation'. And the consequence, they go on to assert, is that 'this matter-flow can only be *followed*' (Deleuze and Guattari 2004: 451). What Deleuze and Guattari call 'matter-flow', I would call *material*. Accordingly, I recast the assertion as a simple rule of thumb: to *follow the materials*.[4]

To apply this rule is to intervene in a world that is continually 'on the boil'. Perhaps it could be compared to a huge kitchen. In the kitchen, stuff is mixed in various combinations, generating new materials in the process that will in turn become mixed with other ingredients in an endless process of transformation. To cook, containers have to be opened, and their contents poured out. We have to take the lids off things. Faced with the anarchic proclivities of his or her materials, the cook has to struggle to retain some semblance of control over what is going on. An even closer parallel might be drawn with the laboratory of the alchemist. The world according to alchemy, as art historian James Elkins explains, was not one of matter that might be described in terms of its molecular composition, but one of *substances* that were known by what they look and feel like, and by following what happens to them as they are mixed, heated or cooled. Alchemy, writes Elkins, 'is the old science of struggling with materials, and not quite understanding what is happening' (Elkins 2000: 19). His point is that this, too, is what painters have always done. Their knowledge was also of substances, and these were often little different from those of the alchemical laboratory. As practitioners, the builder, the gardener, the cook, the alchemist and the painter are not so much imposing form on matter as bringing together diverse materials and combining or redirecting their flow in the anticipation of what might emerge.

In their attempts to rebalance the hylomorphic model, theorists have insisted that the material world is not passively subservient to human designs. They have expressed this, however, by appeal not to the vitality of materials but to the agency of objects. If persons can act on objects in their vicinity, so, it is argued, can objects 'act back', leading persons to act differently from how they might otherwise have done (see Chapter 2, p. 28). The speed bump on the road, to take a familiar example adduced by Bruno Latour, causes the driver to slow down, its agency here substituting for that of the traffic policeman (Latour 1999b: 186–190). We may stare at an object, explains Elkins (with acknowledgement to the psychoanalysis of Jacques Lacan), but the object also stares back at us, so that our vision is caught in a 'cat's cradle of crossing lines of sight' (Elkins 1996: 70). And in a precise reversal of the conventional subject–object relations of hylomorphism, archaeologist Chris Gosden suggests that, in many cases, it is not the mind that imposes its forms on material objects, but rather the latter that give shape to the forms of thought (Gosden 2005: 196). In this endless shuttling back and forth between the mind and the material world, it seems that objects can act like subjects and that subjects can be acted upon like objects. Instead of subjects and objects there are 'quasi-objects' and 'quasi-subjects', connected in relational networks (Latour 1993: 89).

Yet paradoxically, these attempts to move beyond the modernist polarisation of subject and object remain trapped within a language of causation that is founded on the very same grammatical categories and that can conceive of action only as an *effect* set in train by an agent. 'Agents', according to anthropologist Alfred Gell, 'initiate "actions" which are "caused" by themselves, by their intentions, not by the physical laws of the cosmos' (1998: 16). The intention is the cause, the action the effect. Assuming that human beings alone are capable of initiating actions in this sense, Gell nevertheless allows that their agency may be distributed around a host of artefacts enrolled in the realisation of their original intentions. These artefacts then become 'secondary agents' to the 'primary agency' of the human initiators (ibid.: 20–21). Not all would concur with Gell that actions are the effects of prior intentions, let alone with the identification of the latter with mental states. Intentionality and agency, as archaeologist Carl Knappett argues, are not quite the same: 'artifacts such as traffic lights, sleeping policemen, or catflaps might be described as possessing a kind of agency, yet it would be much harder to argue that they manifest intentionality' (2005: 22). It would indeed be foolish to attribute intentions to catflaps. But is it any less so to suggest that they 'possess agency'? Rather that attributing the action to the agency of the flap (in cohort with that of the cat, and of the cat's owner who installed the flap in the door to save her from having to open it herself), would it not make more sense to attribute the operation of the flap to the action into which it was enlisted, of the cat's making its way in or out of doors? Surely, neither the cat nor the flap possess agency; they are rather *possessed by the action*. Like everything else, as I shall now show, they are swept up in the generative currents of the world.

Flying kites

The world we inhabit is not made up of subjects and objects, or even of quasi-subjects and quasi-objects. The problem lies not so much in the *sub-* or the *ob-*, or in the dichotomy between them, as in the *-ject*. For the constituents of this world are not already thrown or cast before they can act or be acted upon. They *are* in the throwing, in the casting. The point may best be demonstrated by means of a simple experiment that I have myself carried out with my students at the University of Aberdeen. Using fabric, matchstick bamboo, ribbon, tape, glue and twine, and working indoors on tables, we each made a kite. It seemed that we were assembling an object. But as soon as we carried our creations outside, they leaped into action, twirling, spinning, nosediving, and occasionally flying. How did this happen? Had some animating principle magically jumped into the kites, causing them to act most often in ways we did not intend? Were we witnessing, in their unruly behaviour, the consequences of interaction between – in each case – a person (the flyer) and an object (the kite), which can only be explained by imagining that the kite had acquired an 'agency' capable of counteracting that of the flyer? Of course not. The kites behaved in the way they did because, at the moment we went out of doors, they were swept up, as indeed we were ourselves, in those currents of air that we call the *wind*. The kite that had lain lifeless on the table indoors, now immersed in these generative currents, had come to life. What we had thought to be an object was revealed as a *thing*.

'An "object"', writes design philosopher Vilém Flusser, 'is what gets in the way': standing before us as a fait accompli, complete in itself, it blocks our path. To continue, we have either to find a way around it, to remove it, or to achieve a breakthrough (Flusser 1999: 58). The thing, by contrast, draws us in, along the very paths of its formation. Each, if you will, is a 'going on' – or better, a place where several goings on become entwined.[5] As Martin Heidegger put it, albeit rather enigmatically, the thing presents itself 'in its thinging from out of the worlding world' (Heidegger 1971: 181). It is a particular gathering together or interweaving of materials in movement. Thus the very 'thinginess' of the kite lies in the way it gathers the wind into its fabric and, in its swooping, describes an ongoing 'line of flight'

(Deleuze and Guattari 2004: 323). This line should on no account be confused with the line connecting the kite with the flyer. For lines of flight, as Deleuze and Guattari insist, do not connect (see Chapter 6, p. 83). Like the stems of plants growing from their seeds, to return to Klee's image, such lines trace the paths of the world's becoming – its 'worlding' – rather than connecting up, in reverse, sequences of points already traversed. Moreover, what goes for the kite-in-the-air, in its thinging, also goes for the flyer-on-the-ground. If the kite is not endowed with an agency that causes it to act, then neither is the human flyer. Like the kite, the human is not a being that acts – an agent – but a 'hive of activity' (Chapter 2, p. 29), energised by the flows of materials, including the currents of air, that course through the body and, through processes of respiration and metabolism, keep it alive.[6] Like the kite's line of flight, so the life trajectory of the flyer follows a course orthogonal to any line we might draw connecting the kite as (quasi-) object with the flyer as (quasi-) subject.

In practice, then, flyer and kite should be understood not as interacting entities, alternately playing agent to the other as patient, but as trajectories of movement, responding to one another in counterpoint, alternately as melody and refrain. We could say the same of the builder, in relation to the brick and mortar of a house under construction, the gardener in relation to the soil in his or her beds, the cook in relation to the ingredients of a pie, and the painter in relation to pigments and oils. Daniel Miller, a leading figure in the study of material culture, has argued that it is by studying 'what people do with objects' that we can best understand how they create worlds of practice (Miller 1998: 19). However, neither brick nor mortar, nor soil, nor the ingredients in the kitchen, nor paints and oils, are objects. They are materials. And what people do with materials, as we have seen, is to follow them, weaving their own lines of becoming into the texture of material flows comprising the lifeworld. Out of this, there emerge the kinds of things we call buildings, plants, pies and paintings. In the very first move that isolates these things as objects, however, theorists of material culture have contrived to obstruct the flows that brought them to life. The 'problem of agency' is thus one that they have created for themselves, born of the attempt to re-animate a world already rendered lifeless by an exclusive focus on the 'objectness' of things. Theirs is a world not of things that exist in the throwing, but in which the die is already cast. It is indeed striking that the more theorists have to say about agency, the less they seem to have to say about life. To rewrite the life of things as the agency of objects is to effect a double reduction, of things to objects, and of life to agency. And the source of this reductive logic lies in the hylomorphic model.

Sawing planks

My aim is to restore things to life and, in so doing, to celebrate the creativity of what Klee (1973: 269) called 'form-giving'. This means putting the hylomorphic model into reverse. More specifically, it means reversing a tendency, evident in much of the literature on art and material culture, to read creativity 'backwards', starting from an outcome in the form of a novel object and tracing it, through a sequence of antecedent conditions, to an unprecedented idea in the mind of an agent. This backwards reading is equivalent to what Alfred Gell has called the *abduction of agency*. Every work of art, for Gell, is an 'object' that can be 'related to a social agent in a distinctive, "art-like" way' (1998: 13). By 'art-like', Gell means a situation in which it is possible to trace a chain of causal connections running from the object to the agent, whereby the former may be said to index the latter. To trace these connections – to look through the work to the agency *behind* it (see Knappett 2005: 128) – is to perform the cognitive operation of abduction. From the argument set out in the previous paragraphs, it should be clear why I believe this view to be fundamentally mistaken. A work of art, I insist, is not an object but a thing and, as Klee argued, the role of the artist – as that of any skilled practitioner – is not to give effect to a preconceived idea, novel or not, but to join with and follow the forces and flows of material that bring the form of the work into being. The work invites the viewer to join the artist as a fellow traveller, to look *with* it as it unfolds in the world, rather than behind it to an originating intention of which it is the final product.

Following, Deleuze and Guattari observe, is a matter not of *iteration* but of *itineration* (2004: 410). Artists – as also artisans – are itinerant wayfarers. They make their way through the taskscape (Ingold 2000a: 194–200) as do walkers through the landscape, bringing forth their work as they press on with their own lives. It is in this very forward movement that the creativity of the work is to be found. To read creativity 'forwards' entails a focus not on abduction but on *improvisation* (Ingold and Hallam 2007: 3). To improvise is to follow the ways of the world, as they open up, rather than to recover a chain of connections, from an end point to a starting point, on a route already travelled. Here are Deleuze and Guattari again:

> One launches forth, hazards an improvisation. But to improvise is to join with the World, or to meld with it. One ventures from home on the thread of a tune. Along sonorous, gestural, motor lines that … graft themselves onto or begin to bud 'lines of drift' with different loops, knots, speeds, movements, gestures, and sonorities.
>
> (2004: 343–344)

Life, for Deleuze and Guattari, issues along such thread-lines or lines of drift (see Chapter 6, p. 83). Along them, points are not connected up but outstripped in the current of movement. This is so even if practitioners are following directions laid down in a plan, score or recipe: indeed the more strictly any performance is specified, the greater the improvisational demands placed on practitioners to 'get it right'.[7] Any formal resemblance between copy and model is not given in advance but is rather a horizon of attainment, to be judged in retrospect (Ingold and Hallam 2007: 5). The same is true, however, even of our most ordinary, routine movements: 'the everyday walk', as Erin Manning has observed, 'is an improvisation before it is a choreography' (2009: 19). As with life itself, the important thing is that it should carry on.

In Chapter 4, I illustrated the difference between iteration and itineration with the example of sawing through a plank of wood. From a point of view external to the action, it may look as though with each stroke of the saw, the carpenter is merely reproducing the same gesture, over and over again, or that sawing is just the repetitive execution of a single step in the operational sequence involved in, say, making a bookcase. However, as Charles Keller has pointed out – by way of the examples of silversmithing and weaving – 'what appears to the observer to be a linear series of steps, a *chaîne opératoire* … is a complex reciprocal process for the practitioner' (2001: 37). Thus the carpenter himself, obliged to follow the material and respond to its singularities, negotiates 'a continuous variation of variables, instead of extracting constants from them' (Deleuze and Guattari 2004: 410). No two strokes of the saw are quite alike, and each – far from following its predecessors like beads on a string – grows out of the one before and prepares the next. Thus the carpenter who has a feel for what he is doing is one who can harmonise the concurrent variations with which he has to deal. This calls for continual correction, in response to an ongoing perceptual monitoring of the unfolding task. That is why every stroke is different, and why sawing has a rhythmic quality.

Let us now imagine the carpenter in his workshop, in a village high in the French Alps, where the critic, novelist and painter, John Berger, has made his home. The workshop, or *charpente*, occupies the second floor of one of the outbuildings of an old farm. Its floor, walls and roof beams have been hewn from timber, just as have the planks on which he now works. You can see in the beams traces of the movements of the axe that cut them, following the grain that reveals the provenance of every beam from a tree once growing in the forest. The *charpente*, Berger observes, is 'filled with time'. There is the time it took for the trees to grow, the time to let their wood dry, the time to build with them and – now that the building has reached the end of its useful life and its planks can fetch a good price elsewhere – the time spent putting away, taking out and pulling down (Berger 2005: 139). But why does Berger choose to include the story of the *charpente* in a dialogue with his daughter Yves on the subject of *drawing*? The clue comes right at the end: '*Le dessinateur comme charpentier. Le dessin comme forêt?*' (ibid.: 144). Could it be that drawing is an activity like carpentry, or even that there is a parallel between the drawn lines of a sketch and the lines of growth of living trees? I believe the parallel is apt, and that a consideration of drawing can serve very well to bring out the itinerant, improvisatory and rhythmic qualities of making as a way of working with lines.

Drawing lines

The act of drawing, Berger argues, is intrinsically dynamic and temporal, leaving its traces 'as eddies on the surface of the stream of time' (ibid.: 124). It is about becoming rather than being. You cannot *be* a mountain, or a buzzard soaring in the sky, or a tree in the forest. But you can *become* one, by aligning your own movements and gestures with those of the thing you wish to draw, as Heidegger would say, in its 'thinging'. 'It's a flowing', says Berger, and at the same time, a 'continuous correcting' (ibid.: 124–125). The draughtswoman with her pencil, just like the carpenter with his saw, must feel where she is going, and must continually adjust her gestures so as to maintain alignment with a moving target. Moreover, as with the mountain path, the buzzard's flight or the tree root, the drawn line does not connect predetermined points in sequence but 'launches forth' from its tip, leaving a trail behind it. Where the path winds, the bird flies and the root creeps, the line follows. Yet it has no end point, for one can never tell when a drawing is finished. In this regard, according to art historian Norman Bryson, drawing differs from painting – or at least from oil painting as it has developed in the western tradition (Bryson 2003: 149).[8] The density and opacity of oil paint is such as to obscure the processes that led up to the work of art. All the revisions, alterations, erasures and false starts that went into making it remain hidden, buried under the surface that meets the eye. We are thus more inclined to treat the work as a finished object, and to treat it as an index of the intentions of the artist, as though the latter were linked to the former by a simple chain of cause and effect. In short, the painting predisposes viewers towards the logic of abduction.

But with drawing it is quite otherwise. For the drawn line is irretractable. Once made it cannot be undone. Other lines may be drawn over or across it, but it is still there for all to see, an indelible record of the pressure of the fingers on the pencil that made it, driven by the impatience, control or anxiety of the maker (Elkins 1996: 227). Thus drawing leaves nowhere to hide (Bryson 2003: 149). Whereas a painting exists 'in the tense of the completed past', in drawing, the time of completion never arrives. It is always ongoing, always work in progress. Every line invites its continuation (ibid.: 150). And so drawing carries on, dicing with the hazards of improvisation, tracing a path that runs not from an image in the mind of a maker to its expression in the material world but orthogonally, looping in and out between mind and paper, rather as a swimmer dives into water and comes back up for air (Berger 2005: 125), or as the embroiderer's thread loops over and under in stitching. The mark on paper, writes Bryson:

> leads as much as it is led: it loops inward from the paper to direct the artist's decision concerning the line that is next to be drawn, and loops back out, as a new trace on paper, *sewing* the mind into the line, binding mind and line in a suturing action … into a knot that grows tighter and tighter … Every drawing that is made re-enacts the same fatal rhythm, following an open expanse … that gradually yields to a network of lines that close in on the drawing and pull the net tight, immobilizing the design.
>
> (2003: 154–155)

What Bryson says of drawing, I suggest, applies generally to the skilled practice of making things. This, in turn, gives us an answer to a key question posed by social anthropologist Karin Barber. In a world of fluid process, how can emergent forms be made to last? What makes things stick (Barber 2007: 25)? Our answer is that it is not because of the inertia of the materials of which they are made that things endure beyond the moment of their emergence, but because of the contrary forces of friction that materials exert on one another when they are ever more tightly interwoven.

In conclusion, however, I return to the 'lineaments' of Alberti. For on the face of it, these abstract, conceptual and intangible lines could not be more different from the marks made by carpentry, drawing or embroidery, with all their vivid presence, dynamism and tactility. The lines of Renaissance art and architecture did indeed come to lie *in between* mind and world, projected onto paper as if on the glass of a window through which the viewing subject fixes his gaze on the objects of his attention. Yet even Alberti imagined these lines as threads, like those of a veil stretched between the eye and the thing seen, and so fine that they could not be split (Alberti 1972: 38). In effect, Alberti's lineaments were threads pulled taut. The taut thread or string, as I have argued elsewhere (Ingold 2007a: 159), was the precursor of the drawn line of architectural design, whose straightness was compared to that of a ray of light. Seventeenth-century treatises on perspective even depicted sight lines as lines of tightly stretched thread, but with loose ends that betrayed their nature (Mitchell 2006: 348–353; see Figure 17.1). The example of Chartres Cathedral, however, shows that the master builders of medieval times were already stringing out lines on the ground, much as methodical gardeners still do today (Turnbull 2000: 53–87). But this string had first to be spun. Spinning, as Victoria Mitchell has pointed out, is itself a ubiquitous form of line-making, 'drawing out through the actions of the fingers and body a continuous trail of

FIGURE 17.1 Sight lines as threads: two engravings by Abraham Bosse, a disciple of the seventeenth-century engineer and mathematician Girard Desargues, from his work of 1647, *Manière Universelle de M. Desargues* (Paris, 1647–1648). The loose ends of the lines betray their thread-like nature. Reproduced courtesy of the Bibliothèque nationale de France.

thread' (Mitchell 2006: 345). In the turn from spinning a thread to stretching it from point to point lies the 'hinge' between bodily movement and abstract reason, between the textilic and the architectonic, between the haptic and the optical, between improvisation and abduction, and between becoming and being. Perhaps the key to the ontology of making is to be found in a length of twine.

18

DRAWING TOGETHER

DOING, OBSERVING, DESCRIBING

Painting and drawing

I have been inspired by an article by the art historian Norman Bryson (2003), written to accompany a major exhibition on the theme of drawing. In it, Bryson compares drawing with painting, or more specifically, with the western tradition of oil painting.[1] One particular aspect of the comparison caught my attention. It starts with the painter or draughtsman poised at that inaugural moment when the hand is about to make its first trace on an initially blank surface. You might think this is a moment that drawing and painting have in common. But in reality, Bryson argues, the perceptions of blankness, and of the potentials it holds, are radically different in each case. The painter perceives a surface that has to be filled throughout its extent, an extent that is nevertheless bounded by the four sides of the frame. This frame exerts a kind of pressure that rebounds inwards on the composition in such a way that every element that is added – every trace of the brush – has to anticipate the totality of the complete picture of which it will eventually form a part. It is, in other words, subject to what Bryson (2003: 150–151) calls 'the law of the all-over'. Drawing, by contrast, is not compelled to observe this law. Instead, although the blank surface of the paper is perceptually present, it does not have to be conceived *as* a surface, as an area that needs to be filled. It becomes rather a 'reserve', a kind of insurance against finality and closure.

Thus the drawn line can unfold in a way that responds to its immediate spatial and temporal milieu, having regard for its own continuation rather than for the totality of the composition. 'The reserve', Bryson writes, 'introduces a principle of non-compositionality, an anti-totalizing force that relieves the drawn line of the responsibility to always put the totality first, to put the collective first, and to assume in relation to the surface a secondary, derivative function' (ibid.: 151). Compared to painting's logic of the all-over, drawing's logic is of 'localized space and time'. Operating with these different logics, the painter's brush and the draughtsman's pencil follow distinctive trajectories. The brush, before it can touch the surface of the canvas, has to hover – to hesitate – while it takes in the sum of marks already made and seeks out an appropriate channel of entry that is consistent with the overall compositional aim. The pencil, by contrast, freed from this 'complex calculus of the totality', does not hover but carries on its way from where the hand is now positioned, responding only to the present conditions in its vicinity rather than to any imagined future state. Indeed the conception of the surface as a reserve ensures that no drawing is ever finished. The last line to have been drawn is never the last that *could* have been drawn: even that final line 'is in itself open to a present that bars the act of closure' (ibid.: 150). Whereas painting moves to completion, drawing carries on, manifesting in its lines a history of becoming rather than an image of being.

Reading Bryson, it struck me that what he says about the processes of art could readily be transposed to those of social life. Metaphorically, the brush and the pencil could stand, respectively, for two ways of thinking about human action, and about the context of that action. One way is to imagine that to act as a responsible social being is to put the totality first, to 'make one's mark on society' (as we say colloquially), by contributing to the overall picture. Society, here, covers the world, within the limits of an institutional frame that rebounds inwardly on the constitution of the person or the self. Another way is to imagine the social world as a tangle of threads or life-paths, ever ravelling here and unravelling there, within which the task for any being is to improvise a way through, and to keep on going. Lives are bound up *in* the tangle, but are not bound *by* it, since there is no enframing, no external boundary. Thus the self is not fashioned on the rebound but undergoes continual generation along a line of growth.

The comparison between these two ways of thinking is of course a heuristic one, and I have no desire to set up a crude dichotomy, let alone to argue that one way is right, and the other wrong. I would venture, however, that the first has been the default position in social anthropology for much of its twentieth-century history, and that it underwrites the discipline's long-held profession to address the *totality* of social phenomena. The second surely has its antecedents too, but it has always remained as something of an undercurrent in a discipline that seems determined to enframe others, to paint them into the picture, and thereby to bring closure to their lives. For my part, however, I have found it profoundly liberating. As Bryson said of the drawing, it is premised on a principle of non-compositionality, and harbours an anti-totalising force that enables us better to understand how lives are lived not in closed social worlds but in the *open*. These lives are social not because they are framed but because they are entwined. All life is social in this sense, since it is fundamentally multi-stranded, an intertwining of many lines running concurrently.

The geographer Torsten Hägerstrand (1976) referred to this characteristic of the life process as the *principle of togetherness*. This is not, he writes, 'just *resting* together. It is also *movement* and *encounter*'. There can be no life that is *not* social, or that evades this principle, for 'what is all the time resting, moving and encountering is … humans, plants, animals and things all at once' (Hägerstrand 1976: 332). Togetherness binds all things, but they are not bound into a totality, or placed within a common frame. Like the lines of a drawing, the lines of social life manifest histories of becoming in a world that is never complete but always in progress. Hägerstrand's call is for a holism which, like that of the drawing, is processual and open-ended and, by the same token, both non-compositional and anti-totalising. My proposal, then, is to redraw anthropology *along these lines*. The drawing is part metaphorical, but also part methodological. Metaphorically, it is about our understanding of persons and other things as drawing together or binding the trajectories of life. Each, we might say, is a *togethering*. Methodologically, it is about the potential of drawing as a way of describing the lives we observe and with which we participate, both in movement and at rest, in what is sometimes called the 'ethnographic encounter'.[2]

Towards a graphic anthropology

It is extraordinary that in all the debate about 'writing culture', the assumption has always been that the *graphic* part of ethnography is writing and not drawing. 'What does the ethnographer do?' Clifford Geertz once asked rhetorically. 'He writes' (Geertz 1973: 19). What a limiting view this is! Given that by all accounts, drawing is an immensely powerful tool of observation, and given also that it combines observation and description in a single gestural movement, why has it been all but forgotten in anthropology? The answer, I suggest, lies in a residual commitment, within the mainstream of the discipline, to a painterly aesthetic that values compositionality and totalisation over improvisation and process. Ethnography remains beholden to the 'law of the all-over', which it satisfies through means that are antithetical to the waywardness of the drawn line. Rather than joining with the togetherings of life, and carrying them forward, its tendency is to want to retroject the fullness of the phenomenal world, caught at a particular moment, *back* upon the surface of the page as if on a blank canvas or screen.

This is what Alfred Kroeber, in a paper published in 1935, meant by 'an endeavour at descriptive integration' that aims, as he put it, to grasp 'the totality of phenomena' (Kroeber 1935: 545–547; see Chapter 19, p. 235). Subsequently endorsed by E. E. Evans-Pritchard (1950: 122) and thence passed to the mainstream of social anthropology, Kroeber's ideal of descriptive integration was a direct heir to the 'art of describing' perfected by Dutch painters in the seventeenth century (Alpers 1983). The objective was to render a moment in the collective life of a people with the same completeness and accuracy with which the Dutch rendered their landscapes. As the painting covers the entire canvas, leaving no space unfilled, so in an ethnographic account that grasps the totality there should be no gaps. Every detail should be filled in. Indeed the very 'thickness' of the ethnographer's description, to use Geertz's term (1973: 6, after Ryle 1971), brings to mind the density and opacity of oil paint that – as Bryson explains (2003: 149) – covers over and obliterates the workings of the picture. All the revisions, alterations and false starts that went into making it remain hidden, buried under the surface that meets the eye, leaving the picture as a completed whole that preserves in its compositional arrangement the totality of phenomena represented. And so, too, the perfect ethnography hides the traces of its inscription, presenting a picture of the lifeworld *as if* it were arrayed, fully formed, upon a surface.

By contrast, an anthropology that takes drawing as its medium – that is, a *graphic* anthropology (Afonso and Ramos 2004: 73) – would appeal to the openness of the reserve rather than the closure of a surface that has been completely filled in. Indeed, in its sights, the lifeworld would have no surface. Finding a way through rather than covering over, the drawn line contrives to make the surface disappear, or as Bryson puts it (2003: 151), to be 'perceptually present but conceptually absent'. Though practically inscribed as traces on a surface, the lines of the drawing appear like threads in a void (Ingold 2007a: 57). If anything, they weave a surface rather than being laid upon it. And like threads, they cannot be erased.[3] Since drawing does not cover, neither can it be covered up. In drawing as in life, what is done cannot be undone. It is, at every moment, a risky endeavour, with no assurance of how things will turn out. Though you may be able to recover from errors, it is impossible to go back and correct them. You can only carry on from where you are now, leaving a trail behind you as evidence of where you have been. Drawing, Bryson writes, is relentless: 'it forces everything into the open, into a field of exposure without shields or screens, with no hiding places, a radically open zone that always operates in real time' (2003: 149).

Observation and description

A graphic anthropology, then, would aim not at a complete description of what is already there, or has already come to pass, but to join together with persons and other things in the movements of their formation. This joining together is a practice of observation. By observation I do not mean the distanced and disinterested contemplation of a world of objects, nor the translation of objects into mental images or representations. I refer rather to the intimate coupling of the movement of the observer's attention with currents of activity in the environment (Ingold 2000a: 108). To observe is not so much to see what is 'out there' as to *watch what is going on*. Its aim is thus not to represent the observed but to participate with it in the same generative movement.

In her fine study of the power of calligraphy in contemporary Chinese society, Yuehping Yen (2005: 89–90) explains that one cannot observe a work of calligraphy, let alone understand its meaning, merely by looking at it. One has to enter *into* it and to join in the process of its production – in other words, to be reunited with the calligrapher in his or her 'inked traces'. Anthropologist and craftsperson Stephanie Bunn has said much the same about understanding pattern, for example in knotwork, knitting and basketry. 'We may see the pattern in our mind's eye, but we do it, we know it, we embrace it through the movement of our bodies' (Bunn 1999: 26). It is similar with patterning in music. On a purely intellectual level it might be possible to apprehend, say, one of Bach's suites for unaccompanied cello as a complete, perfectly formed structure. But as a practising cellist I cannot listen to a performance without feeling the music flowing through my body, arms and fingers as though I were playing it myself. To listen is to unite the process of one's own kinaesthetic attention with a trajectory of sound.

The visual theorist James Elkins makes an identical point in his comparison of the ways in which the historian of art and the practising artist might respond to a drawing:

> A historian, trained with books and colour slides, will stand at a respectful distance and look without moving. An artist, at home with gestures, will want to move a hand over the drawing, repeating the gentleness of the marks that made it, reliving the drag of the brush or the push of the pencil. The drawing has *become* its bodily response, and the body moves in blind obedience to what it senses on the page.
>
> (Elkins 1996: 227)

Elkins exaggerates, however, in describing the body's obedience as 'blind'. As I shall show in a moment, the exaggeration stems from a peculiar tendency, common among theorists of visual culture, to reduce vision to the interpretation of images. Thanks to this reduction, observers whose eyes – as Hägerstrand put it (1976: 332) – are always 'looking around' and wondering where to go next, appear to be groping in the dark, their experience more tactile than visual. My contention, to the contrary, is that it is precisely in this ocular itineration along the paths of the world's becoming that the essence of vision resides. It is a practice of togethering. Thus, far from there being any contradiction between participation and observation, as is often supposed, the one – in the visual as in any other sensory modality – is a *condition* for the other (see also Chapter 10, p. 219). The spectator who stands at a distance, in order to make an objective study, is observationally blind.

It is one thing to observe what is going on; however, quite another to describe it. As I have already noted, anthropologists have long assumed that to describe things is not to draw them but to put them in writing. It is supposed, moreover, that as an art of verbal composition, descriptive writing entails a *turning away* from observation (Clifford 1990: 52). I explore the consequences of this deviation at greater length in the next chapter (p. 241). Suffice it to remark at this point that the conventional bracketing of observation and description under the rubric of 'ethnography' tends to obscure the fact that the production of ethnographic accounts is most often far removed from the contexts of observational engagement. Ethnographers observe in the field but withdraw to the study to describe. The real problem with ethnography, then, lies not in the alleged contradiction between participation and observation, which is a chimera, but in the disconnection of the art of description from observational practice. One way to reconnect them, I suggest, might be to think of description in the first place as a process not of verbal composition but of line-making. And this leads me back to drawing.

Text and image

Drawing is a mode of description that has not yet broken away from observation (see Chapter 19, p. 241). At the same time that the gesturing hand draws *out* its traces upon a surface, the observing eye is drawn *into* the labyrinthine entanglements of the lifeworld, yielding a sense of its forms, proportions and textures, but above all of its movements – of the generative dynamic of a world-in-formation. In recent anthropology, however, the potential of drawing to couple observation and description has been largely eclipsed by an overriding dichotomy between the written text and the visual image. The sub-discipline of visual anthropology, in particular, has invested heavily in this dichotomy. For example, in her influential book *The Ethnographer's Eye*, Anna Grimshaw complains of 'anthropologists committed to language and writing' who want to marginalise, contain and suppress the visual (Grimshaw 2001: 172). For these anthropologists, she alleges, 'images are condemned as seductive, dazzling, deceptive and illusory, and are regarded as capable of wreaking all sorts of havoc with the sobriety of the discipline' (ibid.: 5). She presents no evidence to support this allegation, and I do not believe there is any. What interests me, however, is that the visual anthropology for which she calls should be understood as *alternative* to anthropology in writing. Do we not use our eyes to read and write, just as we do to observe a work of calligraphy or of drawing? Why else does almost every scholar wear spectacles? What does the characterisation of writing as *non*-visual tell us about our understanding of vision?

The only way to sustain the view that the written text is non-visual, as we saw in Chapter 16 (pp. 196–7), is by supposing that vision has nothing to do with eyesight and everything to do with the perusal of images. Thus: no images; no vision. Seeing, then, is not about the optical tracking of marks and traces inscribed or impressed upon surfaces in the world, whether of the ground – as when the hunter follows a trail – or of parchment or paper as in reading a manuscript. It is about eyes opening up to a domain of images. Vision only occurs, in this view, when what meets the eyes is an image of what has already been observed. With this, we return to the peculiar presupposition of Elkins, namely, that eyes that look around, but which do not open up to images, are blind. Elkins is convinced that whatever is not fixed in memory, in the form of what he calls a 'final image', we simply fail to see (Elkins 1996: 219–224). Likewise for Grimshaw, the ethnographer's eye turns out to be not so much an organ of observational engagement as an instrument by which moments of such engagement can be fixed, framed and returned to the viewer for subsequent scrutiny. This is what the camera does, and we soon realise that the 'eye' of Grimshaw's allegory is in fact a camera. It is, in her terms, an 'image-based technology' (2001: 3) that can succeed in capturing the fullness of the world at an instant, within the limits of a frame, and can then *play it back* to the viewer.[4] Filling the frame, the photographic plate is subject to the same 'law of the all-over' as the oil painting. There is no reserve.

Yet as we have already seen, ethnographic 'thick description', although literary, is also subject to this law. It has the same antecedents as does photography in the traditions of landscape painting,[5] and has its foundations in the same commitments to composition and totalisation. Just as in the visual image, the world is played back to the viewer, so in the literary text it is played back to the reader. Whether of text or image, the surface that it covers stands in for the surface of the lifeworld. Drawing, however, subverts the assumptions that underpin the polarity of text and image. Its lines neither solidify into images nor compose themselves into the static verbal forms of the printed text. They do not capture the world in its totality, and render it *back* to the viewer or reader. Rather, they are carried *forward*, in real time, in concert with the movements of the worlding world, in an ever-unfolding relation between observant eyes, gesturing hands and their descriptive trace.

Indeed it is no accident or oversight that a visual anthropology that has so much to say about the camera has virtually dismissed the pencil. In one of the only contributions to the flourishing literature in this field to give any credit to drawing, Ana Isabel Afonso and Manuel Joao Ramos (2004: 74) deplore the willingness of visual anthropologists to cast aside the humble and 'handicrafty' pencil in their haste to embrace the latest in digital imaging technologies. It is a mistake to think that the camera does the same as a pencil, only faster; or that the photographic image achieves the same as the drawing, only with greater accuracy.[6] For the pencil is not an image-based technology, nor is the drawing an image. It is the trace of an observational gesture that follows what is going on. The camera interrupts this flow of visuo-manual activity and cuts the relation between gesture and description that lies at the heart of drawing. Nor is it an accident, or an oversight, that an ethnography that claims – in the idiom of James Clifford (1990: 53) – to be 'graphocentric' does all its writing on a keyboard. For what the camera does for drawing, the keyboard does for writing. Critically, the keyboard ruptures the direct link between perception, gesture and its trace that is crucial to observational description. Its effect is to transform the meaning of description, from a scribal practice in which the writing hand leaves a continuous trace that is always responsive, in the quality of the line, to conditions as they unfold, to a practice of verbal composition in which the aim is to render an account wherein every word is chosen for its fit within the totality (Ingold 2007a: 128).[7] A return to drawing is thus also a return to handwriting, replacing the rigid opposition between image and text with a continuum of scribal practices, or processes of line-making, ranging from handwriting through calligraphy to drawing and sketching, with no clear points of demarcation between them.

Looking back

I began with the difference between painting and drawing, and have ended by contrasting the kind of ethnographic description that sets up an opposition between image and text with the kind that gives us a continuum from drawing to handwriting. The first kind, which has been conventional in anthropology ever since Kroeber introduced his notion of the 'descriptive integration' of phenomena, yields the studies *of* people that comprise the bulk of ethnographic literature. They are integrative, all-over accounts that, in their very completion, establish a separation between ourselves who read them and the others whose lives are portrayed therein. As anthropologists are all too aware, almost to the point of obsession, this kind of writing inevitably involves a process of 'othering'. Even if the people were not other to begin with, they have always become other by the end. My suggestion is that a descriptive endeavour of the second kind, whose instrument is the pen or pencil rather than the camera and keyboard, would yield studies that are *with* people rather than *of* them. Where studying *of* is a process of othering, studying *with* is a process of togethering. The first is transitive, the second intransitive.

I believe that the logic of the study *of* – the logic of the all-over – is largely responsible for the banishment of life from anthropology, leaving the discipline adrift in a ghostly realm of words and images. As I have explained in Chapter 1, my ambition all along has been to bring anthropology back to life. An anthropology thus restored to life is an anthropology *with*. Its holism lies in its appeal not to the totality of structures or systems that are fully joined up, but to the essential continuity of the life process.[8] Always open-ended and never complete, the process is nevertheless implicate in every moment it brings forth. 'The real whole', as Henri Bergson wrote, 'might well be ... an indivisible continuity. The systems we cut out within it would ... not then be *parts* at all; they would be *partial* views of the whole' (Bergson 1911: 32). My argument, then, is not against holism per se, but against the particular conception of part–whole relations implied when holism is equated with totalisation (Ingold 2007c: 209). That the task of life is never finished, and that the world never ceases its worlding, does not mean that lives are half-completed or that the world we inhabit is but half-built. Nor does it mean that lives are fragmented and worlds torn to pieces that, like Humpty Dumpty, can never be reassembled. The alternative to totalisation is not fragmentation, rupture and discontinuity. It is rather a holism that is anti-compositional, fluid, processual and improvisatory. And its key descriptive practice is drawing.

Epilogue

19

ANTHROPOLOGY IS *NOT* ETHNOGRAPHY

Acceptable generalisation and unacceptable history

The objective of anthropology, I believe, is to seek a generous, comparative but nevertheless critical understanding of human being and knowing in the one world we all inhabit. The objective of ethnography is to describe the lives of people other than ourselves, with an accuracy and sensitivity honed by detailed observation and prolonged first-hand experience. My aim, in this final chapter, is to demonstrate that anthropology and ethnography are endeavours of quite different kinds. This is not to claim that the one is more important than the other, or more honourable. Nor is it to deny that they depend on one another in significant ways. It is simply to assert that they are not the same. Indeed this might seem like a statement of the obvious, and so it would be were it not for the fact that it has become commonplace – at least over the last quarter of a century – for writers in our subject to treat the two as virtually equivalent, exchanging anthropology for ethnography more or less on a whim, as the mood takes them, or even exploiting the supposed synonymy as a stylistic device to avoid verbal repetition. Many colleagues to whom I have informally put the question have told me that in their view there is little if anything to distinguish anthropological from ethnographic work. Most are convinced that ethnography lies at the core of what anthropology is all about. For them, to suggest otherwise seems almost anachronistic. It is like going back to the bad old days – the days, some might say, of Alfred Reginald Radcliffe-Brown. For it was he who, in laying the foundations for what – in the early decades of the twentieth century – was the new science of social anthropology, insisted on the absolute distinction between ethnography and anthropology.

He did so in terms of a contrast, much debated at the time but little heard of today, between *idiographic* and *nomothetic* inquiry. An idiographic inquiry, Radcliffe-Brown explained, aims to document the particular facts of past and present lives, whereas the aim of nomothetic inquiry is to arrive at general propositions or theoretical statements. Ethnography, then, is specifically a mode of idiographic inquiry, differing from history and archaeology in that it is based on the direct observation of living people rather than on written records or material remains attesting to the activities of people in the past. Anthropology, to the contrary, is a field of nomothetic science. As Radcliffe-Brown declared in his introduction to *Structure and Function in Primitive Society* – in a famous sentence that, as an undergraduate beginning my anthropological studies at Cambridge in the late 1960s, I was expected to learn by heart – 'comparative sociology, of which social anthropology is a branch, is … a theoretical or nomothetic study of which the aim is to provide acceptable generalisations' (Radcliffe-Brown 1952: 3). This distinction between anthropology and ethnography was one that brooked no compromise, and Radcliffe-Brown reasserted it over and over again. Returning to the theme in his Huxley Memorial Lecture for 1951 on 'The comparative method in social anthropology', best known for its revision of the theory of totemism, Radcliffe-Brown insisted that 'without systematic comparative studies anthropology will become only historiography and ethnography' (1951a: 16). And the aim of comparison, he maintained, is to pass from the particular to the general, from the general to the more general, and ultimately to the universal (ibid.: 22).

The distinction between the idiographic and the nomothetic was first coined in 1894 by the German philosopher–historian Wilhelm Windelband, a leading figure in the school of thought, then known as neo-Kantianism. Windelband's real purpose was to lay down a clear dividing line between the craft of the historian, whose concern is with judgements of value, and the project of the natural science, concerned as it is with the accumulation of positive knowledge based on empirical observation. But he did so by identifying history with the documentation of particular events and science with the search for general laws. And this left his distinction wide open for appropriation by positivistic natural science to denote not its opposition to history but the two successive stages of its own programme: first, the systematic collection of empirical facts; and secondly, the organisation of these facts within an overarching framework of general principles. It was left to Heinrich Rickert, a pupil of Windelband and co-founder with him of the neo-Kantian school, to sort out the confusion by pointing out that there are distinct ways, respectively scientific and historical, of attending to the particular, to each of which there corresponds a specific sense of the idiographic (Collingwood 1946: 165–170). One way treats every entity or event as an objective fact, the other attributes to it some meaning or value.[1] In so far as a geologist setting out to reconstruct the history of a rock formation, or a palaeontologist seeking to reconstruct a phylogenetic sequence on the basis of fossil evidence, necessarily deals in particulars, the reconstruction could – in the *first* of these senses – be deemed to be idiographic. Moreover the same might have been said (and indeed was said) of attempts, predominantly by North American scholars and going under the rubric of ethnology, to reconstruct chronological sequences of culture on the evidence of distributions of what were then called 'traits'.

It was in this sense that Radcliffe-Brown could set aside North American ethnology, which he associated primarily with the work of Franz Boas and his followers, as an idiographic enterprise wholly distinct from his nomothetic social anthropology conceived as a search for general laws governing social life (Radcliffe-Brown 1951a: 15). But while Boasian ethnology was thus being portrayed in Britain as historical rather than scientific, on the other side of the Atlantic it was being criticised for being scientific rather than historical. This critique came from Alfred Kroeber. Thoroughly conversant with the writings of the neo-Kantian school, Kroeber called for an anthropology that would be fully historical and therefore idiographic in the *second* sense. It must, in short, attend to particulars in terms of their value and meaning. Yet no particular – no thing, or happening – can have value and meaning in itself, cut out from the wider context of its occurrence. Each has rather to be understood by way of its positioning within the totality to which it belongs. Thus while preserving the singularity of its phenomena rather than allowing them to be dissolved into laws and generalisations, the historical approach – in Kroeber's words – 'finds its intellectual satisfaction in putting each preserved phenomenon into a relation of ever widening context within the phenomenal cosmos' (Kroeber 1952: 123). He characterised this task, of preservation through contextualisation, as 'an endeavour at descriptive integration' (1935: 545). As such, it is entirely different from the task of theoretical integration that Radcliffe-Brown had assigned to social anthropology. For the latter, in order to generalise, one must first isolate every particular from its context in order that it can then be subsumed under context-independent formulations. Kroeber's disdain for Radcliffe-Brown's understanding of history, as nothing but a chronological tabulation of such isolated particulars awaiting the classificatory and comparative attentions of the theorist, bordered on contempt. 'I do not know the motivation for Radcliffe-Brown's depreciation of the historical approach', he remarked caustically in an article first published in 1946, 'unless that, as the ardent apostle of a genuine new science of society, he has perhaps failed to concern himself enough with history to learn its nature' (in Kroeber 1952: 96).

The sigma principle and the totality of phenomena

Though I am not sure that the terms are the best ones, the distinction between descriptive and theoretical integration is of great importance. For the two modes of integration entail entirely different understandings of the relation between the particular and the general. The theoretician operating in a nomothetic mode imagines a world that is, by its nature, particulate. Thus the reality of the social world, for Radcliffe-Brown, comprises 'an immense multitude of actions and interactions of human beings' (1952: 4). Out of this multitude of particular events the analyst has then to abstract general features that amount to a specification of form. One of the strangest attempts to spell out this procedure appears in a book ominously entitled *The Theory of Social Structure* by the great ethnographer and anthropologist Siegfried Nadel, posthumously published in 1957. Introduced by his friend and colleague Meyer Fortes (in Nadel 1957: xv) as a work 'destined to be one of the great theoretical treatises of twentieth-century social anthropology', it was soon forgotten. Its peculiarity lay in its author's use of notation drawn from symbolic logic in order to formalise the move from the concreteness of actually observed behaviour to the abstract pattern of relationships.

Let us suppose, Nadel postulated, that between persons A and B we observe diverse behaviours denoted by the letters a, b, c … n, but that all index a condition of 'acting towards' – of A acting towards B and of B acting towards A. We denote this condition with the colon (:). It then follows that a formal relationship (r) exists between A and B, under which is subsumed the behavioural series a … n. Or in short:

$$A \text{ r } B, \text{ if}$$
$$A (a, b, c \ldots n): B, \text{ and } \textit{vice versa}$$
$$\therefore r \supset \Sigma \text{ a} \ldots \text{n}$$

(Nadel 1957: 10)

My purpose in recovering this formulation from the rightful oblivion into which it quickly fell is only to highlight the sense of integration epitomised in the last line by the Greek 'sigma', the sign conventionally used in mathematics to denote the summation of a series. The abstract relation, here, takes the form of a covering statement that encompasses every concrete term in the series.

When Kroeber spoke of 'descriptive integration', however, he meant something quite different: more akin, perhaps, to the integration of an artist's picture on the canvas as he paints a landscape. To the artist's gaze, the landscape presents itself not as a multitude of particulars but as a variegated phenomenal field, at once continuous and coherent. Within this field, the singularity of every phenomenon lies in its enfolding – in its positioning and bearing, and in the poise of a momentarily arrested movement – of the entangled histories of relations by which it came to be there, at that position and in that moment. And as the artist tries to preserve that singularity in the work of the brush, so, for Kroeber, does the anthropologist in his endeavours of description. This is what he meant when he insisted that the aim of anthropology – as of history – must be one of 'integrating phenomena as such' (Kroeber 1935: 546). The integration he was after is one of a world that already coheres, where things and events occur or *take place*, rather than a world of disconnected particulars that has to be rendered coherent, or joined up after the fact, in the theoretical imagination. Thus what Kroeber called the 'nexus among phenomena' (loc. cit.) is there to be described, in the relational coherence of the world; it is not something to be extracted from it as one might seek the general features of a form from the range of its concrete and particular instantiations. For precisely that reason, Kroeber thought, it would be wrong to regard the phenomena of the social world as *complex*. Contemplating the landscape, the painter would be unlikely to exclaim 'What a complex landscape this is!' He may be struck by many things, but complexity is not one of them. Nor is it a consideration in the regard of the historically oriented anthropologist. Complexity only arises as an issue in the attempt to reassemble a world already decomposed into elements, as a picture, for example, might be cut up to make a jigsaw puzzle. But like the painter, and unlike the puzzle builder, Kroeber's anthropologist seeks an integration 'in terms of the totality of phenomena' (ibid.: 547) that is ontologically prior to its analytical decomposition.

Yet if the anthropologist describes the social world as the artist paints a landscape, then what becomes of time? The world stands still for no one, least of all for the artist or the anthropologist, and the latter's description, like the former's depiction, can do no more than catch a fleeting moment in a never-ending process. In that moment, however, is compressed the movement of the past that brought it about, and in the tension of that compression lies the force that will propel it into the future. It is this enfolding of a generative past and a future potential in the present moment, and not the location of that moment in any abstract chronology, which makes it historical. Reasoning along these lines, Kroeber came to the conclusion that time, in the chronological sense, is inessential to history. Presented as a kind of 'descriptive cross-section' or as the characterisation of a moment, a historical account can just as well be synchronic as diachronic. Indeed it is precisely to such characterising description that anthropology aspires. 'What else can ethnography be', asked Kroeber rhetorically, 'than … a timeless piece of history?' (1952 [1946]: 102). The other side of this argument, of course, is that the mere ordering of events in chronological succession, one after another, gives us not history but science. Boas, whose painstaking attempts to reconstruct the lines of cultural transmission and diffusion over time had been dismissed by Kroeber as anti-historical, was perplexed. He confessed to finding Kroeber's reasoning utterly unintelligible (Boas 1936: 137). Back in Britain, however, Kroeber's understanding of what a historical or ideographic anthropology would look like fell on the more sympathetic ears of E. E. Evans-Pritchard.

In his Marett Lecture of 1950, 'Social anthropology: past and present', Evans-Pritchard virtually reiterated what Kroeber had written fifteen years previously about the relation between anthropology and history. These were his words:

> I agree with Professor Kroeber that the fundamental characteristic of the historical method is not chronological relation of events but descriptive integration of them; and this characteristic historiography shares with social anthropology. What social anthropologists have in fact chiefly been doing is to write cross-sections of history, integrative descriptive accounts of primitive peoples at a moment in time which are in other respects like the accounts written by historians about peoples over a period of time...
>
> (Evans-Pritchard 1950: 122)

Returning to this theme over a decade later, in a lecture on 'Anthropology and history' delivered at the University of Manchester, Evans-Pritchard roundly condemned – as had Kroeber – the blinkered view of those such as Radcliffe-Brown for whom history was nothing more than 'a record of a succession of unique events' and social anthropology nothing less than 'a set of general propositions' (Evans-Pritchard 1961: 2). In practice, Evans-Pritchard claimed, social anthropologists do not generalise from particulars any more than do historians. Rather, 'they see the general in the particular' (ibid.: 3). Or to put it another way, the singular phenomenon opens up as you go deeper into it, rather than being eclipsed from above. Yet Evans-Pritchard was by no means consistent in this view, for hardly had he stated it than he asserted precisely the opposite: 'Events lose much, even all, of their meaning if they are not seen as having some degree of regularity and constancy, as belonging to a certain type of event, all instances of which have many features in common' (ibid.: 4). This is a statement fully consistent with what, following Nadel, we might call the sigma principle of comparative generalisation, and flies in the face of the Kroeberian project of descriptive integration, or preservation through contextualisation.

In defence of Radcliffe-Brown

The problem is that once the task of anthropology is defined as descriptive integration rather than comparative generalisation, the distinction between ethnography and social anthropology, on which Radcliffe-Brown had set such store, simply vanishes. Beyond ethnography, there is nothing left for anthropology to do. And Radcliffe-Brown himself was more than aware of this. In a 1951 review of Evans-Pritchard's book *Social Anthropology*, in which the author had propounded the same ideas about anthropology and history as those set out in his Marett lecture (see Evans-Pritchard 1951: 60–61), Radcliffe-Brown registered his strong disagreement with 'the implication that social anthropology consists entirely or even largely of ... ethnographic studies of particular societies. It is towards some such position that Professor Evans-Pritchard and a few others seem to be moving' (Radcliffe-Brown 1951b: 365). And it was indeed towards such a position that the discipline moved over the ensuing decade, so much so that in his Malinowski Lecture of 1959, 'Rethinking anthropology', Edmund Leach felt moved to complain about it. 'Most of my colleagues', he grumbled, 'are giving up in the attempt to make comparative generalizations; instead they have begun to write impeccably detailed historical ethnographies of particular peoples' (Leach 1961: 1). But did Leach, in regretting this tendency, stand up for the nomothetic social anthropology of Radcliffe-Brown? Far from it. Though all in favour of generalisation, Leach launched an all-out attack on Radcliffe-Brown for having gone about it in the *wrong way*. The source of the error, he maintained, lay not in generalisation per se, but in comparison.

There are two varieties of generalisation, Leach argued. One, the sort of which he disapproved, works by comparison and classification. It assigns the forms or structures it encounters into types and subtypes, as a botanist or zoologist, for example, assigns plant or animal specimens to genera and species. Radcliffe-Brown liked to imagine himself working this way. As he wrote in a letter to Claude Lévi-Strauss, social structures are as real as the structures of living organisms, and may be collected and compared in much the same way in order to arrive at 'a valid typological classification' (Radcliffe-Brown 1953: 109). The other kind of generalisation, of which Leach approved, works by exploring a priori – or as he put it, by 'inspired guesswork' – the space of possibility opened up by the combination of a limited set of variables (Leach 1961: 5). A generalisation, then, would take the form not of a typological specification that would enable us to distinguish societies of one kind from those of another, but of a statement of the relationships between variables that may operate in societies of *any* kind. This is the approach, Leach claimed, not of the botanist or zoologist, but of the engineer. Engineers are not interested in the classification of machines, or in the delineation of taxa. They want to know how machines work. The task of social anthropology, likewise, is to understand and explain how societies work. Of course, societies are not machines, as Leach readily admitted. But if you want to find out how societies work, they may just as well be compared to machines as to organisms. 'The entities we call societies', Leach wrote, 'are not naturally existing species, neither are they man-made mechanisms. But the analogy of a mechanism has quite as much relevance as the analogy of an organism' (ibid.: 6).

I beg to differ, and on this particular point I want to rise to the defence of Radcliffe-Brown who, I think, has been grievously misrepresented by his critics, including both Leach and Evans-Pritchard. According to Leach, Radcliffe-Brown's resort to the organic analogy was based on dogma rather than choice. Not so. It was based on Radcliffe-Brown's commitment to a philosophy of process. On this he was absolutely explicit. Societies are *not* entities analogous to organisms, let alone to machines. In reality, indeed, there are no such entities. 'My own view', Radcliffe-Brown asserted, 'is that the concrete reality with which the social anthropologist is concerned … is not any sort of entity but a process, the process of social life' (1952: 4). The analogy, then, is not between society and organism as entities, but between social *life* and organic *life* understood as processes. It was precisely this idea of the social as a life process, rather than the idea of society as an entity, that Radcliffe-Brown drew from the comparison. And it was for this reason, too, that he compared social life to the functioning of an organism and *not* to that of a machine, for the difference between them is that the first is a life process whereas the second is not. In life, form is continually emergent rather than specified from the outset, and nothing is ever quite the same from one moment to the next. To support his processual view of reality, Radcliffe-Brown appealed to the celebrated image of the Greek philosopher Heraclitus, of a world where all is in motion and nothing fixed, and in which it is no more possible to regain a passing moment than it is to step twice into the same waters of a flowing river (Radcliffe-Brown 1957: 12).

What his critics could never grasp, according to W. E. H. Stanner (1968: 287), was that in its emphasis on continuity through change, Radcliffe-Brown's understanding of social reality was thoroughly historical. Thus we find Evans-Pritchard, in his 1961 Manchester lecture, pointing an accusing finger at Radcliffe-Brown while warning of the dangers of drawing analogies from biological science and of assuming that there are entities, analogous to organisms, that might be labelled 'societies'. One may be able to understand the physiology of an organism without regard to its history – after all, horses remain horses and do not change into elephants – but social systems can and do undergo wholesale structural transformations (Evans-Pritchard 1961: 10). Yet a quarter of a century previously, Radcliffe-Brown had made precisely this point, albeit with a different pair of animals. 'A pig does not become a hippopotamus… On the other hand a society can and does change its structural type without any breach of continuity' (Radcliffe-Brown 1952 [1935]: 181). This observation did not escape the attention of Lévi-Strauss who, in a paper presented to the Wenner-Gren Symposium on Anthropology in 1952, deplored Radcliffe-Brown's 'reluctance towards the isolation of social structures conceived as self-sufficient wholes' and his commitment to 'a philosophy of continuity, not of discontinuity' (Lévi-Strauss 1968: 304). For Lévi-Strauss had nothing but contempt for the idea of history as continuous change. Instead, he proposed an immense classification of societies, each conceived as a discrete, self-contained entity defined by a specific permutation and combination of constituent elements, and arrayed on the abstract coordinates of space and time (Lévi-Strauss 1953: 9–10). The irony is that it was from Lévi-Strauss, and not from Radcliffe-Brown, that Leach claimed to have derived his model for how anthropological generalisation should be done. Whereas Lévi-Strauss was elevated as a mathematician among the social scientists, the efforts of Radcliffe-Brown were dismissed as nothing better than 'butterfly collecting' (Leach 1961: 2–3). Yet Lévi-Strauss's plan for drawing up an inventory of all human societies, past and present, with a view to establishing their complementarities and differences, is surely the closest thing to butterfly collecting ever encountered in the annals of anthropology. Unsurprisingly, given its ambition, the plan came to nothing.

I do not pretend that Radcliffe-Brown's approach was without contradictions of its own. On the contrary, it was mired in contradiction from the start. Much has been made of Radcliffe-Brown's debt to the sociology of Emile Durkheim (1982 [1917]), and for Durkheim, of course, societies *were* self-contained entities, each with its own individuality, which could nevertheless be classified in terms of the possible combinations of their constituent parts.[2] But where Lévi-Strauss took this principle of discontinuity to its logical extreme, Radcliffe-Brown – influenced as much by Whitehead's (1929) philosophy of organism as by Durkheim's sociology – moved in the opposite direction, to re-establish the principle of continuity. This attempt to refract the process ontology of Whitehead through the classificatory epistemology of Durkheim, though brave, was bound to fail. Inevitably, social life reappeared as the life of society, emergent form as pre-existent structure, the continuity of history as the alternation of stability and change (Ingold 1986: 153–154). Indeed there was no way in which Durkheim's first rule of sociological method, *to consider social facts as things*, could be squared with Radcliffe-Brown's idea of social life as a continuous and irreversible process. Nevertheless I have found more inspiration in this idea of the social as a life process than in all the criticisms that have been levelled against it put together. Divested of the deadweight of Durkheim's sociologism, I believe it is an idea that we can and should take forward from Radcliffe-Brown in forging a conception better suited to our times of what a genuinely open-ended and comparative anthropology could be. Quite simply, it would be an inquiry into the conditions and possibilities of social life, at all times and everywhere. To be more precise, I need to explain what I mean by both 'social' and 'life'.

Social life and the implicate order

In a series of seminars presented at the University of Chicago in 1937, subsequently transcribed and published under the title *A Natural Science of Society*, Radcliffe-Brown dwelt at some length on the distinction between social science and psychology (Radcliffe-Brown 1957: 45–52). The matter was for him absolutely clear-cut. Psychology studies the mind, and mind is a system of relations between states internal to the individual actor. They are, so to speak, 'under the skin'. Social science, however, deals with relations between individuals, not within them. 'The moment you get outside the skin of the individual', Radcliffe-Brown declared, 'you have no longer psychological, but social relations' (ibid.: 47). The deep-seated assumption that mind is an internal property of human individuals that can be studied in isolation from their involvement with one another or with the wider environment continues to reverberate within the field of psychology. It has, however, been widely challenged (see Chapter 6, p. 86). One of the first to issue such a challenge was the great pioneer of psychological anthropology, A. Irving Hallowell. In an extraordinarily prescient paper on 'The self and its behavioral environment', published in 1954, Hallowell concluded that no physical barrier can come between mind and world. 'Any inner-outer dichotomy', he maintained, 'with the human skin as boundary, is psychologically irrelevant' (Hallowell 1955: 88). Fifteen years later, Gregory Bateson made exactly the same point. Mind, Bateson insisted, is not confined within individual bodies as against a world 'out there', but is immanent in the entire system of organism–environment relations within which all human beings are necessarily enmeshed. 'The mental world', as he put it, 'is not limited by the skin' (Bateson 1973: 429). Rather, it reaches out into the environment along the multiple and ever-extending sensory pathways of the human organism's involvement in its surroundings. Or as Andy Clark has observed, still more recently, the mind has a way of leaking from the body, mingling with the world around it (Clark 1997: 53).

I invoke the word 'social' to signify this understanding of the essential interpenetrability or commingling of mind and world. Far from serving to demarcate a particular *domain* of phenomena, as opposed – say – to the biological or the psychological, I take the word to denote a certain ontology: an understanding of the constitution of the phenomenal world itself. As such, it is opposed to an ontology of the particulate that imagines a world of individual entities and events, each of which is linked through an external contact – whether of spatial contiguity or temporal succession – that leaves its basic nature intact. In the terms of the physicist David Bohm (1980), the order of such an imagined world would be *explicate*. The order of the social world, by contrast, is *implicate*. That is to say, any particular phenomenon on which we may choose to focus our attention enfolds within its constitution the totality of relations of which, in their unfolding, it is the momentary outcome.[3] Were we to cut these relations, and seek to recover the whole from its now isolated fragments, something would be lost that could never be recovered. That something is life itself. As the biologist Paul Weiss put it, in a 1969 symposium on the future of the life sciences, 'the mere reversal of our prior analytical dissection of the Universe by putting the pieces together again … can yield no complete explanation of even the most elementary living system'

(Weiss 1969: 7). That is why, to return to my earlier criticism of Leach, a mechanical analogy can offer no account of social *life*. A machine can be constructed from parts, but machines do not live. And this brings me from the meaning of the social to the second of my key terms, namely 'life'. By this I do not mean an internal animating principle that is installed in some things but not others, distinguishing the former as members of the class of animate objects. Life, as Weiss observed, 'is process, not substance' (1969: 8), and this process is tantamount to the unfolding of a continuous and ever-evolving field of relations within which beings of all kinds are generated and held in place. Thus where Radcliffe-Brown drew an analogy between organic life and social life, I draw an identity. Organic life *is* social, and so for that matter is the life of the mind, because the order to which it gives rise is implicate.[4]

In this distinction between explicate and implicate orders lies an echo of the contrast I drew earlier between theoretical and descriptive modes of integration. To recapitulate: the theoretical mode works through the summation of discrete particulars, according to the sigma principle, so as to arrive at covering statements of the general form of social relations. The descriptive mode, on the other hand, seeks to apprehend the relational coherence of the world itself, as it is given to immediate experience, by homing in on particulars each of which brings to a focus, and momentarily condenses, the very processes that brought it into being. Though both modes of integration aspire to a kind of holism, their respective understandings of totality are very different. The first is a totality of *form*: it implies the closure and completion of a system of relations that has been fully joined up. The second, however, is a totality of *process* that, since it is forever ongoing, is always open-ended and never complete, but which is nevertheless wound up in every moment that it brings forth. Now as I mentioned earlier, I am not convinced that the terms 'theoretical' and 'descriptive' are entirely appropriate for these two approaches. The trouble is that the very notion that description is a task somehow opposed to the project of theory has its roots in the first of the two modes. It harks directly back to Radcliffe-Brown's division between ethnography and anthropology: respectively idiographic and nomothetic, descriptive and theoretical. Yet in the opposition between descriptive data and theoretical generalisation the act of description is itself diminished, reduced to a mechanical function of information pick-up. The second mode, on the other hand, refuses this reduction, recognising – as the first does not – that any act of description entails a movement of interpretation. What is 'given' to experience, in this mode, comprises not individual data but the world itself. It is a world that is not so much mapped out as taken in, from a particular vantage point, much as the painter takes in the landscape that surrounds him from the position at which he has planted his easel.

It follows that any endeavour of so-called descriptive integration, if it is to do justice to the implicate order of social *life*, can be neither descriptive nor theoretical in the specific senses constituted by their opposition. It must rather do away with the opposition itself. What then becomes of my initial distinction between ethnography and anthropology? Have I not argued myself out of the very position from which I began? I have certainly argued against the simple alignments of ethnography with data collection and of anthropology with comparative theory. If there is a distinction between ethnography and anthropology, then it must be drawn along different lines. Let me return for a moment to Radcliffe-Brown. In his 1951 lecture on 'The comparative method in social anthropology', he had a word or two to say about armchairs. It is told that long ago, in the days before fieldwork had become established practice in anthropological research, scholars sat in their libraries, ensconced in comfortable armchairs, as they carried out their comparative work. By the middle of the twentieth century, however, the 'armchair anthropologist' had become an object of derision, whose airy speculations were brushed aside by a new generation for whom fieldwork was paramount. For Radcliffe-Brown this was a matter of regret. A social anthropology that aspires to systematic comparison, and that is not content to rest on its ethnographic laurels, must, he thought, allow space for the armchair (Radcliffe-Brown 1951a: 15). Now whether our anthropological ancestors actually sat in armchairs as they worked, I do not know. But the reason why this particular piece of furniture has earned its central place in the disciplinary imagination is plain. For it seems to cocoon the scholar in a sedentary confinement that insulates him almost completely from any kind of sensory contact with his surroundings. Being-in-the-armchair, if you will, is the precise inverse of being-in-the-world.[5]

Here is where I differ from Radcliffe-Brown: I do not think we can do anthropology in armchairs. I can best explain why in terms of the difficulty that I, along with many colleagues (Sillitoe 2007: 150), routinely face in introducing what our subject is about, especially to novice students. Perhaps it is the study of human societies – not just of our own society, but of all societies, everywhere. But that only begs further questions. You can see and touch a fellow human being, but have you ever seen or touched a society? We may think we live in societies, but can anyone ever tell where their society ends and another begins? Granted that we are not sure what societies are, or even whether they exist at all, could we not simply say that anthropology is the study of *people*? There is much to be said for this, but it still does not help us to distinguish anthropology from all the other disciplines that claim to study people in one way or another, from history and psychology to the various branches of biology and biomedicine.

What truly distinguishes anthropology, echoing our conclusion from the last chapter, is that it is not a study *of* at all, but a study *with*. Anthropologists work and study *with* people. Immersed with them in an environment of joint activity, they learn to see things (or hear them, or touch them) in the ways their teachers and companions do. An education in anthropology, therefore, does more than furnish us with knowledge *about* the world – about people and their societies. It rather educates our *perception* of the world, and opens our eyes and minds to other possibilities of being. The questions we address are philosophical ones: of what it means to be a human being or a person, of moral conduct and the balance of freedom and constraint in people's relations with others, of trust and responsibility, of the exercise of power, of the connections between language and thought, between words and things, and between what people say and what they do, of perception and representation, of learning and memory, of life and death and the passage of time, and so on and so forth. Indeed the list is endless. But it is the fact that we address these questions in the world, and *not* from the armchair – that this world is not just what we think *about* but what we think *with*, and that in its thinking the mind wanders along pathways extending far beyond the envelope of the skin – that makes the enterprise anthropological and, by the same token, radically different from positivist science. We do our philosophy out of doors. And in this, the world and its inhabitants, human and non-human, are our teachers, mentors and interlocutors.

Anthropology as art and craft

In a recent, somewhat wistful essay, Maurice Bloch (2005) asks rhetorically, 'Where did anthropology go?' Echoing a complaint that has rumbled on ever since the collapse of the nineteenth-century certainties of evolutionary progress, he worries that in the absence of any 'generalizing theoretical framework', anthropology is left 'without the only centre it could have: the study of human beings' (ibid.: 2, 9). He suggests a return to functionalism, taken in a broad sense as an understanding grounded in the circumstances of real human beings, in specific places, and embedded in the wider ecology of life. I am sympathetic, having myself put forward something similar under the rubric of the 'dwelling perspective' (Ingold 2000a). As Bloch (2005: 16–17) says of his functionalism, this is not a theory so much as an attitude – let us say, a way of knowing rather than a framework for knowledge as such. Fundamentally, as a way of knowing it is also a way of being. The paradox of the armchair is that in order to *know* one can no longer *be* in the world of which one seeks knowledge. But anthropology's solution, to ground knowing in being, in the world rather than the armchair, means that any study *of* human beings must also be a study *with* them. Indeed, Bloch offers a fine example of how this might be done, recalling a discussion of a deeply philosophical nature with his hosts during fieldwork in a small Malagasy village. He describes the discussion as a seminar (ibid.: 4). I am sure we can all recall similar conversations. They shape the way we think.

A moment ago I referred to the work of Hallowell – a profound contribution to the philosophy of the self, consciousness and perception. As we know, however, this philosophy was shaped more than anything by endless conversations with his hosts, the Ojibwa people of north-central Canada. One thing he learned from them is particularly worthy of consideration here. It concerns dreaming. The world of one's dreams, Hallowell's mentors told him, is precisely the same as that of one's waking life. But in the dream you perceive it with different eyes or through different senses, while making different kinds of movements – perhaps those of another animal such as an eagle or a bear – and possibly even in a different medium such as in the air or the water rather than on land. When you wake, having experienced an alternative way of being in that same world in which you presently find yourself, you are wiser than you were before (Hallowell 1955: 178–181). To do anthropology, I venture, is to dream like an Ojibwa. As in a dream, it is continually to *open up* the world, rather than to seek closure. The endeavour is essentially comparative, but what it compares are not bounded objects or entities but ways of being. It is the constant awareness of alternative ways of being, and of the ever-present possibility of 'flipping' from one to another, that defines the anthropological attitude. It lies in what I would call the 'sideways glance'. Wherever we are, and whatever we may be doing, we are always aware that things might be done differently. It is as though there were a stranger at our heels, who turns out to be none other than ourselves. This sensibility to the strange in the close-at-hand is, I believe, one that anthropology shares with art. But by the same token, it is radically distinguished from that of normal science, which defamiliarises the real by removing it altogether from the domain of immediate human experience.

Turning from its underlying sensibilities to its working practices, anthropology is perhaps more akin to craft than art.[6] For it is characteristic of craft that both the practitioner's knowledge *of* things, and what he does *to* them, are grounded in intensive, respectful and intimate relations *with* the tools and materials of his trade. Indeed, anthropologists have long preferred to see themselves as craftsmen among social scientists, priding themselves on the quality of their handiwork by contrast to the mass-produced goods of industrial data processing turned out by sociologists and others. Rarely, however, have they sought to spell out exactly what craftsmanship entails. Rather ironically, introducing an edited volume entitled *The Craft of Social Anthropology* published in 1967, Max Gluckman explained that its purpose is to provide a guide to modern fieldwork methods. The contributing authors, who broadly represented the so-called 'Manchester School' of social anthropology, had all tried, wrote Gluckman, 'to set techniques in the framework of theoretical problems, so that those who use the book may remind themselves of what they are aiming at when they collect their material' (Gluckman 1967: xi). The irony is that the language of data collection, hypothesis testing and theory building used throughout the book could hardly be further removed from the practice of craft, and in fact the term, so prominently displayed in the book's title, is never mentioned again. That anthropology is a craft seems to have been something that its contributors simply took for granted. A decade previously, however, C. Wright Mills had concluded his book *The Sociological Imagination* (1959) with an appendix that tackles the issue head-on. Apart from its presumption that all social scientists are men, Mills's essay 'On intellectual craftsmanship' remains as relevant today as it was fifty years ago. Though addressed to social scientists in general rather than anthropologists in particular, it contains more words of wisdom than any number of theoretical treatises and methodological manuals.

This is how Mills begins:

> To the individual social scientist who feels himself a part of the classic tradition, social science is the practice of a craft. A man at work on problems of substance, he is among those who are quickly made impatient and weary by elaborate discussions of method-and-theory-in-general; so much of it interrupts his proper studies.
>
> (1959: 215)

Thus the first thing about intellectual craft, for Mills, is that there is no division between method and theory. Against the idea that you start by setting a theoretical agenda, and then test it empirically by means of data collected in accordance with standard protocols, Mills declares: 'Let every man be his own methodologist; let every man be his own theorist; let theory and method again become part of the practice of craft' (ibid.: 246). The second thing about intellectual craft, then, is that there is no division, in practice, between work and life. It is a practice that involves the whole person, continually drawing on past experience as it is projected into the future. The intellectual craftsman, as Mills puts it, 'forms his own self as he works towards the perfection of his craft' (ibid.: 216). What he fashions, through his work, is a way of being. And thirdly, to assist him in this project, he keeps a journal, which he periodically files, sorts and scrambles for new ideas. In it, he notes his experiences, his 'fringe-thoughts' that have come to him as by-products of everyday life, snatches of overheard conversations, and even dreams (ibid.: 216–217). It is from this heterogeneous reservoir of raw material that the intellectual craftsman shapes his work.

Mills's portrayal of craftsmanship certainly seems to fit, so far as anthropology is concerned. I am confident that most anthropologists would be happy to sign up to it, even if it goes against the grain of much of what has been published on the subject of theory and method. But what has become of ethnography? If theory and method are to come together again in craft, as Mills recommends, then should not every anthropologist be his or her own ethnographer, and vice versa? We can still recognise today the figure of the 'social theorist', sunk in his armchair or more likely peering from behind his computer screen, who presumes to be qualified, by virtue of his standing as an intellectual, to pronounce upon the ways of a world with which he involves himself as little as possible, preferring to interrogate the works of others of his kind. At the other extreme is the lowly 'ethnographic researcher', tasked with undertaking structured and semi-structured interviews with a selected sample of informants and analysing their contents with an appropriate software package, who is convinced that the data he collects are ethnographic simply because they are qualitative. These figures are the fossils of an outmoded distinction between empirical data collection and abstract theoretical speculation, and I hope we can all agree that there is no room for either in anthropology. But what of the detailed descriptions of other people's lives, informed by prolonged fieldwork, that are characteristic of ethnography at its best? Should we not leave some space for them? Indeed we should. But something happens when we turn from the being *with* of anthropology to the ethnographic description *of*. And to explain what this is I must return to the notion of description itself.

Writing and correspondence

Earlier I likened the anthropological mode of descriptive integration to the integration of a landscape painting as it takes shape upon the artist's canvas. In painting, as also in drawing, observation and description go hand in hand. This is because both painting and drawing entail a direct coupling between the movement of the artist's visual perception, as it follows the shapes and contours of the land, and the gestural movement of the hand that holds the brush or pencil, as it leaves a trace upon a surface. Through the coupling of perception and action, the artist is drawn *in* to the world, even as he or she draws it *out* in the gestures of description and the traces they yield.[7] As I have already mentioned, there is much in common between the practices of anthropology and art. Both are ways of knowing that proceed along the observational paths of being *with*, and both, in doing so, explore the unfamiliar in the close at hand. But by and large, ethnographers neither paint nor draw. As noted in the last chapter, the entire debate that has accompanied the so-called 'crisis of representation' has been founded on the premise that the graphic part of ethnography is not drawing but writing. Moreover it is writing understood not as a practice of inscription or line-making but as one of verbal composition, which could be done just as well on a keyboard as with a pencil or pen. It is for this reason that James Clifford, for example, can assert that description involves 'a turning *away* from dialogue and observation towards a separate place of writing, a place for reflection, analysis and interpretation' (Clifford 1990: 52).

There is nothing intrinsically wrong with this, but the separation deserves to be noted. Conventionally we associate ethnography with fieldwork and participant observation, and anthropology with the comparative analysis that follows after we have left the field behind. I want to suggest, to the contrary, that anthropology – as an inquisitive mode of inhabiting the world, of being *with*, characterised by the 'sideways glance' of the comparative attitude – is itself a practice of observation grounded in participatory dialogue. It could perhaps be characterised as a *correspondence*. In this sense, the anthropologist's observations answer to his experience of habitation. The correspondence may be mediated by such descriptive activities as painting and drawing, which can be coupled to observation. It can also, of course, be mediated by writing. But unlike painting and drawing, anthropological writing is *not* an art of description. We do not call it 'anthropography', and for good reason. The anthropologist writes – as indeed he thinks and speaks – *to* himself, to others and to the world. This verbal correspondence lies at the heart of the anthropological dialogue. It can be carried out anywhere, regardless of whether we might imagine ourselves to the 'in the field' or out of it. Anthropologists, as I have insisted, do their thinking, talking and writing in and with the world. To do anthropology, you do not have to imagine the world as a field. 'The field' is rather a term by which the ethnographer retrospectively imagines a world from which he has *turned away* in order, quite specifically, that he might *describe it in writing*. His literary practice is not so much one of *non-descriptive correspondence* as one of *non-correspondent description* – that is, a description which (unlike painting or drawing) has broken away from observation. Thus if anyone retreats to the armchair, it is not the anthropologist but the ethnographer. As he shifts from inquiry to description he has of necessity to reposition himself from the field of action to the sidelines.

It has long been customary to divide the process of anthropological research into three successive phases: of observation, description and comparison. In practice, as Philippe Descola has pointed out, this three-phase model offers 'a purified definition of operations that are most often intertwined' (Descola 2005: 72). One cannot say where one ends and the next begins. An overall movement is nevertheless assumed from ethnographic particulars to anthropological generalities. It might seem from the foregoing that I have reversed this order, placing anthropology before ethnography rather than after it. But that is not really my intention. I do not believe that anthropology is any more *prior* to ethnography than the other way round. They are just different. It may be hard to carry on both at once, because of the different positionalities they entail, but most of us probably swing back and forth between them, like a pendulum, in the course of our working lives. My real purpose in challenging the idea of a one-way progression from ethnography to anthropology has not been to belittle ethnography, or to treat it as an afterthought, but rather to liberate it, above all from the tyranny of method. Nothing has been more damaging to ethnography than its representation under the guise of the 'ethnographic method'. Of course, ethnography has its methods, but it *is not* a method. It is not, in other words, a set of formal procedural means designed to satisfy the ends of anthropological inquiry. It is a practice in its own right – a practice of verbal description. The accounts it yields, of other people's lives, are finished pieces of work, not raw materials for further anthropological analysis. But if ethnography is not a means to the end of anthropology, then neither is anthropology the servant of ethnography. To repeat, anthropology is an inquiry into the conditions and possibilities of human life in the world; it is not – as so many scholars in fields of literary criticism would have it – the study of how to write ethnography, or of the reflexive problematics of the shift from observation to description.

This is a message that has critical implications for the way anthropology is taught. Too often, it seems to me, we disappoint our students' expectations. Rather than awakening their curiosity towards social life, or kindling in them an inquisitive mode of being, we force them into an endless reflection on disciplinary texts that are studied not for the light they throw upon the world but for what they reveal about the practices of anthropologists themselves and the doubts and dilemmas that surround their work. Students soon discover that having doubled up on itself, through its conflation with ethnography, anthropology has become an interrogation of its own ways of working.[8] As educators based in university departments, most anthropologists devote much of their lives to working with students. They probably spend considerably more time in the classroom than anywhere they might call the field. Some enjoy this more than others, but they do not, by and large, regard time in the classroom as an integral part of their *anthropological* practice. Students are told that anthropology is what we do with our colleagues, and with other people in other places, but not with them. Locked out of the powerhouse of anthropological knowledge construction, all they can do is peer through the windows that our texts and teachings offer them. It took the best part of a century, of course, for the people once known as 'natives', and latterly as 'informants', to be admitted to the big anthropology house as master collaborators, that is as people we work *with*. It is now usual for their contributions to any anthropological study to be fulsomely acknowledged. Yet students remain excluded, and the inspiration and ideas that flow from our dialogue with them unrecognised. I believe this is a scandal, one of the malign consequences of the institutionalised division between research and teaching that has so blighted the practice of scholarship. For indeed, the epistemology that constructs the student as the mere recipient of anthropological knowledge produced elsewhere – rather than as a participant in its ongoing creative crafting – is the very same as that which constructs the native as an informant. And it is no more defensible.

Anthropology is *not* ethnography. Ethnographers describe, principally in writing, how the people of some place and time perceive the world and how they act in it. In our dreams we might once have supposed that by adding up, comparing and contrasting the ways that people of all places and times perceive and act, we might be able to extract some common denominators – possible candidates for human universals. Any such universals, however, are abstractions of our own, and as Whitehead was the first to point out, it is a fallacy to imagine that they are concretely instantiated in the world as a substrate for human variation.[9] With its dreams of generalisation shattered, where should anthropology go? Should it continue to accumulate disparate but thematically oriented ethnographic case studies between the covers of edited volumes, in the hope that some kinds of generalisation might still fall out? Should it abandon its project for the work of philosophers who have never mustered the energy or the conviction to leave their armchairs? Should it, on the other hand, join with the literary critics in their own arcane ruminations on the ethnographic project? Anthropology has tried all these things. Yet every direction leads off at a tangent from the world we inhabit. It is no wonder, then, that anthropologists are left feeling isolated and marginalized, and that they are routinely passed by in public discussions of the great questions of social life. I have argued for a discipline that would return to these questions, not in the armchair but in the world. We can be our own philosophers, but we can do it better thanks to its embedding in our observational engagements with the world and in our collaborations and correspondences with its inhabitants. What, then, should we call this lively philosophy of ours? Why, *anthropology*, of course!

NOTES

1 Anthropology comes to life

1 Here, as elsewhere in this volume, I employ the third-person singular pronoun in its masculine form. This has no significance for my argument, and readers are welcome to substitute the feminine form if they wish.

2 This was the 1982 Malinowski Lecture, delivered at the London School of Economics.

3 I recall a seminar at the University of Manchester, sometime in the early 1980s, on the ecology of perception. The participants were mainly philosophers and psychologists; I was the only anthropologist present. I was brimming with my newly kindled enthusiasm for Bergson. The philosophers, however, blanched at the mention of his name. It was all very well for me as an anthropologist, they said, but they had their careers to think about.

2 Materials against materiality

1 I hasten to add that, of course, the greater part of archaeology is dedicated precisely to the study of materials and the ways they have been used in processes of production. Even in anthropology, there is some ethnographic work on the subject. My point is simply that this work does not seem to impinge significantly on the literature on materiality and material culture. For scholars who have devoted much of their energies to the study of materials, this literature reads more like an escape route into theory – one which, I confess, I have previously used myself. Thus, my argument is directed as much at myself as at anyone else, and is part of an attempt to overcome the division between theoretical and practical work.

2 The proceedings of the conference were subsequently published as DeMarrais et al. (2004).

3 I address many of these questions concerning landscape, sky and weather in Chapters 9 and 10.

4 This phrase was coined by Karl Marx, in the *Communist Manifesto* of 1848. He was referring metaphorically to the evaporation, in bourgeois society, of the 'fixed, fast-frozen relations' of pre-capitalist modes of production, and not to any process of nature (Marx and Engels 1978: 476).

5 I do not pretend to offer a comprehensive critique of Hetherington's argument, which is mainly focused elsewhere. In any case I concur with much of it. I cite it here simply as an exemplary instance of the role that the concept of materiality plays in arguments of this kind.

6 The fact that materials outlast the objects made from them establishes, in turn, the possibility of recycling. This possibility arises at the moment when our focus shifts from finished objects to the stuff of which they are made, seeing in it the potential for further transformation. In this sense, as Bunn remarks, recycled materials 'are a "grey area", on the edge of material and object' (Bunn 1999: 21).

7 In the words of philosopher Gilbert Simondon, 'Living matter is far from being pure indetermination or pure passivity. Neither is it a blind tendency; it is, rather, the vehicle of informed energy' (Simondon 1980: 66).

8 I return to the critique of the concept of agency in Chapter 17 (pp. 213–14).

9 I have found Gibson's tripartite scheme a useful starting point for thinking about the inhabited environment. But it is by no means without its problems, which I explore in later chapters (see especially Chapters 9 and 10).

10 I return to the distinction between existence and occurrence in Part IV of this volume.

11 Philosopher Arnold Berleant draws precisely the same distinction. 'Stone has two sides', he writes. There is the 'hard side': this is the stone, for example, of the geologist, armed with hammer and chisel. But stone also has a 'soft side', consisting in 'the range of meanings that stone holds for us, the values we find in it, the metaphors by which stone figures in our understanding, its influence on our imagination, and the powers we attribute to it'. Berleant makes the distinction, however, only to dissolve it by folding the hard side of stone into the soft. Because the world we inhabit is necessarily a *human* world, he argues, everything about stone that we intuitively take to be hard is in fact already screened through the social and cultural layers that enfold us. Thus, Berleant concludes, 'stone has only one side, a soft side' (2010: 110–111). For reasons that will become clear below, I reject this argument, which merely displaces the problem of the 'two sides' from the constitution of stone to the constitution of humanity.

3 Culture on the ground

1 Balzac's 'Theory of walking' (*Théorie de la demarche*) was originally published in 1833. The translation of this passage is mine.

2 Many more examples could have been adduced. Devine (1985) has drawn attention to the frequency with which early travel accounts, missionaries' reports and ethnographic literature allude to the dexterity of the toes and the prehensile powers of the feet among 'primitive' people accustomed to going barefoot.

3 The pliancy of the soles was achieved through the use of caoutchouc, later known as India rubber (Dowie 1839: 407–408). In the United States, a way of attaching India rubber soles to boots and shoes had been patented in 1832. But the natural rubber did not wear well in the cold winters and warm summers of North America. It became hard and brittle in freezing weather, and soft and sticky in heat. Only after Charles Goodyear's invention of a method of treating the rubber so that it became serviceable at all temperatures did the rubber-soled shoe industry really take off (Tenner 2003: 83).

4 These connotations probably have their source in the division of military rank between pedestrian foot soldiers and the equestrian cavalry.

5 There is some evidence to suggest that baby walkers actually delay the onset of upright posture, as they restrict infants' freedom to explore and interact with their environment (Tenner 2003: 9–10).

6 The goose step has its origins in marching styles developed by the Prussian army in the early eighteenth century, and survived for almost three centuries until it was abolished by the East German Ministry of Defence in 1990 (Bremmer 1992: 15; Flesher 1997).

7 Writing in 1791 and citing Rousseau in his support, Adam Walker opined that 'there is but one way of Travelling more pleasant than riding on horseback, and that is on foot; for then I can turn to the right or the left' (cited in Jarvis 1997: 9, 29).

8 While walking side by side, pedestrians can remain aware of and coordinate each other's gait and pace through peripheral vision, which is especially sensitive to movement, even though they may not 'see' one another directly (on the role of peripheral vision in the detection of movement, see Downey 2007). In a recent study of pedestrian behaviour on the streets of the city of Aberdeen, in north-east Scotland, Lee and Ingold (2006) found that side-by-side walking was generally experienced as a particularly companionable form of activity. Even while conversing, as they often did, companions would rarely make direct eye contact, at most inclining their heads only slightly towards one another. Direct face-to-face interaction, by contrast, was considered far less sociable. Crucially, in walking together, companions share virtually the same visual field, whereas in face-to-face interaction each can see what is behind the other's back, opening up the possibility for deceit and subterfuge. When they sit and face one another, rather than moving

along together, conversers appear to be engaged in a contest in which views are batted back and forth rather than shared.

9   From *When We Were Very Young*, by A.A. Milne (1936: 12–13). The drawing by Ernest H. Shepard that accompanies this rhyme shows Christopher Robin wearing knee-length lace-up boots and striding like a true soldier!

10 For an example from the hyper-modern city of Brasilia, see Ribeiro (1996: 149).

11 The foot is a very sensitive organ. For every square inch of sole, there are no fewer than 1,300 nerve endings (Tenner 2003:52).

12 In the simple act of walking along the street to the bus stop, as Erin Manning suggests, the 'backgrounded ground … appears only insofar as it is expressed as something else (steadiness of movement, for instance)'. Should you happen to lose your footing and trip, however, the ground suddenly rears up in the foreground, whilst you are 'horizontalized'! 'Facedown: the bus stop is momentarily backgrounded' (Manning 2009: 76).

13 The difference between these modes of knowledge integration, respectively 'along' and 'up', is further explored in Chapter 13.

14 The hard, rigid boots employed in sports such as skating, skiing and football present a particular puzzle. For far from reducing the foot to a stepping or pedalling machine, these boots enable the wearer to perform movements of great skill and dexterity. These movements, however, are not prehensile, and do not involve curling the toes. Rather, the boot appears to convert the foot into a rigid extension of the ankle. The victory of Hungary over England at Wembley stadium in 1953, in what is often taken to be the match that invented modern football, has been attributed, among other things, to the fact that the Hungarian players – to the utter astonishment of their English counterparts – wore boots that were cut away below the ankles.

15 From *The Memoirs of Sherlock Holmes* by Sir Arthur Conan Doyle (Doyle 1950: 146). One wonders what Holmes would have made of the bipedal footprints left in volcanic ash from 3.5 million years ago at the East African site of Laetoli (see Tuttle et al. 1992).

16 See, for example, the series of photographs from the Muybridge collection reproduced in Napier (1967).

4 Walking the plank

1   Pye's distinction between the workmanships of certainty and of risk thus precisely parallels my own between transport and wayfaring, which I explore further in Chapter 12.

2   Drawing his examples from silversmithing and weaving, Keller has argued in terms ostensibly similar to mine. What might appear to the observer as a 'linear series of steps' is, for the artisan, a 'complex reciprocal process' (Keller 2001: 37). But behind the similarity lies a fundamental difference of approach. For Keller remains wedded to a mentalist view of action according to which for every movement there is a corresponding 'kinaesthetic image'. The challenge for the practitioner, then, is to coordinate the images rather than harmonise the movements themselves. I return to this theme in Chapter 17 (pp. 216-17).

5 Rethinking the animate, reanimating thought

1   Here, I am using the word 'thing' in the Kantian rather than the Heideggerian sense, that is, as a completed object rather than a gathering of the threads of life (on this distinction, see Chapter 17, pp. 214–15). Only in this sense can things be understood as belonging to a priori categories.

2   Erin Manning writes, in similar vein, that 'to experience is always to exist on the cusp of appearance and reality: it is to co-live the present as a pastness of emergence that will only be known in its future-pastness-becoming-present' (Manning 2009: 69).

3   I have excluded so-called actor-network theory from this list, as I deal with it in the following two chapters (6 and 7).

4   It will also do for places, as we shall see in Chapter 12 (p. 148).

5   This theme is explored at greater length in Chapter 14.

6   I return to this theme in Chapter 10, p. 128.

6 Point, line, counterpoint

1 Gibson's reasoning on this point is spelled out in greater detail in Chapter 9 (p. 116).
2 I return to this passage, and to Deleuze's view of improvisation, in Chapter 17 (p. 216).
3 I use the notion of 'fluid space', here, in deference to its originators. However, for reasons set out in Chapter 12, I do not like the term 'space', and wish that Mol and Law could have used some other word to get their idea across. 'Space', for me, signifies absence rather than co-presence. The volume to which Mol and Law refer, however, is not a vacuum but a plenum. It is not really space, but an environment or a world (see Ingold 2006).

7 When *ANT* meets *SPIDER*

1 The notion of 'wideware' is taken from Andy Clark. 'The relation between the biological organism and the wideware', writes Clark, 'is as important and intimate as that of the spider and the web' (1998: 274). Elsewhere, art historian James Elkins draws on the metaphor of the web to describe the 'skein of vision' within which every human being catches the objects of his or her attention (or is alternatively caught). 'I am not the spider who weaves the web, and I am not even the fly caught in the web: I am the web itself, streaming off in all directions with no center and no self that I can call my own' (Elkins 1996: 75).
2 Sarah Whatmore, for example, calls for 'hybrid geographies' that would study 'the *living* … spaces of social life, configured by numerous, interconnected agents' (2007: 339, original emphasis). Such geographies would be characterised, she writes, by 'a shift in analytical emphasis from reiterating fixed surfaces to tracing points of connection and lines of flow' (ibid.: 343). Lines that connect points are one thing, however; lines of flow are quite another. As Pearson points out (after Deleuze and Guattari), 'hybrids simply require a connection of points and do not facilitate a passing between them' (Pearson 1999: 197). Studying the living, fluid spaces comprised by lines – such as those of the spider's web – that pass between, rather than from point to point, calls for geographies not of hybridity but of *mixture* (Mol and Law 1994: 660). Far from tracing the connections that link heterogeneous but nevertheless discrete material elements into networked assemblages, geographies of mixture would aim to *follow the materials* through those processes of amalgamation, distillation, coagulation and dispersal that both give rise to things and portend their dissolution (see Chapter 17, p. 213).
3 The notion of the 'dance of agency' is taken from the work of the sociologist of science, Andrew Pickering (1995: 21–22).
4 Andy Clark (1998: 272) illustrates this point with the example of the tuna fish. 'The real swimming machine', he suggests, 'is thus the fish *in its proper context*: the fish plus the surrounding structures and vortices that it actively creates and then maximally exploits.' The 'proper context', in this case, is a fluid material medium with its pressure gradients and lines of force. It is not an assemblage of discrete material objects.
5 On the mind-dust of 'agency', see Chapter 2, p. 28.
6 From the literature, one can infer that the philosopher on whose lecture SPIDER eavesdropped was Steven Collins (1985).
7 This crude pun identifies SPIDER's interlocutor as a double of Bruno Latour, one of the principal architects of actor-network theory (e.g., Latour 1993, 2005). I admit that the double is something of a caricature, for the real Latour has been an inconsistent critic of much that has been passed off as applications of ANT, to the extent of denying that it is a theory at all, and that it actually deals with networks (Latour 1999). SPIDER's views, naturally, bear an uncanny resemblance to my own.

8 The shape of the earth

1 It is worth bearing in mind that the Illinois countryside, to which the children were accustomed, is for the most part monotonously flat.
2 It is important not to confuse the scientific concept of atmosphere with its phenomenological meaning as a field of sentience akin to an aura, as when we speak of the 'atmosphere' evoked by a gathering or by a performance of music. I elaborate on the concept in this latter sense in Chapter 10 (p. 134). See also Böhme (1993).

3 The words quoted here, along with all subsequent quotations from Saint Augustine, are drawn directly from the 1943 translation of his *Confessions* by F. J. Sheed (Augustine 1943). For the sake of presentation, however, I have excluded ellipses where words have been omitted without altering the sense. For ease of comparison with other editions, I have included in the text references both the pagination from the Sheed edition and the original book and chapter numbers, indicated respectively with upper and lower case Roman numerals.
4 The first version of this essay was delivered as a lecture at Freiburg in 1935.

9 Earth, sky, wind and weather

1 On the distinction between the material world and the world of materials, and for a fuller account of Gibson's tripartite division of the inhabited environment into substances, medium and surfaces, see Chapter 2.
2 Gibson's conclusion bears comparison with that of Gilles Deleuze, who asks us to imagine a world without others. In such a world, epitomised by Robinson Crusoe's island, 'only the brutal opposition of sky and earth reigns with an unsupportable light and an obscure abyss' (Deleuze 1984: 56). However, for Deleuze this brutality, or desolation, is not assuaged merely by the presence of furniture. In a world that is furnished, yet devoid of others, objects rise up menacingly ahead or strike from behind. One experiences this as the force and pain of collision – of constantly bumping into things along their hard edges. When others are present, by contrast, there can be a sharing of viewpoints – a convergence of visual attention from multiple positions – that enables one to see around things, softening their outlines and allowing them 'to incline towards each other' (loc. cit). For Gibson, however, the presence of others makes no difference: 'the environment surrounds all observers in the same way that it surrounds the single observer' (1979: 43). This is because observations are taken not from points at all, but along paths of movement. Over time one can be in all places, just as all others can be in the place where one is now. It is the movement around, according to Gibson, and not the pooling of observations from multiple fixed points, that softens the edges of things, making possible what Deleuze (1984: 56) calls 'the margins and transitions in the world', regulating 'variations of depth' and preventing 'assaults from behind'.
3 On the concept of inversion, see Chapter 5, p. 68.
4 For a vivid account of what it feels like to climb a hill, see Wylie (2002).
5 Hayden Lorimer (2006) offers a fine account of the conjoint reading of country by reindeer and herdsmen in Scotland's Cairngorm Mountains, distinguished by its attention to meteorological phenomena, and especially to the ways gusts of wind – to which the animals are supremely sensitive – are funnelled by the clefts and gullies of the landscape. 'What wells up', Lorimer writes, 'is a biotic account of the herd enrolling winds, stones, tors, trees and mosses into a territory of patterned ground' (ibid.: 516–517). The importance of wind and weather, and of the ability of both people and animals to read it, receives similar emphasis in Anna Järpe's (2007) recent study of Sámi reindeer herding in Swedish Lapland.
6 This particular riddle is also mentioned by Nelson in his ethnography of the Koyukon, but is given a rather free translation:

> *Wait, I see something: My end sweeps this way and that way and this way around me.*
> *Answer: Grass tassles moving back and forth in the wind, making little curved trails in the snow.*
> (Nelson 1983: 44)

10 Landscape or weather-world?

1 Geographer and climatologist John Thornes notes that while the sky takes up 40 per cent of Constable's celebrated painting *The Haywain* (1821), 'it is hardly ever mentioned and is taken for granted by most art historians and cultural geographers in discussing the picture' (Thornes 2008: 573).
2 On the difference between Gothic masonry and post-Renaissance architecture, see Chapter 17, p. 211.
3 This is taken to its extreme in a recent book by Erin Manning (2009). An evangelically Deleuzoguattarian meditation on the philosophy of art and movement, the book bears the

unfortunate title *Relationscapes*. I admit, however, that my own concept of 'taskscape' (Ingold 2000a: 195) is just as awkward.

4 The implication of the concept of embodiment, writes dance philosopher Maxine Sheets-Johnstone, is that 'we perceive others and experience ourselves precisely as *packaged*'. In having recourse to the concept, she complains, 'we avoid coming to terms with … what is actually there, sensuously present in our experience' (Sheets-Johnstone 1998: 359, 360–361).

11 Four objections to the concept of soundscape

1 The concept of soundscape was introduced by the Canadian composer R. Murray Schafer (1994), and has since been widely adopted.

2 One of the main ways in which a landscape is audible is in running water. 'Streams and rivers', as Gaston Bachelard has pointed out, 'provide the sound for mute country landscapes, and do it with a strange fidelity' (Bachelard 1983: 15).

3 Mikkel Bille and Tim Flohr Sørensen (2007) have recently proposed an argument in support of the concept of lightscape. It is an argument, however, that proceeds by treating light not as a phenomenon of lived experience but as an object endowed with agency.

12 Against space

1 As Paul Harrison notes, the 'taking place' of dwelling, in Heidegger's thought, presupposes that a being is already *in* place, '*such that the event of taking-place is itself reined in and contained*' (Harrison 2007: 634, original emphases). What then, Harrison asks rhetorically, 'of the world and of Heidegger's words on openness' (ibid.)?

2 This section presents, in summary form, an argument that I have developed at greater length in *Lines* (Ingold 2007a: 72–84).

3 Based on fieldwork among the Inuit of Igloolik, Claudio Aporta writes that travelling 'was not a transitional activity between one place and another, but a way of being … Other travellers are met, children are born, and hunting, fishing and other subsistence activities are performed' (Aporta 2004: 13).

4 This is not to deny that people may also travel by sea. But marine travel raises special issues in part because of the way the liquid medium erases all trace of the activities that have taken place there. The wake of a small, non-motorised boat fades rapidly, as does the sound of the spoken word. Thus land is to sea travel rather as writing is to speech.

5 To me, as a relatively inexperienced user, navigating the internet is a matter of activating a sequence of links that take me, almost instantaneously, from site to site. Each link is a connector, and the web itself is a network of interconnected sites. Travel through cyberspace thus resembles transport. Experienced users, however, tell me that as they 'surf' the net, they follow trails like wayfarers, with no particular destination in mind. For them, the web may seem more like a mesh than a net. How, precisely, we should understand 'movement' through the internet is an interesting question, but it is beyond the scope of this chapter, and most certainly beyond my own competence, to address it further here.

6 The same advice was given by Samuel Johnson to readers of his tour of the Western Isles of Scotland. See Chapter 3 (p. 38).

7 From *We're Going on a Bear Hunt*, retold by Michael Rosen, illustrated by Helen Oxenbury (Rosen 1989).

8 The example that follows is loosely based on a project in which I was marginally involved. This was the EU-funded TUNDRA project (Tundra Degradation in the Russian Arctic), which ran for three years from 1998 to 2000, coordinated by the University of Lapland's Arctic Centre. The project set out to assess feedbacks from the Russian Arctic to the global climate system through changes in greenhouse gas emissions and in freshwater run-off, and to understand the relations between climate change, carbon and hydrological cycles, industrial pollution and social awareness. The study was carried out in the Usa river basin, in the north-eastern part of the territory of the Komi Republic, just to the west of the Ural Mountains.

9 James Fox, in reference to Austronesian ethnography, has introduced the term *topogeny* to refer to a story that goes along from place to place, and that is recited as an ordered succession of place names. Thus the kinds of stories I refer to here could be called topogenic (Fox 1997).

10 I return to this conclusion in Chapter 13, p. 163.

13 Stories against classification

1 There seems, at first glance, to be a contradiction between the assertions: on the one hand, that culture is acquired in the lifetime of individuals, and on the other, that the acquisition of culture precedes their life in the world. Orthodox culture theory resolves the contradiction by supposing that enculturation takes place in sequestered spaces of observation that present a simulacrum of the world rather than exposing novices to its actuality. Every novice, it is supposed, must spend time in these nurseries of cultural acquisition before being let loose to apply what they have learned in the 'real world'.

2 On this distinction, see Jablonka (2000: 39) and Ingold (2002: 60–62).

3 Initially I had followed Edward Casey (1996: 30) in contrasting *vertical* and *lateral* modes of integration. 'Lateral', however, suggests sideways displacement *across* a surface. Here, however, I mean the tracing of a path *through* the world. For reasons that will become clear later on, it is important that these should not be confused.

4 Here, and in the remainder of this paragraph, I recapitulate an argument that I have spelled out at greater length elsewhere (Ingold 2007a: 90).

5 The same is true of the meanings of words, which are, in effect, highly compressed and abridged, miniature stories. As Jean Briggs has shown, in her study of word meanings in the Inupiaq language, 'knowledge is personal and experiential, and can best be communicated by sharing one's own experiences and allowing learners to participate in constructing meanings in whatever ways they are capable of' (Briggs 2002: 80).

6 The text was based on lectures that Kant originally presented in Königsberg in 1775. See Richards (1974).

14 Naming as storytelling

1 Semiotician Thomas Sebeok has raised the intriguing possibility that in playful behaviour, even non-human animals may recognise and address one another by the non-verbal equivalents of singular proper names (Sebeok 1986: 82–96).

2 This immediately invalidates Scott Atran's claim (1990: 47) 'that living kinds are everywhere ranked into transitively structured taxonomies'. The claim is founded on a circularity, since it is couched in terms of a categorical opposition between cognitive universals and cultural particulars which – as we have seen in Chapter 13 (p. 158) – already presupposes that knowledge takes the form of a classification.

3 For another example, see Chapter 9, p. 121.

4 I have already introduced and discussed this distinction in Chapters 12 (p. 154) and 13 (p. 160). I take the notion of 'languaging' from Alison Phipps (2007: 12).

15 Seven variations on the letter A

1 Curated by Wendy Gunn, the exhibition was held at Aberdeen Art Gallery from 6 April to 4 June 2005, and its opening was timed to coincide with that year's conference of the Association of Social Anthropologists, hosted by the University of Aberdeen, on *Creativity and Cultural Improvisation* (see Hallam and Ingold 2007; Gunn 2009).

2 I have excluded discussion of the remaining five panels, since I have already considered the issues they raise elsewhere (Ingold 2007a), and have nothing further to add. The excluded panels are: an **A** formed from the edges of overlapping sheets of decorated wallpaper; an **A** made of sticks – following the example of Eeyore in *The House at Pooh Corner*; an **A** made of spliced three-ply rope; three **A**s on a slate – one added with chalk, the other two scratched at knife-point; and a hand-carved letter **A** from a set of wooden blocks for printing.

3 I would draw a parallel here, from a much earlier period, with the 90 degree rotation of the originally pictographic signs of the Sumerian cuneiform script. This was almost certainly due to the change from writing on small square clay tablets to large rectangular ones (Powell 1981).
4 On the hand as a compendium of gestures, see Chapter 4 p. 58.
5 I return to this severance in Chapter 18, p. 225.
6 On this kind of line, and its connection with wayfaring, see Chapter 12, p. 150.

16 Ways of mind-walking

1 I return to this puzzle in Chapter 18 (pp. 224–5).
2 I am the first to admit that my choice of these sources is an accident of circumstances wholly unconnected with the writing of this chapter. But more often than not, the serendipitous juxtapositions thrown up by such accidents, rather than examples carefully selected to prove a point, turn out to be most productive of unexpected insights.
3 In Chapter 14 we reached a very similar conclusion regarding the perception of animals among Koyukon people in Alaska. For them, too, animals are compendia of stories told, names uttered, and actual sightings of creatures engaged in their characteristic life activities.
4 The line reproduced here is taken from the Appendix to Kandinsky's essay, *Point and Line to Plane*, Diagram 16.

17 The textility of making

1 In his essay *On the Mode of Existence of Technical Objects*, the philosopher Gilbert Simondon advanced much the same argument with the example of another woodworking tool, the adze. 'This tool', he writes, 'is not merely a block of homogeneous metal shaped to a particular form. It has been forged, which means that the molecular chains in the metal have a certain orientation that varies in different places, like a wood with fibres so disposed as to give the greatest solidarity and the greatest elasticity' (Simondon 1980: 83–84).
2 John Protevi (2001: 169) comments likewise on how the 'tenaciously deep-rooted' philosophical prejudices of hylomorphism have led to 'the privilege of the architect's vision and the invisibility or denigration of artisanal sensitivity'.
3 Precisely because 'technology' *is* an ontological claim, it makes no sense to treat technology as a subject *about* which ontological claims can be made. If the claim embodied in the concept is without foundation, then so is the concept itself.
4 I mean following to be understood here in an active rather than passive sense. It is not blind. The hunter following a trail must remain ever alert to visual and other sensory cues in an ever-changing environment and must adjust his course accordingly. In following materials the practitioner does the same. The consequence of failure would be that the work goes off track and cannot be carried on.
5 Further reflection led us to conclude that the kite had never been an object in the first place, although it had seemed like one. Instead, we came to think differently about our process of making. We saw it less as an assembly of elementary components into a final composite, and more as a binding of materials each of which had particular dynamic properties – of runniness, stickiness, rigidity, flexibility and so on – calling in our work for specific bodily postures, gestures and manoeuvres.
6 In this sense, of course, there is no opposition between persons and things. Rather, persons are things too, or as Timothy Webmoor and Christopher Whitmore put it, 'Things are us!' (Webmoor and Whitmore 2008).
7 In practice, then, planned action and itineration are not alternative procedures. The practitioner does not have to choose between one and the other, or to find some way to combine them. This is because directions do not, in themselves, tell practitioners what to do. A signpost means nothing until it is placed somewhere in the terrain. Likewise, every direction draws its meaning from its placement in a taskscape that is already familiar thanks to previous experience. Only when so placed does it indicate a trail that can practicably be followed. And to proceed from one direction marker to the next, practitioners have to find their way, attentively and responsively, but without further recourse to explicit instruction (Ingold 2001a: 137–138).

7   I return in the next chapter (pp. 200–1) to Bryson's elucidation of the differences between drawing and painting.

18   Drawing together

1   Whether Bryson's comparison is strictly accurate in art historical terms is not my concern here. No doubt there have been draughtsmen who have 'painted' with their pencils, and painters who have 'drawn' with the brush. For the purposes of my argument, the key to the comparison lies in the relation between mark and surface rather than in the technicalities of the instruments used. 'Brush' and 'pencil' thus stand for different forms of this relation.
2   For the time being, I shall defer the question of the difference between ethnography and anthropology, which I consider in depth in Chapter 19. In brief, I shall show that graphic anthropology is really a kind of 'anthropography', which differs from ethnography in so far as it is founded in a relation of correspondence. Drawing makes possible a *descriptive correspondence*, as distinct from the *non-descriptive correspondence* of written anthropology, and the *non-correspondent description* of written ethnography.
3   It is true that lines drawn with a pencil can be rubbed out. But as an action, this has a quite different quality from drawing. The movement entailed is one of scrubbing rather than tracing, and is oriented to surface rather than line. It is in this sense akin to painting over. Complete erasure, however, is almost impossible, since the pencil leaves its mark as a groove in the paper.
4   On the idea of playback in the apprehension of visual images and aural recordings, and its relation to notions of landscape and soundscape, see Chapter 11 (pp. 136–7).
5   On the derivation of photography from the Dutch art of describing, see Jay (1988: 15).
6   This is not to deny that in skilled hands, a camera can be used like a pencil, to conduct an engagement with what is going on that is at once observational and generative. Indeed, many visual anthropologists would describe their practice in precisely these terms (Pink 2007; Grimshaw and Ravetz 2009). But in that case, the camera should be regarded as an instrument of drawing and not as an image-based technology.
7   In an interview, dating from 1971, the poet Pablo Neruda tells of how a broken finger compelled him to revert to handwriting. He found that poetry written by hand was more sensitive. 'The typewriter separated me from a deeper intimacy with poetry, and my hand brought me closer to that intimacy again' (Neruda 1971: 59).
8   I return to the contrast between the alternative holisms of structure and process in Chapter 19 (p. 237).

19   Anthropology is *not* ethnography

1   Contemporary readers will immediately recognise in this a forerunner of the so-called etic/emic distinction.
2   Starting from the premises (a) that every society is a structured combination of parts, and (b) that these parts can combine in only a limited number of possible ways, Durkheim thought that it should be possible in theory to construct a table of essential social types prior to seeking out their empirical manifestations in the form of particular societies. 'Thus', Durkheim concluded, 'there are social species for the same reason as there are biological ones. The latter are due to the fact that organisms are only varied combinations of the same anatomical unity' (Durkheim 1982 [1895]: 116). Durkheim was alluding here to the biology of Georges Cuvier. A firm believer in the fixity of species, Cuvier had proposed – under his principle of the 'correlation of parts' – that each and every naturally existing organism manifests one of the total set of logically possible working combinations of basic organs.
3   As we saw in Chapter 13, this contrast between explicate and implicate orders also distinguishes the world according to classification from the storied world, and their modes of integration – respectively vertical and 'alongly'.
4   The converse of this, as we saw in Chapter 18 (p. 221), is that there is no life that is *not* social.
5   On the history of the chair, and its contribution to the imagined insulation of intellectual work from activity on the ground, see Chapter 3 (p. 39).

6 This is not the place for a discussion of the differentiation of art and craft, and I attach no particular significance to it here.

7 On the potential of drawing to couple observation and description, see Chapter 18, p. 224.

8 The same doubling up is all too apparent, as well, in many fields of art, and the consequences of this involution are as damaging for art as they are for anthropology. An art that addresses nothing but its own practice will contribute little to human understanding. If the scope of collaboration between art and anthropology is marked out in terms of their mutual self-interrogation, then both will sink together. Much of the inherent potential of this collaboration is, I believe, being squandered on account of the confusion between anthropology and ethnography. Art and ethnography do not combine well. The former compromises ethnography's commitment to descriptive accuracy; the latter shies away from the immediacy of art's observational engagement. Mixing art and ethnography is probably a recipe for bad art, and for bad ethnography. Combining art and anthropology, by contrast, could greatly enhance the power of both.

9 This is the 'fallacy of misplaced concreteness', by which one comes 'to mistake a conceptual abstraction for an actual vital agent' (Whitehead 1938: 66).

REFERENCES

Afonso, A. I. and J. Ramos 2004. New graphics for old stories: representations of local memories through drawings. In *Working Images: Visual Research and Representation in Anthropology*, eds S. Pink, L. Kurti and A. I. Afonso. London: Routledge, pp. 72–89.

Agamben, G. 2004. *The Open: Man and Animal*, trans. K. Attell. Stanford, CA: Stanford University Press.

Alberti, L. B. 1972. *On Painting*, trans. C. Grayson, ed. M. Kemp. Harmondsworth: Penguin.

Alberti, L. B. 1988. *On the Art of Building in Ten Books*, trans. J. Rykwert, N. Leach and R. Tavernor. Cambridge, MA: MIT Press.

Allen, N. J. 1998. The category of substance: a Maussian theme revisited. In *Marcel Mauss: A Centenary Tribute*, eds W. James and N. J. Allen. New York: Berghahn, pp. 175–191.

Alpers, S. 1983. *The Art of Describing: Dutch Art in the Seventeenth Century*. London: Penguin.

Anderson, D. 2000. *Identity and Ecology in Arctic Siberia*. Oxford: Oxford University Press.

Aporta, C. 2004. Routes, trails and tracks: trail breaking among the Inuit of Igloolik. *Études/Inuit/Studies* 28(2): 9–38.

Ashizawa, K., C. Kumakura, A. Kusumoto and S. Narasaki 1997. Relative foot size and shape to general body size in Javanese, Filipinas and Japanese with special reference to habitual footwear types. *Annals of Human Biology* 24: 117–129.

Atran, S. 1990. *Cognitive Foundations of Natural History: Towards an Anthropology of Science*. Cambridge: Cambridge University Press.

Augustine, Saint 1943. *The Confessions of Saint Augustine*, trans. F. J. Sheed. New York: Sheed and Ward.

Bachelard, G. 1964. *The Poetics of Space*. Boston, MA: Beacon Press.

Bachelard, G. 1983. *Water and Dreams: An Essay on the Imagination of Matter*, trans. E. R. Farrell. Dallas, TX: Pegasus Foundation.

Balzac, H. de 1938. *Oeuvres Diverses de Honoré de Balzac*, Vol. 2 (1830–1835). Paris: Louis Canard.

Banks, M. 2001. *Visual Methods in Social Research*. London: SAGE.

Barber, K. 2007. Improvisation and the art of making things stick. In *Creativity and Cultural Improvisation*, eds E. Hallam and T. Ingold. Oxford: Berg, pp. 25–41.

Bateson, G. 1973. *Steps to an Ecology of Mind*. London: Granada.

Berger, J. 2005. *Berger on Drawing*, ed. J. Savage. Cork: Occasional Press.

Bergson, H. 1911. *Creative Evolution*, trans. A. Mitchell. London: Macmillan.

Bergson, H. 1991. *Matter and Memory*, trans. N. M. Paul and W. S. Palmer. New York: Zone Books.

Berleant, A. 2010. *Sensibility and Sense: The Aesthetic Transformation of the Human World*. Exeter: Imprint Academic.

Bernstein, N. A. 1996. On dexterity and its development. In *Dexterity and its Development*, eds M. Latash and M. T. Turvey. Mahwah, NJ: Lawrence Erlbaum Associates, pp. 3–244.

Bidney, D. 1953. *Theoretical Anthropology*. New York: Columbia University Press.

Bille, M. and T. F. Sørensen 2007. An anthropology of luminosity: the agency of light. *Journal of Material Culture* 12(3): 263–284.

Billeter, J. F. 1990. *The Chinese Art of Writing*, trans. J.-M. Clarke and M. Taylor. New York: Rizzoli International.

Bloch, M. 2005. *Essays on Cultural Transmission*. Oxford: Berg.

Boas, F. 1936. History and science in anthropology: a reply. *American Anthropologist* 38: 137–141.

Bohm, D. 1980. *Wholeness and the Implicate Order*. London: Routledge and Kegan Paul.

Böhme, G. 1993. Atmosphere as the fundamental concept of a new aesthetics. *Thesis Eleven* 36: 113–126.

Boivin, N. 2008. *Material Cultures, Material Minds*. Cambridge: Cambridge University Press.

Bradley, C. 2002. Travelling with Fred George: the changing ways of Yup'ik star navigation in Akiachak, Western Alaska. In *The Earth is Faster Now: Indigenous Observations of Arctic Environmental Change*, eds I. Krupnik and D. Jolly. Fairbanks, AK: Arctic Research Consortium of the United States, pp. 240–265.

Brand, S. 1994. *How Buildings Learn: What Happens to Them After They're Built*. Harmondsworth: Penguin.

Braverman, H. 1974. *Labor and Monopoly Capital: The Degradation of Work in the Twentieth Century*. New York: Monthly Review Press.

Bremmer, J. 1992. Walking, standing and sitting in ancient Greek culture. In *A Cultural History of Gesture*, eds J. Bremmer and H. Roodenburg. Oxford: Polity Press, pp. 15–35.

Briggs, J. L. 2002. Language dead or alive: what's in a dictionary? In *The Power of Traditions: Identities, Politics and Social Sciences*, ed. M. Nagy. Topics in Arctic Social Sciences 4, Quebec: International Arctic Social Sciences Association (IASSA), pp. 69–82.

Brown, L. B. and R. H. Thouless 1965. Animistic thought in civilized adults. *The Journal of Genetic Psychology* 107: 33–42.

Brown, T. 1978. *The Tracker: The Story of Tom Brown, Jr. as Told by William Jon Watkins*. New York: Prentice Hall.

Bryson, N. 2003. A walk for walk's sake. In *The Stage of Drawing: Gesture and Act*, ed. C. de Zegher. London: Tate Publishing; New York: The Drawing Center, pp. 149–158.

Bunn, S. 1997. Animal products. In *Encyclopedia of Vernacular Architecture of the World*, Vol. 1, ed. P. Oliver. Cambridge: Cambridge University Press, pp. 195–197.

Bunn, S. 1999. The importance of materials. *Journal of Museum Ethnography* 11: 15–28.

Canguilhem, G. 2008. *Knowledge of Life*, trans. G. Geroulanos and D. Ginsburg. New York: Fordham University Press.

Caplan, R. 1978. His perspective, chairs as symbols of civilization and cultures. In *Chair: The Current State of the Art, with the Who, the Why and the What of it*, prod. P. Bradford, ed. B. Prete. New York: Thomas Y. Crowell, pp. 8–19.

Carlsöö, S. 1972. *How Man Moves*. London: Heinemann.

Carruthers, M. 1990. *The Book of Memory: A Study of Memory in Medieval Culture*. Cambridge: Cambridge University Press.

Carruthers, M. 1998. *The Craft of Thought: Meditation, Rhetoric and the Making of Images, 400–1200*. Cambridge: Cambridge University Press.

Casey, E. S. 1996. How to get from space to place in a fairly short stretch of time: phenomenological prolegomena. In *Senses of Place*, eds S. Feld and K. H. Basso. Santa Fe, NM: School of American Research Press, pp. 13–52.

Certeau, M. de 1984. *The Practice of Everyday Life*. Berkeley, CA: University of California Press.

Clark, A. 1997. *Being There: Putting Brain, Body and the World Together Again*. Cambridge, MA: MIT Press.

Clark, A. 1998. Where brain, body and world collide. *Daedalus: Journal of the American Academy of Arts and Sciences* (special issue on the brain) 127(2): 257–280.

Clark, W. B. 2006. *A Medieval Book of Beasts: The Second-Family Bestiary.* Woodbridge, Suffolk: Bydell Press.

Clifford, J. 1990. Notes on (field)notes. In *Fieldnotes: The Makings of Anthropology*, ed. R. Sanjek. Ithaca, NY: Cornell University Press, pp. 47–70.

Collingwood, R. G. 1946. *The Idea of History.* Oxford: Clarendon Press.

Collins, S. 1985. Categories, concepts or predicaments? Remarks on Mauss's use of philosophical terminology. In *The Category of the Person: Anthropology, Philosophy, History*, eds M. Carrithers, C. Collins and S. Lukes. Cambridge: Cambridge University Press, pp. 46–82.

Connerton, P. 1989. *How Societies Remember.* Cambridge: Cambridge University Press.

Cooney, G. 2003. Introduction: seeing the land from the sea. *World Archaeology* 35(3): 323–328.

D'Andrade, R. G. 1981. The cultural part of cognition. *Cognitive Science* 5: 179–195.

Darwin, C. 1874. *The Descent of Man, and Selection in Relation to Sex* (second edition). London: John Murray.

Darwin, C. 1950. *On the Origin of Species by Means of Natural Selection, or, The Preservation of Favoured Races in the Struggle for Life.* London: Watts [reprint of first edition of 1859].

Deleuze, G. 1984. Michel Tournier and the world without others. *Economy and Society* 13: 52–71.

Deleuze, G. and F. Guattari 2004. *A Thousand Plateaus: Capitalism and Schizophrenia*, trans. B. Massumi. London: Continuum [originally published as *Mille Plateaux*, vol. 2 of *Capitalisme et Schizophrénie*, Paris: Minuit, 1980].

DeMarrais, E., C. Gosden and C. Renfrew (eds) 2004. *Rethinking Materiality: The Engagement of Mind with the Material World.* Cambridge: McDonald Institute for Archaeological Research.

Derrida, J. 1974. *Of Grammatology*, trans. G. C. Spivak. Baltimore, MD: Johns Hopkins University Press.

Descartes, R. 1988. *Descartes: Selected Philosophical Writings*, trans. J. Cottingham, R. Stoothoff and D. Murdoch. Cambridge: Cambridge University Press.

Descola, P. 2005. On anthropological knowledge. *Social Anthropology* 13(1): 65–73.

Devine, J. 1985. The versatility of human locomotion. *American Anthropologist* 87: 550–570.

Diener, P., D. Nonini and E. E. Robkin 1980. Ecology and evolution in cultural anthropology. *Man* (N.S.) 15: 1–31.

Dillon, M. C. 2007. Merleau-Ponty and the ontology of ecology or apocalypse later. In *Merleau-Ponty and Environmental Philosophy: Dwelling on the Landscapes of Thought*, eds S. L. Cataldi and W. S. Hamrick. Albany, NY: State University of New York Press, pp. 259–272.

Dobzhansky, T. 1965. Mendelism, Darwinism, and evolutionism. *Proceedings of the American Philosophical Society* 109(4): 205–215.

Dowie, J. 1839. Observations on boots and shoes, with reference to the structure and action of the human foot. *Edinburgh New Philosophical Journal* 26: 401–409.

Downey, G. 2007. Seeing with a 'sideways glance': visuomotor 'knowing' and the plasticity of perception. In *Ways of Knowing: New Approaches in the Anthropology of Experience and Learning*, ed. M. Harris. Oxford: Berghahn, pp. 222–241.

Doyle, A. C. 1950. *The Memoirs of Sherlock Holmes.* Harmondsworth: Penguin.

Dreyfus, H. L. 1991. *Being-in-the-world: A Commentary on Heidegger's 'Being and Time, Division I'.* Cambridge, MA: MIT Press.

Durkheim, E. 1982. *The Rules of Sociological Method*, trans. W. D. Halls, ed. S. Lukes. London: Macmillan.

Eisenberg, L. 1972. The human nature of human nature. *Science* 176: 123–128.

Elden, S. 2006. Heidegger's animals. *Continental Philosophy Review* 39: 273–291.

Elkins, J. 1996. *The Object Stares Back: On the Nature of Seeing.* New York: Simon & Schuster.

Elkins, J. 2000. *What Painting Is.* London: Routledge.

Engels, F. 1934. *Dialectics of Nature*, trans. C. Dutt. Moscow: Progress.

Evans-Pritchard, E. E. 1950. Social anthropology: past and present. *Man*, 198: 118–124.

Evans-Pritchard, E. E. 1951. *Social Anthropology.* London: Cohen and West.

Evans-Pritchard, E. E. 1961. *Anthropology and History.* Manchester: Manchester University Press.

Farnell, B. M. 1994. Ethno-graphics and the moving body. *Man* (N.S.) 29: 929–974.

Farnell, B. M. 2000. Getting out of the habitus: an alternative model of dynamically embodied social action. *Journal of the Royal Anthropological Institute* (N.S.) 6: 397–418.

Feld, S. and K. H. Basso (eds) 1996. *Senses of Place*. Santa Fe, NM: School of American Research.

Fienup-Riordan, A. 1994. *Boundaries and Passages: Rule and Ritual in Yup'ik Eskimo Oral Tradition*. Norman, OK: University of Oklahoma Press.

Flesher, M. M. 1997. Repetitive order and the human walking apparatus: Prussian military science versus the Webers' locomotion research. *Annals of Science* 54(5): 463–487.

Flusser, V. 1999. *The Shape of Things: A Philosophy of Design*. London: Reaktion.

Foucault, M. 1973. *This is not a Pipe*, trans. J. Harkness. Berkeley, CA: University of California Press.

Fox, J. J. 1997. Genealogy and topogeny: towards an ethnography of Rotinese ritual place names. In *The Poetic Power of Place: Comparative Perspectives on Austronesian Ideas of Locality*, ed. J. J. Fox. Canberra: Research School of Pacific and Asian Studies, Australian National University, pp. 91–102.

Friedman, T. and A. Goldsworthy 1990. *Hand to Earth*. Leeds: W. S. Maney.

Gay, J. 1974. *Poetry and Prose*, Vol. I, ed. V. A. Dearing. Oxford: Clarendon.

Geertz, C. 1973. *The Interpretation of Cultures*. New York: Basic Books.

Gell, A. 1998. *Art and Agency: An Anthropological Theory*. Oxford: Clarendon.

Gibson, J. J. 1979. *The Ecological Approach to Visual Perception*. Boston, MA: Houghton Mifflin.

Gluckman, M. 1967. Introduction. In *The Craft of Social Anthropology*, ed. A. L. Epstein. London: Tavistock.

Godelier, M. 1986. *The Mental and the Material*, trans. M. Thom. London: Verso.

Godelier, M. 1989. Incest taboo and the evolution of society. In *Evolution and its Influence*, ed. A. Grafen. Oxford: Clarendon Press, pp. 63–92.

Goffman, E. 1971. *Relations in Public: Microstudies of the Public Order*. London: Allen Lane.

Goodall, J. 1990. *Through a Window: My Thirty Years with the Chimpanzees of Gombe*. New York: Houghton Mifflin.

Gosden, C. 1999. *Anthropology and Archaeology: A Changing Relationship*. London: Routledge.

Gosden, C. 2005. What do objects want? *Journal of Archaeological Method and Theory* 12(3): 193–211.

Graves-Brown, P. M. (ed.) 2000. *Matter, Materiality and Modern Culture*. London: Routledge.

Griffin, D. R. 1984. *Animal Thinking*. Cambridge, MA: Harvard University Press.

Grimshaw, A. 2001. *The Ethnographer's Eye: Ways of Seeing in Modern Anthropology*. Cambridge: Cambridge University Press.

Grimshaw, A. and A. Ravetz 2009. Rethinking observational cinema. *Journal of the Royal Anthropological Institute* (N.S.) 15(3): 538–556.

Gunn, W. (ed.) 2009. *Fieldnotes and Sketchbooks: Challenging the Boundaries Between Descriptions and Processes of Describing*. Frankfurt am Main: Peter Lang.

Guthrie, S. 1993. *Faces in the Clouds: A New Theory of Religion*. Oxford: Oxford University Press.

Hägerstrand, T. 1976. Geography and the study of the interaction between nature and society. *Geoforum* 7: 329–334.

Hallam, E. and T. Ingold (eds) 2007. *Creativity and Cultural Improvisation*. Oxford: Berg.

Hallowell, A. I. 1955. *Culture and Experience*. Philadelphia, PA: University of Pennsylvania Press.

Hamel, C. de 1992. *Scribes and Illuminators*. London: British Museum Press.

Harrison, P. 2007. The space between us: opening remarks on the concept of dwelling. *Environment and Planning D: Society and Space* 25: 625–647.

Harvey, J. 1974. *Cathedrals of England and Wales*. London: B. T. Batsford.

Heidegger, M. 1971. *Poetry, Language, Thought*, trans. A. Hofstadter. New York: Harper and Row.

Heidegger, M. 1992. *Parmenides*, trans. A. Schuwer and R. Rojcewicz. Bloomington, IN: Indiana University Press.

Heidegger, M. 1995. *The Fundamental Concepts of Metaphysics: World, Finitude, Solitude*, trans. W. McNeil and N. Walker. Bloomington, IN: Indiana University Press.

Helander, E. and T. Mustonen (eds) 2004. *Snowscapes, Dreamscapes: Snowchange Book on Community Voices of Change*. Tampere Polytechnic Publications, Series C, Study Materials 12. Vaasa: Fram Oy.

Henry, M. 2009. *Seeing the Invisible: On Kandinsky*, trans. S. Davidson. London: Continuum [originally published as *Voir l'invisible*, Éditions François Bourin, 1988].

Hetherington, K. 2003. Spatial textures: place, touch, and praesentia. *Environment and Planning A* 35: 1933–1944.

Hill, M. R. 1984. *Walking, Crossing Streets, and Choosing Pedestrian Routes: A Survey of Recent Insights from the Social/Behavioral Sciences*, New Series 66. Lincoln, Nebraska; University of Nebraska Studies.

Hillman, M. and A. Whalley 1979. *Walking is Transport*. Vol. XLV, No 583. London: Policy Studies Institute.

Hodges, H. 1964. *Artefacts: An Introduction to Early Materials and Technology*. London: Duckworth.

Hopkins, G. M. 1972. *Look Up at the Skies!*, ed. R. Warner. London: Bodley Head.

Huxley, T. H. 1894. *Man's Place in Nature, and Other Anthropological Essays*. London: Macmillan.

Iguchi, K. 2008. Reading music/playing music: the musical notations of the Kyoto Gion festival and the *Noh* flute. *Ethnomusicology Forum* 17(2): 249–268.

Ingold, T. 1983. The architect and the bee: reflections on the work of animals and men. *Man* (N.S.) 18: 1–20.

Ingold, T. 1986. *Evolution and Social Life*. Cambridge: Cambridge University Press.

Ingold, T. 1989. The social and environmental relations of human beings and other animals. In *Comparative Socioecology*, eds V. Standen and R. A. Foley. Oxford: Blackwell Scientific, pp. 495–512.

Ingold, T. 1992. Culture and the perception of the environment. In *Bush Base: Forest Farm. Culture, Environment and Development*, eds E. Croll and D. Parkin. London: Routledge, pp. 39–56.

Ingold, T. 1993. The art of translation in a continuous world. In *Beyond Boundaries: Understanding, Translation and Anthropological Discourse*, ed. G. Palsson. Oxford: Berg, pp. 210–230.

Ingold, T. 1994. Humanity and animality. In *Companion Encyclopedia of Anthropology: Humanity, Culture and Social Life*, ed. T. Ingold. London: Routledge, pp. 14–32.

Ingold, T. 1997. Life beyond the edge of nature? Or, the mirage of society. In *The Mark of the Social*, ed. J. B. Greenwood. Lanham, MD: Rowman and Littlefield, pp. 231–252.

Ingold, T. 1999. 'Tools for the hand, language for the face': an appreciation of Leroi-Gourhan's *Gesture and Speech*. *Studies in the History and Philosophy of Biological and Biomedical Science* 30: 411–453.

Ingold, T. 2000a. *The Perception of the Environment: Essays on Livelihood, Dwelling and Skill*. London: Routledge.

Ingold, T. 2000b. Making culture and weaving the world. In *Matter, Materiality and Modern Culture*, ed. P. M. Graves-Brown. London: Routledge, pp. 50–71.

Ingold, T. 2001a. From the transmission of representations to the education of attention. In *The Debated Mind: Evolutionary Psychology Versus Ethnography*, ed. H. Whitehouse. Oxford: Berg, pp. 113–153.

Ingold, T. 2001b. From complementarity to obviation: on dissolving the boundaries between social and biological anthropology, archaeology and psychology. In *Cycles of Contingency: Developmental Systems and Evolution*, eds S. Oyama, P. E. Griffiths and R. D. Gray. Cambridge, MA: MIT Press, pp. 255–279.

Ingold, T. 2002. Between evolution and history: biology, culture and the myth of human origins. *Proceedings of the British Academy* 112: 43–66.

Ingold, T. 2003. Two reflections on ecological knowledge. In *Nature Knowledge: Ethnoscience, Cognition, Identity*, eds G. Sanga and G. Ortalli. New York: Berghahn, pp. 301–311.

Ingold, T. 2004. Buildings. In *Patterned Ground: Entanglements of Nature and Culture*, eds S. Harrison, S. Pile and N. Thrift. London: Reaktion, pp. 238–240.

Ingold, T. 2005a. The eye of the storm: visual perception and the weather. *Visual Studies* 20(2): 97–104.

Ingold, T. 2005b. Landscape lives, but archaeology turns to stone. *Norwegian Archaeological Review* 38(2): 122–126.

Ingold, T. 2006. Review of Doreen Massey, *For Space*. *Journal of Historical Geography* 32(4): 891–893.

Ingold, T. 2007a. *Lines: A Brief History*. London: Routledge.

Ingold, T. 2007b. Earth, sky, wind and weather. *Journal of the Royal Anthropological Institute* (N.S.) (2007 special issue): S19–S38.

Ingold, T. 2007c. Movement, knowledge and description. In *Holistic Anthropology: Emergence and Convergence*, eds D. Parkin and S. Ulijaszek. Oxford: Berghahn, pp. 194–211.

Ingold, T. 2010. Footprints through the weather-world: walking, breathing, knowing. *Journal of the Royal Anthropological Institute* (N.S.) (2010 special issue): S121–S139.

Ingold, T. and E. Hallam 2007. Creativity and cultural improvisation: an introduction. In *Creativity and Cultural Improvisation*, eds E. Hallam and T. Ingold. Oxford: Berg, pp. 1–24.

Ingold, T. and T. Kurttila 2000. Perceiving the environment in Finnish Lapland. *Body and Society* 6(3/4): 183–196.

Jablonka, E. 2000. Lamarckian inheritance systems in biology: a source of metaphors and models in technological evolution. In *Technological Innovation as an Evolutionary Process*, ed. J. Ziman. Cambridge: Cambridge University Press, pp. 27–40.

James, W. 1982. *Psychology*. New York: Henry Holt.

Järpe, A. 2007. 'Ever against the wind…': lifescapes and environmental perception among Sámi reindeer herders in Västerbotten, Sweden. Unpublished PhD thesis, University of Aberdeen.

Jarvis, R. 1997. *Romantic Writing and Pedestrian Travel*. London: Macmillan.

Jay, M. 1988. Scopic regimes of modernity. In *Vision and Visuality*, ed. H. Foster (Dia Art Foundation Discussions in Contemporary Culture, No 2). Seattle, WA: Bay Press, pp. 3–23.

Jetté, J. 1908–1909. On Ten'a folklore. *Journal of the Royal Anthropological Institute* 38: 298–367; 39: 460–505.

Jetté, J. 1911. On the superstitions of the Ten'a Indians. *Anthropos* 6: 95–108, 241–259, 602–615, 699–723.

Jetté, J. 1913. Riddles of the Ten'a Indians. *Anthropos* 8: 181–201, 630–651.

Johanson, E. 1994. Gait laboratory: structure and data gathering. In *Human Walking* (second edition), eds J. Rose and G. G. Gamble. Baltimore, MD: Williams and Wilkins, pp. 201–224.

Johnson, S. and J. Boswell 1924. *Johnson's Journey to the Western Islands of Scotland, and Boswell's Journal of a Tour to the Hebrides with Samuel Johnson, LL.D.*, ed. R. W. Chapman. London: Oxford University Press.

Jones, D. 1964. *An Outline of English Phonetics* (ninth edition). Cambridge: Heffer.

Kandinsky, W. 1982. *Kandinsky: Complete Writings on Art, Vols. 1 (1901–1921) and 2 (1922–1943)*, eds K. C. Lindsay and P. Vergo. London: Faber & Faber.

Kant, I. 1933. *Immanuel Kant's Critique of Pure Reason*, trans. N. K. Smith. London: Macmillan.

Kant, I. 1970. A translation of the Introduction to Kant's *Physische Geographie*. In *Kant's Concept of Geography and its Relation to Recent Geographical Thought*, ed. J. A. May. Toronto: University of Toronto Press, pp. 255–264.

Kawada, J. n.d. Postures de portage et de travaux manuels – en rapport avec d'autres domaines de la vie japonaise. Unpublished paper presented at the colloquium, *Culture et Usages du Corps*, Saint Germain en Laye, 1–4 March 1996.

Keller, C. M. 2001. Thought and production: insights of the practitioner. In *Anthropological Perspectives on Technology*, ed. M. B. Schiffer. Albuquerque, NM: University of New Mexico Press, pp. 33–45.

Kirby, P. W. (ed.) 2009. *Boundless Worlds: An Anthropological Approach to Movement*. Oxford: Berghahn.

Klee, P. 1961. *Notebooks, Volume 1: The Thinking Eye*, ed. J. Spiller, trans. R. Manheim. London: Lund Humphries.

Klee, P. 1973. *Notebooks, Volume 2: The Nature of Nature*, ed. J. Spiller, trans. H. Norden. London: Lund Humphries.

Knappett, C. 2005. *Thinking Through Material Culture: An Interdisciplinary Perspective*. Philadelphia, PA: University of Pennsylvania Press.

Kroeber, A. L. 1935. History and science in anthropology. *American Anthropologist* 37(4): 539–569.

Kroeber, A. L. 1952. *The Nature of Culture*. Chicago, IL: University of Chicago Press.

Larson, F., A. Petch and D. Zeitlyn 2007. Social networks and the creation of the Pitt Rivers Museum. *Journal of Material Culture* 12(3): 211–239.

Latash, M. 1996. The Bernstein problem: how does the central nervous system make its choices? In *Dexterity and its Development*, eds M. Latash and M. T. Turvey. Mahwah, NJ: Lawrence Erlbaum Associates, pp. 277–303.

Latour, B. 1993. *We Have Never Been Modern*, trans. C. Porter. Hemel Hempstead: Harvester Wheatsheaf.

Latour, B. 1999a. On recalling ANT. In *Actor Network Theory and After*, eds J. Law and J. Hassard. Oxford: Blackwell, pp. 15–25.

Latour, B. 1999b. *Pandora's Hope: Essays on the Reality of Science Studies*. Cambridge, MA: Harvard University Press.

Latour, B. 2005. *Reassembling the Social: An Introduction to Actor-Network Theory*. Oxford: Oxford University Press.

Lazier, B. n.d. Earthrise, or the globalization of the world picture. Unpublished manuscript.

Leach, E. R. 1961. *Rethinking Anthropology*. London: Athlone Press.

Lee, J. and T. Ingold 2006. Fieldwork on foot: perceiving, routing, socialising. In *Locating the Field: Space, Place and Context in Anthropology*, eds S. Coleman and P. Collins. Oxford: Berg, pp. 67–85.

Lefebvre, H. 1991. *The Production of Space*, trans. D. Nicholson-Smith. Oxford: Blackwell.

Lefebvre, H. 2004. *Rhythmanalysis: Space, Time and Everyday Life*. London: Continuum.

Leroi-Gourhan, A. 1993. *Gesture and Speech*, trans. A. Bostock Berger, intr. R. White. Cambridge, MA: MIT Press.

Leudar, I. and A. Costall 1996. Situating action IV: planning as situated action. *Ecological Psychology* 8: 153–170.

Lévi-Strauss, C. 1953. *Race and History*. Paris: UNESCO.

Lévi-Strauss, C. 1968. *Structural Anthropology*. Harmondsworth: Penguin.

Lewis, N. 2001. The climbing body, nature and the experience of modernity. In *Bodies of Nature*, eds P. MacNaghten and J. Urry. London: Sage, pp. 58–80.

Lewontin, R. C. 1982. Organism and environment. In *Learning, Development and Culture*, ed. H. C. Plotkin. Chichester: Wiley.

Lingis, A. 1998. *The Imperative*. Bloomington, IN: Indiana University Press.

Löfgren, O. 2000. Motion and emotion: the microphysics and metaphysics of landscape experiences in tourism. In *Negotiating Nature: Culture, Power, and Environmental Argument*, eds A. Hornborg and G. Pálsson. Lund: Lund University Press, pp. 17–35.

Lorimer, H. 2006. Herding memories of humans and animals. *Environment and Planning D: Society and Space* 24: 497–518.

Low, C. 2008. Khoisan wind: hunting and healing. In *Wind, Life, Health: Anthropological and Historical Perspectives*, eds C. Low and E. Hsu. Oxford: Blackwell, pp. 65–83.

Low, C. and E. Hsu (eds) 2008. *Wind, Life, Health: Anthropological and Historical Perspectives*. Oxford: Blackwell.

Macauley, D. 2005. The flowering of environmental roots and the four elements in presocratic philosophy: from Empedocles to Deleuze and Guattari. *Worldviews: Environment, Culture, Religion* 9(3): 281–314.

Malafouris, L. and C. Knappett (eds) 2008. *Material Agency*. Berlin: Springer.

Malpas, J. E. 1999. *Place and Experience: A Philosophical Topography*. Cambridge: Cambridge University Press.

Manning, E. 2009. *Relationscapes: Movement, Art, Philosophy*. Cambridge, MA: MIT Press.

Marx, K. 1930. *Capital*, Vol. 1, trans. E. Paul and C. Paul. London: Dent.

Marx, K. 1973. *Grundrisse*, trans. M. Nicolaus. Harmondsworth: Penguin.

Marx, K. and F. Engels 1977. *The German Ideology*, ed. C. J. Arthur. London: Lawrence & Wishart.

Marx, K. and F. Engels 1978. Manifesto of the Communist Party. In *The Marx-Engels Reader* (second edition), ed. R. C. Tucker. New York: W. W. Norton, pp. 469–500.

Massey, D. 2005. *For Space*. London: SAGE.

Mauss, M. 1979. Body techniques. In *Sociology and Psychology: Essays*. London: Routledge and Kegan Paul, pp. 97–123.

Medawar, P. 1960. *The Future of Man*. London: Methuen.

Merleau-Ponty, M. 1962. *Phenomenology of Perception*, trans. C. Smith. London: Routledge & Kegan Paul.

Merleau-Ponty, M. 1964. Eye and mind, trans. C. Dallery. In *The Primacy of Perception, and Other Essays on Phenomenological Psychology, the Philosophy of Art, History and Politics*, ed. J. M. Edie. Evanston, IL: Northwestern University Press, pp. 159–190.

Melville, H. 1972. *Typee: Narrative of a Four Months' Residence Among the Natives of a Valley of the Marquesas Islands; or, a Peep at Polynesian Life*. Harmondsworth: Penguin [originally published in 1846].

Miller, D. (ed.) 1995. *Acknowledging Consumption*. London: Routledge.

Miller, D. 1998. Why some things matter. In *Material Cultures: Why Some Things Matter*, ed. D. Miller. London: UCL Press, pp. 3–20.

Miller, D. (ed.) 2005. *Materiality*. Durham, NC: Duke University Press.

Mills, C. W. 1959. *The Sociological Imagination*. New York: Oxford University Press.

Milne, A. A. 1936. *When We Were Very Young* (twenty-eighth edition). London: Methuen.

Mitcham, C. 1978. Types of technology. *Research in Philosophy and Technology* 1: 229–294.

Mitchell, V. 1997. Textiles, text and techne. In *Obscure Objects of Desire: Reviewing the Crafts in the Twentieth Century*, ed. T. Harrod. London: Crafts Council, pp. 324–332.

Mitchell, V. 2006. Drawing threads from sight to site. *Textile* 4(3): 340–361.

Mol, A. and J. Law 1994. Regions, networks and fluids: anaemia and social topology. *Social Studies of Science* 24: 641–671.

Morphy, H. 1991. *Ancestral Connections: Art and an Aboriginal System of Knowledge*. Chicago, IL: University of Chicago Press.

Mulligan, H. 1997. Cave shelter. In *Encyclopedia of Vernacular Architecture of the World*, Vol. 1, ed. P. Oliver. Cambridge: Cambridge University Press, pp. 238–240.

Nadasdy, P. 1999. The politics of TEK: power and the 'integration' of knowledge. *Arctic Anthropology* 36: 1–18.

Nadel, S. F. 1957. *The Theory of Social Structure*. London: Cohen and West.

Napier, J. 1967. The antiquity of human walking. In *Human Variations and Origins: Readings from the Scientific American*. San Francisco, CA: Freeman.

Naveh, J. 1975. *Origins of the Alphabet*. London: Cassell.

Nelson, R. K. 1983. *Make Prayers to the Raven: A Koyukon View of the Northern Forest*. Chicago, IL: University of Chicago Press.

Neruda, P. 1971. Interview in 'Writers at work'. *The Paris Review* (fifth series).

Nobes, G. and G. Panagiotaki 2007. Adults' representations of the Earth: implications for children's acquisition of scientific concepts. *British Journal of Psychology* 98: 645–665.

Nobes, G. and G. Panagiotaki 2009. Mental models or methodological artefacts? Adults' 'naïve' responses to a test of children's conceptions of the earth. *British Journal of Psychology* 100: 347–363.

Nobes, G., A. E. Martin and G. Panagiotaki 2005. The development of scientific knowledge of the Earth. *British Journal of Developmental Psychology* 23: 47–64.

Ogborn, M. 1998. *Spaces of Modernity: London's Geographies, 1680–1780*. London: Guildford Press.

Olsen, B. 2003. Material culture after text: re-membering things. *Norwegian Archaeological Review* 36(2): 87–104.

Olwig, K. 2002. The duplicity of space: Germanic 'raum' and Swedish 'rum' in English language geographical discourse. *Geografiska Annaler* 84 B (1): 1–17.

Olwig, K. 2008. Performing on the landscape versus doing landscape: perambulatory practice, sight and the senses of belonging. In *Ways of Walking: Ethnography and Practice on Foot*, eds T. Ingold and J. Lee Vergunst. Aldershot: Ashgate, pp. 81–91.

Ortega y Gasset, J. 1941. *History as a System and Other Essays Towards a Philosophy of History*. New York: Norton.

Oyama, S. 1985. *The Ontogeny of Information: Developmental Systems and Evolution*. Cambridge: Cambridge University Press.

Oyama, S. 1989. Ontogeny and the central dogma: do we need the concept of genetic programming in order to have an evolutionary perspective? In *Systems in Development: The Minnesota Symposia on Child Psychology*, Vol. 22, eds M. Gunnar and E. Thelen. Hillsdale, NJ: Erlbaum.

Pearson, K. A. 1999. *Germinal Life: The Difference and Repetition of Deleuze*. London: Routledge.

Pelegrin, J. 1993. A framework for analysing prehistoric stone tool manufacture and a tentative application to some early stone industries. In *The Use of Tools by Humans and Non-Human Primates*, eds A. Berthelet and J. Chavaillon. Oxford: Clarendon Press, pp. 302–314.

Pelegrin, J. 2005. Remarks about archaeological techniques and methods of knapping: elements of a cognitive approach to stone knapping. In *Stone Knapping: The Necessary Conditions for a Uniquely Hominin Behaviour*, eds V. Roux and B. Bril. Cambridge: McDonald Institute for Archaeological Research, pp. 23–33.

Pels, P. 1998. The spirit of matter: on fetish, rarity, fact, and fancy. In *Border Fetishisms: Material Objects in Unstable Spaces*, ed. P. Spyer. London: Routledge, pp. 91–121.

Phipps, A. 2007. *Learning the Arts of Linguistic Survival: Languaging, Tourism, Life*. Bristol: Multilingual Matters.

Pickering, A. 1995. *The Mangle of Practice: Time, Agency and Science*. Chicago, IL: University of Chicago Press.

Pink, S. 2007. Walking with video. *Visual Studies* 22(3): 240–252.

Pollard, J. 2004. The art of decay and the transformation of substance. In *Substance, Memory, Display*, eds C. Renfrew, C. Gosden and E. DeMarrais. Cambridge: McDonald Institute for Archaeological Research, pp. 47–62.

Powell, M. A. 1981. Three problems in the history of cuneiform writing: origins, direction of the script, literacy. *Visible Language* 15: 419–440.

Preston, B. 2000. The functions of things: a philosophical perspective on material culture. In *Matter, Mind and Modern Culture*, ed. P. M. Graves-Brown. London: Routledge, pp. 22–49.

Protevi, J. 2001. *Political Physics: Deleuze, Derrida and the Body Politic*. London: Athlone Press.

Pye, D. 1968. *The Nature and Art of Workmanship*. Cambridge: Cambridge University Press.

Pye, D. 1978. *The Nature and Aesthetics of Design*. London: Herbert Press.

Quintilian, M. F. 2001. *The Orator's Education, Books 1–2*, ed. and trans. D. A. Russell. Cambridge, MA: Harvard University Press.

Radcliffe-Brown, A. R. 1951a. The comparative method in social anthropology. *Journal of the Royal Anthropological Institute* 81: 15–22.

Radcliffe-Brown, A. R. 1951b. Review of E. E. Evans-Pritchard's *Social Anthropology*. *British Journal of Sociology* 2: 364–366.

Radcliffe-Brown, A. R. 1952. *Structure and Function in Primitive Society*. London: Cohen and West.

Radcliffe-Brown, A. R. 1953. Letter to Lévi-Strauss. In *An Appraisal of Anthropology Today*, ed. S. Tax. Chicago, IL: University of Chicago Press.

Radcliffe-Brown, A. R. 1957. *A Natural Science of Society*. New York: Free Press.

Rawson, P. 1979. *Seeing Through Drawing*. London: British Broadcasting Corporation.

Rayner, A. D. M. 1997. *Degrees of Freedom: Living in Dynamic Boundaries*. London: Imperial College Press.

Rée, J. 1999. *I See a Voice: A Philosophical History of Language, Deafness and the Senses*. London: Harper Collins.

Reed, E. S. 1982. Darwin's earthworms: a case study in evolutionary psychology. *Behaviourism* 10: 165–185.

Reid, A. 1978. *Weathering: Poems and Translations*. Edinburgh: Canongate.

Renfrew, C. 2001. Symbol before concept: material engagement and the early development of society. In *Archaeological Theory Today*, ed. I. Hodder. Cambridge: Polity, pp. 122–140.

Renfrew, C. 2004. Towards a theory of material engagement. In *Rethinking Materiality: The Engagement of Mind with the Material World*, eds E. DeMarrais, C. Gosden and C. Renfrew. Cambridge: McDonald Institute for Archaeological Research, pp. 23–31.

Reuleaux, F. 1876. *The Kinematics of Machinery: Outline of a Theory of Machines*. London: Macmillan.

Revel, N. 2005. Palawan Highlanders and Dayaks of Borneo: human beings and birds, their relation. In *Animal Names*, eds A. Minelli, G. Ortalli and G. Sanga. Venice: Istituto Veneto di Scienze, Lettere ed Arti, pp. 401–417.

Ribeiro, G. 1996. Action, dwelling and squatting: an ecological approach to the relation between person and urban environment. *Ecological Psychology* 8: 131–151.

Richards, P. 1974. Kant's geography and mental maps. *Transactions of the Institute of British Geographers* (N.S.) 11: 1–16.

Richerson, P. J. and R. Boyd 1978. A dual inheritance model of the human evolutionary process, I: Basic postulates and a simple model. *Journal of Social and Biological Structures* 1: 127–154.

Rogoff, I. 2002. Studying visual culture. In *The Visual Culture Reader* (second edition). London: Routledge, pp. 24–36.

Rosen, M. 1989. *We're Going on a Bear Hunt*, illustrated by H. Oxenbury. London: Walker Books.

Rubin, D. 1988. Go for the skill. In *Remembering Reconsidered: Ecological and Traditional Approaches to the Study of Memory*, eds U. Neisser and E. Winograd. Cambridge: Cambridge University Press, pp. 374–382.

Ryle, G. 1971. The thinking of thoughts: what is 'le penseur' doing? In his *Collected Essays*, Vol. 2. London: Hutchinson, pp. 480–496.

Sahlins, M. 1976. *Culture and Practical Reason*. Chicago, IL: University of Chicago Press.

Sapir, E. 1944. Grading: a study in semantics. *Philosophy of Science* 11: 93–116.

Schafer, R. M. 1994. *The Soundscape*. Rochester, VT: Destiny Books.

Scott, C. 1989. Knowledge construction among Cree hunters: metaphors and literal understanding. *Journal de la Société des Américanistes* 75: 193–208.

Sebeok, T. 1986. Naming in animals, with reference to playing. In *I Think I am a Verb: More Contributions to the Doctrine of Signs*, by T. A. Sebeok. New York: Plenum Press, pp. 82–96.

Sheets-Johnstone, M. 1998. *The Primacy of Movement*. Amsterdam: John Benjamins.

Shepherd, N. 1977. *The Living Mountain: A Celebration of the Cairngorm Mountains of Scotland*. Aberdeen: Aberdeen University Press.

Sigaut, F. 1993. How can we analyse and describe technical actions? In *The Use of Tools by Humans and Non-human Primates*, eds A. Berthelet and J. Chavaillon. Oxford: Clarendon Press, pp. 381–397.

Sigaut, F. 1994. Technology. In *Companion Encyclopedia of Anthropology: Humanity, Culture and Social Life*, ed. T. Ingold. London: Routledge, pp. 420–59.

Sillitoe, P. 2007. Anthropologists only need apply: challenges of applied anthropology. *Journal of the Royal Anthropological Institute* (N.S.) 13: 147–165.

Simondon, G. 1980. *On the Mode of Existence of Technical Objects*, ed. J. Hart, trans. N. Mellamphy. Unpublished manuscript, University of Western Ontario [translation of *Du Mode d'existence des Objects Techniques*. Paris: Aubier Montaigne, 1958]

Sirén, O. 2005. *The Chinese Art of Painting: Texts by the Painter Critics, from the Han Through the Ch'ing Dynasties*. Mineola, NY: Dover Publications [originally published by Henri Vetch, Beijing, 1936].

Siza, A. 1997. *Architecture Writings*, ed. A. Angelillo. Milan: Skira Editore.

Sloterdijk, P. 2005. Forward to the theory of spheres. In *Cosmograms*, eds M. Ohanian and J. C. Royaux. New York: Lukas and Sternberg, pp. 223–241.

Solnit, R. 2001. *Wanderlust: A History of Walking*. London: Verso.

Sperber, D. 1996. *Explaining Culture: A Naturalistic Approach*. Oxford: Blackwell.

Stanner, W. E. H. 1968. A. R. Radcliffe-Brown. *International Encyclopaedia of the Social Sciences* 13: 285–290. New York: Crowell Collier and Macmillan.

Stewart, S. 1972. Footgear – its history, uses and abuses. *Clinical Orthopaedics and Related Research* 88: 119–122.

Stoczkowski, W. 2002. *Explaining Human Origins: Myth, Imagination and Conjecture*, trans. M. Turton. Cambridge: Cambridge University Press.

Strunk, O. (ed.) 1950. *Source Readings in Music History: From Classical Antiquity Through the Romantic Era*. New York: W. W. Norton.

Suzuki, T. 1986. *The Way of Acting: The Theatre Writings of Tadashi Suzuki*, trans. J. T. Rimer. New York: Theatre Communications Group.

Tenner, E. 2003. *Our Own Devices: The Past and Future of Body Technology*. New York: Alfred A. Knopf.

Thelen, E. 1995. Motor development: a new synthesis. *American Psychologist* 50: 79–95.

Thomson, J. A. 1911. *Introduction to Science*. London: Williams and Norgate.

Thornes, J. 1999. *John Constable's Skies*. Birmingham: University of Birmingham Press.

Thornes, J. 2008. Cultural climatology and the representation of sky, atmosphere, weather and climate in selected works of Constable, Monet and Eliasson. *Geoforum* 39: 570–580.

Tilley, C. 1994. *A Phenomenology of Landscape: Places, Paths and Monuments*. Oxford: Berg.

Tilley, C. 2004. *The Materiality of Stone: Explorations in Landscape Phenomenology*. Oxford: Berg.

Tilley, C. 2007. Materiality in materials. *Archaeological Dialogues* 14(1): 16–20.

Toren, C. 1999. *Mind, Materiality and History*. London: Routledge.

Turnbull, D. 1991. *Mapping the World in the Mind: An Investigation of the Unwritten Knowledge of Micronesian Navigators.* Geelong: Deakin University Press.

Turnbull, D. 2000. *Masons, Tricksters and Cartographers.* Amsterdam: Harwood Academic.

Tuttle, R. H., D. M. Webb, N. I. Tuttle and M. Baksh 1992. Footprints and gaits of bipedal apes, bears, and barefoot people: perspectives on Pliocene tracks. In *Evolutionary Biology, Reproductive Endocrinology and Virology* (Topics in Primatology Vol. 3), eds S. Matano, R. H. Tuttle, H. Ishida and M. Goodman. Tokyo: University of Tokyo Press, pp. 221–242.

Tylor, E. B. 1881. *Anthropology: An Introduction to the Study of Man and Civilization.* London: Macmillan.

Uexküll, J. von 1982. *The Theory of Meaning*, trans. B. Stone and H. Weiner from *Bedeutungslehre* (ed. T. von Uexküll). *Semiotica* 42(1): 25–82 [originally published in 1940].

Uexküll, J. von 1992. A stroll through the worlds of animals and men: a picture book of invisible worlds. *Semiotica* 89(4): 319–391 [originally published in 1934].

Urry, J. 2000. *Sociology Beyond Societies: Mobilities for the Twenty-First Century.* London: Routledge.

Vernant, J. P. 1983. *Myth and Thought Among the Greeks.* London: Routledge and Kegan Paul.

Vico, G. 1948. *The New Science of Giambattista Vico* [1744], ed. and trans. T. G. Bergin and M. H. Fisch. Ithaca, NY: Cornell University Press.

Vološinov, V. N. 1973. *Marxism and the Philosophy of Language*, trans. L. Matejka and I. R. Titunik. Cambridge, MA: Harvard University Press.

Vosniadou, S. 1994. Universal and culture-specific properties of children's mental models of the earth. In *Mapping the Mind: Domain Specificity in Cognition and Culture*, eds L. A. Hirschfeld and S. A. Gelman. Cambridge: Cambridge University Press, pp. 412–430.

Vosniadou, S. and W. F. Brewer 1992. Mental models of the earth: a study of conceptual change in childhood. *Cognitive Psychology* 24: 535–585.

Vosniadou, S., I. Skopeliti and K. Ikospentaki 2004. Modes of knowing and ways of reasoning in elementary astronomy. *Cognitive Development* 19(2): 203–222.

Wagner, R. 1986. *Symbols that Stand for Themselves.* Chicago, IL: University of Chicago Press.

Wallace, A. D. 1993. *Walking, Literature and English Culture.* Oxford: Clarendon.

Warner, M. 1996. Forms into time: the works of David Nash. In *David Nash: Forms into Time.* London: Academy Editions.

Watanabe, H. 1971. Running, creeping and climbing: a new ecological and evolutionary perspective on human evolution. *Mankind* 8: 1–13.

Weber, K. 2004. *Unfold! You cul de sac.* Frankfurt: Revolver Verlag.

Webmoor, T. and C. L. Whitmore 2008. Things are us! A commentary on human/thing relations under the banner of a 'social' archaeology. *Norwegian Archaeological Review* 41(1): 53–70.

Weiss, P. 1969. The living system: determinism stratified. In *Beyond Reductionism: New Perspectives in the Life Sciences,* eds A. Koestler and J. R. Smythies. London: Hutchinson.

Wendrich, W. 1999. *The World According to Basketry: An Ethno-archaeological Interpretation of Basketry Production in Egypt.* Leiden: University of Leiden, CNWS.

Whatmore, S. 2007. Hybrid geographies: rethinking the 'human' in human geography. In *The Animals Reader*, eds L. Kalof and A. Fitzgerald. Oxford: Berg, pp. 337–348.

Whitehead, A. N. 1929. *Process and Reality: An Essay in Cosmology.* Cambridge: Cambridge University Press.

Whitehead, A. N. 1938. *Science and the Modern World.* Harmondsworth: Penguin [first published in 1926].

Wiebe, R. 1989. *Playing Dead: A Contemplation Concerning the Arctic.* Edmonton, Canada: NeWest.

Wolff, M. 1973. Notes on the behavior of pedestrians. In *People in Places: The Sociology of the Familiar*, eds A. Birenbaum amd E. Sagarin. New York: Praeger, pp. 35–48.

Wolin, R. (ed.) 1993. *The Heidegger Controversy.* Cambridge, MA: MIT Press

Wylie, J. 2002. An essay on ascending Glastonbury Tor. *Geoforum* 33: 441–454.

Yen, Y. 2005. *Calligraphy and Power in Contemporary Chinese Society.* London: Routledge Curzon.

Zuckerkandl, V. 1956. *Sound and Symbol: Music and the External World*, trans. W. R. Trask. Bollingen Series XLIV. Princeton, NJ: Princeton University Press.

INDEX

actor-network theory 64, 85, 94
affordance 11, 78-9, 82
agency 28-9, 130, 213-15; abduction of 215; and actor-network theory 85, 90-2; dance of 92-3; versus intelligence 93-4; versus intentionality 214; versus life 215; versus materiality 73, of objects 16-17, 28-9, 213-15
air 21, 88, 130, 138-9; circulations of 122; of heaven 109; medium of 22-3, 92, 111; open 95, 115; versus space 145; *see also* atmosphere; sky
Alberti, Leon Battista 211-12, 218
alchemy 213
alphabet 183, 193
animals, non-human 8, 174; domestic 165-6, 170; European and Japanese understandings of 41; Heidegger on 10-11; learning by 156; medieval understandings of 200; names of 169-75; natural histories of 7; and production 4, 6; sources of environmental meaning for 64, 76-7, 80; as sources of materials 24-5
animism 28-9, 63, 67-8, 73-4; versus fetishism 28; versus science 75; and totemism 198
anthropology 10, 20, 138, 181, 229, 238-43; and the concept of culture 142; and developmental systems theory 9; drawing in 177; ecological 76; experimental nature of 15-16; graphic 179, 222-3; and life 3-4, 14, 226; Marxian approach to 7; psychological 236; social 221-2, 230, 233-4, 238; and sound 136; teaching of 242-3; visual 179, 196, 224-5
anthropomorphism 165, 174
archaeology 16, 20, 120, 130, 136, 177, 229
architecture 9, 123, 136, 177, 181, 211-12

Aristotle 99, 104-5, 210
art 181, 201, 239, 241; abstract 178, 206-8; and agency 215-16; of describing 126-7, 136, 177, 222
artefacts 20, 21-2, 183, 214
astonishment, versus surprise 63-4, 74-5
astronomy 67-8, 99, 104, 114
atmosphere 73, 111, 132, 134-5; scientific concept of 104, 107; versus sky 96, 108; *see also* air; sky
Augustine, Saint 109-10, 112-13
availableness, versus occurrentness 80-1

Bateson, Gregory 86, 236
behaviour: versus action 77, 93; versus comportment 82
Berger, John 217
Bergson, Henri 13, 87, 226
bestiary 200-2, 204
biodiversity 163
bipedalism 33-5, 41, 48-9
Bloch, Maurice 238-9
Boas, Franz 230, 232
body 12, 16-17, 22-3, 37, 135, 166, 223; as an instrument 57; and machine 61; techniques 39, 46, 48-50, 57
Bohm, David 160, 236
boots 16-17, 35-7, 39-40, 44, 46-8, 50
brain, human 33-4
Bryson, Norman 217-18, 220-2
building 24, 84-5, 199-200, 211-12; versus dwelling 6, 9-10, 44; *see also* dwelling

calligraphy 184-5, 188, 223, 225
camera 177, 225-6
captivation, Heidegger's concept of 81

carpentry 179, 211, 216-18
Carruthers, Mary 198-200
cartography 127, 141, 149, 168, 199
chairs 39, 44-5; arm- 237-8
chimneys 123
Ching Hao 197-8, 207-8
Clark, Andy 86, 236
classification 142-3, 153-5, 158-60, 162-4,
    166-8; versus network 167, 175; of societies
    234-5; versus stories 159-60, 173
clouds 104, 106-7, 116-18, 122, 127-8
concentration 18, 60-1
copying 179, 216; of letters 185, 195
correspondence 241-3
counterpoint 83, 88, 215
craft 212, 222-3, 239-40
creativity 10, 13, 178-9, 215-16
culture 156, 162, 164; concept of 142; and
    practical reason 76-7; versus science 155

Darwin, Charles 7, 34-5, 47, 84, 163
Deleuze, Gilles 3, 13-14, 64, 83-5, 88, 132-4,
    174, 210-11, 213, 215-16
description 237; and correspondence 241-2; and
    observation 179, 222, 224, 242
developmental systems 9, 49
dexterity 18, 36, 58-9
Dobzhansky, Theodosius 124
drawing 147, 150-1, 177-9, 181, 221, 224,
    226; and carpentry 217; the earth 101-5,
    107, 111-12, 114, 197; as observation 179;
    versus painting 217-18, 220-1, 226, 241; and
    wayfaring 178; versus writing 178, 181, 188,
    195, 222, 241-2
dreaming 28, 137, 239-40
Dreaming, Australian Aboriginal concept of 198,
    202-4, 206
Durkheim, Emile 235
dwelling 3, 4, 6, 9-12, 44, 122-3, 147, 239;
    see also building

ears 95, 137
earth: as ground 113-14; Heidegger on 113, 118,
    120; and sea 132; shape of 95-6, 99-111, 113-
    14, 116; and sky 73-4, 87-8, 95, 97, 112-13,
    117-23, 131, 178; and space 145; surface of
    24, 131, 167-8; see also ground; land
ekphrasis 200
elements, in painting 207-8
Elkins, James 197, 213, 223-5
embodiment 134-5, 138-9
embroidery 178, 193-5, 218
Engels, Friedrich 3, 4-7, 10
environment 64, 70-1, 76-9, 84, 95-6; built 123;
    in ecological psychology 116-17; versus
    globe 96; and space 145; versus world 11, 30,
    77, 81, 111; see also landscape

erasure 54, 194, 217, 222
ethnography 67, 169, 179, 222, 224-6, 232;
    versus anthropology 229, 233, 237, 240-3
Evans-Pritchard, E. E. 222, 233-5
Evenki, of Siberia 149
evolution 8-9, 49-50, 124, 164; versus history 4,
    7, 50; human 33-5, 156
excavation 23-4
existence, versus occurrence 141, 143, 154, 160,
    175, 191
experiments: in anthropology 15-16; in
    handwriting 188; in kite flying 214; in line
    drawing 147, 150; to reveal understandings
    of the shape of the earth 100-1, 105-6, 109,
    114; in sorting objects 21
explicate (versus implicate) order 160, 236-7
eye: as bodily instrument 57; in haptic vision
    133; and mind 197; and posture in walking
    40, 43-4; as screen 137; training of 95; and
    the visual image 224-5; see also vision

feeling 129-30, 132, 134, 138
feet 17, 33-42, 46-8
fire 21, 117, 119, 122
footprints 47, 197

gait 17, 40, 47-9
Geertz, Clifford 3, 39, 76, 156-7, 222
Gell, Alfred 213-14, 215
genealogical model 142-3, 157-60, 162, 164
genes 97
genotype, and culture-type 157-8; versus
    phenotype 8-9, 97, 157, 160, 163
geography 110, 138, 141-2, 154, 164
gesture 17, 56-60, 150-1, 177, 179; and
    calligraphy 184-5, 188; and description 225
Gibson, James 109; on earth and sky 82, 87, 96,
    111-12, 116-18, 127-9, 131-2, 134; and the
    ecological approach to perception 11-12,
    22, 45-6, 77-9, 96, 112, 127; on medium,
    substances and surfaces 22-4, 30, 124; theory
    of affordances of 64, 77-9; on the weather
    119
globe 96, 106, 109, 164
Gluckman, Max 239-40
Godelier, Maurice 7-8, 9, 20-2
ground 16, 119, 121, 130-2; versus earth 102-5,
    107-8, 112-14; of habitation 87, 111, 115; of
    perception 45, 96; and space 145; texture of
    116; see also earth; land
growth 6-8, 13, 69, 120, 124, 164

habitation, versus occupation 10, 12, 71, 123-4,
    145, 147, 149-51, 162, 168, 173
haecceities 64, 84, 86, 88
Hägerstrand, Torsten 9, 14, 84, 221, 223
Hallowell, A. Irving 236, 239

hand: as a compendium of gestures 58, 188; and feet 33-5, 37, 41, 46; in handwriting 178, 187-8, 190; as instrument 57; in sawing 17, 52-3, 57; in world forming 82

hearing 136; and sound 132, 138; tuning of 95; and vision 39, 45, 128-9, 200-2

heaven 109-11, 113-14

Heidegger, Martin: on dwelling 3, 9-12, 112, 147; on earth and sky 112-13, 118-21, 124; on the hand 82, 190; on humans and animals 10-11, 64, 81-2; on the open 80-2, 96, 147; on the typewriter 190; on the worlding world 130, 214

Henry, Michel 198, 207-8

history 4, 6-9, 13, 46, 64, 75; versus anthropology 232-3, 235; versus science 230-2

holism 179, 221, 226, 237

Hopkins, Gerard Manley 120-1

human being 3, 4-8, 10-11; and agency 29, 214; versus animal existence 11, 82; and anthropology 229; and being human 113-14; and culture 156; and drawing 177; and human becoming 9, 12; and human nature 31; naming of 143, 165-6

hunters and gatherers 166, 169

Huxley, Thomas Henry 33-4, 35-6

hybridity 91-3

hylomorphic model 178, 210-11, 213, 215

idiographic, versus nomothetic 229-30, 237

image: and artefact 183; as back projection 97, 133, 225; figurative 200; and imagination 197, 208; versus object 5-6, 9-10, 14, 22, 134, 136, 159, 178, 181, 206-7, 210; in riddles 173; and text 177-9, 200, 224-6; in visual culture studies 136-7, 196

imagination 196-8, 208

immersion 10, 24, 80, 115, 128, 130, 135, 137

implicate (versus explicate) order 160, 236-7

improvisation 10, 62, 84, 162, 178-9, 221, 226; versus abduction 216, 219

ink 21, 26, 209

inscription 178, 193; versus embroidery 195

Inuit, of the Canadian Arctic 72, 149-50

invariants 112

inversion 63, 68-70, 73, 97, 117, 145, 147-8, 151, 155

itineration, versus iteration 216

kairos 54

Kandinsky, Wassily 178-9, 197-8, 205-9

Kant, Immanuel 96, 109-11, 116, 164, 167

keyboard 177-8, 225-6, 241

Khoisan, of southern Africa 121

kites 130, 135, 139, 179, 214-15

Klee, Paul 120, 150, 191, 210, 215-16

knowledge 15, 17, 142-3, 145; anthropological 242-3; innate and acquired 156, 164; inside versus outside 203; integration of 153-5, 158-9, 167-8, 231; and language 161; limits of 110-11; and practice 159; traditional 155

Koyukon, of Alaska 72, 119, 121-2, 143, 169-75

Kroeber, Alfred 222, 230-3

labour 5-6, creativity of 10

land 119-21, 126-7, 131-4, 145, 151; *see also* earth; ground

landscape 21, 31; etymology of 126; formation of 47; medieval and modern senses of 126-7, 133-4; painting 74, 127, 232, 237; perception of 129-30, 133-4, 136; as scenery 38, 152; and space 145; versus weather-world 73, 96-7, 132-3, 135, 138, 198-202, 204; *see also* environment

language 161-2, 175, 193, 195; of animals 174

Latour, Bruno 64, 85, 213

Leach, Edmund 233-5, 237

learning: cultural 156-7, 161; to write 183-4

Lefebvre, Henri 60, 84

Leroi-Gourhan, André 57, 60

letters 178, 181, 195, 200-1, 207; evolution of 185-7; shapes of 183-4, 188, 190, 197

Lévi-Strauss, Claude 234-5

life: animals as manifestations of 170; and animism 28-9, 67-70; and anthropology 3-4, 14, 226; binds medium and substances 120, 124; and DNA 73, 97; generative potential of 198, 210; and the implicate order 236; and inversion 145; lines of 83, 208; and movement 72, 178; primacy of 6-7; and room 146-7; social and organic 234, 237; and story 161; and time 13, 142

light 21, 74, 96-7, 128-30, 132, 134, 136-8

lightscape 134, 138

lines 3, 4, 13-14, 63, 148-50; of becoming (or flight) 83, 85, 214-15; dotted 150-1, 191; drawn 177, 217-18, 220-21; and fish 208; of growth 71, 120, 150, 168, 210, 221; as lineaments 211-12, 218; of movement 121, 148, 153; and shapes 181; and surface 181; as threads 218-19; of writing 178, 189-91

Lingis, Alphonso 114-15, 128

locomotion 12, 49; and cognition 17, 35, 46

machine 18, 46, 59, 61-2

Magritte, René 118, 182-3, 185

making 6, 10, 20, 177-8, 210-12, 218

maps 127, 168, 199, 204-5

Marx, Karl 3, 5-7, 9-10, 46, 62

Massey, Doreen 141-2, 146

material culture 23; studies of 10, 16, 20, 23, 28, 30, 138, 215

material world 130; definition of 21-2, 30-1

materials 10, 16, 20, 24–8, 210, 215; from
animals and plants 24–6; following 179,
213; versus materiality 16, 20, 23, 27, 31,
179; properties of 29–30, 212; *see also*
substances
Mauss, Marcel 39, 41, 48–9, 57
medium: fluxes of (versus conformation
of surfaces) 129, 134, 138; rendered
immaterial 73, 97, 130; versus substances
22–3, 30, 87, 111, 118, 120–2, 124, 127;
volatility of 87, 139; and weather 73–4, 119
memory 57, 152, 159, 161
Merleau-Ponty, Maurice 12, 69, 96, 128–9,
134, 137
meshwork 42–3, 149, 155, 191; versus network
63–4, 70, 84–5, 92–3, 151–2, 154, 163, 168,
178
Miller, Daniel 20, 215
Mills, C. Wright 240
mind 16–17, 20–1, 31, 86, 236; versus body 39,
77, 93, 116; versus matter 22, 30, 111, 137
monasticism, in medieval Europe 178, 197–
200, 206–7, 209
moon 21, 72, 74, 101–4, 110, 113, 117–18, 132,
134
Morphy, Howard 202–4
movement 17, 142, 145, 147–50, 152, 154; as
knowing 160, 162; lines of 121, 148, 153;
and perception 11, 46, 59–60, 94, 152;
primacy of 12, 72–4; and process 159–60;
and togetherness 221
music 83, 193, 205–7, 223
Mussorsky, Modest 205–7
mycelium, fungal 86, 124–5

Nadel, Siegfried 231, 233
naming 143, 165–75
Nash, David 27
natural selection 7–8, 34–5, 68
nature 84; and art 179, 208–9; versus society 3,
4, 8–9, 21, 31, 166
needle 194–5
network 70, 85, 90–1, 143, 167; versus
meshwork 63–4, 70, 84–5, 92–3, 151–2,
154, 163, 168, 178
niche, ecological 78, 80, 82, 87
nomothetic, versus idiographic 229–30, 237
notation 181; logical 231; musical 192–3,
nouns, common and proper 165–8, 173, 175

objectivity 152
objects: agency of 16–17, 28–9, 213–15; clouds
as 118, 127; versus enclosures 23–4, 87;
externality of 207; as furnishing 82, 87,
116; versus images 5–6, 9–10, 14, 22, 134,
136, 159, 178, 181, 206–7, 210; materiality
of 16, 20, 26, 28; on and of the earth 131;

and subjects 213–15; versus things 179, 214–
15; world without 117, 131–2
observation 12, 15, 75, 129, 137, 179, 197, 223;
and description 179, 222, 224, 242; and
participation 223–4, 241
occupation, versus habitation 10, 12, 71, 123–4,
145, 147, 149–51, 162, 168, 173
occurrence, versus existence 141, 143, 154, 160,
175, 191
occurrentness, versus availableness 80–1
Ojibwa, of north-central Canada 239
Olwig, Kenneth 141, 147
Ortega y Gasset, José 3, 7
Oyama, Susan 8–9

painting 69, 74, 127, 129, 178, 183, 200, 205–9,
213; versus drawing 179, 197, 217–18, 220–1,
241; figurative versus geometric 202–5, 207;
and landscape 74, 127, 145, 198, 232, 237;
and photography 136, 225
Palawan Highlanders, of the Philippines 135
path 4, 12, 121, 196; of observation 12, 46, 112;
way of life as 162
paving 17, 37, 41–4, 123–4
pebbles 117, 131
pen 26, 178, 187–8, 195
perception 117–18, 128, 130, 238; and action
17, 53, 58–61, 65, 77, 79–80, 97, 152, 241;
ecological approach to 11–12, 22, 45–6, 77–9,
96, 112, 127 (*see also* Gibson, James); haptic
versus optical 133–4, 219
phenotype, versus genotype 8–9, 97, 157, 160,
163
philosophy 13–14, 93–4, 238, 243
photography 127, 136, 183, 225
Piaget, Jean 109
pitch, musical 181, 192–3
place 23, 166, 168; and movement 149–50, 154,
160; naming 143, 166; versus path 12, 148;
and sensory experience 134, 139; and space
141, 145–7, 149, 152, 155
posture, upright 33–4, 39–41, 48; bodily 58
print 178, 190
production 3, 4–6, 8–10, 12; versus consumption
5, 9–10, 14, 26; versus transport 12
psychology 68, 137, 236; cognitive 11, 77, 159;
developmental 95–6, 99, 109; ecological
11–12, 22, 45–6, 77–9, 96, 112, 127
Pye, David 29–30, 56, 59
Pythagoras 99

Quintilianus, Marcus Fabius 183–4, 187

Radcliffe-Brown, Alfred Reginald 229–31,
233–8
rain 21, 116, 129–30, 138
reading 196–7, 208

Reid, Alastair 166, 175
relatedness, genealogical 163
relations 69-71, 85-6, 91, 124, 141, 231-2; and
    stories 160-1
respiration 96, 115, 120, 215
rhythm 18, 46, 55, 60-1, 217
riddles 121-2, 143, 169, 172-4
roads 17, 37
room 141, 145-6, 155

Sahlins, Marshall 5, 76
sawing 17, 51-5, 58-60, 179, 216-17
science 113-14, 153-5, 156, 174, 239; versus
    animism 75; and the earth 95-6, 100; and
    life 97; and objectivity 152
scopic regime 126
scribes 178, 185, 188, 191, 199-200
sea 131-2
sewing 178
Siza, Alvaro 212
skill 16, 18, 30, 58-9, 61-2, 94, 211
skin 86-7
sky 72, 74, 107-8, 115, 130-2; drawing of 96,
    101, 103-8, 112; and earth 73-4, 87-8,
    95, 97, 112-13, 117-23, 131, 178; Gibson
    on 96, 111-12, 116-17, 127, 128-9; and
    heaven 109; Heidegger on 112-13, 118-19;
    and landscape 21, 127, 135; perception of
    128-9, 134, 138; and space 145; see also air;
    atmosphere
smell 22, 42, 95, 121, 136
smoke 21, 122-3
snow 21, 119, 121-3, 130
society 3, 4, 7-8, 21, 221, 238; versus nature 3, 4,
    8-9, 21, 31, 166; versus organism 234-5, 237
sound 97, 129-30, 132, 134, 136-9; and letters
    192-3
soundscape 97, 134, 136-8
space 141-2, 145-8, 164; empty (terra nullius)
    166; fluid 64, 86-8; outer 96, 104, 107-9,
    113-14; striated versus smooth 132-4
speed 152
spider 5, 64-5, 80, 83, 85, 91-3, 119
spirit 29
stars 21, 73, 101-3, 110, 117-18, 132
stone 16, 19, 23, 30-2, 80-1, 117, 131; knapping
    211
stories 142, 155, 161, 199; versus classification
    159-60, 173; and materials 30-2; as names
    168, 170-2; and place 154; and tools 54-7
storytelling 143, 161-2, 164, 169, 171-2, 195;
    and tool-use 54-7
substances 22, 27-8, 124, 213; and media 22-3,
    30, 87, 111, 118, 120-2, 124, 127; see also
    materials
sun 21, 72-4, 95, 110, 117-18, 132, 134
sunlight 21, 129-30, 138

surfaces: between medium and substances 22-4,
    30, 87, 118, 127; conformation of (versus
    fluxes of medium) 129, 134, 138; of the earth
    74, 87; of the ground 87, 116, 127; hard
    17, 124-5 (see also paving); in painting and
    drawing 220-2; and perception 12, 22-3, 129;
    of wood 27; in and of the world 47, 71, 111,
    119, 151
surprise, versus astonishment 63-4, 74-5

technology 61-2, 212; image-based 225
text 178, 191, 196; versus image 177-9, 200,
    224-6; and landscape 199; versus texture 84
things 11, 81; versus objects 179, 214-15; as
    relations 70
thread: versus trace 121, 181, 194-5; spinning
    218-19
Tilley, Christopher 30-1, 129-30, 148
time 13, 142, 152, 164, 217-18, 232
togetherness, principle of 221, 223, 226
tools 17, 34, 46, 53-5, 56-8; functions of 56-7
topics 154, 160
touch 23, 42, 95, 136; versus feeling 129-30, 132,
    138; haptic and optical 133; pedestrian 45
trace: versus thread 121, 181, 194-5; and gesture
    181, 190
tracks 121, 149, 151, 197
transmission: cultural 142-3, 145, 157-62, 164;
    genetic 157-8, 164
transport 17, 37-8, 85, 124, 145; versus
    production 12; versus wayfaring 59, 149-52,
    162-3
travel 37-8, 44, 149-50, 152, 196, 198, 202
Tylor, Edward Burnet 29, 36-7
typewriting 181, 189-91

Uexküll, Jakob von 64, 77, 79-81, 83
umbrella plan 54
Umwelt 80-1
use: versus manufacture 27; of tools 56-8

van Gogh, Vincent 121-2
verbs, names as 168-9, 175
vision 95, 136, 152, 179, 199, 223-4; and the
    experience of light 97, 128-9, 132, 137; and
    eye-to-eye contact 43-4; haptic and optical
    133; and hearing 39, 45, 128-9, 200-2; in
    walking 42-3, 196-7; and the weather 96,
    132; see also eye
visual culture, studies of 97, 136-7, 179, 196-7,
    223-4
Vygotsky, Lev 109

Walbiri, of the Australian Central Desert 151
walking 16-17, 33, 37-44, 47-50, 177, 208, 216;
    and drawing 178; and painting 202; and

reading 199, 202; and sawing 53; and writing 190, 196-7
way of life 4, 12
wayfaring 12, 148, 211, 216; and drawing 178; and the integration of knowledge 154-5; and monastic practice 198-9; versus transmission 143; versus transport 59, 149-52, 162-3
weather 21, 73-4, 118-19, 121-2, 130, 138; and wind 113, 115, 121-2; *see also* weather-world
weather-world 96-7, 115, 120, 131-2, 134; *see also* weather
weaving 9, 10, 60, 84, 126, 178, 211; versus felting 133; and text 191
web: of life 63, 70; of the spider 64-5, 80, 85, 91, 93, 119
Weber, Klaus 124-5
Whitehead, Alfred North 13, 77, 235, 243

wind 17, 21, 73-4, 119-22, 130, 214; and the body 139; and feeling 129-30, 134-5, 138; and weather 113, 115, 121-2
Windelband, Wilhelm 230
wood 16-17, 20, 27-8, 54-5
words 197, 200; as assemblies 183; and pictures 200-1; sonority of 193
workmanship 18, 29-30, 59
writing 50, 84, 133, 177, 208; versus drawing 178, 181, 188, 195, 222, 241-2; by hand 178, 188-9, 225; as line-making 179

Yolngu, on north-east Arnhem Land, Australia 178, 197, 202-4, 209

Zuckerkandl, Victor 129, 138